"Allan Abbass has masterfully integrated the work of his mentors with his own research, theory, and clinical learning into an organized and graceful approach to short-term psychotherapy. The book is practical and clear in its recommended psychotherapeutic approach that is supported by both theory and empirical research. It is also rich in clinical examples. Dr. Abbass's ideas are very helpful to practitioners of all levels."

> —Raymond A. Levy, PsyD, Clinical Director, Massachusetts General Hospital Psychotherapy Research Program, Harvard University

"The internationally recognized master clinician and researcher Dr. Allan Abbass offers readers one of the most clearly articulated descriptions of how to conduct intensive psychotherapy. Using extensive case material and clear descriptions of the technique and process, Abbass demonstrates how to expertly transform the lives of those suffering with crippling psychological disturbances. A must-read for psychotherapists who want to improve their effectiveness and reach the most treatment refractory patients."

> —Jeffrey J. Magnavita, PhD, ABPP, Past President, Society for the Advancement of Psychotherapy, and coeditor of the *Journal of Unified Psychotherapy and Clinical Science*

"Dr. Abbass's work springs from a profound and nuanced psychoanalytic understanding of his patients, combined with a highly innovative approach to engaging the patient in corrective emotional experiences. He offers wonderful examples of how to engage patients to lead them to the point where they have transformative experiences. This revolutionary book will richly repay those who devote their time to really study it."

> —Sherwood Waldron, MD, Chair, Psychoanalytic Research Consortium

"One of the perennial problems for psychotherapists is the paradoxical situation in which the patient often resists the help offered by the therapist. In this superb new volume, Allan Abbass provides a systematic approach to dealing with that inevitable resistance. Both beginning and advanced therapists will benefit from the clinical wisdom in these pages."

> —Glen O. Gabbard, MD, author of *Long-Term Psychodynamic Psychotherapy: A Basic Text*

"This is a wonderful book on how to work to reach toward people beneath their blocks and encourage maximal treatment engagement. Filled with both theoretical innovations and a myriad of interventions you can use to help patients build psychological strength, become more relationally competent, and process difficult feelings, this book will help you be a more effective therapist."
—Leslie S. Greenberg, Distinguished Research Professor Emeritus, Department of Psychology, York University

"Using compelling clinical illustrations, Dr. Abbass has crafted a conceptually rich, empirically robust, and technically clear guide to the practice of intensive short-term psychotherapy."
—Molyn Leszcz, MD, FRCPC, Professor and Interim Chair, Department of Psychiatry, University of Toronto

"This book is desperately needed in our field. Written in clear language, this volume is packed with research data, as well as detailed illustrations and case vignettes that bring the concepts to life. This is a sophisticated text for therapists who, like Abbass himself, are dedicated to going all out to help even the most troubled and treatment-resistant patients. It is ultimately a book of hope."
—Patricia Coughlin, PhD, Clinical Professor, UNM School of Medicine, and author of *Intensive Short-Term Dynamic Psychotherapy* and coauthor of *Lives Transformed*

"Abbass presents in clear and jargon-free prose an approach to therapy that some may find congenial, some may find challenging, and many will experience as a highly stimulating blend of both. Richly illustrated with clinical detail, the book presents an active version of psychodynamic therapy that has been tested in the crucible of systematic research."
—Paul L. Wachtel, PhD, Distinguished Professor, Doctoral Program in Clinical Psychology, City University of New York

"Allan Abbass unveils his process of conducting ISTDP by providing clear and concise guidelines that are useful to the beginner, intermediate, and master clinician. He presents vignettes from psychotherapy sessions for almost any scenario a therapist and patient might face together when working deeply with emotions. This book is a must-read for learning the art and science of ISTDP!"
—Kristin A. R. Osborn, MA, LMHC, Harvard Medical School, and President, International Experiential Dynamic Therapy Association

"*Reaching through Resistance* provides an excellent update on intensive short-term dynamic therapy . . . The book builds on the rich clinical experience of the author and is full of very helpful examples for psychotherapeutic interventions using ISTDP. A must for therapists treating patients with various levels and forms of resistance."
　　—Falk Leichsenring, University of Giessen, Germany

"Many patients do not respond to an appropriate course of therapy. In this book, Dr. Allan Abbass describes a systematic way to address such cases of 'treatment resistance.' I particularly liked the detailed case vignettes, which illustrate how to connect to the person who is suffering beneath the symptoms."
　　—Michael Thase, MD

"Abbass has presented an approach to short-term psychodynamic psychotherapy that is both sophisticated and readable. The copious use of case material adds to the interest and accessibility of the book."
　　—George Stricker, PhD, Professor, American School of Professional
　　　Psychology, Argosy University, Washington DC

"Dr. Abbass offers a model of understanding early attachment patterns, trauma, emotions, anxiety, and bodily reactions in psychotherapy. In addition, he provides some of the most extensive clinical vignettes used to illustrate the many varied technical interventions presented that I have ever seen. This provides readers with a very clear understanding of how they might intervene in relation to the model of therapy being presented, which makes the book a useful resource for clinicians at any level of experience."
　　—Mark Hilsenroth, Professor, Adelphi University

"Dr. Allan Abbass is a giant in the field of short-term dynamic therapy, and this book is a tour de force. The combination of detailed cases and comprehensive explanatory material from a preeminent researcher and teacher makes *Reaching through Resistance* a must-read."
　　—Howard Schubiner, MD, author of *Unlearn Your Pain*; Director,
　　　Mind-Body Program, Providence Hospital, Southfield, Michigan; and
　　　Clinical Professor, Wayne State University

"In the tradition of Davanloo and Malan, Abbass is exploring methods to rapidly get beyond resistance to modify central conflicts. The intense focus on the current relationship between therapist and patient provides an avenue for both assessment of levels of pathology and change."
　　—John F. Clarkin, Clinical Professor of Psychology in Psychiatry, Weill
　　　Cornell Medical College

Reaching through Resistance

Advanced Psychotherapy Techniques

Allan Abbass, MD

Seven Leaves Press

Seven Leaves Press
4520 Main Street, #700
Kansas City, MO 64111
www.sevenleavespress.com

Ordering Information

Quantity sales. Special discounts are available on quantity purchases by corporations, associations, and others. For details, contact the "Special Sales Department" at the address above.

Orders by US trade bookstores and wholesalers. Please contact BCH: (800) 431-1579 or visit www.bookch.com for details.

Printed in the United States of America

Abbass, Allan.
   Reaching through resistance : advanced psychotherapy techniques / Allan Abbass, MD. — First edition.
   pages cm
   Includes bibliographical references and index.
   LCCN 2014959405
   ISBN 978-0-9883788-6-5 (print)
   ISBN 978-0-9883788-7-2 (ebook)

   a. Resistance (Psychoanalysis) 1. Title.
RC489.R49A23 2015   616.89'14
QBI15-600052

First Edition
19 18 17 16 15   10 9 8 7 6 5 4

Cover image: Kristina Sobstad
Cover design: VMC Art & Design
Interior design: Marin Bookworks

To my parents

Contents

Acknowledgments

This book is the work of more than twenty years of case study coupled with the study of Dr. Habib Davanloo's work and that of colleagues. My first note of gratitude is to Dr. Davanloo for teaching me over the past twenty years and for developing and disseminating his methods for over forty years now. Among other short-term dynamic psychotherapy pioneers, I also wish to thank Dr. David Malan for his support and encouragement to research and teach this method. Further thanks go to my research colleagues of all stripes around the world whom I've been privileged to collaborate with and learn from: this network has been a great, warm, and supportive family.

I have been privileged to work with many patients and learners who have provided me personal benefit and enjoyment through witnessing their developments while experiencing my own. I want to thank each of you for allowing me to take this journey with you. Many of my former learners from around the world are now accomplished teachers, and I'm very proud to have been part of their development: as David Malan once wrote me, I pass to you "more strength to your arm" going forward.

I also want to thank my international colleagues who have encouraged me to extend my thinking and consider the importance of certain factors in the intensive short-term dynamic psychotherapy treatment process. In particular, several colleagues have developed models that underscore the importance of positive feelings and self-directed compassion within the treatment framework. These and other exposures have changed how I teach and interact with patients, and you will see this reflected in this book. Although I have always known intensive short-term dynamic psychotherapy and psychotherapy in general to be acts of love, this fact has become more crystallized in my mind over the past fifteen years.

I want to thank my loving family for allowing me the time to master and disseminate this approach at the expense of personal time away

from home. A special thank you to Jon Frederickson (2013) who provided a great deal of guidance to me after his successful publication
of *Co-Creating Change*. I also want to thank those who reviewed this
manuscript, including my colleagues Jasen Elliott, Dion Nowoweiski,
and Joel Town, and my sister, author Lori Gosselin.

Introduction

I am pleased to provide this volume to assist you in understanding and working with psychoneurotic and fragile patient groups. These populations are extremely common, representing the vast majority of treatment-resistant patients in mental health clinics and a large portion of those on chronic medications for psychological and physical symptom disorders.

For a range of reasons, these people suffer chronically and find themselves being bounced between disparate parts of the medical and mental health systems at great cost to society. The long-term suffering is masked by short assessments, medical procedures, and referrals, so nobody but the patient himself and his family know about his chronic misery. He may end up in jail or institutionalized or he may suffer in silence in his own cave. After these patients had experienced years of childhood deprivation and abuse, the system often re-creates thwarted attachment efforts and adds to their burdens.

Finally, the patient has been referred to you. He brings trunkloads of misery, symptoms, and a spectrum of mechanisms by which he keeps a distance from you and he hurts himself. You can feel the heaviness as he hauls this luggage into your office. He is lucky to get to meet you, even if only for a few meetings. And the process begins.

How can you provide a compassionate, corrective experience to help remove some of his burden? How can you reach through to the person underneath, the person as he was meant to be before all this adversity?

In this volume we will review in detail the theoretical underpinnings and steps you can take to reach through to the person beneath the resistance. After decades of case-based research we can outline specific treatment ingredients to assist you with this process.

The intensive short-term dynamic psychotherapy (ISTDP) framework centers on key common ingredients of interest in psychotherapy today, including use of video for quality improvement, a rapid evaluative procedure, cognitive restructuring as needed, a high degree of emotional engagement, and a here-and-now focus, among others. Moreover, this framework includes novel processes such as monitoring unconscious signals in the body, rapid handling of defenses, the somatic experience of emotions, and the potent healing force: the *unconscious therapeutic alliance* (Davanloo 1987a). These common psychotherapy factors, coupled with unique components, are woven into a seamless fabric allowing you to work with an extremely broad range of clients. About forty published research studies show that ISTDP can be highly effective to the majority of psychiatric patients with benefits that persist in long-term follow-up (Abbass, Town, and Driessen 2012, 2013). Thus is it a *transdiagnostic* treatment, likely affecting brain regions known to be dysfunctional in diverse mental illnesses. It performs very well in treatment-resistant and complex populations (Winston et al. 1994; Abbass 2006; Abbass, Sheldon, et al. 2008; Abbass, Town, and Bernier 2013; Solbakken and Abbass 2014). Moreover, its specific ingredients, such as emotional experiencing and defense work, are related to treatment outcomes (Abbass 2002a; Town, Abbass, and Bernier 2013; Johansson, Town, and Abbass 2014). Now numerous studies show the treatment to be cost-effective, offsetting the excessive cost burden these patients place on medical, occupational, and social systems (Abbass and Katzman 2013; Abbass, Town, and Bernier 2013).

If you are new to this approach, I hope it will be understandable and the amount of new terminology tolerable. If you are coming from a cognitive behavioral therapy background, it may help to consider this as a unique exposure model with cognitive restructuring and response prevention in cases as needed: this exposure is to internal emotions and can lead to generalized benefits. If you are coming from other psychodynamic schools, I trust the core elements and processes will have enough familiarity to bridge to novel accelerating components of this approach: psychodynamic therapy going efficiently with rapid mobilization of the unconscious will have common therapy ingredients described herein regardless of the school of therapy.

I will introduce and describe specific intervention types that have different neurobiological and psychological effects. Interventions such as *bracing* and *recapping* are used to build capacities, while *clarification*, *challenge,* and *head-on collision* are used to interrupt defensive behaviors. The mainstay intervention, *pressure,* is used to continually reach to the person beneath the resistance and to encourage maximal treatment engagement and self-compassionate efforts. These interventions combined are a palette of tools you can use to help patients build psychic strength, gain relational capacity, bear difficult feelings, and extract themselves from long-held self-destructive patterns.

I have broken the book down into two main parts. The first reviews a new metapsychology of the unconscious derived from thousands of case studies and goes into great detail in the theoretical and technical basis of the approach. The second part focuses on the clinical application of this metapsychology. This part begins with the initial process, including psychodiagnostic evaluation, and moves into the process of mobilizing and working with the unconscious of patients from across the two spectra. The appendix reviews the current state of evidence for short-term psychodynamic psychotherapy and intensive short-term dynamic psychotherapy.

My hope is that this book will support you in your capacity to care for the people you will be privileged to meet. I also hope it will provide a supportive challenge to master your own self as a therapeutic instrument.

PART 1

A New Metapsychology of the Unconscious

CHAPTER 1

Attachment Trauma, Transference, and Countertransference

Imagine a mother and baby, face to face; the baby is having "whole body smiles" in response to a warm and equally responsive mother. You feel good seeing this. Why? Something good is happening: attachment, with all the biological and psychological benefits that result. A child who grows up with this uninterrupted parental bond will be able to relate to others without undue fear, anxiety, or defensiveness.

However, what happens if this bond is interrupted by a parent's mental illness, death, abuse, or separation? This *attachment trauma* causes painful feelings. If the child can process the pain with a loved one, he will continue to develop normally and have close relationships later in life. If he is unable to process these feelings with a loved one, he will avoid his feelings and the relationships that trigger them. He will suffer from anxiety over closeness and intimacy.

The intense pain of loss may also mobilize rage directed at the lost, absent, or abusive parent. Unable to depend on his parent to help him process his feelings, the child, with his immature mind, must depend on his defenses instead. Because his conscious rageful feelings cause suffering, eventually he buries them in his *unconscious*. But, believing his feelings are the same as deeds, the child will live as if he had acted out his rage, as if he had damaged or murdered his parent. As a result, he has complex feelings of love, pain, rage, longing, and guilt about the rage buried in his mind. Now he fears to be close to his feelings or to the people that trigger them.

A child who shuts down his complex feelings can grow into an adolescent who experiences interpersonal avoidance, self-destructiveness, physical illness, depression, anxiety, or anorexia. The earlier the trauma, the more severe the pain, rage, and guilt will be and, thus, the greater the defenses and self-destructiveness. (See chapter 3.) The link between these trauma and long-term difficulties has been observed in diverse research about adverse childhood events (Felitti et al. 1998).

If a parent cannot or does not respond to the child, the child's attachment longings will be frustrated. Children without secure attachment will suffer from patterns of pathology such as fragile character structure (Davanloo 1995a) and borderline personality organization (Kernberg 1976). They will suffer from the consequences of massive pain, rage, and guilt due to their attachment efforts being thwarted. They rely on primitive defenses including projection, splitting, and projective identification, leading to a poor ability to maintain an integrated self. Their unconscious anxiety manifests as mental confusion and a range of neurological symptoms, leading to poor anxiety tolerance.

TRANSFERENCE

The complex emotions related to attachment trauma are mobilized in a patient's current relationships, especially in psychotherapy. Why? You are a caring person, offering a potential attachment and expressing positive regard for your patient. You, looking into his eyes, remind him of his early attachments, interrupted attachments and failed attachment efforts.

This process of activating emotions, anxiety, and defenses in the therapy relationship is *transference*. While transference does not represent the totality of all sources of emotional reactions in patients, it is the central focus of ISTDP and most forms of psychodynamic therapy.

As a matter of terminology, Habib Davanloo (1990) has also used the term transference to connote the therapy relationship itself. It is the *T* of the classic *Triangle of Person* (Malan 1979) where *C* is current people and *P* is past people (fig. 1.1).

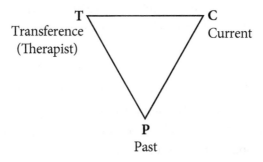

Figure 1.1 The triangle of person

COUNTERTRANSFERENCE

The term *countertransference* has many different meanings. Otto Kernberg (1965) offers what is known as a totalistic definition of countertransference to account for all the feelings a therapist might experience with a patient. He proposes three kinds of countertransference that are all highly relevant to ISTDP:

- *Objective countertransference:* The patient evokes emotional reactions in the therapist that most people would have. For example, if the patient curses repeatedly, most therapists and others would be objectively irritated at such conduct.

- *Subjective countertransference:* The patient evokes feelings in the therapist that tell the therapist something about the patient's inner life. Kernberg (1965) describes two types of subjective countertransference:

  - *Concordant countertransference* where the therapist is identified with the patient's experience. This process, a product of empathic attunement, leads the therapist to feel something the patient is feeling. As a social species, we are able to sense other people's emotions and can experience the same visceral experience in some detail. For example, if you are the therapist, you may feel something in your stomach telling you the patient's anxiety is going into the smooth muscle of his stomach. You may feel a rise of heated rage in your chest, telling you that the patient's rage is coming to the surface.

  - *Complementary countertransference* occurs when the therapist feels the patient's feelings in the patient's transference resistance. For example, the patient rejects you as he was rejected and you feel angry as the patient did when he was rejected in the past.

- *Neurotic countertransference:* The therapist has feelings toward the patient that are based on his own unresolved attachment trauma. Specifically, the past unresolved feelings in the therapist are activated while connecting with the patient and manifest in some combination of unconscious anxiety and defense.

Therapists providing intensive therapies must be aware of these reactions to use them therapeutically and to avoid negative consequences for patients. Countertransference issues in relation to different patient categories will be discussed in chapters 13–17.

Attachment trauma is the central pathogenic force in a wide range of illnesses. Transference occurs when a patient's unresolved past feelings are activated in relation to the therapist and other current people. Objective countertransference occurs when the patient evokes feelings most people would have. Subjective countertransference occurs when the patient evokes feelings in the therapist that relate to the patient's inner life. Neurotic countertransference occurs when the therapist unconsciously transfers unresolved feelings onto the patient. Countertransference responses can be helpful cues that can guide the therapist.

CHAPTER 2

Unconscious Anxiety and Defenses

Attachment trauma–based unconscious pain, rage, and guilt trigger unconscious anxiety and unconscious defenses against that anxiety (fig. 2.1). This relationship is referred to as the *Triangle of Conflict* (Malan 1979). That is why we say that unconscious anxiety and defenses are *signals* of unconscious feelings.

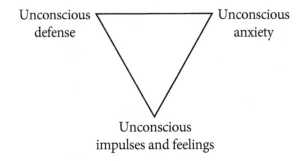

Unconscious defense   Unconscious anxiety

Unconscious impulses and feelings

Figure 2.1 The triangle of conflict

Let's review the different patterns of unconscious anxiety and corresponding patterns of unconscious defense you will see.

STRIATED (VOLUNTARY) MUSCLE UNCONSCIOUS ANXIETY

The first pattern is *striated muscle unconscious anxiety* (Davanloo 2001; Abbass 2005). Striated muscle is the voluntary muscle of the body—muscle you can move on purpose. Anxiety in the striated muscle starts in the thumb and goes up the hand, arm, shoulder, and neck. Then it goes to the chest, abdomen, legs, and feet. This neurobiological process follows a progression up the side of the cerebral cortex. When it is activated, you will see hand clenching and sighing respirations as the muscles of the chest and diaphragm contract and relax.

A person with anxiety in this pathway will have spasms, pains, and aches such as seen in fibromyalgia, headache, backache, neck pain, shoulder pain, chest pain, and abdominal wall pain. A person can experience hyperventilation with dizziness, tingling in the hands and feet, and a sense of shortness of breath as is seen with panic. Further, choking sensations, vocal problems, tics, and tremors can be caused or worsened by unconscious anxiety in the relevant striated muscle. A partial list of medical presentations related to striated muscle anxiety is shown in table 2.1.

Table 2.1 Striated-muscle-related medical presentations

Tension headaches	Chest pain
Jaw pain, teeth grinding	Shortness of breath
Choking sensations	Abdominal wall pain
Vocal and other tics	Leg pain
Neck pain	Cramps
Fibromyalgia	Tremors
Back pain	

Case Vignette: Striated Muscle Unconscious Anxiety

A man with fibromyalgia, with chronic pain related to stiff muscles, is sitting with hands firmly clenched while describing a conflict with his wife.

Therapist (Th): What kind of conflict was it? [*Pressure to be specific.*]

Patient (Pt): Um, well, problems with the neighbors. My wife's opinion was that I spent too much time arguing with this man, and she was probably right.

Th: So she brought this up again in the incident? [*Pressure to be specific.*]

Pt: Um-hmm.

Th: And how did you feel? [*Pressure to identify feelings.*]

Pt: Well, I'm getting tired of hearing about this.

Th: How do you feel toward her? [*Pressure to identify feelings.*]

Pt: [*Sighs deeply.*] Mad.

Th: Mad, like you mean angry? [*Clarification.*]

Pt: Angry, yeah.

Th: How do you experience the anger inside, physically inside your body? [*Pressure to experience rage.*]

Pt: I'm very, very tense.

Th: That's tension. That's anxiety. [*Clarification.*]

Pt: Anxiety, yeah.

Th: But how did you experience the anger toward her? [*Pressure to experience rage.*]

Pt: It's hard to explain.

Th: You became anxious, did you? [*Clarification.*]

Pt: Yeah, I became anxious.

Th: Do you become tense when you have anger, become anxious when you have anger inside? [*Clarification.*]

Pt: Yeah, and then I start to ignore her.

Th: That's a mechanism you use to deal with the anger? [*Clarification.*] But how do you experience the anger underneath? [*Pressure to experience rage.*]

Pt: Like I say, it's really hard to put a word on that. I get really mad, okay.

Th: So it's like rage, you mean.

Pt: It's like rage, yeah.

Th: How do you experience the rage? [*Pressure to experience rage.*]

Pt: [*Sighs deeply.*]

In this segment, focus or pressure on the patient to identify his feelings toward his wife activated unconscious anxiety in the striated muscle: rather than feel the feelings, he just became tense and sore in his body.

ISOLATION OF AFFECT

Was this man able to intellectually tell me how he felt toward his wife? When I said how did you feel toward her, what did he say? He said "Mad."

He is able to intellectually label his feeling, but does he experience the feeling in his body? No, he just becomes frozen with tension. Does he notice this? No. He can describe the intellectual label (anger) but not the physical experience of his feeling. This is called *isolation of affect.* When the person can intellectualize and isolate his affect from his experience, anxiety is discharged into the striated muscle. This capacity is parallel to the ability to self-reflect through activation of the dorsolateral prefrontal cortex. Davanloo calls the groups of defenses against the experience of murderous rage operating in treatment sessions *major resistances.* Isolation of affect is the first one.

Anxiety in the striated muscle is the best pattern to have, except in this patient's case the degree of chronic tension he had caused a lot of muscle pain. When he experienced the underlying rage and guilt, his tension and pain dropped rapidly.

SMOOTH MUSCLE UNCONSCIOUS ANXIETY

The second pathway of unconscious anxiety involves the *smooth muscle.* Smooth muscle is involuntary muscle over which a person has no control, located in the airways, bowel, and blood vessels. The muscle in the bladder is similar but is called *transitional muscle.* People with a lot of anxiety channeled to this muscle suffer from many somatic symptoms requiring referral to medical specialists. A partial list of these common presentations is shown in table 2.2.

Table 2.2 Smooth-muscle-related medical presentations

Medical specialty	Smooth-muscle-related condition
Cardiology	Hypertension, coronary spasm, flushing, hypotension with loss of consciousness
Respirology	Asthma, coughing, choking symptoms
Gastroenterology	Irritable bowel syndrome, gastroesophageal reflux disease, functional vomiting, unexplained abdominal pain
Urology	Bladder dysfunction, interstitial cystitis
Neurology	Migraine

If unconscious anxiety goes into smooth muscle when the therapist focuses on emotions, he will see no striated muscle tension. These patients seem relaxed because they don't exhibit visible muscle tension. Since they don't look anxious, they end up in medical settings rather than psychologists' offices. Patients with unconscious anxiety in this pathway frequently have two or more of the conditions listed: in our own large sample (Johansson, Town, and Abbass 2014), one half of the patients with migraine headaches also have irritable bowel syndrome.

Case Vignette: Smooth Muscle Unconscious Anxiety

A middle-aged woman with migraines and irritable bowel syndrome is sitting looking very calm with no visible muscle tension.

Th: Can you tell me an example of when you had a conflict so we can see how it affects your symptoms? [*Pressure to be specific, pressure to task.*]

Pt: If I ever get in a conflict with someone, I get a headache. [*Suggestion of link to complex feelings.*]

Th: Can you describe a specific time this happened? [*Pressure to be specific.*]

Pt: It happens with my husband sometimes.

Th: Can you tell me an example of when that happened? [*Pressure to identify feelings.*]

Pt: Yes, once when my husband had spent all our money on a trip and we had none left for our rent, I was so mad I yelled at him. A while later I got a headache and nausea.

Th: So you did the action of yelling, but how did you feel toward him? [*Clarification of action versus feeling, pressure to identify feelings.*]

Pt: I thought, "I'm not a good wife." [*No display of signals of striated muscle anxiety.*]

Th: You mean you became critical of yourself? [*Clarification.*]

Pt: Yes, I was. My stomach doesn't feel good right now.

Th: Can you tell me what you notice in your stomach? [*Intellectual review to reduce anxiety and isolate affect.*]

Pt: There are cramps here, like bloating coming on. [*Points to her middle abdomen.*]

Th: So when we talk about this situation of conflict and frustration, your stomach reacts. Is that what happened? [*Recap: feelings-anxiety.*]

Pt: Yes, it seems to.

Th: So is this a way that frustration with your husband goes, to your stomach or to a headache somehow? Because when you start to talk about your frustration toward him, your stomach reacts here and out there you got a headache. [*Repeat of recap.*]

Pt: Yes, it did.

Th: Can we examine that? How that happens here? [*Pressure to task and patient's will.*]

Pt: I would sure like to.

Monitoring of Response

The therapist observes that the patient looks completely relaxed with no striated muscle tension. This woman's anxiety is not discharged into the striated muscle but is being *repressed* into the smooth muscle in the gastrointestinal tract. In the actual event it appeared to produce a headache. The patient also has a tendency to self-criticize when she has anger with someone else, another typical finding in patients with *repression*. To confirm that anxiety is channeling to the smooth muscle and to ascertain the level of anxiety intolerance this patient has, the therapist repeats the process with another focus.

> *Th:* Can you tell me what happens when we are here together? What feelings come up here with me as we talk together? [*Pressure to identify feelings.*]
>
> *Pt:* Well, I don't know. [*Smiles but shows no visible tension.*]
>
> *Th:* Let's see what feelings come up here generating this stomach effect. [*Repeat of pressure.*]
>
> *Pt:* I . . . my stomach is reacting again. [*Again appears totally relaxed with no striated muscle response.*]
>
> *Th:* So again when you speak of your feelings, your stomach reacts with cramps. [*Recapitulation, linking of feelings with anxiety.*]

Assessment

The therapist confirmed that this woman's unconscious anxiety was not discharged to the striated muscle but rather into the smooth muscle of her bowel. She had limited ability to isolate affect or intellectualize about her emotions. These findings show that rapid mobilization of unconscious feelings could worsen her gastrointestinal symptoms because her anxiety exceeded the threshold of her anxiety tolerance. Hence, before helping her to be able to tolerate her unconscious emotions, the therapist needs to build her anxiety tolerance through the *graded format of ISTDP* reviewed in chapter 15 (Davanloo 1995b, c; Whittemore 1996; Abbass and Bechard 2007).

REPRESSION

Was this woman able to identify which emotions she was feeling? No. She started to talk about when she was irritated but ended up talking about where the feelings went—into the stomach. The emotions were *instantly repressed*. The feelings did not reach consciousness but instead were repressed into the body. Recent research suggests this process is mediated at least in part by the subgenual part of the anterior cingulate cortex. Depressed patients with overactivity in this region do not respond to cognitive therapy, cognitive behavioral therapy, or certain antidepressants (Abbass, Nowoweiski, et al. 2014).

Repression is the second category of major resistance. Repression is an unconscious process where emotions are shunted away from consciousness. This is different than *suppression*, where the patient consciously avoids emotions.

COGNITIVE-PERCEPTUAL DISRUPTION

Cognitive-perceptual disruption occurs when unconscious anxiety interrupts a person's special senses and ability to think. Some of the many manifestations of this anxiety pathway include interruption of vision or hearing with what is better known as *sensory conversion*. A person can transiently go completely blind or deaf. The mind goes blank and the person can even lose consciousness with a fainting attack or a pseudoseizure type of event. The person can hallucinate when anxious: thus, he may actually experience transient psychotic phenomena. These patients end up seeing the neurologist and having special tests like magnetic resonance imaging scans, and some patients are misdiagnosed as having psychosis. A partial list of clinical presentations of cognitive-perceptual disruption is in table 2.3.

Table 2.3 Cognitive-perceptual-disruption-related medical presentations

Visual blurring, visual loss, tunnel vision
Hearing impairment or loss
Memory loss, mental confusion
Loss of consciousness
Pseudoseizure
Dissociation
Hallucination in all five senses

If a person has significant anxiety in the form of cognitive-perceptual disruption and the therapist focuses on unconscious feelings, this patient will become mentally confused or develop some of these other phenomena.

Case Vignette: Cognitive-Perceptual Disruption

A man with paranoid personality disorder arrived in a treatment session rubbing his eyes but with absolutely no visible striated muscle anxiety.

Pt: You'll have to excuse me a little today; I'm a little foggy.

Th: Foggy? [*Clarification of the experience.*]

Pt: Yeah.

Th: Is your thinking kind of foggy, cloudy? [*Clarification of the experience.*]

Pt: Foggy and cloudy.

Th: How's your vision? [*Clarification of the experience.*]

Pt: Cloudy.

Th: Is it tunnel vision, or is it like looking through a screen? [*Clarification of the experience.*]

Pt: More tunnel vision.

Th: More like it's hard to see the outside of your visual field, but you can see straight ahead in the room. [*Clarification of the experience.*]

Pt: Yeah.

Th: When did that start? [*Pressure to be specific.*]

Pt: Um, two, maybe two days ago relatively . . . like I just noticed it this morning.

Th: So this is what we looked at as anxiety, right? [*Pressure to remember previously learned material.*]

Pt: Yeah.

Th: And the last two days, all day? [*Clarification of the experience.*]

Pt: Actually more or less just today when I woke up.

Th: Okay, so why are you anxious right now? [*Pressure to identify causes.*]

Pt: Is it anxiety?

Th: That's what we figured when we've met before. [*Pressure to remember previously learned material.*]

Pt: It's more of a completely stoned type of feeling.

Th: It's a disconnection kind of thing. Disconnected from what's going on. [*Clarification.*]

Pt: Yeah.

Th: And any thoughts about why you're anxious this morning? [*Pressure to identify causes.*]

Pt: I don't think it has anything to do with coming here.

Th: You don't think it has anything to do with coming in?

Pt: Not to do with coming to see you, no.

Th: You weren't anxious about it?

Pt: No, I don't think so.

Th: How do we account for that anxiety then? How are you accounting for it? [*Pressure to identify causes.*]

Pt: I've got school tomorrow and I was thinking about school last night.

Th: Why today though? [*Pressure to identify causes.*]

Pt: Um, I don't know. You're right, cause it's kind of subsiding!

Th: It's just come down now?

Pt: Yeah.

In this vignette, the patient has no anxiety in the striated muscle. Could he tell the therapist about the emotions? No. He wasn't conscious of his feelings or even his anxiety. This is why we call it *unconscious* anxiety. Since they are unaware of their feelings or anxiety, these patients often seek medical attention for these somatic symptoms.

PROJECTION, PROJECTIVE IDENTIFICATION, AND SPLITTING

In the early sessions, this patient projected his rage onto others and then feared them. By this treatment session, he had ceased projecting and was exploring his own feelings and the anxiety they triggered. As he trusted me and faced his feelings, anxiety began in the form of cognitive-perceptual disruption. Projection is a major defense against cognitive-perceptual disruption. By projecting his anger onto others, he did not have to experience unconscious anxiety over the intense rage within himself but he instead suffered conscious fear and rage about the rage he expected from others.

Like projection, projective identification goes with cognitive-perceptual disruption. Projective identification in this frame is the projection of aspects of oneself, such as the abuser, the neglector, or the critic. These projected parts may produce a concordant (we are both critics) or complementary reaction in others (you are controlling so I will defy you). *Splitting* refers to holding one-dimensional views of people and events to preclude any complex feelings and anxiety. Examples of splitting include idealization and devaluation of the self or others. This set of primitive defenses used in session is a third category of major resistance.

Patients with dissociative and psychotic disorders, at times, have these manifestations of major resistance. (See chapters 16–17.)

MOTOR CONVERSION

Another somatic pattern related to unconscious feelings and impulses is motor conversion. When motor conversion is active, instead of striated muscle tensing up, the patient goes weak and flat, losing power in one or more muscle groups. For example, the patient may lose the ability to move his arms, legs, or vocal cords. Sometimes, as in the case of tremor, the patient experiences excess tension alternating with weakness in rapid cycles.

When the patient's anxiety goes into conversion, he looks relaxed because he has no striated muscle tone. This is the well-known phenomenon of "la belle indifference" where the person appears relieved despite paralysis. The patient is neither anxious nor defensive because the anxiety and defense both are converted into weakness.

To clarify, many neurologists also refer to striated muscle symptoms of unconscious anxiety as conversion, but the mechanism is obviously different. Patients with anxiety in the striated muscle rarely show la belle indifference; patients with motor conversion usually do. Patients with anxiety in the striated muscle will show signaling of a rise of unconscious feeling and anxiety; patients with motor conversion do not. Patients with anxiety in the striated muscle will be tense and strong; patients with motor conversion will show no tension and lots of weakness. Patients with anxiety in the striated muscle will use tactical defenses and isolation of affect; patients with motor conversion will show few defenses since all the feelings and anxiety are repressed, manifesting as weakness. Obviously, the treatment of these two categories of conversion will differ greatly.

Case Vignette: Motor Conversion

A man with episodic weakness with falling and becoming at times paralyzed for hours or days comes to the office by wheelchair. He is having a great deal of weakness and spasms and moving from side to side in the chair as if he could fall out.

> *Th:* I understand you saw the neurologist about some problems and he suggested that we meet. What are the difficulties that you're experiencing at this point in time? [*Pressure to be specific.*]
>
> *Pt:* [*Display of large-amplitude upper body spasms.*]
>
> *Th:* You're experiencing physical symptoms right now? [*Clarification of symptoms, encouragement to self-reflect.*]
>
> *Pt:* Yes.
>
> *Th:* What are you experiencing in your body, at this point, right now? What is it that you observe from inside? [*Pressure to self-reflect.*]
>
> *Pt:* Uh, well, I'm coherent. [*Self-reflection with a clear head.*]
>
> *Th:* Um-hmm, what is it that you're noticing in your body? [*Encouragement to self-reflect.*]
>
> *Pt:* Okay. [*Self-reflection.*]
>
> *Th:* Are you aware of being anxious? [*Encouragement to self-reflect.*]
>
> *Pt:* No, I'm not anxious.
>
> *Th:* Do you notice muscle tension? [*Encouragement to self-reflect.*]
>
> *Pt:* You mean as far as being tense coming into the building?
>
> *Th:* Muscle tension within your body. [*Encouragement to self-reflect.*]
>
> *Pt:* Oh yeah, I know that's there.
>
> *Th:* Why is that there right now when you're coming here to see me; what's causing that? What feelings are driving that tension in the body? [*Pressure to identify feelings.*]

Response to Focused Process

After seven minutes of focusing on the bodily experiences and what underlying emotions he had, the patient becomes much more relaxed and the spasms stop. He has no sighing and hand clenching, suggesting the emotional forces are manifesting as conversion. He begins to focus on conflict with his new wife that predated these symptoms, which began one year prior.

> Pt: My wife likes to have things a certain way, and sometimes she goes off yelling and cursing.
>
> Th: Um-hmm.
>
> Pt: And it really pisses me off.
>
> Th: So this was a certain time when you were home and that happened? [Pressure to be specific.]
>
> Pt: I could hear her walking around the hallway swearing.
>
> Th: How did you feel toward her? [Pressure to identify feelings.]
>
> Pt: Very angry!
>
> Th: How does that feel in your body when you think about that—in your body? [Pressure to experience rage.]
>
> Pt: In my body. [Self-reflection.]
>
> Th: Thinking about it now, what are you noticing that tells you that you feel very angry inside? [Pressure to experience rage.]
>
> Pt: Gosh! [Self-reflection; draws a large sigh.]

Conversion to Striated Muscle Anxiety

This patient's sigh is a marker of a shift from conversion to the striated muscle anxiety pathway. This transition is a direct product of focused pressure to mobilize his unconscious emotions, coupled with efforts for him to observe his body and isolate affect. When he started to isolate affect, the emotional forces shifted from conversion to striated muscle anxiety. From this state he went on to experience some complex feelings about his wife, including a small amount of somatic anger and guilt. These feelings with his wife became linked to complex feelings about his mother from past verbal abuse. His mother is now a nice, older woman: the conflict with his wife has mobilized this unresolved rage and guilt.

At the end of the session, the patient is quite strong in all his limbs and walks out with no need for his cane or wheelchair. What took place is the process of replacing motor conversion with emotional experience. We explored feeling gradually to change the pathway of anxiety discharge from motor conversion into the striated muscle. Chapter 15 describes this "graded format" in great detail, but the principle is this: if the therapist helps the patient isolate affect, unconscious anxiety shifts to the striated muscle.

MAJOR RESISTANCE OF GUILT

A fourth category of major resistance is resistance of guilt or the punitive superego (punishing conscience), a force that Davanloo calls the *perpetrator of the unconscious* (Davanloo 1987b, 1988, 2005). This resistance of guilt refers to a built-in need to defeat and sabotage the treatment process to avoid the experience of unconscious impulses and feelings. This resistance is driven by intense guilt about murderous and primitive rage toward loved ones and is seen in highly resistant and fragile patients. Unconscious guilt drives an overbuilt conscience that punishes the patient for his complex feelings: the patient harms himself to avoid guilt over his wish to harm others. The result is damage to relationships, reduced insight into oneself, loss of productivity and limited enjoyment of life. Anytime the therapist approaches the patient's complex feelings, the resistance of the superego will interrupt the session. This resistance is a formidable foe to the therapy process, requiring extensive efforts to turn the patient against it; it is the essence of treatment resistance in psychiatric conditions. The patient cannot let himself succeed in the bond with the therapist due to massive guilt about rage toward loved ones. In response, use well-timed pressure, challenge, and head-on collision to overcome this powerful resistance. (See chapter 15.)

SUMMARY: MAJOR DEFENSES AND SOMATIC PATTERNS

Thus, we see specific somatic patterns of unconscious anxiety and the defense of motor conversion. These four patterns (striated muscle, smooth muscle, cognitive-perceptual disruption, and conversion) correspond to patterns of major resistance. Recognition of these patterns can directly inform how to proceed with psychotherapy. (See table 2.4.) Some patients have different anxiety pathways predominant at different times, so we will review interventions used to manage each of these.

Table 2.4 Corresponding somatic and resistance patterns

Somatic pattern	Corresponding resistance
Striated (voluntary) muscle	Isolation of affect
Smooth muscle	Repression
Motor conversion	Repression
Cognitive-perceptual disruption	Projection, projective identification, splitting, repression
Any of the above patterns	Resistance of guilt (punitive superego)

TACTICAL DEFENSES

In contrast to major defenses, tactical defenses are loosely held and easily penetrated or bypassed—they are satellites around the major defenses or can constitute the entire set of defenses a patient uses (Davanloo 1996a, b). Rather than a dichotomy, these defenses are on a continuum from tactical to major defenses. (See fig. 2.2.)

Tactical defense   **Major defense**

Tactical defense	Major defense
More apparent	Less apparent
Dystonic	Syntonic
Loosely held	Tightly held
Easily handled	Difficult to handle

Figure 2.2 Continuum of tactical to major defenses

Several types of tactical defenses exist, including the following:
Cover words: using words to hide one's true feelings
> *Cover words for anger:* "It bugged me" or "I'm annoyed."
> *Confusion as a tactical defense:* "I'm confused."
> *Cover words for murderous rage:* "I'm frustrated."
> *Cover words for emotional closeness:* "I'm embarrassed."
> *Covers words like silly or dumb:* "It was a silly situation to be in."

Defensive weeping: using regressive defenses

Blanket statements: saying for example "I was completely overwhelmed."

Use of jargon: making statement such as "I was full of existential angst."

Indirect speech: stating for example "I was probably mad."

Rumination: rambling nonspecifically without a focus or target

Vagueness: responding to a question with a vague statement

Rationalization: explaining the reason for a feeling rather than the feeling itself

Intellectualization: giving a description devoid of emotional experience

Generalization: being nonspecific

Diversification: avoiding the focus

Not remembering: suppressing and ignoring emotions

Denial: not acknowledging what one is actually experiencing or doing

Externalization: blaming others for internal problems

Obsessional indecisiveness: not committing to specifics about problems or emotions

Stubbornness, defiance: exhibiting oppositional conduct

Tangents: avoiding specific focus on feelings or problems

Somatization: describing symptoms rather than actual feelings

Talking to avoid the experience of feelings: continuing to speak so feelings are not felt

Body movement as defense against feelings: avoiding eye contact for example

Passive compliance: going along with the therapist

To determine whether a defense is a tactical defense versus part of the major resistance, the therapist should interrupt or ignore it and see whether it goes away. If the defense keeps coming back, it is likely part of the tightly maintained major resistances against murderous rage.

There are many ways to handle tactical defenses including clarifying, pressuring, ignoring, blocking, and challenging (Davanloo 2005). In general, tactical defenses can be ignored so long as there is continued rise in unconscious signals and access to feelings. If the patient keeps using a tactical defense, it is more a part of major resistance and it will need to be clarified and challenged directly.

Low resistance patients use only tactical defenses. *Moderately resistant patients* use both tactical and major defenses. *Highly resistant patients* with repression and *fragile character structure patients* may lack tactical defenses, so they succumb to major defenses of repression and projection.

CONSCIOUS VERSUS UNCONSCIOUS FEELINGS AND ANXIETY

As described above, patients are unaware of unconscious anxiety and what drives it. In contrast, conscious anxiety is noticed and experienced. For example, when first visiting a surgeon, patients will be anxious about what will happen and what the outcome will be. This type of anxiety is primarily cognitive in the form of worry and may be accompanied by some muscle tension in anticipation of pain or bad news. This anxiety is adaptive and matches the context; it is also transitory. This anxious event may also activate unconscious anxiety and result in, for example, diarrhea prior to such an appointment; in this case, both conscious and unconscious anxiety are present.

Similarly, conscious emotions are experienced and linked to conscious stimuli. For example, conscious anger is experienced by someone being provoked by harsh comments from a critical boss. Such conscious experiences are devoid of unconscious anxiety and defense. This conscious anger may, however, activate unconscious unprocessed feelings, such as guilt-laden rage from childhood criticism; in this case, unconscious anxiety and defense will be activated.

> *There are four main formats of somatic manifestation of activated unconscious impulses and feelings and corresponding categories of major resistance. Many forms of tactical defenses may exist separately or be more or less part of major resistance. Tactical and major defenses are on a continuum. These defenses are all signals of activated unconscious impulses and feelings. Conscious feelings and anxiety are triggered by conscious stimuli and do not have unconscious anxiety or defense as a component.*

CHAPTER 3

Spectra of Suitable Patients

This chapter reviews the categories of patients suitable for ISTDP (Davanloo 1995b, 2001). These categories of patients relate to the degree and nature of defense and anxiety. (See fig. 3.1.)

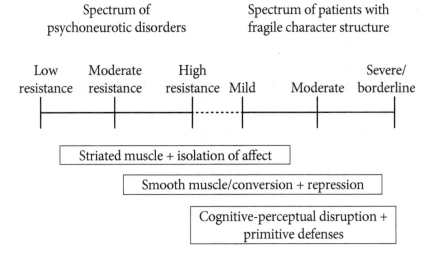

Figure 3.1 Spectra of patients suitable for ISTDP

These categories also relate to the intensity of underlying unprocessed feelings and impulses, which in turn relates to the age of trauma. (See fig. 3.2.)

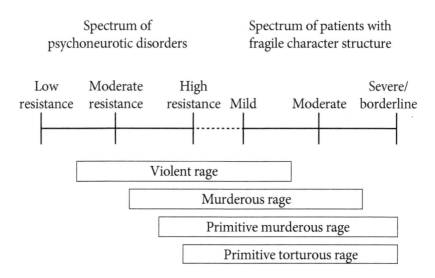

Figure 3.2 Underlying guilt-laden aggressive impulses

SPECTRUM OF PSYCHONEUROTIC DISORDERS

The first of two spectra is the spectrum of psychoneurotic disorders (Davanloo 1995a). This spectrum goes from low to moderate to high resistance.

Low resistance patients are highly responsive with a single focus of loss with unresolved grief. These losses have typically occurred after the age of seven. These patients present with only minor tactical defenses; they do not have unconscious rage and guilt so they have no major resistance. (See chapter 12.)

Moderately resistant patients present a moderate degree of symptom and character problems. They have experienced attachment trauma, usually after age five, resulting in unprocessed pain, murderous rage, guilt about this rage, and grief. Unconscious anxiety is discharged to the striated muscle, and the primary major defense is isolation of affect, although they can also experience some repression. These patients have some insight into the problems and defenses, but are moderately impaired socially and functionally due to resistances against emotional closeness and habitual character defenses. (See chapter 13.)

On the right side of the spectrum, highly resistant patients have complex symptoms and character problems. These patients have

endured trauma early in life typically starting before age four, resulting in layers of intense grief, rage, and guilt about the rage. They also
have layers of guilt and grief due to losses resulting from the defenses.
These feelings tend to be fused together and hard to experience sepa-
rately. If the rage has a sexualized component (e.g., urge to rape) it is
highly fused with primitive rage and guilt. Highly resistant patients
have a punitive superego due to buried primitive murderous rage and
guilt about the rage. They use *syntonic* character defenses, meaning
they do not see their defenses as problematic. These patients also have
resistances against emotional closeness. Repression and isolation of
affect are typical major resistances. They can be extremely detached
or defensive, or they can suffer from self-destructive behavior disorders. They can also suffer from severe symptom disturbances. Friends,
family, and health professionals have usually given up trying to reach
through to these patients.

SPECTRUM OF PATIENTS WITH FRAGILE CHARACTER STRUCTURE

The next spectrum comprises patients with fragile character structure (Davanloo 1995a). They comprise one-quarter of psychiatric private office referrals (Abbass 2002a). These patients have intense, unconscious, primitive murderous rage, primitive torturous rage, guilt,
and grief related to figures in the past who failed to consolidate or heal
ruptured bonds with the patient. The major resistances of fragile patients are primarily primitive defenses such as projection, projective
identification, splitting, and repression. Unconscious anxiety occurs as
cognitive and perceptual disruption in the forms of mental confusion,
dissociation, fainting, or hallucination. They have much dysfunction
and often land in jail or the hospital because of physical injury. They
cannot tolerate their own emotions, so they need preparatory work to
help them build capacity before they can face underlying feelings.

At the mild end of this spectrum are fragile patients who experience these primitive phenomena only at a high level of anxiety; these
patients can tolerate a moderate amount of anxiety. At the severe end
of the spectrum are patients with borderline personality structure
who use projection and projective identification at a very low level of

anxiety. Moderately fragile patients fall between these two extremes. (See chapters 16–17.)

CONTRAINDICATIONS TO ISTDP TRIAL THERAPY

In general, relatively few absolute contraindications exist to having an ISTDP trial therapy. Because the model includes close monitoring of patient response and techniques to bring down anxiety, it is generally a safe procedure, even with patients with more severe mental disorders. However, the following relative contraindications are worth noting.

First, patients with active *mania* should not be provided a trial therapy: there is significant likelihood of increased symptomatology. Likewise, patients with *unstable psychotic* symptoms should not be offered a trial therapy until stabilized. Even then, psychosis is a contraindication to this model in the hands of most therapists with even a moderate degree of experience. Patients with active *ulcerative colitis, Crohn's disease, multiple sclerosis, and rheumatoid arthritis* should be treated with great caution when using this approach as any increase in anxiety caused by treatment could exacerbate these autoimmune disease processes.

Active *substance dependence* is a relative contraindication to this treatment. Patients who come to sessions intoxicated or who are unable to function without alcohol in their systems may require medical detoxification and a period of abstinence prior to being able to benefit significantly from this treatment. Patients using marijuana daily can undergo a trial therapy without any significant difficulties or concerns about withdrawal.

Patients who are actively *suicidal* can have a trial therapy so long as they can (in the therapist's opinion) make an honest commitment to not act on these impulses in the service of trying treatment. If any doubt exists about willingness or ability to make this commitment, the patient should be assessed for more intense care including hospitalization, medications, and emergency services.

CAUTION REGARDING THE USE OF INTENSIVE SHORT-TERM DYNAMIC PSYCHOTHERAPY

Even with the safeguards built into this treatment approach, therapists should work within their level of skill, confidence, and knowledge. This guideline is a basic matter for all regulated therapists and is at the core of professional ethics codes. An anxious therapist is more likely to induce misalliance and adverse effects. Video-recording-based training is recommended so therapists can learn to read defenses and body markers showing that this accelerated treatment effort is safe. Moreover, therapists should only work with more complicated patients, including patients with repression, depression, conversion, and cognitive disruption, under supervision or with close scrutiny through video-recording and some sort of peer review process. Being in over one's head can result in adverse effects in both therapist and patient (Abbass 2004).

The majority of patients seeking psychiatric services fall into two broad spectra of patients suitable for ISTDP. Patients with fragile character structure have had deficient early attachments plus trauma, resulting in cognitive-perceptual disruption and primitive defenses. Patients with psychoneurotic disorders had more secure attachments and do not routinely employ these primitive defenses. A cautious approach is warranted in applying the model in certain cases.

CHAPTER 4

Complex Transference Feelings and the Unconscious Therapeutic Alliance

I n all but the low resistance patients, direct access to the unconscious can be achieved through the mobilization and direct experience of the *complex transference feelings*, a process that effectively reduces *resistance* and activates the healing force within the patient that Davanloo (1987a) called the *unconscious therapeutic alliance*.

TRIPLE FACTORS

Davanloo (2005) discovered the key relationship between the complex transference feelings, unconscious therapeutic alliance, and resistance. These complex feelings toward the therapist resonate with pain, rage, and guilt about the rage from past attachment trauma. When these unconscious complex feelings are activated with the therapist, unconscious anxiety and defenses (resistance) are mobilized. The direct experience of the complex feelings overrides the anxiety and defenses. Through this process, the unconscious therapeutic alliance rises in proportion. This entire process is referred to as *unlocking the unconscious* (Davanloo 1995d).

COMPLEX TRANSFERENCE FEELINGS

Complex transference feelings are mobilized when the therapist reaches to the person who is stuck underneath the defenses. Trying to connect to the person and helping him battle his defenses evokes complex feelings, which include warm feelings or appreciation coupled with irritation and anger toward the therapist. The anger will have an element of guilt attached to it because of the positive feelings toward the therapist. The degree to which these complex feelings are experienced is in direct proportion to both the removal of resistance and the dominance of the unconscious therapeutic alliance.

Simply put, the degree to which a person can experience love, rage, and guilt combined equals the degree to which the unconscious therapeutic alliance can be activated. This capacity to tolerate ambivalence is the central key to ISTDP and needs to be optimized. Without this capacity, the unconscious will stay shut, and emotions will stay buried.

This same capacity must be present in the therapist: he must be able to simultaneously feel *both continuous positive regard for the patient and disdain for the resistances* that hurt the patient.

Together, the patient and the therapist can safely tolerate only as much rage as they can experience love at the same time: combined, these experiences enable the experience and working through of guilt, the central pathogenic force in all but low resistance patients. If the therapist or patient cannot tolerate this ambivalence, the process will become split with elements of idealization and devaluation resulting in either limited treatment effects or adverse events (Abbass 2004).

UNCONSCIOUS THERAPEUTIC ALLIANCE

The therapeutic alliance is composed of conscious and unconscious components. Conscious therapeutic alliance refers to rapport, shared objectives, shared therapy effort, and other ingredients of an effective collaborative process. A conscious therapeutic alliance is inadequate to bring up unconscious material for processing in all but lower resistance patients; another more powerful force is required to battle higher degrees of resistance.

Davanloo's major discovery is that of the unconscious therapeutic alliance (Davanloo 1987a). When working with highly resistant patients and mobilizing the unconscious, Davanloo observed that the patients were experiencing visual imagery in the form of damaged or dead bodies of attachment figures or other disturbing images. He discovered this was a manifestation of a dynamic force in the patient working to bring unconscious feelings and impulses to consciousness to be healed. He called this force the *unconscious* therapeutic alliance since it was not functioning volitionally, and it operated differently than conscious components of therapeutic alliance.

When the unconscious therapeutic alliance is working at a high level, visual imagery of the unconscious is indeed experienced within and between the treatment sessions. However, it is more common for the unconscious therapeutic alliance to only be mobilized to a partial level so that these more dramatic or obvious manifestations are absent. For help in recognizing these lower level manifestations of unconscious therapeutic alliance, figure 4.1 describes a *spectrum of the unconscious therapeutic alliance* (Abbass 2012). The therapist's goal is to recognize when the unconscious therapeutic alliance is developing and work with the alliance rather than disagree with the alliance or become frightened by what it produces.

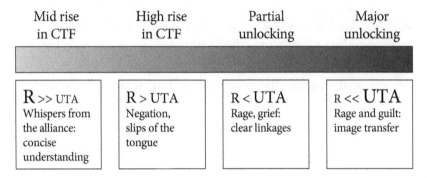

Figure 4.1 Spectrum of unconscious therapeutic alliance
R: resistance, UTA: unconscious therapeutic alliance,
CTF: complex transference feelings

Whispers from the Alliance

I refer to the very first signs of the unconscious therapeutic alliance as *whispers from the alliance*—these occur when the patient offers short statements reflecting concise understanding of her difficulties and inner obstacles to treatment. She speaks softly but with deep meaning. Whispers from the alliance occur at a mid rise in the complex transference feelings: they are the first communications from the unconscious therapeutic alliance. At this stage, the unconscious therapeutic alliance is mobilized but mostly overpowered by the resistance and anxiety.

One patient who always felt herself a victim declares with a small voice something that summarized her difficulty.

Pt: I've been getting in my own way.

A chronically self-punitive man says the following:

Pt: Maybe I am not such a bad person.

A highly resistant man simply makes a statement about his feelings:

Pt: I bottle them up!

These communications are markers of a mobilized unconscious: a shifting in favor of alliance over resistance.

Negation and Slips

The next level of unconscious therapeutic alliance appears in the form of negation and slips of the tongue, as originally described by Freud. Negation simultaneously reveals and denies the unconscious wishes. Negation occurs at a high rise in the complex transference feelings where the unconscious therapeutic alliance is growing but still somewhat weaker than the resistance.

One man at a high rise in complex feelings makes a declaration:

Pt: I never hit anybody in my life.

And three seconds later he adds to his statement.

Pt: I did but I missed him and hit the wall! Yeah! I broke my hand.

A middle-aged man declares the following after a partial passage of complex feelings.

Pt: I can't think of a specific time and day I felt angry with my father.

Th: You can't think of one?

Pt: Yes, I can! On my seventh birthday he was drinking and fell over right on the table.

A young man with depression has this to say at a high rise in complex feelings.

Pt: I never wanted to kill anyone.

Th: You mean you wanted to kill people?

Pt: Yes, I did!

As you see, at this level of rise in complex transference feelings and unconscious therapeutic alliance, the patient is nearly ready to declare feelings he had not previously been clearly aware of.

Linkages

The next level of unconscious therapeutic alliance occurs in the form of crystal-clear linkages the patient makes between his past and current complex feelings. These linkages occur during a first break-through or partial unlocking of the unconscious after the patient experiences some components of the complex transference feelings. The unconscious therapeutic alliance, now higher than the resistance, can direct us to the underlying complex feelings.

A middle-aged woman after experiencing violent rage and guilt about the rage toward the therapist declared:

Pt: No. No. I feel terrible to have thought of hitting you . . . I remember my mother did that to me once. I think I could have killed her that day.

A young man after passage of violent rage and guilt toward the therapist declared:

Pt: I just remember my father did something to me. My sister and I were arguing, and he put me in the basement in the dark. I was so furious about that.

Transfer of Images

At the next level, the unconscious therapeutic alliance results in the transfer of visual imagery. When the person experiences murderous rage and guilt in the therapeutic relationship, the visual imagery will transfer to the person in the past where those feelings belong. When murderous rage breaks through to the therapist for example, the image of the therapist might convert into the blond-haired, blue-eyed mother from the past. Then the patient will feel guilt and other emotions toward her mother. This process is a *major unlocking of the unconscious*. The experience of the rage clears out the anxiety and drops the resistance; then the unconscious therapeutic alliance dominates the weakened resistance. When the unconscious is thus mobilized, patients often see powerful imagery during and between sessions. Davanloo called this process *dreaming while awake* (Davanloo 2005).

Here is an example of dreaming while awake: After a session one patient saw an image of her mother's dead body floating in the harbor. As she kept walking along the waterside, her mother's dead body floated beside her all the way home. The same image kept rising up across her visual field "like a slide" until this patient had a major passage of guilt about the rage toward the mother.

WORKING WITH THE UNCONSCIOUS THERAPEUTIC ALLIANCE

The forthcoming chapters contain many case vignettes illustrating how to work with the mobilized unconscious therapeutic alliance. A few of the central themes to note are as follows:

- *Recognize the unconscious therapeutic alliance at its lower levels:* The first step is detection of the unconscious therapeutic alliance so you don't accidentally counter and obstruct it. Then you will go to a mode of listening for what the unconscious therapeutic alliance is saying versus working to mobilize it. One not uncommon technical issue in new learners is missing the unconscious therapeutic alliance and challenging it rather than following it. In one example the therapist kept challenging the patient's unconscious therapeutic alliance that was bringing a clear incident from the past with the father: the therapist kept pressing to feelings in the transference, thereby blocking access to the unconscious.

- *Follow it! You are now the copilot:* When the unconscious therapeutic alliance is mobilized, your job is to follow it, help the patient maximize his emotional experiences, and recap what is learned with the unconscious therapeutic alliance. You have done the job of mobilizing this powerful force; now the task is for a partnership of two copilots to fly over regions of the unconscious that need examining and experiencing.

- *Educate it—recapitulate:* After you complete segments of emotionally focused work, recapitulate what is learned in great detail to bolster the unconscious therapeutic alliance. To recapitulate, actively link all the information together in terms of feelings-anxiety-defense and all people, past and present. Make this a shared process with the patient, and be sure each piece is correct by verifying it with her. This linking work fuels the unconscious therapeutic alliance, which is then empowered with a deeper understanding of psychodynamics and the treatment pathway. This understanding allows you and the patient to collaboratively paint the portrait of the person's overall self. Cases in chapters 13–17 illustrate the techniques and functions of recapitulation.

- *Maintain it:* If anxiety and resistance overtake the unconscious therapeutic alliance, your job is to repower the unconscious therapeutic alliance through pressure, challenge, and head-on collision to reactivate the complex transference feelings and unconscious therapeutic alliance. If the unconscious therapeutic alliance is weak, the patient will try to move the process into the transference, as if it is a gas station, for more fuel.

UNCONSCIOUS THERAPEUTIC ALLIANCE VERSUS PSYCHOSIS

Signs of the unconscious therapeutic alliance can be mistaken for a psychotic breakdown or major cognitive disturbance. In fact, a patient whose unconscious therapeutic alliance is mobilized is doing well in her life. She is generally working, functioning, relating well to others, and experiencing decreased symptoms. In contrast to a psychotic breakdown, signals of the unconscious therapeutic alliance have clear dynamic links that, when worked through, lead to the experience of the complex feelings and therapeutic effects.

The complex transference feelings include deep appreciation and irritation toward the therapist for his efforts to reach through the patient's resistance. The unconscious therapeutic alliance is seen along a spectrum from low levels to a position of dominance over the resistance when it shines light on the unconscious impulses and feelings to allow healing. The unconscious therapeutic alliance is mobilized in direct proportion to the complex transference feelings: reaching through resistance brings the unconscious therapeutic alliance into force.

CHAPTER 5

Somatic Experience
of Emotions

etailed videotaped case studies reveal direct physiologic concomitants of unconscious impulses and feelings. This chapter reviews these somatic pathways.

POSITIVE FEELINGS

Positive feelings, including love, are experienced with warmth or an upward moving energy and an urge to reach out and embrace. An urge to smile and touch or hold the other person exists, leading to a sensation of calm. Positive feelings cause a reduction of anxiety and defenses.

RAGE

The somatic pathway of rage begins at the bottom of the body, in the feet or lower abdomen and moves causing a sensation like energy, heat, or a volcano. This sensation moves toward the neck and the sides of the head and down the arms to the hands, creating an urge to grab and perform some form of violence. Thus, it moves up each spinal level from the thoracic (back) to the cervical (neck) nerves. The experience of this urge displaces any unconscious anxiety. Thus, the person goes from being tense and restrained to being activated and free to move. Rage arises in waves that sequentially increase and then decrease. When rage is higher, anxiety is lower and vice versa.

If the rage has a sexual component, such as an urge to rape, the patient will feel some degree of genital sexual arousal alongside the somatic pathway of rage. Both male and female patients may feel as if they have some degree of an erect penis that can perform the act of a rape. Because sexualized rage is generally contained in the deeper zones of the unconscious, therapists seldom see this type of rage before they work in those unconscious zones.

GUILT

Guilt manifests itself somatically as upper chest and neck pain with intense sobbing and strong ideas of remorse attached to imagery of rage toward loved ones. Guilt passes in distinct, solid waves that come and go. When the guilt is present, the person finds it impossible to speak as he is in the grips of this intense emotion. Between the waves, the person is able to speak (Davanloo 2005).

GRIEF

In contrast to guilt, grief is not necessarily seen in distinct, solid waves—there is not the severe physical pain seen with guilt. The person's thoughts relate to loss rather than remorse. You will tend to feel empathic grief with the patient when she is feeling this. Sometimes grief and guilt are felt within moments of each other, and the result is combinations of these pathways.

COGNITIVE TO AFFECTIVE CONTINUUM

Davanloo described and we have corroborated the direct relationship between the experience of emotions and treatment outcome (Abbass 2002a; Town, Abbass, and Bernier 2013; Johansson, Town, and Abbass 2014). There is a continuum from cognitive awareness to affective experience of emotions. In treatment, we always aim for higher levels of affective experience versus cognitive awareness of emotions. On a brain level, we activate limbic structures and memory systems as highly as possible to override defensive regions, including those of the prefrontal cortex. This process is necessary to bring not just symptom reduction but enduring character change for our neurotically disturbed patients. (See fig. 5.1.) Upcoming chapters will include many vignettes to illustrate emotional experiences and the processes to mobilize them.

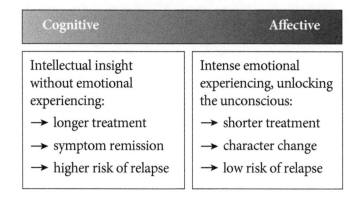

Figure 5.1 Cognitive to affective continuum

Emotions and impulses each have specific somatic concomitants. There is a spectrum from cognitive awareness to somatic experiencing of emotions. In ISTDP we are always aiming for greater affective versus cognitive experiences of feelings.

PART 2

Clinical Application

CHAPTER 6

Initiating
Treatment

nitiating the process of ISTDP requires knowledge of the metapsychology we reviewed in part 1. Part 2 reviews a step-by-step process that allows you to determine the format and pace of treatment tailored to your patient's capacities.

Initiating this approach to accessing unconscious, unprocessed feelings begins with a three-step process that includes *handling barriers to initial engagement*, detecting the *front of the system* and performing a *psychodiagnostic assessment*. *Five key parameters* inform your subsequent interventions.

STEP 1: HANDLE BARRIERS TO INITIAL ENGAGEMENT

To begin psychotherapy the patient must have

- a problem
- located within himself
- that he wants to deal with
- now *and* with you

You cannot treat a patient who has no problem or a problem he believes other people create. A person with highly syntonic defenses may not be aware of a problem but may wish to explore this lack of awareness with you: this is a problem that you and he can focus on. You also cannot treat a patient who doesn't want to address his problem at this time. Finally, you cannot work effectively with a patient who doesn't want to work with you: conscious defiance blocks unconscious mobilization.

Lack of a Problem

To address the lack of a declared problem, explore with the patient what problems there appear to be.

Th: It isn't clear what the problem is then. [*Pressure against the defense of externalization.*]

Pt: [*Sighs.*] I think it has to do with my wife. She is always criticizing me about working harder and making more money.

Externalization

To deal with externalization, focus on how this is a problem within the patient: alternatively focus on the feelings *he has toward the person* he appears to be blaming for the problem. This procedure produces an internal focus.

Th: How do you feel toward her? [*Pressure to identify feelings.*]

Pt: [*Sighs, clenches hands.*] I ignore her and try to get out of the house.

Th: That is how you deal with the feelings. [*Clarification of defense.*] But how do you feel toward her when she is critical? [*Pressure to identify feelings.*]

Defiance: Lack of Willingness

To make sure the patient wants to deal with the problem, ask her directly and put pressure on her will to do something good for herself.

Th: Is it your wish to look into how you handle these feelings and the impact that has on your relationship? [*Pressure to the will.*]

Pt: [*Sighs, clenches hands.*] I *have* to deal with this.

Th: But do you want to on your own will? [*Pressure to the will.*]

Pt: [*Sighs.*]

Other defenses can create a tacit lack of willingness.

Pt: I hate myself. I don't deserve to do well.

Th: Self-hating, hmm. Let's see what we can do about that. [*Pressure to positive self-regard.*]

Pt: It's the first thought I have when you ask about my feelings. I can't stand myself. [*Self-hatred.*]

Th: So let's see what we can do about that, because if you hate yourself then you won't allow yourself to benefit here. You won't allow yourself to get better. This is what we have to address before we do anything else. [*Pressure to positive self-regard, clarification of the damaging impact of the defense.*]

Pt: [*Clenches hands and starts to break eye contact.*] I have to deserve to get better.

In these cases, signs of unconscious signaling tell you that the barriers to engage are being penetrated. As you can see, the process of addressing barriers to engagement often proceeds quickly to the next steps in the initial evaluative process.

Procrastination

Similarly, to be certain the patient wants to deal with the problems now and with you, ask him. This work will interrupt defenses including procrastination and passive compliance or defiance.

Th: So you've had this problem for fifteen years. Is it your wish *now* to look at this problem together with me so we can do something to help you with this? [*Pressure against procrastination.*]

Following are two longer illustrative case vignettes of patients presenting with barriers to initial engagement.

Barriers to Engagement: Vignette 1

A teenage girl arrived with no signs of unconscious anxiety.

Th: Can you tell me what difficulties you want help with?

Pt: What difficulties I have? I have a difficulty respecting authority. No one should be able to tell me what to do.

Th: How is that a difficulty for you? [*Pressure to internal problem.*]

Pt: I do what I want to do, go out when I want to, and stay out all night when I want to.

Th: How is this a difficulty for you? [*Pressure to internal problem.*]

Pt: Well, it isn't really a difficulty for me.

Th: So what you are saying is you don't identify a difficulty within yourself?

Pt: Not really. [*Smiles.*]

Th: So what brought you here today? [*Pressure to internal problem.*]

Pt: My mother and the doctor.

Th: So is there something you hope you and I can do together? Is there any problem within you that we can look at and understand? [*Pressure to internal problem.*]

Pt: [*Sighs.*]

Stay Focused on Initial Barriers

Here we see barriers to engagement including externalization, passive compliance/defiance, and a lack of an internal focus. The process here is to continue to focus on internal problems, and monitor the unconscious anxiety and defenses that will become mobilized in the transference. Continue to undo defiance by asking what the patient wishes to do; focus on her will and stay out of the shoes of pressuring parents or doctors who arranged the appointment.

Th: It sounds like you are here because of being pushed to be here, but, I don't see how that can help you with your problems. [*Clarification.*]

Pt: But I want to be here for me. I don't like how my life is going with people. When they reject me I get anxious, so I just dump people before they can dump me. [*Sighs.*]

Th: Can you tell me about a time that happened? [*Pressure to specific incident.*]

Vignette Summary

The simple act of showing your patient that you will not control her, will not be part of a sadomasochistic act, brings a rise in complex feelings and a budding capacity for her to self-reflect for her own sake. Note that this will not be the end of externalizing, passive defiance, or compliance but rather a beginning of building both a necessary conscious and unconscious alliance. These kinds of challenges to engage are normal with adolescents, highly resistant, and fragile patients, but they are rare with low to moderately resistant patients.

Barriers to Engagement: Vignette 2

A woman with chronic depression arrives with ambivalence and hopelessness.

Th: Can you tell me about the difficulties you have?

Pt: [*Lowers head, looks despondent.*] I don't know what to do. I've had several treatments. Nothing has helped me.

Th: You mean you tried treatments before? How do you think it will go with us doing something now? [*Clarification.*]

Pt: I really don't know if it can do anything. It's kind of "what's the point?"

Th: So the first thing you are telling me is you don't have much in the way of hope about this. Is that right? What can we do about that? [*Pressure to her will and to counter hopelessness.*]

Pt: [*Raises head.*] Well, it definitely may help me. [*Sighs, clenches hands.*]

Th: And the thing to consider is your wish. Because it sounds like you're ambivalent about even trying. [*Clarification.*]

Pt: [*Sighs, sits up.*]

Th: Because if you're ambivalent and have one foot in and one foot out the door, then where will we get to? [*Clarification of the impact of the resistance.*]

Pt: [*Sighs.*]

Th: What can we do about your ambivalence? [*Pressure against ambivalence.*]

Pt: A better question is what *I* can do about my ambivalence. [*Stated with increasing confidence, raised head, more engagement.*]

Th: That's for sure! So what will you do about it? [*Pressure against ambivalence.*]

Vignette Summary

Here we see a person with resistances of ambivalence and hopelessness precluding engagement. When I focused on these defenses, clarified the effects, and pressured her to engage, she started to signal with hand clenching, sighing, and becoming more engaged. Had I not focused this way, she could have become less engaged, more depressive, and more hopeless.

STEP 2: FIND THE FRONT OF THE SYSTEM

Once the patient is in agreement with and focused on an internal problem, you can begin to mobilize the unconscious in a collaborative fashion. To know where to focus, find the *front of the system*. The front of the system is the unconscious defenses, unconscious anxiety, and unconscious feelings activated in the therapeutic relationship.

The patient can have one of *four fronts* requiring matching interventions.

1. *Activated and avoided complex feelings:* Focus on the cognitive and somatic experiences of the underlying complex feelings.

A man arrives angry because I'm late in starting the session. The front of the system is avoided complex feelings in the transference: we focus on these feelings.

Th: Can you tell me what you would like help with?

Pt: Well, right now I'm frustrated. I just want to be put to sleep and never wake up. [*Clenches hands.*]

Th: Can you tell me how you feel right now with me when you come into the office? [*Pressure to identify feelings.*]

Pt: Well, what came to my mind is "I was here on time so why couldn't you be?"

Th: How do you feel toward me about that? [*Pressure to identify feelings.*]

Pt: Frustrated, but not too bad. [*Smiles and clenches hands, sighs; minimization.*]

Th: How do you experience this frustration with me in your body? [*Pressure to experience rage.*]

2. *Active defenses at the front:* Turn him against the defenses in the room and focus on underlying feelings.

A man is pressed to come by his employer because of customer complaints. The front of the system is global emotional and interpersonal detachment: we focus on this to help him see and turn against these defenses.

Pt: [*Sits with tense posture and stares out the window, avoiding the therapist.*]

Th: Can you tell me what difficulties you are having?

Pt: My boss says I don't relate to customers, but I don't see a problem in that. [*Stares out the window the entire time.*]

Th: When you come in, I notice you seem preoccupied within yourself. [*Clarification.*] Is this what happens with people—that you become uncomfortable and close up?

Pt: [*Sighs.*]

3. *Active unconscious anxiety:* Focus on the underlying feelings. If anxiety is too high, reduce it by recapping or reviewing bodily symptoms. (See chapter 15.)

A man with chronic pain and fibromyalgia comes in. The front of the system is unconscious anxiety in striated muscle activating tactical defenses. He has very good anxiety tolerance, so we focus on mobilizing the underlying complex feelings.

Pt: [*Appears very tense; clenches hands and sighs.*]

Th: I noticed when you came in that you are tense. Do you notice that? [*Pressure to be conscious of anxiety.*]

Pt: [*Smiles slightly and sits up straight.*] Yeah, I get tense and I get sore muscles.

Th: Can we look at what feelings create that tension? What feelings do you have here with me? [*Pressure to identify feelings.*]

Pt: [*Smiles and sighs.*] Well, I *was* a *little bit* nervous about coming in. [*Tactical defenses and striated muscle tension.*]

Th: Can we look beneath this anxiety at how you feel here with me? [*Pressure to identify feelings.*]

4. *Flat with no activation:* Take the patient's history. Explore problem areas looking for signs of anxiety and resistance.

A woman with chronic depression arrives. In this case, passivity at the front of the system is working so well as a defense that she has no anxiety whatsoever. I have to keep helping to turn her against this passivity. In chapter 7 we focus on the many factors that can cause this flat response.

Pt: [*Sits with no motion, passively looking at the therapist.*]

Th: Can you tell me what problems you want us to focus on? [*Pressure for her to be active.*]

Pt: The other therapist sent me to you because I'm not responding to *her* treatment. [*Passive response.*]

Th: Do you have any thoughts on what we can do that would help you? [*Pressure for her to be active.*]

Pt: I don't know. I was hoping you knew. [*Passive response.*]

Th: When you come in are you looking to me to know what to do? Are you waiting for me? [*Clarification of passivity.*]

Pt: Yes, you're the one who knows!

STEP 3: PSYCHODIAGNOSTIC EVALUATION

Once you have removed barriers to engagement and are working with the front of the system, the next step is to perform a *psychodiagnostic evaluation.* This process involves further pressure on feelings or defenses (chapter 9) to mobilize the complex transference feelings. (See fig. 6.1.) These complex transference feelings mobilize unresolved complex feelings from past relationships, which then activate unconscious anxiety, defenses, and the unconscious therapeutic alliance in proportion. Hence, this process is both evaluative and therapeutic. The four case vignettes in chapter 2 are all psychodiagnostic evaluations showing the different anxiety and defense patterns.

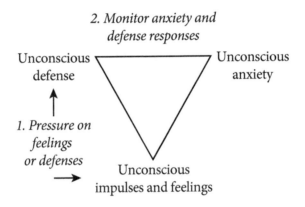

Figure 6.1 Psychodiagnostic evaluation

Specific possible responses to pressure occur with regard to the patient categories along the two spectra: the patient can either *feel feelings, defend, go flat,* or have *no response.* We will review each of these in turn.

The algorithm in figure 6.2 outlines the basic response patterns that determine the patient's place on the treatment spectra (Abbass, Arthey, and Nowoweiski 2013).

1. *Feeling feelings with inquiry alone*

If the patient shows only minor tactical defenses and has break-throughs of grief about loss when the therapist focuses the interview, he is low resistance.

These patients do not have buried rage and guilt and only have tactical defenses. (See chapter 12.)

2. *Defending: moderate resistance*

If the patient brings some defenses that need to be clarified but responds primarily to pressure with a breakthrough of complex transference feelings, he is moderately resistant. (See chapter 13.)

3. *Defending: major wall and barrier*

If pressure results in a major wall of defense in the office requiring extensive challenge to help the client turn against this defense, then he is highly resistant. (See chapter 14.)

4. *Going flat: repression*

If he goes flat with depression, smooth muscle anxiety, or conversion at some level of rise in complex transference feelings, the client has high resistance with repression. (See chapter 15.)

5. *Going flat: cognitive-perceptual disruption or primitive defenses*

If the client cognitively disrupts or uses primitive defenses at some level of rise in complex transference feelings, he has a fragile character structure. If this occurs at a low level of rise in feeling, he has severe fragility, at a moderate level he has moderate fragility, and at a high level he has mild fragility. (See chapters 16–17.)

6. *Having no response*

If you see no response, then either technical problems exist or some other pattern or pathway is open requiring evaluation. Stop and address the cause. (See chapter 7.)

OVERVIEW AND FIVE PARAMETERS TO INFORM INTERVENTIONS

Thus, we have reviewed the process of initial mobilization of the unconscious and psychodiagnostic evaluation. This treatment model gives you the ability to simultaneously monitor signals of unconscious operations to inform your next intervention. Five key parameters follow:

1. *Active unconscious anxiety discharge pathways:* striated muscle, smooth muscle, or cognitive-perceptual disruption. (See chapter 2.)

2. *Active major defense patterns:* isolation of affect, repression, projection, and resistance of guilt (superego). (See chapter 2.)

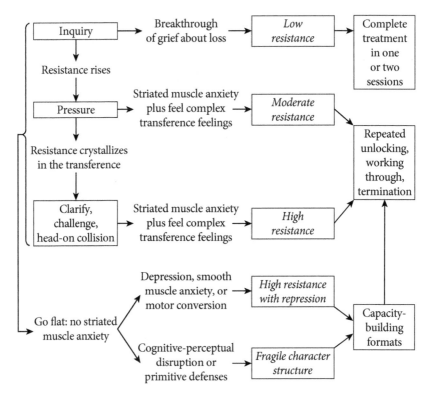

Figure 6.2 Psychodiagnostic algorithm

3. *Degree to which resistances are syntonic versus dystonic:* how much the patient identifies with her defenses. (See chapters 8, 10, and 14.)

4. *Degree of rise in the transference:* low, mid, high rise in complex transference feelings or an already mobilized unconscious therapeutic alliance. (See chapters 4 and 8.)

5. *Presence and height of thresholds:* low, moderate, or high threshold to smooth muscle anxiety, cognitive-perceptual disruption, repression, or primitive defense. (See chapters 15–17.)

The patient's status regarding these five parameters will directly dictate how to proceed in order to mobilize the unconscious. Monitoring will help you determine the evolving front of the patient's defensive system and how to engage it. Specific technical interventions to mobilize the unconscious will be illustrated in upcoming chapters.

THE TIME FOR INQUIRY

Inquiry focuses on problem areas and the impact they have on your patient and his life. When is it best to do inquiry at the start of trial therapies?

The primary initial treatment objective is to reach the person beneath the resistance. If the patient presents with activated feelings, anxiety, or defenses, put inquiry aside and respond to these signals from the patient first. Gather information about problems as you proceed with this focused emotional activation and later in the session. It is preferable to gather this information later in the session when the patient is calm and his memory systems are activated.

If a person presents with no signs of activated feelings, anxiety, or defense, then inquire into problem areas first. Through this focus you can determine the range of problems and the damage they cause. Gathering information (Step 1) can mobilize the unconscious, unprocessed impulses and feelings; hence, inquiry can flow directly into finding system fronts (Step 2) and performing a psychodiagnostic evaluation (Step 3) if the patient has no barriers to engagement. If barriers to engagement are encountered in inquiry, they should be addressed according to Step 1.

A systemic evaluation is required to safely access the unconscious impulses and feelings. Initial evaluation includes handling barriers to engagement, recognizing the front of the system, performing a psychodiagnostic evaluation, and monitoring five parameters. Inquiry should be performed first when there are no signals of active feelings, anxiety, or defenses. These steps provide you a road map to the unconscious.

CHAPTER 7

Why No Signals?

The practice of ISTDP requires a visible signaling system of the unconscious for you to direct your next intervention. If at any time in the treatment process a patient becomes "flat" with no obvious activation of unconscious anxiety in striated muscle, you must determine where his psychodynamic forces are going. This chapter describes elements that prevent, or preclude the need for, striated muscle anxiety.

THE ABSENCE OF AN UNCONSCIOUS PROBLEM

If a person has no evident unconscious conflict with unprocessed emotions, no unconscious anxiety or defense will rise. For instance, people experiencing external stressors such as social or financial difficulties may have no unconscious anxiety or defense.

UNCONSCIOUS ANXIETY GOING OTHER PLACES

If unconscious anxiety is not manifesting in the striated muscle, the patient will not exhibit visible signs of such tension. Anxiety may be going into the following:

Cognitive-perceptual disruption: If the person's unconscious anxiety is manifesting as cognitive-perceptual disruption (visual blurring, mental confusion, or hallucinations), you will see no striated signaling.

Smooth muscle anxiety: If unconscious anxiety is going into the smooth muscle of the bowel, airway, or blood vessels, you will see little or no striated signaling.

Other somatic manifestations: If a person's unconscious anxiety goes into physical systems beyond the striated muscle, such as the immune system, she will look relatively relaxed with low levels of muscle tension.

Muscular discharge: If the person is actively discharging striated muscle anxiety through tensing and relaxing his muscles, chewing gum, or generating large muscle group movements in the body (e.g., shaking his legs or twisting his body), you will see little or no striated signaling with hand clenching and sighing.

Hiding the tension: A person may consciously hide striated muscle tension by body movements or holding herself still. You must address the patient's conscious defense against allowing you to see her anxiety.

CHARACTER DEFENSES BLOCKING RISE IN COMPLEX TRANSFERENCE FEELINGS

Character defenses are the habitual behaviors a person uses to control his emotions and interactions with others. If the patient uses a high degree of character defense, you may see no striated signaling. Examples of character defenses follow:

Ambivalence: The person using the defense of noncommitment will not signal any anxiety.

Defiance: The person opposes the therapist's efforts to get to know her and to help her resolve her difficulties.

Compliance: Under the guise of being a very willing patient, compliant patients will control the process and prevent any rise in the complex transference feelings through active compliance. Compliance is another variant of defiance where the perceived will of the therapist is defied.

Externalization: While the person blames others for the problem he creates, he will show no striated signaling.

Passivity: The patient who takes a very passive expectant position waiting for the therapist to solve her problems will not manifest unconscious anxiety. Passivity may be evident with the patient maintaining good eye contact and silently waiting.

Hopelessness: The person who adopts a hopeless position and sees no point in making a therapeutic effort will show no striated signaling.

Helplessness: The person who adopts a helpless position, feeling incapable of engaging in the therapeutic task, will show no striated signaling.

Major intellectualization: A massive amount of intellectualization may prevent any striated signaling.

Denial: Rapid denial of emotions and internal processes will prevent any striated signaling.

Syntonic defenses: The patient with syntonic defenses cannot see his defenses and the feelings that are warded off. Thus, you will see no striated signaling until the syntonicity is penetrated.

ORGANIC, BRAIN, AND OTHER FACTORS

Significant brain dysfunction or mental confusion for any reason will not result in any activation of striated signaling or formal defenses. Examples of these conditions follow:

Intellectual impairment: A person with a low intellectual capacity and cognitive difficulties may be flooded with conscious anxiety but not manifest unconscious anxiety or defense.

Physical illness and exhaustion: A physically depleted person may lack the energy required for striated signaling or defense to be mobilized.

Substance use: The sedating and chemical effect of street drugs or excess alcohol may prevent any striated signaling.

Sedating medications: Sedative medications such as benzodiazepines or antipsychotic medications may prevent striated signaling, and the person may not be able to use formal and intellectualized defenses.

Confusion about the process: The person who is truly experiencing confusion about the therapy process for any reason will not exhibit any striated signaling or formal defense.

PROJECTION, PROJECTIVE IDENTIFICATION, OR SPLITTING

When a person uses projection or projective identification, feelings or characteristics of the patient are projected out and interacted with. Thus, when these defenses are active, you will not see any striated muscle anxiety signaling. In projection, for example, feelings are projected onto others so the patient will experience no feelings internally that could evoke anxiety. In projective identification, aspects of the self, such as an abusive part of the self, are projected outward so there is no internal conflict about these parts. Similarly *splitting*—such as the idealization or devaluation of the self or others—prevents any internal complexity of emotions.

REPRESSION

Repression of emotions prevents striated muscle anxiety, so other formal defenses are unnecessary. Examples of repression follow:

Major depression: The process of major depression occurs when the person becomes physically and mentally exhausted, self-punitive, and physically depleted. The depressive process may develop over seconds or minutes, but usually progresses over a longer period of time. Major depression may manifest itself in the form of low mood, loss of interest, loss of sex drive, and loss of or increases in appetite. An acute depressive episode may also occur leading to mental depletion as a manifestation of the depressive process. In such severe depression, striated signaling may be absent.

Conversion: A person with active conversion will not have any striated muscle unconscious anxiety. Rather, the unconscious impulses and feelings will activate weakness in a set of muscles (motor conversion) or cognitive-perceptual disruption (sensory conversion). (See chapter 2.)

SUICIDAL OR HOMICIDAL PLANS

Prior to completed suicide the person appears unusually relaxed, calm, and even peaceful during her last visit to the family doctor. Always investigate the absence of anxiety in a chronically self-destructive person. This lack of anxiety can be a marker of active suicidal planning. When the person decides not to kill herself, unconscious anxiety and other defenses will rise. If someone with suicidal or homicidal ideation has no signaling of unconscious anxiety, admit her for observation regardless of what she says. (See the barriers to engagement in major depression case in chapter 15, page 201.)

The patient with homicidal ideation may also show no striated anxiety signaling or other defense. He may need intervention by psychiatric services or legal authorities as a matter of safety for himself and society. Patients with serious homicidal ideation are not candidates for ISTDP: no psychotherapy can solve an external problem the patient wishes to solve through violence.

TECHNICAL ISSUES

Multiple technical issues can block the mobilization of striated signaling and formal defenses. (See chapters 12–17.) Some examples of technical issues follow:

Absence of pressure: If the level of pressure is too low or in the wrong place, no signaling will occur. For instance, pressure on defenses or feelings that are not present will generate no signals and could cause misalliance. (See chapter 9.)

Premature challenge: When you challenge defenses at too low of a rise in complex feelings, the patient will experience you as critical. As a result, positive feelings, complex transference feelings, anxiety signaling, and the unconscious alliance will drop. The proper timing of challenge is reviewed in chapter 10.

Transference activation: The patient interacts with attributes of past people she projects onto the therapist. For example, the patient projects her controlling father upon the therapist, and then the patient defies the father/therapist. In a complementary fashion through projective identification, the therapist experiences himself as if he *is* the controlling father. This process must be deactivated through some combination of clarification and challenge.

When neither signals of unconscious anxiety in striated muscle nor obvious defenses appear, stop and search for where the dynamic forces are going. The dynamic forces may manifest as other anxiety or defensive channels. Otherwise, you may have medical, chemical, or technical issues to address. A new onset lack of signals may reflect unexpressed suicidal or homicidal ideation. In all cases stop pressure and explore what is happening.

CHAPTER 8

Low versus Mid versus High Rise in the Transference

This chapter reviews the different degrees of mobilization of the unconscious: the degree of activation of the triple factors of the complex transference feelings, transference component of the resistance, and unconscious therapeutic alliance (Davanloo 1999a). (See figs. 8.1 and 8.2.)

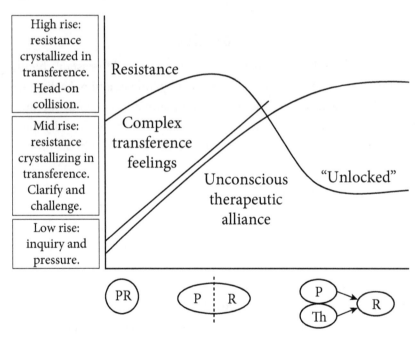

Figure 8.1 Low, mid, and high rise in the transference
P: patient healthy aspects, R: resistance, Th: therapist

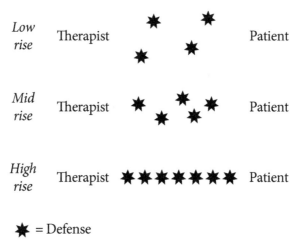

Figure 8.2 Degree of crystallization of resistances by level of rise

LOW RISE

A low rise in the transference with moderately resistant, highly resistant, and fragile patients is revealed by little emotional activation and thus, few defenses. The patient can maintain eye contact because he is not anxious. A low rise occurs because the therapist and patient are not focusing on activating internal feelings. As a result, the process is flat and lifeless. Defenses, if present, are not in response to the therapy because the therapist is not uncovering enough unconscious emotions to mobilize the triple factors central to the treatment process.

Therapy at a low rise results in cognitive understanding, symptom reduction (in some cases), and high relapse rates. It also results in lesser reductions in symptoms, work dysfunction, medication amounts, and medical system costs (Abbass 2002a; Town, Abbass, and Bernier 2013; Johansson, Town, and Abbass 2014).

Thus, at a low rise in the transference, little to no activation of the complex transference feelings, transference component of the resistance, and unconscious therapeutic alliance occurs: the emotional roots of the problems and unconscious healing forces are not being activated.

MID RISE IN THE COMPLEX TRANSFERENCE FEELINGS

At a mid rise in the transference feelings, the complex transference feelings, transference component of the resistance, and unconscious therapeutic alliance are partially activated, giving rise to unconscious anxiety.

In response to this activation, the patient shifts from warding off feeling to warding off you: her defenses crystallize, forming a barrier in the transference. This active detachment is the hallmark of mid rise in the transference. This detachment takes forms that include the patient's breaking of eye contact, becoming slow, and ruminating to herself. Character defenses that were present will increase; for example, the patient will become more passive, more defiant, or more compliant.

At this mid rise in the transference, pressure alone—inviting the patient to focus and be present with you—is not adequate to mobilize the unconscious. At this point, you must start to question, clarify, and challenge the defenses that are making a barrier between the patient and you.

To mobilize the unconscious further, you must help the patient separate from and ultimately hate the resistances that are ruining the therapy and every other relationship in his life. Thus, the patient's *syntonic* defenses must become *dystonic*. This defense work plus increased pressure can bring direct access to the unconscious in a moderately resistant patient. However, this work will result in increased resistance in the highly resistant patient. Thus, you must now challenge these activated obstructive defenses.

HIGH RISE: RESISTANCE IN THE TRANSFERENCE

At a high rise in the complex transference feelings, the anxiety rises, creating increased resistance in the transference: the patient's defenses are coalescing to create a barrier between the patient and you. With this increased crystallization, all of the patient's character defenses are operating. Internally, the unconscious alliance is activated as well. Now the complex feelings are high, the resistance is high, and the unconscious therapeutic alliance is mobilized resulting in an intrapsychic crisis.

At a high rise, a patient will exhibit some or all of the features outlined below.

Physically she may avoid eye contact, turn her body away, close her hands and legs, or lie back in her seat. Physical tension is typically high with hand clenching and frequent sighs. Verbally, she may become slow or even silent. Outright defiance or passive compliance may be present. Sarcasm and other more malignant defenses may attempt to thwart the therapeutic attachment.

The therapist's job at this point is to more emphatically turn the patient against her defenses. You achieve this by drawing attention to the reality of the situation, pointing out your limits, emphasizing the patient's will, underscoring the partnership, clarifying the task at hand, and providing a high degree of pressure for the patient to overcome this destructive system.

This high degree of pressure and challenge constitutes a *head-on collision* (Davanloo 1999b): a realistic and honest examination of the resistance, the potential of the alliance, the limits of the therapist, and the potential of the therapy process. (See chapter 11.) If well timed and constructed, this powerful intervention will lead to a breakthrough of unconscious complex feelings and direct access to the unconscious.

In chapters 9–11, we will review the techniques of pressure, clarification, challenge, and head-on collision with a case example.

Low rise in the transference, characterized by a flat process, requires pressure to mobilize the unconscious feelings and defenses. Mid rise is observable with defenses crystallizing in the transference: now is the time to clarify and challenge these defenses. High rise is observable with an intrapsychic conflict and a high degree of defenses crystallized in the transference: now is the time to increase the challenge and head-on collide with this resistance.

CHAPTER 9

Pressure: Reaching through Resistance

ressure is the most important intervention in ISTDP and perhaps in all psychotherapy methods (Davanloo 1999a). Pressure is all your efforts to help the patient to be emotionally present, identify processes and emotions, and overcome her defenses.

Pressure is the central means by which you *reach through resistance* to connect to the person stuck underneath: it is an unmistakable declaration of your deep concern for your patient. Such effort mobilizes complex transference feelings and, secondarily, the unconscious therapeutic alliance. The converse is also true: dropping pressure drops the rise in complex transference feelings and reduces the unconscious therapeutic alliance: the patient will experience you as disconnecting from her.

PRESSURE VERSUS CHALLENGE

Pressure means *encouraging the person to do something* for the sake of his healing. In contrast, *challenge* is suggesting or telling him to *stop* doing something that interferes with his healing. This critical difference distinguishes pressure interventions from challenge interventions. Different brain regions (limbic versus inhibitory brain regions) may be involved in these two interventions with pressure saying "start or continue" and challenge saying "stop" (Davanloo 1999c).

FORMATS OF PRESSURE

Some of the categories of pressure are described and summarized in table 9.1.

Table 9.1 Examples of pressure

Types of pressure	Examples	Defense being worked upon
Pressure to feelings	How do you feel? How do you experience the feeling? What does the rage want to do?	Emotional avoidance and repression
Pressure to task	Can we examine how this problem affects you? Can we explore how this anxiety affects your body?	Self-neglect, tendency to be unfocused
Pressure to be specific	Can you describe a specific example of when you had the symptoms?	Vagueness
Pressure to the person's will	Is it your wish that we examine this?	Compliance and defiance
Pressure to positive regard for oneself	Let's see what we can do so you will have a good feeling about yourself and what you are doing for yourself.	Self-hatred and resistance of guilt
Pressure to encourage active collaboration	How do you suggest we approach this problem?	Passivity and compliance
Pressure against character defenses	Are you sure now is the time to solve this problem?	Character defenses such as procrastination, habitual nonverbal avoidance, externalization

Pressure to Identify, Experience, and Express Feelings

One of the most common forms of pressure is to focus on avoided impulses and feelings. You may ask, for instance, "How do you feel here with me?" or "How do you feel toward (someone else)?" to identify feelings. You may follow up with, "How do you experience these feelings physically?" to assist in the somatic experience of the feelings. When the patient is experiencing the feelings, you may then pressure to portray the impulse of a loving feeling or rage by asking, "What does this rage want to do?" Thus, any such focus on feelings, the body's experience, and the patient's impulse constitutes pressure and yields therapeutic benefits.

Pressure to the Task

Pressure to the task encourages the patient to focus on the current therapeutic task. The therapist will ask, "Could we take a look at this problem?" or "Shall we take a look at the feelings underneath this anxiety?" This work counters any tendencies to be unfocused or to ignore one's own internal processes.

Pressure to Be Specific

Examining specific situations and specific emotions to activate feelings and impulses and to counter intellectualized vagueness is pressure to be specific. For instance you may ask, "Can you describe a specific time this anxiety happened?"

Pressure to the Person's Will

Pressure to the will is focusing on what the person *wants* to do. Pressure to the will deactivates defiance before defiance becomes entrenched in the therapeutic relationship. Questions that demonstrate pressure to the will are, "What do you want to do about this problem?" or "Is it your will to work on this problem?"

Pressure to Positive Self-Regard

Patients who are self-hating require pressure to have a positive self-regard. This pressure, as all other forms, mobilizes appreciation for this support but also irritation because the self-punitive aspects of the patient resent your support and demand self-punishment. Use a statement like this: "Let's see what we can do so you will have a good feeling about yourself and take good care of yourself."

Pressure to Active Collaboration

Many passive patients will defer to you and look to your leadership. Invite active partnership and collaboration to counter this resistance with questions such as this: "What do you think we should do next?"

Pressure against Specific Character Defenses

You can apply pressure against any of a patient's habitual character defenses. Through this pressure you encourage a person to move away from these old defenses and to collaborate with you in a healthy way. Like other forms of pressure, this mobilizes complex feelings, anxiety, and other defenses that can be clarified and challenged. Using pressure against these defenses at a low rise in complex transference feelings is the best way to activate a patient without the risks of misalliance that come with challenge that is applied at too low a rise. (See chapter 10.) Examples of this form of pressure include the following:

Procrastination: "Are you sure now is the time to solve this problem?"

Continuous eye avoidance: "What happens when you look at my eyes?"

Externalization: "Can we look at how you feel toward her when she rejected you?"

EFFECTS OF PRESSURE ACROSS THE SPECTRA

The effects of pressure differ across the spectra of suitable patients. In low resistance patients, pressure is enough to allow breakthroughs of unconscious grief. (See chapter 12.) In moderately resistant patients, complex transference feelings, transference components of resistance, and unconscious therapeutic alliance are mobilized resulting in eventual breakthrough to the unconscious. In highly resistant patients pressure brings rise in these three dynamic forces resulting in crystallization of the resistances in the transference. (See chapter 14.) In fragile patients (chapters 16–17) and those with repression (chapter 15), pressure brings a rise in somatic symptoms, cognitive-perceptual disruption, or primitive defenses.

TIMING OF PRESSURE

Since pressure is the key to mobilizing the unconscious therapeutic alliance, pressure should be present at all times as long as resistance is active. Thus, other than when feelings are breaking through and the unconscious therapeutic alliance is dominant, use pressure.

Case Example: The Sixty-Two-Year-Old Accountant

The patient is a sixty-two-year-old married accountant with chronic depression and emotional detachment. Following inquiry into the problem areas, pressure to a specific example allows us to understand how his symptoms formed when he was removed from some contracted accounting work. In this vignette, the pressure is to identify feelings that preceded his depression. He was sitting with hands clenched and some striated muscle tension.

Th: How did you feel toward the man who had terminated your contract? [*Pressure to identify feelings.*]

Pt: Well, I felt sorry for him. [*Intellectual answer, denial of any anger.*]

Th: How did you feel toward the guy about terminating you though? [*Pressure to identify feelings.*]

Pt: I felt sorry for him.

Th: How did you feel toward him? [*Pressure to identify feelings.*]

Pt: Toward him? [*Clenches his hands.*]

Th: Yeah.

Pt: Felt sorry for him; he's having a terrible time. [*Intellectualizing, rationalizing.*]

Th: But how did you feel about him cutting you off in the middle of the contract? [*Counter to tactical defenses, pressure to feelings.*]

Pt: Yeah. [*Nonresponse to question.*]

Th: Let's see how you feel toward him about that. [*Pressure to identify feelings.*]

Pt: I had no bad feelings toward him. [*Denial.*]

Th: But how do you feel toward him about the action of cutting you off in the contract? [*Pressure to identify feelings.*]

Pt: [*Takes a big sigh.*] I was ambivalent really. [*Tactical defense: cover words.*]

Th: But what feelings do you have because you say you got tired and depressed around then, right? [*Linking to his problems, pressure to feelings.*]

Pt: Yeah.

Th: When you look back now, how do you feel toward him? [*Pressure to identify feelings.*]

Pt: I certainly feel sorry for him. He's having a rough time.

Th: How else do you feel toward him besides being sorry for him? [*Pressure to identify feelings.*]

Pt: [*Takes a big sigh.*]

Pressure in this case is mobilizing complex feelings, unconscious anxiety in striated muscle, and intellectualized defenses.

TECHNICAL PROBLEMS IN APPLYING PRESSURE

You can run into several potential areas of difficulty in applying the phase of pressure. These areas include the following:

Lack of pressure: One of the most common difficulties therapists have is a lack of pressure. Examples of therapist behaviors that amount to a lack of pressure include excessive intellectualized inquiry, too slow a pace, too much explaining and intellectualizing about the process, movement from zone to zone without any clear rationale, and a lack of examination of specific incidents. This lack of expressed efforts to reach through to the person stuck underneath the resistances can result in symptom increase, stagnation, and misalliance.

Pressure in the wrong place: Another difficulty is applying pressure but in the wrong zone. For example, if the therapist presses to feelings rather than pressing on the defenses when the patient is in a highly resistant position, no rise of complex feelings and unconscious alliance will occur. Rather, there may be a risk of confusion and misalliance.

Splitting: If the therapist preferentially focuses only on anger or only on positive feelings to the exclusion of the other activated mixed feelings, complex transference feelings will not rise. This selective focus invalidates the other feelings or impulses that are being mobilized by the therapeutic process and reinforces primitive defenses of splitting, externalization, idealization, and devaluation. In this model *all the avoided emotions* must be recognized, validated, and experienced.

Pressure is any intervention encouraging a person to do the best she can for her own health. Pressure has many forms including pressure to feelings, to the will, to the task, and to be specific and focused. Pressure reaches through to the person who is struggling beneath the resistances and mobilizes the unconscious therapeutic alliance.

CHAPTER 10

Clarification and Challenge

Before challenging any defense, clarify its nature, function, and damaging effects. Clarification points out the nature of the defense and its effect upon the therapeutic relationship and the person's life (Davanloo 1999c) and begins to turn the patient against his own defenses. Clarification is a necessary ingredient when working with moderately and highly resistant patients.

TIMING OF CLARIFICATION

Clarify the resistance when it moves into the transference or becomes relevant to the therapeutic relationship. Thus, at mid rise in the transference, clarification is necessary to further mobilize the unconscious in moderately and highly resistant patients. (See fig. 8.1.)

EFFECTS OF CLARIFICATION

In addition to helping the patient understand and turn against her defenses, clarification mobilizes the complex transference feelings, transference components of the resistance, and the unconscious therapeutic alliance. In low and moderately resistant patients, clarification can result in a breakthrough to the unconscious. In highly resistant patients, clarification helps the resistance crystallize in the transference: then you and the patient can collaboratively challenge the resistance.

NATURE OF CHALLENGE

Once clarified, defenses can be actively challenged *in concert with the patient*. In contrast to pressure, which encourages a person to *do something* good for himself, challenge *discourages and stops* a person from doing something bad to himself.

Through challenge, the therapist helps the patient stop defensive behavior. Before the patient can stop that defense, however, he must see it and its price. That is why *adequate clarification must precede challenge.*

TIMING OF CHALLENGE

Challenge is also delivered at mid to high rise in complex transference feelings when the resistances are crystallizing in the transference. *It is critical that defenses be clarified before challenging them so the patient knows you are challenging her defensive behaviors, not her as a person.* (See fig. 8.1.)

EFFECTS OF CHALLENGE

Combined, clarification and challenge muster the conscious and unconscious therapeutic alliance to battle the resistance. Thus, challenge weakens the resistance. Challenge is not necessary for low resistance patients because they do not bring resistances into the transference. In moderately resistant patients, challenge, coupled with persistent pressure, causes a direct breakthrough of complex transference feelings that leads to dominance of the unconscious therapeutic alliance. In highly resistant patients, challenge mobilizes complex transference feelings and unconscious anxiety and causes further crystallization of resistance in the transference. At this point, the therapist uses more powerful forms of challenge and head-on collision.

Case of the Sixty-Two-Year-Old Accountant, Continued

As noted in the previous vignette, rather than a breakthrough of feeling in this case of a resistant patient, anxiety and defenses rose and he became increasingly detached. At this point I began to clarify these defenses.

> *Th:* What do you feel though? You see, "sorry for him" is a thought in your mind. It's an idea. [*Clarification of feelings versus thought.*] How do you feel toward him when he cut you out of the contract? How do you feel toward him? [*Pressure to identify feelings.*]
>
> *Pt:* I never really had any feelings. [*Denial; sighs.*]

Th: Did you notice you just took a big sigh? [*Pressure to notice unconscious anxiety.*]

Pt: Yeah.

Th: There is tension in your body. It's anxiety. But how do you feel underneath all that? Your wish is there that we get a good grasp of why is this happening to you, right? [*Pressure to the will.*] I mean you get depressed, you get anxious, and you get shut down. [*Linking of feelings to his problems.*]

Pt: Yeah.

Th: But what's happening? Do you want us to look into that? [*Pressure to the will.*]

Pt: Well, it would be nice to know . . .

Th: Okay. Let's see how you felt toward that guy. [*Pressure to identify feelings.*]

Pt: I don't think I have any feelings toward him.

Th: No, but you get depressed and anxious. What happens to how you feel toward him? How do you feel toward the guy when he cuts you off? [*Pressure to identify feelings.*]

Pt: Yeah. [*Nonresponse to the question.*]

Th: We still don't see how you feel toward him when the guy cuts you out of the contract. I mean, you feel bad for him, but how else do you feel toward him? [*Pressure to identify feelings.*]

Pt: I don't really think I have any feelings!

Th: Yeah, but you got tense and depressed. [*Clarification of the damaging effect of not feeling.*] What emotions do you feel toward the guy when he cut you off? [*Pressure to identify feelings.*]

Pt: Well, I guess I was frustrated. [*Tactical defenses: indefinite terms, past tense, and minimization.*]

Th: You're not sure if you were. [*Challenge, blocking of the defense.*]

Pt: No, I'm not.

Th: You say you "guess" and you're "frustrated," but . . . [*Challenge, blocking of tactical defenses.*]

Pt: I don't recollect having any feelings toward him!

Th: How do you feel when you look at it now though? When you look back on the picture now, how did you feel toward him when you got the notice he was cutting you off? [*Pressure to identify feelings.*]

Pt: [*Takes a big sigh and begins avoiding eye contact and slowing down.*]

Th: What's happening here in the room while we're talking about this because you seem to be slowing down a lot? Did you notice you're slowing down a lot? You're slowing down and you have tension here when we talk, right? [*Clarification of resistance in the transference.*]

At this point we are definitely at mid rise in the complex feelings: the resistances he uses against feelings are becoming resistances against engagement with me. Clarification and challenge to the resistances in the transference are now necessary. Challenge is increased as resistance increases. You will see that clarification is used as needed to be clear about what is being challenged.

Pt: Well, I'm trying to think about the anger. [*Intellectualization.*]

Th: Yeah, but what feelings do you have here with me when we talk because you get slowed down here with me and tense? [*Pressure coupled with clarification.*] How do you feel here with me if you don't slow down or go away, don't remove yourself, how do you feel? [*Pressure and challenge.*]

Pt: Well, I feel a sense of hopelessness not being able to come up with the answers. [*Intellectual answer.*]

Th: How do you feel about the question? [*Pressure to identify feelings.*]

Pt: Well, it is a good question.

Th: How do you feel? What emotions do you have inside because you get slowed down. [*Pressure to identify feelings and clarification of defense.*]

Pt: Yeah.

Th: How do you feel toward me? Back there with those guys, you don't feel the anger, you get slowed down and hopeless and anxious and tense, okay? [*Recap: current-transference relationships.*]

Pt: Yeah.

Th: You don't feel any of that anger about what they were doing. You get slowed down, right? Now here with me you're getting tense and slowed down. [*Clarification of defense.*] But how do you feel here with me? [*Pressure to identify feelings.*] I'm asking you a hard question. This is a hard question for you, but how do you feel about it? [*Pressure to identify feelings.*]

Pt: Well, maybe I don't understand what feelings are. [*Whisper from the unconscious therapeutic alliance.*]

Th: Well, that's one thing we're seeing, but how do you feel about me asking how you feel? [*Pressure to identify feelings.*]

Pt: Well, I feel we're probably getting to the root of the problem. [*Communication from the unconscious therapeutic alliance.*]

Th: So what emotions are stirred up when we work together here to figure this out because you get tensed up, slowed down, and hopeless thoughts? [*Pressure to identify feelings.*]

Pt: I can feel the tension building now. [*Ruminating, detaching.*]

With continued pressure and clarification the patient is increasingly detaching in the room, avoiding eye contact, slowing down, and ruminating to himself. The resistance is crystallizing in the transference.

Th: Now how do you feel here with me? There's a positive feeling because we're working hard and we're doing something. But how do you feel because you are slowing down, and slowing down blocks the feelings. Am I right? [*Clarification and pressure.*] And I think you're measuring everything in your mind, too, censoring yourself. Do you get what I mean? [*Clarification.*] You're filtering everything, am I right? [*Clarification.*]

Pt: Right.

Th: Okay, now if you don't filter yourself, how do you feel? [*Challenge and pressure.*]

Notice, I constantly maintain pressure. Pressure is the lifeline to the person stuck beneath the resistance, encouraging him to do his best to reach back to me. Never let the pressure drop when the resistance is activated.

Clarification and challenge are required to mobilize the unconscious in resistant patients who erect a major wall and barrier in therapy. This clarification and challenge need to be done at mid and high rise in the complex transference feelings when resistances crystallize, making a major obstacle to the breakthrough of feelings.

CHAPTER 11

Head-On Collision

A fter receiving pressure and challenge, highly resistant patients further crystallize their defenses in the transference rather than experiencing complex feelings. This crystallization of resistance is an obstacle in the treatment unless handled.

Through extensive case-based research, Davanloo (1990) discovered that at this high rise in resistance, the complex transference feelings and the unconscious therapeutic alliance are mobilized in direct proportion to the resistance. He discovered a critical fact about unconscious operations in resistant patients: they must *meet the resistance head on and win the internal battle* against it. This "unlocking" event brings lasting change in psychic function, loosening overinhibited brain operations. Through studying videotapes of this critical juncture, Davanloo discovered ISTDP's most powerful intervention: the head-on collision (Davanloo 1999b).

NATURE OF HEAD-ON COLLISION

Head-on collision clarifies the reality of the therapeutic process at the moment it occurs. Tailored specifically to the patient's unconscious therapeutic alliance and resistance and the demands of reality necessary to accomplish the goal in this moment, head-on collision is composed of ingredients that reflect an honest statement delivered by the therapist of the state of affairs. Following is a list of some typical elements of head-on collision (Davanloo 1999b).

1. Clarifying the problem and its effect on the patient's life.

   Th: You have come here with a set of symptoms that include anxiety, depression, and a self-defeating pattern of relating to yourself.

2. Keeping the responsibility for change within the patient: undoing the notion of the omnipotent therapist who can magically heal the patient.

   Th: And these problems are your problems, meaning they are not caused by your wife or anyone else.

3. Emphasizing the patient's will: the patient and not the therapist is the prime mover in seeking help.

   Th: And your will is to do something about it for your own benefit and to benefit those you love.

4. Emphasizing the therapeutic task and the patient's goals in treatment.

   Th: Your wish is to overcome this blockage of emotions and the tendency to distance others and hurt yourself by turning anger on yourself.

5. Emphasizing the partnership between the patient and the therapist. The shared task that "we" are undertaking.

   Th: Together, you and I could get to the root of these problems, to break through to the underlying driving emotional forces.

6. Pointing out and emphasizing the nature of the types, format, and effects of resistance.

   Th: We see that even though part of you wants badly to overcome these problems, another part of you continues to go passive, detached, and helpless and keeps avoiding me.

7. Pointing out the consequences of the resistance if it remains in place.

   Th: As long as you keep doing this, I am useless to you. This wall defeats our efforts together.

8. Challenging and emphasizing the self-destructive nature of the resistance in the transference.

   Th: This is a major self-destructive action for a bright young person like you to take.

9. Emphasizing parallels between self-defeating and self-sabotaging patterns in the transference and all other relationships.

   Th: We know you have put up these same barriers and walls with others and that has badly damaged your marriage and relationship with your children.

10. Emphasizing the masochistic component of the patient's character resistance including the need for self-defeat and self-sabotage. Direct challenge at the forces maintaining the resistance, which may include rhetorical communication to the unconscious.

    Th: Which is to live like a criminal and we don't know what crimes you did to deserve this punishment. [*Rhetorical communication to the unconscious.*]

11. Deactivating of the transference by refusing the transferential role the patient wants to assign to the therapist.

    Th: At the same time, this passive position comes as if somehow I can solve this set of problems on my own, but obviously I can't.

12. Deactivating defiance.

    Th: Yet, part of you keeps this position as if to say "there is no way I'm going to move, I'm going to sabotage his (the therapist's) goal."

13. Challenging the dependent transference pattern: the need to use the therapist as a crutch.

    Th: As long as you continue in this crippled, passive position, this process is doomed to failure.

14. Challenging and pressuring to the resistance against the emotional closeness.

    Th: If you continue to maintain this wall and barrier with me, I will be useless and this will be defeated. Your destructive system will have been victorious over you.

15. Pressuring to the unconscious therapeutic alliance encouraging the patient to do his ultimate best in the battle for freedom.

    Th: So let's see what you are going to do about this massive self-destructive wall and barrier and this passive position here with me.

Rather than offering a formulaic intervention, tailor the head-on collision to the patient's unconscious therapeutic alliance, resistance, and goals for therapy in language that makes sense to the patient. Make sure the patient understands what you are saying and what your statements mean. The patient should exhibit both conscious (nodding and verbal descriptions of concordance) and unconscious (sighing, rise in resistance, or breakthrough of feelings or impulses) markers that he deeply understands you.

FUNCTION OF HEAD-ON COLLISION

The head-on collision mobilizes the complex transference feelings and unconscious therapeutic alliance and turns the patient against the resistance. Some head-on collisions are built to lead directly to breakthrough to the unconscious, while others are built to further mobilize the unconscious forces of complex transference feelings, unconscious therapeutic alliance, and resistance.

FORMATS OF HEAD-ON COLLISION

Davanloo (2005) describes several formats of head-on collisions that have specific timing and function.

Short-Range Head-On Collision

The short-range head-on collision is a short communication about defenses at a mid rise in complex transference feelings. For example, when an ambivalent patient is unclear about what she wants to do, the therapist can point out how her ambivalence paralyzes the process and interrupts any therapeutic progress. These short interventions focus on a specific defense or cluster of defenses operating at the time.

An example of how to deal with persistent nonspecificity would be to say something like this: "So far we are unclear about your problems because you cannot describe specific examples. Until we have a clear understanding of the problem, we cannot solve it. So can we look at a specific example of when you had this problem?"

Head-On Collision to Turn Syntonic Defenses to Dystonic

When the person does not see his defenses and their destructiveness, a head-on collision can help him see their damaging effect in therapy and his life. This realization often brings a breakthrough of grief that further turns the patient against his defenses.

Following is a typical head-on collision and treatment process for highly resistant patients with syntonic defenses.

Case of the Sixty-Two-Year-Old Accountant, Continued

This segment illustrates a head-on collision at high rise in the transference built to turn the patient against his own resistance and make a first breakthrough to the unconscious.

Pt: [*Sits tensely with hands firmly clasped, eyes fully avoiding mine.*]

Th: How do you feel emotionally here with me if you don't avoid me? [*Pressure and challenge.*] And your hands are like that, too, by the way. [*Clarification and challenge.*] They're closed up, and you're closing yourself. How do you feel if you don't shut down? [*Pressure and challenge.*]

Pt: Well, I'm going to have to learn how to open up, aren't I? [*Somewhat sarcastic and passive comment.*]

Th: Well, let's see what we can do about it at this point because part of you shuts you down and the rest of you is trying to open up. [*Head-on collision: emphasizing conflict between alliance and resistance.*]

Pt: Right.

Th: But what can we do about that so you don't shut down anymore [*head-on collision: pressure and challenge*] because shutting down would paralyze you, depress you, make you anxious, and then shut you off. [*Head-on collision: consequences of resistance.*] Let's see what we can do about that shut-down system that you have. What are we going to do about it? [*Head-on collision: pressure to alliance.*]

Pt: Well, that shut-down system has been around for years, perhaps sixty years. [*Whisper from the unconscious therapeutic alliance.*]

Th: Sixty or so? How much has that been hurting you? [*Head-on collision: consequences of the resistance.*]

Pt: I never realized it until you pointed it out, but I think you're right.

Th: How much has it hurt you? You don't let people get close to you. [*Head-on collision: consequences of resistance.*]

Pt: I've been told that.

Th: But here with me there's part of you that wants to put up a wall that keeps me out and then I can't get in to help you, right? [*Head-on collision: consequences of resistance against emotional closeness.*] It keeps me out of there. Do you follow me? Part of you puts up a wall . . . [*Head-on collision: nature of the resistance.*]

Pt: Yeah.

Th: That limits what I can do, and that defeats what you're trying to do here with me. [*Head-on collision: undoing the notion of omnipotent therapist, deactivating defiance, emphasizing the destructiveness of the resistance.*] What are we going to do, because part of you wants to sabotage what you're trying to do with me here, to defeat it? [*Head-on collision: emphasizing the partnership and resistance of the guilt.*] To hurt your effort . . .

Pt: So what causes that? [*Unconscious therapeutic alliance.*]

Th: And hurt what you're trying to do here with me, and we don't know why you would want to do something against yourself. [*Head-on collision: destructiveness of resistance, limits of the therapist.*] What can we do about this because otherwise the risk is that you would hurt yourself; you wouldn't get the best for yourself. Part of you would defeat what you're trying to do with me. [*Head-on collision: consequence of defeat if the resistance stays.*] So what are we going to do? [*Head-on collision: pressure to partnership.*]

Pt: Why does that happen? [*Unconscious therapeutic alliance.*]

Th: What can we do about it right now? [*Head-on collision: pressure to battle his own resistance.*]

Pt: I don't know.

Th: But ultimately you have to break through this. [*Head-on collision: undoing notion of omnipotent therapist, deactivating passive compliance.*]

Pt: I appreciate that.

Th: But what can we do? Because if you keep a wall with me, we won't break through it. [*Head-on collision: consequence of resistances.*] Because part of you still wants to avoid me so you detach. You cover up with me. [*Head-on collision: highlighting the specific defenses.*]

Pt: But I, I feel I've been pretty open with you.

Th: Besides words, though, part of you wants to detach from the emotions that you have here with me. [*Head-on collision: emotional wall and barrier.*]

Pt: That's the result of many years of practice. [*Unconscious therapeutic alliance.*]

Th: I wonder how do you feel about that. Because how many years have you kept yourself from your own true emotions . . . from being your *self.*

Pt: [*Becomes teary-eyed.*] Well, I'm saying it's been sixty years; that's my first reaction. Sixty years and sure it's damaged me probably more than I realize. [*Unconscious therapeutic alliance.*] And maybe you know as a result of the cancer (seven years prior), I knew something was wrong, but I didn't know how to deal with it. I knew something wasn't right, and I was frustrated with "hey, life is short. I've got to get through this." But I didn't know what it was and didn't know how to get through it.

Th: Part of you didn't want to go to the end detached. You didn't want to go through your life as not a feeling person.

Pt: Right.

Th: You didn't want to die that way.

Pt: [*Becomes more tearful, displays palpable painful feeling, and is much more open and relaxed.*]

This vignette illustrates a breakthrough of grief about the destructiveness of the resistance. This breakthrough is a direct response to heavy pressure to reach the person stuck under the resistance and challenge to help him battle the defenses. Head-on collision was also required to enable this breakthrough and to turn him against his defenses. This is typical of early process work with highly resistant patients. (See chapter 14.)

Interlocking Chain of Head-On Collisions

Highly resistant patients may need a series of head-on collisions with increased intensity, breadth, and focus at each level of rise in complex transference feeling. This intensive education about the patient's resistance involves very high pressure to mobilize the conscious and unconscious alliances to do battle with the resistance. (See chapter 14.)

Comprehensive Head-On Collision

Use a comprehensive head-on collision when resistances are heavily focused between you and the patient, or "crystallized" in the room, preventing a breakthrough to the unconscious. Such head-on collisions may have many elements to be delivered over many minutes, highlighting the complete resistance, the potential of the alliance, the limitations of the therapist, and other elements of the therapeutic process.

Case of the Sixty-Two-Year-Old Accountant: Comprehensive Head-On Collision

This occurred some minutes after the last segment where he had a breakthrough of grief about his defenses. Now he has reverted to a detached, defiant, passive position of leaning back in his seat with arms crossed with eye avoidance and closed posture. The resistance is fully crystallized in the transference in the form of a major wall of defenses.

Pt: But I don't know. I've got to learn what feelings are. [*Passive position.*]

Th: What are we going to do here right now, you and me? [*Pressure to be active.*]

Pt: Don't I have to learn what feelings are? [*Passive response.*]

Th: Well, let's see what we're going to do right now though. [*Pressure to be active.*]

Pt: I don't know. What do you want me to do? [*Passive response, irritated tone of voice.*]

Th: Let's see what we're going to do right now. [*Pressure to be active.*]

Pt: Yeah, what are we going to do? [*Passive position.*]

Th: About this detachment here from the feelings, about the shutting down.

Pt: Well, you see that's just normal to me. [*Reverts to a syntonic position.*]

Th: Yeah, but what are we going to do about that? See, because part of you will want to carry it all through your life, right. [*Head-on collision: highlighting the destructive part of him and the impact of continuing to defend.*] You're detached, disconnected, and then getting symptoms, too—depressed and anxious on top of it. [*Head-on collision: damaging effects of his resistance.*] Okay? But now what are we going to do about that here? [*Head-on collision: major pressure to battle the resistance.*] What are we going to do about the detachment here because there's still a barrier here with me? [*Head-on collision: challenge to the wall and detachment.*]

This means I'm on the outside and you're on the inside. [*Head-on collision: effects of wall.*]

Pt: You see, I don't see that barrier.

Th: How do you feel right now here with me?

Pt: I feel fine. [*Irritated tone of voice and use of a cover word.*]

Th: But "I feel fine"' doesn't say how you actually feel toward me. [*Counter to defense of cover word.*]

Pt: Then I come back to saying that maybe I don't understand what feelings are.

Th: Yeah, so what are we going to do about that? [*Pressure to alliance.*]

Pt: I'll have to get an understanding of what feelings are. [*Defiance and passivity.*]

Th: But how are we going to do that? [*Pressure against passive position.*]

Pt: I have no idea. [*Smiles; helpless and passive position.*]

Th: That's a helpless position. [*Challenge.*] You have a smile there, but if you level with yourself, how do you feel underneath the smile here with me? I mean leveling to tell you and me how you actually feel with me right now. [*Pressure to identify feelings.*]

Pt: [*Shakes head and is silent and still closed up.*]

Th: You're censoring yourself still. How do you feel with me right there? [*Challenge and pressure.*]

Pt: Fine! [*Irritated tone of voice.*]

Th: How else do you feel? [*Pressure to identify feelings.*] I think you would totally paralyze yourself rather than say you were frustrated right now. I think you'd totally put a wall between you and me rather than say that. I think you would get depressed rather than to say that. [*Head-on collision: clarification and challenge to the wall and censoring.*]

Pt: [*Avoids eyes further, sighs, clenches hands, and closes up posture.*]

Th: See, you're detaching from me. Your eyes detached and you just took a big sigh, and your hands are tense, and the smile is there, and you're closed up and inside you have some feelings. But part of you says "there's no way I'm going to let him see what my feelings are. I'm going to keep them all bottled inside myself." [*Head-on collision: destructiveness of defiance.*]

Pt: Well . . .

Th: And then sabotage would be assured; defeat would be assured. But then I'd have to ask myself "why does he need to sabotage and defeat himself and then go beyond what I could do to help him?" [*Head-on collision: deactivation of the transference, undoing notion of omnipotence, effects of the resistance.*]

Pt: Maybe there's a fear about . . .

Th: But the problem is what are we going to do about this detachment and this wall and barrier you're putting up here with me right now? [*Head-on collision: problem of the wall, pressure, and challenge.*]

Pt: I don't see the wall.

Th: But right now, it's very specific: it's like that. [*Therapist points to his lie-back posture, which is a nonverbal defense.*] You are totally closed up, tense, smiling, and avoiding me. [*Head-on collision: nature of resistance.*] You're totally avoiding me and covering up. Now here's the issue: part of you (unconscious therapeutic alliance) wants to get to the bottom of this. And part of you (resistance) wants to put up this wall and sabotage and defeat yourself and keep the problems inside and not let me get in to help you out. [*Head-on collision: effects of the resistance.*] But then I'm limited. Right? I'm limited, but then I'd have to say I could only do what I could do. Right? And then I would have to say I failed. But then I can afford to fail because I can't always get there. Because sometimes I can't get through; we can't get through. [*Head-on collision: undoing notion of omnipotence.*] But one question is "can you afford to carry this any longer?" Do you want to carry this any longer, this wall, this detachment, this sabotaging of yourself like that? [*Head-on collision: appeal to the unconscious therapeutic alliance.*] Why do you want to have it like that? [*Head-on collision: pressure to unconscious therapeutic alliance.*]

Pt: I don't see . . .

Th: Take a look here. [*Head-on collision: pointing to his nonverbal defense.*] You're totally closed up here with me. You're disconnected from how you feel here. You're anxious and tense and you're avoiding me and we still don't know how you feel here with me. [*Head-on collision: clarification of the state of resistance, high pressure.*]

Pt: [*Ruminates to himself, still displays detachment.*]

Th: See, you're thinking, but how do you feel? Your mind is blotting the whole thing out, but how do you feel if you don't do that? [*Pressure and challenge.*] See you're avoiding me. More specifically you're avoiding my eyes. [*Identification of detachment, pressure.*]

Pt: I am now because I'm thinking about . . .

Th: Yeah, but most of the time you avoid me and you're slowed down and closed up. You put a wall up between you and me, but let's see what are we going to do about that. [*Head-on collision: nature of resistance, pressure to task and partnership.*] What are we going to do about the wall here between you and me and maybe part of you says "he can ask all day but I'm not going to tell him how I actually feel, I've kept it sixty-two years; I'll keep it the next thirty years or whatever there is." [*Head-on collision: high pressure.*]

Pt: But I'm not doing that consciously. [*Unconscious therapeutic alliance.*]

Th: Consciously or unconsciously doesn't matter. It's happening, and only you can control it. [*Head-on collision: deactivating the transference, pressure.*] But let's see what are we going to do about this because so far it wants to sabotage.

Pt: But then I . . . [*Begins to ruminate.*]

Th: But now you want to explain, but if you don't . . . [*Blocking of rumination.*] You're explaining why you want to keep a wall; part of you wants to keep it.

Pt: If I don't see the wall, how can I defeat it? [*Bounces back and is more active but still leaning back.*]

Th: Yeah, but so far this wall is still here. Your smile is part of the wall. [*Challenge to nonverbal defense.*]

Pt: I don't see the wall. [*Actively moves and gestures, appears irritated.*]

Th: Closed up is part of the wall and holding yourself like that is part of the wall. [*Pointing out his leaning-back posture: challenge to nonverbal defense.*]

Pt: But if I don't see the wall, how do I get rid of it? [*Slaps hands down on legs.*]

Th: But now you're saying "if I don't see the wall."

Pt: Well, I don't. I feel I'm being quite open with you. [*Smiles and looks defensive.*]

Th: Yeah, but your smile is here right now. But what do you feel here with me right now underneath that? You're covered up, but how do you feel toward me? [*Pressure to identify feelings.*]

Pt: I told you, I feel fine! [*Obviously irritated tone of voice.*]

Th: But how else do you feel toward me? Your voice doesn't sound "fine." Your voice is probably the true feeling. How do you feel toward me there? [*Pressure to declare feelings.*]

Somatic Pathway of Rage

The patient finally sits forward and engages eye contact. He is giving up his defenses and allowing the impulse to break through.

Th: I think you'd be crippled to say you're angry, and you would close up and sabotage and become hopeless and anxious and put up a wall and barricade and cripple yourself and shut down rather than to say how you actually feel. [*Head-on collision: crippling effect of resistances, deactivating defiance, high pressure and challenge.*]

Pt: But I don't feel angry! [*Unconscious therapeutic alliance: negation. Moves arms in a very active thrusting motion: tension has dropped and somatic pathway of rage is activated.*]

Th: How do you feel right there? You say you don't feel angry. But, how do you feel right there inside your body? [*Pressure to identify feelings.*]

Pt: Well, the moment I said it, I felt angry!

Unlocking the Unconscious

The patient has reached the beginning of a partial unlocking of the unconscious (Davanloo 1990), brought about through systematic and well-timed, relentless pressure, challenge, and head-on collision. Notice he used negation, as part of the unconscious therapeutic alliance, right up to the breakthrough of the impulse. The unconscious therapeutic alliance then became stronger than the resistance. This event was followed by an extensive recapitulation to fuel the unconscious therapeutic alliance and the unconscious was explored.

Head-on collisions can be short range, comprehensive, or provided in interlocking chains. They are tailored to the moment to present the reality of the therapy situation and implore the patient to overcome his resistance. Head-on collisions are perhaps the most powerful intervention in ISTDP, effectively placing a wedge between the patient and long-held defenses and simultaneously mobilizing the complex transference feelings and unconscious therapeutic alliance.

CHAPTER 12

The Low Resistance Patient: The Open Door

L ow resistance patients are at the extreme left end of the spectrum of psychoneurotic disorders. These patients have only grief about past losses (typically after age seven) without any rage in the unconscious. Thus, they have no unconscious guilt about rage and no self-destructive system. They have only minor tactical defenses and no major defenses (Davanloo 1995a). (See fig. 12.1.)

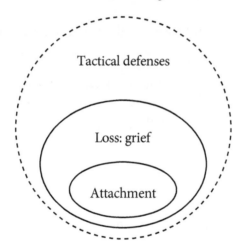

Figure 12.1 The low resistance patient

Low resistance patients' main complaints are obsessional symptoms, worry, anxiety, or mild dysphoria. These symptoms typically activate when patients form or lose close relationships.

Metaphorically, this patient is like a person sitting on her front porch who appears to be welcoming you in. Inside the house are the photos of loved ones who have died. She allows you in the house, but when you ask about the pictures, she changes the subject as if she has no feelings about the deceased. Even though all the signs indicate she wants to talk about the loss, she diverts, minimizes, and avoids your efforts while standing beside the pictures she invited you in to see.

These quite healthy patients can be treated in fewer than five one-hour sessions and typically in only a single session. They rarely are found in secondary and tertiary clinical settings, constituting less than 1 percent of outpatient psychiatric referrals. Of about three thousand cases reviewed to 2014, only about 10 (0.33 percent) were low resistance.

TREATMENT PROCESS FOR LOW RESISTANCE PATIENTS

The treatment process in these cases is one or two sessions to handle tactical defenses and allow the experience of grief about past losses. (See table 12.1.)

Table 12.1 Treatment Process with Low Resistance Patients

Process	Task
Initial process	Inquiry into problem areas, psychodiagnostic evaluation
Dynamic focus on losses	Communication with the conscious therapeutic alliance, handling of tactical defenses
Experience of grief	Breakthrough of grief about losses
Recapitulation	Summarizing the process, linking feelings to anxiety and defenses
Concluding the process	Closure of the process in one or two sessions

Initial Process

These patients arrive with a conscious therapeutic alliance and can describe how they avoid emotions that are triggered in relationships with people. Their unconscious anxiety is in the striated muscle without any smooth-muscle or cognitive-perceptual symptoms. The level of striated muscle anxiety is so low that they do not suffer pain or other symptoms related to this tension. (See fig. 12.2.)

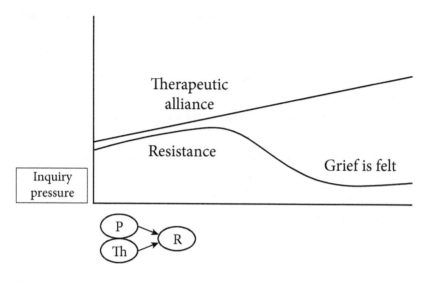

Figure 12.2 Low resistance patient: treatment process
P: patient, Th: therapist, R: resistance

These patients often state right away that they have had a loss and that they have emotions about this loss. When asked about those feelings, the patient will use tactical defenses. For example, she may say "I *may* have *had* a *little* sadness about that." These defenses are arrows signaling that you are focusing in the correct area.

Manage Tactical Defenses

Manage tactical defenses by persistently exploring grief over losses and help the person experience the grief. For instance, ask the patient to describe the positive feelings and close relationship he had with the deceased. "Unlocking the unconscious" does not apply to these patients as the unconscious is already open.

Case Vignette: Unresolved Grief

A twenty-five-year-old woman presents with unresolved grief triggered by recent changes in her life. The process begins with inquiry.

> Pt: My father died when I was twelve years old and lately I've started to mourn his death. I've been very emotional, and my boyfriend told me to get myself together.

> Th: What do you mean by emotional? [*Pressure to be specific.*]

Pt: I'll cry at the slightest provocation. When I see someone happy, I cry.

She went on to describe that when she sees happy shows on television or sees parents with children, she feels the urge to cry. The therapist then summarized the problem she described.

Th: The difficulties then have to do with how you feel about your father's death?

Pt: My mother thinks that's the focal point of my reactions. [*Tactical defense: "mother thinks."*]

Th: What do you think it is? [*Pressure, counter to tactical defense.*]

Pt: I don't know what it is, but it just seems like everything has come to a head with my boyfriend, and I'm just getting very frustrated. [*Tactical defense: denial.*]

Th: So you're not sure what the problem is? [*Taking the side of the tactical defense.*]

Pt: I think [*tactical defense: indefinite terms*] it is partly [*tactical defense: qualifying, minimizing*] to do with my father's death. I mean, I never ever cried about it until the past year. But I don't talk to my mom about it. I can't.

Th: Why? [*Pressure and interruption of tactical defenses.*]

Pt: Because I don't want to put her through that and my brother and sister don't understand because they weren't there when he died. [*Tactical defense: rationalization.*]

Th: What happened?

Pt: He had a stroke. I was sleeping when I heard a scream. My mom told me to go back to bed but I couldn't. He died at the hospital but I was there and held his hand.

Th: Um-hmm.

Pt: I don't know why all this is coming up. [*Therapeutic alliance: negation.*] I guess maybe it was because I have my first boyfriend and I kept thinking that my Dad is not going to be there and see me if I marry him.

Th: What was your relationship like with your father? [*Pressure to recall the attachment.*]

Pt: I guess it was good. [*Tactical defense: indefinite terms.*] We were very close. But I don't remember him. I don't remember what it's like to have a dad. [*Tactical defense: selective memory.*]

Th: You don't remember him? [*Counter to tactical defense.*]

Pt: I can't remember what it was like when I was small. I have pictures, but that doesn't help. I just don't remember.

Th: So when you're talking about this, you're saying you wish he had been there for your graduation and to meet your boyfriend?

Pt: Yeah, I wish he were there to see me grow up. [*Looks increasingly sad, becomes tearful.*]

Th: You have a lot of sadness when you talk about that. [*Facilitation of grief.*]

Pt: Yeah. I'm trying not to cry. [*Weeps.*]

Th: Why? You have a very painful feeling about this. [*Pressure to experience grief.*]

Pt: [*Cries.*] It's really hard to talk about.

Th: It's very painful. [*Pressure to experience grief.*]

Pt: [*Cries.*] He also doesn't have a grave, so I can't go and visit him or talk to him.

Pt: And I know how hard it is for my mom so it's not easy. I feel I have to be strong for her. [*Cries; clarification of her own tactical defense.*]

Concluding the Process

Low resistance patients are usually treatable in one or two sessions. Thus, you will have no formal phase of unlocking, working through, or termination. The session can conclude with a summary recapitulation and with wishing the patient well. A short follow-up meeting can confirm that the process of accessing grief and symptom removal is adequately done.

Pt: This really helped me understand all this. For years I've been swerving around this pain and sadness. It was making me irritable with my boyfriend. I liked getting to understand and put all this together.

CHALLENGES IN WORKING WITH THE LOW RESISTANCE PATIENT

The most common technical problem with low resistance patients is overreading the defenses. If you read tactical defenses as if they are major resistances, you may use challenge when it is not required. This can produce a misalliance, but these patients are quite healthy and will tell you that you are misreading things.

Related to this, you may assume the patient has buried rage and try to "dig" for it. The result will be the same; the patient will become irritated and try to correct the process. This is one situation where listening to the patient's words will help you greatly because the conscious therapeutic alliance is active.

OUTCOMES

These patients' self-report measures are normal at both the start and end of treatment. The small sample of these rare patients from a private psychiatry office study (Abbass 2002a) all did well with one- to two-session treatments. None relapsed or returned for further therapy. All were able to work and function both before and after treatment.

> *Low resistance patients only have grief and minor tactical defenses. Focus on the lost attachment to facilitate the experience of the grief. The treatment is short and all patients do well. The most common technical problem encountered is overreading the defenses and challenging when not required.*

CHAPTER 13

The Moderately Resistant Patient: The Guarded Cellar

oderately resistant patients constitute about one-sixth of out-patient psychiatric referrals (Abbass 2002a). These patients had secure attachments that were interrupted by significant trauma, typically between the ages of four and seven. The trauma produced murderous rage and guilt. These patients have a moderate degree of self-defeating behavior. They present with major resistance in the form of isolation of affect and unconscious anxiety manifesting primarily in the form of striated muscle unconscious anxiety (Davanloo 1995b). (See fig. 13.1.)

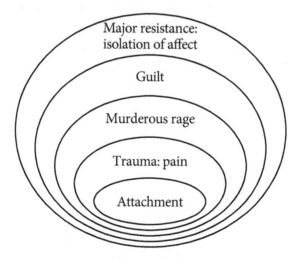

Figure 13.1 Moderately resistant patient

The moderately resistant patient lives as if he has the bodies of murdered loved ones stored in his cellar: no one is allowed to visit his house. Your attempt to know him is met with guilt-induced anxiety and efforts to push you off the property. However, your pressure, experienced as encouragement, assures him of your good intentions: your efforts to reach him encourage him to let you see the cellar.

These patients present significant resistance that can thwart traditional psychotherapy efforts. The conscious therapeutic alliance, overpowered by resistance, needs the unconscious therapeutic alliance to come into force through mobilization of the complex transference feelings.

TREATMENT PHASES FOR MODERATELY RESISTANT PATIENTS

Over a brief treatment course, treatment phases include psychodiagnostic evaluation, repeated unlocking of the unconscious, working through and termination. Table 13.1 illustrates the phases and tasks.

Table 13.1 Treatment phases for moderately resistant patients

Phase	Task
Trial therapy	Initial evaluation, psychodiagnosis, and unlocking the unconscious using primarily pressure
Repeated unlocking	Partial and major unlockings of the unconscious
Working through	Mobilization and experience of residual rage, guilt, and grief
Termination	Closure of the therapy relationship over one or two sessions

TRIAL THERAPY IN MODERATELY RESISTANT PATIENTS

These patients seldom present with barriers to initial engagement. They are able to describe and are usually distressed by their problems (dystonic). The front of the system is almost always striated muscle anxiety and avoided feelings, so pressure to feelings is the typical first intervention. They respond to pressure with striated muscle anxiety, tactical defenses, major defenses of isolation of affect, and some detachment with some crystallization in the transference. To undo this detachment, you will need some clarification and challenge to the resistance. Continued pressure will unlock the unconscious with a breakthrough of the complex transference feelings leading to dominance by the unconscious therapeutic alliance over the resistance. (See fig. 13.2.)

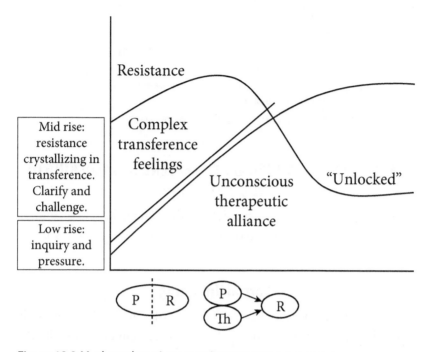

Figure 13.2 Moderately resistant patient: treatment process
R: resistance, P: patient healthy aspects, Th: therapist

When unlocked, the unconscious therapeutic alliance brings clear linkages to or images of past trauma with attachment figures. Thereafter, dynamic exploration of the unconscious, experience of the underlying feelings, recapitulation, and consolidation will complete the trial therapy. This interview is typically two to three hours in length. These elements constitute the central dynamic sequence of *unlocking the unconscious* (Davanloo 2001). (See table 13.2.)

Table 13.2 Central dynamic sequence of unlocking the unconscious

Phase	Process
1	Inquiry: exploring the patient's difficulties and ability to respond
2	Pressure: mobilizing the unconscious and psychodiagnosis
3	Challenge: working on the resistance mobilized in the transference
4	Transference resistance: manifesting some degree of crystallization of resistances

5	Partial, major, or extended unlocking the unconscious: experiencing of the complex transference feelings and activation of the unconscious therapeutic alliance
6	Analysis of the transference: focusing on extensive recapitulation to link all the material into a seamless understanding of the psychodynamics
7	Dynamic exploration of the unconscious: examining the emotional effects of past attachments and attachment trauma
8	Consolidation: reviewing the process and planning treatment

PARTIAL VERSUS MAJOR VERSUS EXTENDED UNLOCKING OF THE UNCONSCIOUS

Davanloo (1995d, 2001) has defined three main degrees of unlocking or degrees of dominance of the unconscious therapeutic alliance over resistance.

Partial Unlocking

In partial unlocking, the complex transference feelings are only partially experienced, and most of the rage and guilt are not felt. The main experience is grief. At this level the unconscious therapeutic alliance brings linkages to past attachment trauma or more recent events with parallel emotions (Davanloo 1995d).

One variant of partial unlocking is called a *first breakthrough*. This term refers to "the first dominance" of the unconscious therapeutic alliance over resistance (Davanloo 2001). These breakthroughs are common when turning a highly resistant patient against her defenses and are primarily composed of grief and little evidence of rage or guilt. (See chapter 11 for a clinical example.)

Major Unlocking

In contrast, major unlockings include the passage of murderous rage in the transference with a transfer of the image to the attachment figure of the past. Guilt about this rage is then experienced face-to-face with the figure of the past. Here we see a major dominance of the unconscious therapeutic alliance over resistance (Davanloo 2001).

Extended Unlocking

The term *extended unlocking* has been used in different ways (Davanloo 2001), but I reserve this term for when the murderous rage is directly experienced with the figure of the past after the rage began in the transference. For example, the rage starts toward you, but as soon as the patient sees his hands attack you, the image becomes his mother from the past. A prolonged passage of rage toward the mother and a prolonged passage of waves of guilt follows. The unconscious therapeutic alliance is completely dominant over the resistance, enabling powerful unfettered experiences of intense rage and guilt.

Case Vignette: Moderately Resistant Patient and Unlocking the Unconscious

The following vignette illustrates the process of trial therapy, psychodiagnosis, and mobilization of the unconscious therapeutic alliance in a moderately resistant patient.

Initial Phase and Psychodiagnostic Evaluation

A woman with chronic worry and tension arrives quite tense with hands clenching. She is engaged and presents a pleasant demeanor.

Th: Can you tell me about the difficulties that you're experiencing?

Pt: Um, tension is one thing, ah. [*Thinks for a moment, sighs.*]

Th: I noticed when you were coming in that there's some anxiety. Did you notice that? [*Pressure to notice unconscious anxiety.*]

Pt: [*Nods agreement.*]

Th: What do you experience physically with the anxiety? [*Pressure to self-reflect.*]

Pt: I'm relaxed, but inside I feel all tense. [*Unconscious anxiety.*]

Th: Where is that? Within your whole body?

Pt: Within my body . . . it just . . . I feel tense.

Th: When you're anxious, in what ways does it affect your body? You get a certain amount of it here, but can you get more anxiety than this? [*Pressure, focusing on the process.*]

Pt: Um . . . yeah, I shake a lot more. But when I get really stressed, really angry or really upset, I feel way more tense.

Th: So what emotions drive the anxiety that you have right now? What's beneath it? [*Pressure to identify feelings.*]

Pt: Why am I anxious?

Th: Yeah. Right now. [*Pressure to identify feelings.*]

Pt: I'm really busy with my family. Is that what you mean?

Th: What feelings are underneath the anxiety when you're here? What feelings come up that get you tense when we're talking here? [*Pressure to identify feelings.*]

Pt: I don't feel tense, see. [*Laughs.*]

Th: So you don't actually feel anxious? The tension you're getting is a bodily reaction. It's not like you're anxious but your body is. [*Clarification of unconscious anxiety.*]

Pt: [*Shakes head.*] Yeah, but I don't notice that. [*Confirmation of unconscious anxiety.*]

Th: You don't notice that piece?

Pt: No. To me I'm relaxed. Like I'm not nervous about talking to you or anything like that.

Th: You feel fine about meeting me, but at that same time this tension is there. [*Clarification of unconscious anxiety.*]

Pt: Yeah. [*Sighs.*]

Th: What emotions drive that anxiety you have? What else is beneath that when we're here talking? [*Pressure to identify feelings.*]

Pt: My problem is that I don't feel tense [*Sighs.*]

Th: What feelings cause you to have this sighing? [*Pressure to identify feelings.*]

Pt: When I first came in?

Th: And just now.

Pt: I don't even notice I'm doing it. [*Unconscious anxiety.*]

Th: Yeah, so what are the emotions that get activated before your body goes tense? Why does that happen? [*Pressure to identify feelings.*] Do you want us to try and figure how that works? [*Clarification of the task and pressure to her will.*]

Pt: I would love to know.

Th: It's unconscious. You're not doing it, but your body does it. [*Brief recap: unconscious anxiety.*]

Pt: And I don't even realize my body's doing it. That's my problem.

Th: Yeah, if we can notice that and see what drives that, do you want us to try for that? [*Pressure to the task and her will.*]

Pt: Okay.

Th: What are the emotions you have here beneath that? What are the feelings you have here with me? [*Pressure to identify feelings.*]

Pt: It's just that, I guess, underneath I'm probably wondering what's going to happen.

Th: Okay, these are some thoughts you have. [*Clarification of thought versus feelings.*]

Pt: Just thoughts I have.

Th: What are the feelings that you have in there? [*Pressure to identify feelings.*]

Pt: [*Shakes head, laughs.*] I'm no good at this!

Th: Do you have trouble identifying different emotional states when you have them? [*Clarification of the problem with emotions.*]

Pt: Obviously, because I can't do it.

Th: So can we try to sort out what is happening? How you're affected so you can reduce or stop anxiety from affecting you? [*Pressure to her will and the task.*]

Pt: Okay. [*Waits passively.*]

Th: Okay, how do we do that? Any thoughts on where we can focus? [*Pressure to encourage active collaboration.*]

Pt: I don't know. [*Breaks eye contact, ruminates to herself, and detaches.*]

Psychodiagnostic Evaluation

After several pressure interventions a rise occurs in the complex transference feelings and unconscious anxiety, and resistance is crystallizing in the transference. Thus, in response to pressure, the patient has defended rather than have a breakthrough of feeling (low resistance) or "go flat" (fragile character structure or high resistance with repression). She appears to be moderately or highly resistant but could still have a threshold where anxiety would go to the smooth muscle or cognitive-perceptual field. We need to continue to mobilize the unconscious to determine her capacity to tolerate anxiety.

The process is at mid rise so now we must begin to clarify and challenge the resistances that are in the room. If we don't do this, the process will stagnate.

Th: Let's see how you feel right now here with me. [*Pressure to identify feelings.*] What are the emotions that are there as we talk? I notice, and I'm not sure if you notice this, that you are tending to withdraw when we're talking. You tend to think and go inward toward yourself. Do you know what I mean by that? It's like you are detaching yourself. [*Clarification of the resistance in the transference.*]

Pt: I didn't know I did that. I know sometimes when I'm thinking, I have to concentrate on what I'm saying.

Th: So when we're here talking, you're tending to think.

Pt: I'm always like that. [*Syntonic defense of emotional detachment.*]

Th: Okay, so feelings are somewhere else other than the thoughts, right. What do you feel inside right now while we're here talking? What are the emotions that you have in there that you're tense about? [*Pressure to identify feelings.*]

Pt: See, that's my problem. I can't identify—to me emotion is anger. [*Sighs.*] I'm not angry. I'm not. [*Unconscious therapeutic alliance: negation.*]

Th: But you've got some anxiety in you though. [*Linking of feelings to anxiety.*]

Pt: I have.

Th: So anxiety is always there at a certain level. But why is that happening to you? Why you've got that working against you? [*Communication with the person stuck under the anxiety and defenses.*]

Pt: Could that be from lifestyle? That's what I don't understand. Like when I'm at my sales work, I've got to be moving fast all the time. [*Firmly clenches hands.*]

Th: You mean the pressure of work? [*Pressure to be specific.*]

Pt: Pressure at work all the time.

Th: Who puts the pressure on you? [*Pressure to be specific.*]

Pt: The job itself. The sales manager. And I put pressure on myself; I try to work fast when I'm doing things.

Th: So what are the emotions you have under this anxiety that push you to do these things and push you and stress you? What are the emotions that are stressing you? [*Pressure to identify feelings.*]

Pt: [*Sighs and firmly clenches hands.*]

Th: You notice you took a sigh there. [*Clarification of nonverbal cues.*]

Pt: I know because that one was a big one.

Th: Yeah, and your arms are tense. I don't know if you noticed that they're clenching. [*Clarification of nonverbal cues.*]

Pt: I didn't, yeah!

Th: So what are the emotions? [*Pressure to identify feelings.*]

Pt: [*Pries her hands apart.*] When you said it, I noticed my fingers are actually hurting each other because I was squeezing so hard.

Th: So what are the emotions beneath the tension you feel right now here as we talk, if you don't go away from me? [*Pressure and challenge.*]

Pt: [*Thinks, clenches hands, and avoids eyes.*]

Th: If you don't go away—because you're tending to detach into yourself. See if you don't do that, because if you detach, it blocks off what we're trying to do, right? [*Short-range head-on collision.*]

Handling Resistance

This is a short-range head-on collision (chapter 11) with the resistances in the transference as evidenced by the resistances against emotional closeness, passivity, and rumination. The negative effect of these resistances is highlighted and pressure is applied for the patient to not do this to herself. The therapist implies that the therapist cannot help the patient if she is detached behind a wall.

Th: Let's see what emotions cause you to tense up and detach. If you don't go detached—if you don't go away . . . [*High pressure and challenge.*]

Pt: I'm tired, if that's an emotion. I'm tired of having to put up with the tension . . .

Th: So let's see what we can do here together. [*Pressure on partnership.*] What are the feelings that make you tense up right now here as we talk? The emotions that are trying to come up that make you tense just when we're talking? [*Pressure to identify feelings.*]

Pt: I hold my emotions in. [*Whisper from the unconscious therapeutic alliance. Patient speaks confidently and quietly but with deep meaning.*]

Unconscious Therapeutic Alliance

This is a whisper from the unconscious therapeutic alliance. In these few words the patient has summarized both the problem and the solution.

Th: Yeah, but your doing that is going to hurt you, isn't it? Doesn't that hurt you to do that to your body and yourself—to hold, lock in the emotions? Let's see what's happening. [*Reply to unconscious therapeutic alliance.*]

Pt: I'm getting tight in my head and arms. They are getting tighter.

Th: So the anxiety's going up as we speak, right?

Pt: Yeah.

Th: We're talking and the anxiety goes up. So what are the feelings beneath all these responses? The feelings that are activating, that you tend to block off, you said? [*Continued and constant pressure.*]

Pt: I try to not have them (feelings).

Th: Is that why you get tensed up though? [*Clarification of the cause of her problem.*]

Pt: That's probably it, and I don't even realize that I'm tense. [*Unconscious therapeutic alliance: she is becoming irritated with her defenses.*]

Th: Okay, so when we're talking here, things are happening. You're trying to be here. You come here for us to do our best to understand what's happening and hopefully to get to the roots of what drives the anxiety, right? And at the same time, when you're trying to do that, this part of you blocks the feelings off; it tends to block you up or you become tense and more detached from yourself. [*Head-on collision: problem, task, patient as the prime mover, partnership, nature of resistance.*]

Pt: And my body just feels like it's getting harder and harder and harder.

Th: Okay, let's see what's happening.

Pt: My muscles, actually, my muscles are tightened up: my sides are hurting. [*Striated muscle anxiety.*]

Th: Okay, let's see what we can do to see what's driving this—what are the feelings that you feel here with me as we talk. The emotions that are just rising up in there. [*Pressure to identify feelings.*]

Pt: [*Thinks, breaks eye contact.*]

Th: If you don't detach from me, if you don't detach from the feelings . . . [*Challenge to resistances against emotional closeness.*]

Pt: I keep detaching. I don't know how not to. I don't know how. [*Very tensely presses all fingers on one another.*]

Th: Let's see how you feel just now inside when we're talking here. The emotions toward me. Do you see the way your hands are? [*Pressure and pointing out of nonverbal cues.*]

Pt: I can't. I can't sit still. [*Helpless position.*]

Th: What are the feelings in there? What are the emotions? [*Pressure to identify feelings.*]

Pt: Tightness.

Th: Yeah, what else is in there? [*Pressure to identify feelings.*]

Pt: Shakiness. [*Laughs.*]

Th: What are the feelings beneath all these things? [*Pressure to identify feelings.*]

Relentless Pressure

This relentless pressure is necessary for any resistant patient because it is the lifeline to the person stuck underneath the resistance. This pressure is the direct connection that brings the unconscious therapeutic alliance and assures the patient that you truly want to see the dead bodies in her cellar and that you are comfortable with whatever feelings or impulses arise.

Pt: I don't have feelings. [*Laughs.*] No. I don't know. [*Sits on her hands as if to keep them from moving.*]

Persisting

The patient is staying in this helpless position stating she "doesn't know." Persist. Trust the process and don't be taken in by the words of the resistance. If this were only a minor tactical defense, then it would have ceased with my bypassing it as in the previous chapter. But this defense did not cease so it is more a part of the major resistance and requires stronger interventions. If I don't deal with this, she would stay in a helpless position.

> *Th:* If you don't let yourself think that you can't feel [*clarification and challenge*], and if you don't let yourself go helpless, if you don't go detached, and if you don't get blocked, let's see how you feel here with me as we talk. [*Pressure to identify feelings.*] What emotions are coming up here toward me as we speak right now? [*Pressure to identify feelings.*]
>
> *Pt:* [*Breaks eye contact.*]
>
> *Th:* You're going away from me again. Do you see that? [*Clarification.*]
>
> *Pt:* Yeah. [*Covers her face.*] I don't know how to answer your question, and it's making me tense. I know that.
>
> *Th:* How do you feel about what I'm asking? What emotions come up about my asking you that? [*Pressure to identify feelings.*]

Complex Transference Feelings

The very active and challenging process we just witnessed mobilizes complex feelings toward the therapist. These in turn activate the complex transference feelings tied to the unprocessed complex attachment related feelings that in turn mobilize the unconscious anxiety and defense we are seeing.

> *Pt:* Frustration. [*Moves hands freely with drop in anxiety; finally declares feelings with the therapist.*]
>
> *Th:* Toward whom?
>
> *Pt:* Toward you, a bit, because . . . [*Tactical defenses: "a bit" is minimizing; "because" is the beginning of rationalizing.*]
>
> *Th:* How do you experience the frustration and anger toward me in your body? How do you experience that feeling? [*Bypassing of the tactical defenses.*]
>
> *Pt:* Tightness.
>
> *Th:* That's anxiety.
>
> *Pt:* I'm tightening up because I can't give you the answers you're looking for and the more you ask, the more frustrated I get, and my voice is rising. [*Hands move freely with a drop in tension and an obvious rise in energy.*]
>
> *Th:* So you experience somewhere in your body a feeling of frustration or anger? [*Bypassing of the tactic of saying "you're looking for"*

> *because breakthrough is imminent and this tactic was not obstructing anything.*]

Pt: [*Nods head.*]

Somatic Pathway of Rage

With clear evidence the patient is almost in touch with the impulse, seeing a drop in tension, motoric activation, and expression of the feeling, I moved to press to the experience of the rage.

Th: But your body gets all clamped up with anxiety. Okay, let's see how you experience the anger as a feeling in the body. If we move aside the anxiety, how do you just feel anger in the body, physically, if you don't go detached? [*Pressure to experience rage and challenge to remaining defenses.*] How do you feel if you don't let it turn into anxiety? [*Pressure to experience rage and challenge.*] If you don't let it go back at you, how do you feel the body reaction of anger in here when we're talking? [*Challenge and pressure to experience the rage.*]

Pt: I don't know, I guess.

Th: In your arms there, in your body, how do you know there's some anger there in you? [*Pressure to experience rage.*]

Pt: Just because they go tight, because I get fidgety.

Th: Tightness is the anxiety. Somewhere in there you say there's anger, so how do you feel it? [*Pressure to experience rage.*]

Pt: The way I identify anger is that I want to holler; I want to scream. [*Moves hands around.*]

Th: You want to show it somehow.

Pt: Yeah, I don't hit, not like that sort of thing. [*Unconscious therapeutic alliance: negation.*]

Th: But you feel that way? [*Pressure to experience rage.*]

Pt: Yeah, it's like "just give me the damn answer." [*Moves arms freely.*]

Th: You feel some of it right now? [*Pressure to experience rage.*]

Pt: I do! I feel a lot of it! [*Moves freely, meaning the anxiety has dropped; this signals that the impulse is being experienced.*]

Th: Where was it located at in your body? [*Pressure to experience rage.*]

Pt: In my arms, my head.

Th: Your arms have that in them? [*Pressure to experience rage.*]

Pt: In my legs, they feel strong when I'm angry, and I just—yeah, my chest. Like when I think about it that way. [*Moves arms freely with drop in tension.*]

Portraying the Rage

With the somatic pathway or rage activated, I now switch to pressure to portray the rage. Each pressure raises the complex transference feelings and unconscious therapeutic alliance to higher levels.

Th: In what way does it want to come out? Let me put it this way: if you were an aggressive person who doesn't hold back the anger, what is the urge if you didn't constrain it? If you just went completely blind what comes out? What does it want to do here with me? [*Pressure to portray the rage.*]

Pt: I'd holler; I'd scream. [*Moves arms a great deal.*]

Th: So what do your arms feel like they want to do if you went berserk, if you couldn't protect me from them? [*Pressure to portray the rage.*]

Pt: They just go like this. [*Clasps hands.*]

Th: What did they want to do to me though? [*Pressure to portray the rage.*]

Pt: Nothing. Physically, I couldn't touch a person.

Facilitating the Expression of the Impulse

Realizing this is inside the first twenty minutes of meeting the therapist and the resistance is still in operation is important. Help your client by separating her from the impulse that she holds back. In some cases bringing in a brutal third person with no conscience to act out the impulse helps at these early moments of treatment; this is much easier for her to see than to see herself being violent.

Th: But if you separate it out from you, what would the anger do? If you watch it, what does it want to do if it comes at me? That feeling that you have to hold back so bad. What are you afraid it will do, you know, if that animal came out for a second and you couldn't constrain it? [*Pressure to portray rage.*]

Pt: Then I'd smash you!

Th: If you were an aggressive man who comes in and has that anger in him, what would it be like? [*Pressure to portray rage.*]

Pt: Oh my God. That's scary.

Th: What do you see in that picture? [*Pressure to portray rage.*]

Pt: I see real anger. Fists balled up. [*Closes fists and makes punching motions.*]

Th: Fists punching.

Pt: Yeah. Somebody's really angry; I could see them like . . .

Th: Punching. [*Motions punches toward therapist's head.*]

Pt: Punching. I can't see myself doing that, but yes, with anger I see that.

Th: So how many punches do you think there were loaded into your arms?

Pt: Two of them.

Th: Then what happens?

Pt: Then I would be deflated; that would take the energy out of me.

Focusing on the Guilt

Now the rage has been experienced partially, and the body is quiet. The focus now is on the other feelings about the impulse. We also look for further signs of the unconscious therapeutic alliance.

Th: What happens to me in that picture in your mind? What happens to my head? Am I knocked out or something?

Pt: No, probably bruised.

Th: Bruised. Anything else?

Pt: But I don't, I don't like to think about it; I don't like . . . [*Becomes teary-eyed, looks sad and guilty.*]

Th: How do you feel to see that in your mind, if I'm all bruised up? [*Pressure to experience guilt.*]

Pt: No, it's not good, and it's not something I would do. [*Sniffles.*]

Unconscious Therapeutic Alliance

At this point the complex feelings, including positive feelings, a rage to punch, and some degree of guilt, have passed. Now the unconscious therapeutic alliance is free to take an upper position over the resistance.

Pt: I can picture other people doing it. When I was a child, my mother did it to my sister. She used to beat my sister with a stick. She used to beat her and she threatened me once with it.

Th: She used to threaten you with a stick.

Pt: Yeah, and she used to beat my sister with the stick, so I'm really . . .

Following the Unconscious Therapeutic Alliance

Now the unconscious therapeutic alliance has arrived with an image of a specific incident of this woman's mother beating her sister. At this point the patient has not felt the feelings toward the mother, and my role is to help her to experience these feelings that the unconscious therapeutic alliance has delivered to consciousness.

Th: How do you react to that when you think about it right now? How do you feel toward her with the stick intimidating you? [*Pressure to identify feelings.*]

Pt: Scared. [*Anxious response.*]

Th: How do you feel toward her though? Right now how do you feel toward her? [*Pressure to identify feelings.*]

Pt: I almost go numb, like I . . . [*Detachment.*]

Th: What's your gut reaction though inside? [*Pressure to identify feelings.*]

Pt: Yeah, my stomach's really tight. [*Striated anxiety.*]

Th: What do you feel like? [*Pressure to identify feelings.*]

Pt: I don't even realize it. [*Unconscious therapeutic alliance: negation.*] Angry at her. [*Clenches fist.*]

Pressure: The Engine to Unconscious Therapeutic Alliance

In this case, the unconscious therapeutic alliance is present but so were unconscious anxiety and defenses. I needed to continue to press, trusting that the unconscious therapeutic alliance would bring the feelings to experience, and the resistance would be further weakened.

Th: How do you feel that anger right now when you think about it? [*Pressure to identify feelings.*]

Pt: I'd like to be able to hit her.

Th: How does your body feel that anger in it, that urge when you think about it now? What is the anger like right now in your body? [*Pressure to experience rage.*]

Pt: I'd love to hit her . . . she's dead.

Th: But back in that time? [*Pressure to experience rage.*]

Pt: Back in that time I wanted to be strong enough that I could hit her and . . . [*Clenches fist.*]

Th: Like pound her again? [*Pressure to portray rage.*]

Pt: Pounding her again, and I wanted to be able to pound her a lot.

Th: How many poundings do you put on her? [*Pressure to portray rage.*]

Pt: Until I knock her out.

Th: So you would beat her unconscious there. How does that feel if it goes?

Pt: Not good. [*Starts to experience some guilt.*]

Th: Does that get it out of your arms?

Pt: It might get it out of my arms, but it wouldn't make me feel good to knock somebody unconscious. [*Unconscious therapeutic alliance: negation as there is satisfaction about the rage.*]

Th: Your mother. [*Counter to the tactic of "somebody."*]

Pt: Yeah.

Somatic Experience of Guilt

Somatic rage has been felt so now the therapist facilitates the passage of guilt.

Th: If she were beaten unconscious on the floor there, how would that have been for you?

Pt: Not good, not good, that's not good. [*Unconscious therapeutic alliance: negation, tears in eyes with guilt.*]

Th: It's a painful feeling for you. To see her eyes there, all beaten down, unconscious. How does that feel? [*Pressure to feel guilt.*]

Pt: No, awful. That makes me feel sick inside.

Th: It's a painful feeling. [*Pressure to feel guilt.*]

Pt: Yeah.

Th: To see that.

Pt: But when I see my sister and what she did to my sister . . .

Th: Then you feel good. You feel good for a second don't you? To beat her unconscious.

Pt: If I could. The ideal situation would be to protect my sister and not have to hurt my mom. Not have anybody hurt. It feels bad. It should never have happened.

Th: How terrible would that be if you had to look at your mother beaten unconscious and her eyes are there looking up at you? [*Pressure to feel guilt.*]

Love for the Mother and Guilt

Focus on the mother's eyes activates feelings about the earliest mother-child attachment. This pressure to see the love for the mother mobilizes guilt about the rage. The experience of guilt is the central healing process in ISTDP and perhaps all of psychotherapy for resistant patients.

Pt: Oh jeez. Not just because it's mom's but anybody. I don't like violence. I don't like to see it. [*Unconscious therapeutic alliance: negation.*]

Th: There's a painful feeling in there to have that rage in you. You see there's a very painful feeling to have rage toward your own mother about things that she was doing, as if you were the one battering her. [*Recap: complex feelings.*]

Positive Feelings

From there we explore and help her experience complex feelings toward the sister and father. Later in the meeting positive feelings with the mother emerge.

Pt: I had a lot of nice times with my mother.

Th: Oh yeah?

Pt: I remember . . . it's weird; just now I remember a long sunny, winter day when we were making all the Christmas goodies. I feel the sun coming through the window, and she's laughing and giving me the nicest hug. [*Memory brought by unconscious therapeutic alliance; becomes teary-eyed.*]

Th: It's a nice memory.

Pt: It's a very nice memory. [*Weeps.*]

Th: It's painful, too.

Empathy for Self and Family

Mobilizing the rage and guilt also mobilizes compassion for the family members and herself.

Pt: Kids will be kids and will agitate their parents.

Th: Yes.

Pt: We should all have had counseling so many years ago.

She further describes the mother's behavior problems, this time with empathy for the mother.

Pt: I don't know why, but my mom had a lot of anger in her. [Unconscious therapeutic alliance: negation.]

Th: What was that from?

Pt: Her mother died when she was a little girl, and she was adopted out. It must have hurt her so much.

Positive Memory of Mother

This patient had no positive memories of the mother before this therapeutic event: she could only recall the mother's hostile moments. This therapeutic event, seen so frequently in treatment, validates the concept that under each pocket of buried rage is love that generates guilt. By experiencing the rage and guilt, the loving feelings are freed up.

Complex Feelings toward the Father

Then the process moved to complex feelings toward the father. Recall the unconscious therapeutic alliance stating she didn't like violence and could never hit anyone.

Pt: I can't imagine having any anger with Dad. [Unconscious therapeutic alliance: negation; clenches hands.]

Th: How do you feel the anger toward him about this? [Pressure to experience rage.]

Pt: I don't want to hit him. [Unconscious therapeutic alliance: negation, sigh.]

Th: How do you feel toward him? [Pressure to identify feelings.]

Pt: It just flashed in my mind a time I actually did hit him! [Unconscious therapeutic alliance: imagery.]

Th: What was happening then?

Pt: I was a teenager, and he was yelling at my sister, and it looked like he was going to hit her.

Th: How do you experience this anger in your body? [*Pressure to experience rage.*]

Pt: It just, it wants to come up! [*Somatic pathway of rage: moves hands up the body from abdomen to head with drop in tension.*]

Th: How much anger is in you right now? [*Pressure to experience rage.*]

Pt: It would slap him hard. Then grab and shake him like ugh, ugh, ugh. [*Shakes back and forth.*]

Th: How much is he damaged from this?

Pt: He falls down. This is terrible.

Th: How do you feel to see him down there? [*Pressure to feel guilt.*]

Pt: Awful. Awful. [*Becomes tearful with guilt.*]

Th: A lot of painful feeling.

Consolidation

The therapist and patient do an extensive and collaborative recapitulation and consolidation of the process and plan follow-up meetings. The key ingredients of this consolidation phase include linking all the corners of the two triangles, highlighting the complex feelings toward the various people, underscoring the destructive effects of resistance, recognizing the relief with the experience of the feelings and the potential for making gains.

Th: How do you feel right now?

Pt: I feel relaxed. That tension has stopped.

Th: So we see that you have had a lot of feelings held inside yourself over the years. [*Recap: complex feelings.*]

Pt: Yes, for sure.

Th: Mixed feelings toward your father, your sister, and your mother. And all of these have been blocked, stored up, and held in. [*Recap: two triangles.*]

Pt: Yes, and I could never talk to my family about these things. I wish I could have, but I was too anxious.

Th: It's as if you were afraid of attacking them. And is this the same thing at work or with your children today: these feelings come up and make you tense? Then you end up avoiding the feelings and just worrying. [*Recap: triangle of conflict.*]

Pt: Yes.

Th: And the same responses came up here with me. You became tense: hands clenching and then detached from me. But underneath all this, these mixed feelings of love, rage, guilt, and sadness were rising up, just by being here with me. [*Recap: triangle of person, transference-current-past links.*]

Pt: I see all this now. I wish I had known about this years ago.

Th: How about if I arrange a series of follow-up sessions to look further into these processes?

Pt: Yes. For sure.

Treatment after Trial Therapy

After trial therapy, the process includes repeated unlocking of the unconscious, working through, and termination.

Repeated Unlocking of the Unconscious

With moderately resistant patients, the phase of repeated unlocking of the unconscious includes a series of partial or major unlockings. This process may range anywhere from a few to up to twenty unlockings over a treatment course of five to twenty sessions. These repeated unlockings open access to guilt, grief, and loving feelings. During this phase symptoms typically cease, psychiatric medications are stopped, and patients make a return to work if they had been disabled.

Vignette: Repeated Unlocking of the Unconscious

Following is a typical treatment session with a moderately resistant patient after the trial therapy. This is the eighth treatment hour. The patient has no barriers to engagement, and the front of the system is anxiety with avoided feelings: the pathway to the unconscious is clearly pressure to the feelings.

Pt: Since last night I'm feeling very anxious.

Th: Anxious?

Pt: The tension is right here. [*Sighs deeply and clenches hands.*]

Th: Your stomach?

Pt: Yeah.

Th: Since last night? [*Pressure to be specific.*]

Pt: Yeah, Matthew and I had a bit of a, I guess not really a fight. [*Tactical defenses.*]

Th: That came first or the anxiety came first? [*Pressure to be specific.*]

Pt: Yeah. All night and all day I've been feeling very, um, just tense.

Th: How did you feel toward Matthew? [*Pressure to identify feelings.*]

Pt: I'm not angry now, I don't . . . [*Sighs deeply.*]

Th: You have tension and anxiety though. [*Pressure with elements of challenge.*]

Pt: I have tension though; I have a lot of tension right now.

Th: But, what do you feel besides anxiety? [*Pressure with challenge.*]

Pt: I really can't . . . [*Smiles and giggles using tactical defense.*]

Th: You're laughing though. [*Challenge.*]

Pt: I mean, I guess I didn't identify it as anger.

Th: So what is it that tells you that you have anger inside you? [*Pressure to experience rage.*]

Pt: Just the feeling of the fighting. The feeling of anger.

Th: How do you experience it, physically? What is it that tells you it's anger that you're experiencing? [*Pressure to experience rage.*]

Pt: Just instead of the anxiety or being anxious it kind of stops when I talk about it and get angry. [*Description of the rage displacing the unconscious anxiety.*]

Th: Yeah, what do you experience physically that tells you it's anger, right now? [*Pressure to experience rage.*]

Pt: Just a, just a physical rush of adrenaline rushing from my stomach up just . . . [*Somatic pathway of rage; moves hands upward quickly.*]

Th: Do you experience that right now though? [*Pressure to experience rage.*]

Pt: A little.

Th: How about if we see the whole experience because some part of you wants to push that away and make you anxious instead. [*Clarification of resistance, pressure.*]

Pt: It was a split second. [*Snaps fingers, tension is low.*]

Th: Yeah, in that split second how did you experience the rush? [*Pressure to experience rage.*]

Pt: It just came over me and I just . . . it was just . . . [*Moves hands in expressive fashion.*]

Pressure to Portray the Rage

This patient's reactions give enough data to show that she is experiencing the rage: tension dropping, energized state, and cognitive components of rage with an impulse. I keep pressing until the somatic rage displaces the anxiety as much as possible because this will ensure a strong unlocking of the unconscious with dominance of the unconscious therapeutic alliance.

Th: Yeah, if this whole rage had blasted out of you, what way was this rage going if it went out—in your thoughts if it went out. If this whole animal came out, blasted out like that . . . [*Pressure to portray the rage.*]

Pt: It would have been hitting him. [*Forms hand into a fist and punches it into the other hand.*]

Th: In what way though would this sense of the animal come out? [*Pressure to portray the rage.*]

Pt: It would be hitting him on the head with my fist.

Th: What else? [*Pressure to portray the rage.*]

Pt: On his chest.

Th: On his chest. How much force is in you when you do this? [*Pressure to portray the rage.*]

Pt: A lot!

Th: What would you like to do to his head? [*Pressure to portray the rage.*]

Pt: Cut him.

Guilt

A few minutes later, she is becoming visibly guilty with tears in her eyes.

Th: Punching and hitting—I sense you have a painful feeling about this rage inside, too. [*Pressure to feel guilt.*]

Pt: My Matt. [*Sobs.*]

Th: For a split second there was a real murderous rage in there.

Pt: Yeah.

Unlocking the Unconscious

The patient is now totally calm and looking at the image of her battered husband. The breakthrough of the complex transference feelings has removed the unconscious anxiety and resistance: now the unconscious therapeutic alliance is in command of the process.

Pt: I had a picture of my father just now. I don't know why. [*Unconscious therapeutic alliance brings image.*]

Th: How do you mean?

Pt: I thought of him just now.

Th: He just comes to your mind?

Pt: He just came to my mind and I don't know why. [*Unconscious therapeutic alliance: negation.*] I haven't thought about him for days.

Th: What makes him come to your mind right now? When you look at Matt's body, you mean?

Pt: No, not when I looked at his body. Matt's body left my head, and then I saw my father. Not my father's dead body but my dad. Just like a picture. [*Moves hand from the top to the bottom of her visual field, illustrating that this picture appeared in front of her visual field.*]

Unconscious Therapeutic Alliance Brings Link

From there the unconscious therapeutic alliance brought a specific incident from her past where the father had beaten the mother. This woman experienced the identical complex feelings toward the father, including rage to smash his head, that had been mobilized toward the husband. At the end of the session she is entirely relaxed and describes a major relief.

Th: And you're also someone that gets headaches sometimes.

Pt: [*Smiles.*] Actually, I had a headache last night.

Th: Because all that rage is focused on the head of your father and Matthew, too. To what extent are those all mechanisms to deal with the rage and the guilt? [*Clarification of projective identification and symptom formation; her headache is linked to urge to damage loved ones' heads. (See chapter 14.)*]

Pt: I never thought of it that way. That makes a lot of sense, but right now I feel a lot of relief . . .

Th: There's no headache now.

Pt: There's no headache, my back's not sore, and my muscles are relaxed. I'm not tense here or here. [*Points to stomach and chest.*] My stomach muscles are relaxed.

Summary of Vignette

The process is relatively straightforward. This patient had few defenses by this point in therapy, so she was able to experience these emotions relatively easily. The unconscious therapeutic alliance had good strength from the start of the session and took a dominant position later in the session.

Working Through

In moderately resistant patients, the phase of working through is closely linked to the phase of repeated unlocking and termination. This phase consolidates gains, deepening the patient's understanding of himself and his family of origin and his processing of residual emotions. In this phase more grief and some pockets of rage and guilt are mobilized as successful termination is impending. The patient has grief about the damage the defenses have caused and grief about the suffering of parents and other family members. He has grief about other losses. Reunion with family members is normal in this phase: if loved ones are dead, then the reunion is imagined but very real and meaningful. This work opens the door for termination.

Vignette in the Working Through Phase

After repeated breakthroughs of rage and guilt toward the father, the same young patient had a vivid dream that the father came to visit her and said a tender goodbye. This is a product of the unconscious therapeutic alliance. That week she was having vivid images of the funeral of her father that she had attended at age nine. She was dressed in black during this session as if at the funeral.

Pt: I can see myself clinging onto the coffin. They had to pull me off of it. I was so desperate. [*Becomes teary-eyed.*]

Th: How do you feel right now when you see this? [*Pressure to feel grief.*]

Pt: It's so painful. [*Weeps.*] I never got to say goodbye to him.

Th: It's very painful. [*Pressure to feel grief.*]

Pt: [*Weeps.*]

Th: How would you say goodbye if you had a moment with him right now. [*Pressure to feel grief.*]

Pt: I'd say "I love you so much" . . . "I miss you so much." [*Weeps heavily.*]

Th: Very painful. [*Pressure to feel grief.*]

Another young patient arrived at his sixteenth session after a three-hour bus ride from his parents' home.

Pt: I was sitting on the bus after I left home, and there was so much sadness, I cried the whole way here. [*Weeps.*]

Pt: I was thinking of my dad and my sister and how I love them so much. [*Weeps more.*]

Pt: It's been so hard over the years with her and me fighting and how that put a wall up with my dad. It's so great. Dad and I spent the whole day together yesterday.

Termination

The phase of termination with moderately resistant patients is generally only one or two sessions where the process is concluded. The therapist and patient will look forward to whatever adverse events are likely to come up in life and how the person is going to handle them. If some work remains to be done this will be underscored and the patient will be encouraged to continue to process emotions after treatment ends. It is typical for patients to make further gains after these short treatment courses (Town, Diener, et al. 2012).

Vignette: Termination Session

The young woman from the first vignette of the working through phase arrived in the tenth session dressed in a white shirt and skirt, reporting gains in her functioning at work and her relationships, and an absence of any symptoms. She exhibited no signals of unconscious anxiety or defense.

Pt: Everything seems to be good. I was thinking of what to talk about and nothing came to mind. Work is going well, and things have settled down with my husband. I haven't had any anxiety for a few weeks, and I really understand what was happening. My father's death and conflict with my mom were the center of everything. From what I can see, everything came from that—all the rage, pain, and frustration.

She went on to describe the resolution of the grief about her father's death.

Pt: Yes, now I'm able to see that he didn't die on purpose. He didn't do that to us; it just happened. I've let go of that now. [*Absence of any unconscious anxiety.*] Now I know I've said goodbye. His birthday is coming up, and in the past I was so defensive on that day. Now I only have positive memories about him, remembering the nice family times I couldn't recall in the past.

She went on to make a comment and express her appreciation.

Pt: You always knew what I was feeling and helped me to not avoid those hard feelings. I could never lie to you. Before this, with people, I could just dance around feelings, and I would never let anything out. But you helped me to stick there and feel those feelings. Thank you for that.

CHALLENGES IN WORKING WITH MODERATELY RESISTANT PATIENTS

The most common technical problems therapists have working with these patients include the following.

Inadequate Psychodiagnostic Phase

If we do not apply enough pressure to be certain about the anxiety and defense pathways, the patient may be viewed as fragile, extremely resistant, or low resistant. Thus, we need to apply adequate pressure to accurately read the degree and nature of resistance.

Lack of Clarification before Challenge

If the therapist challenges the patient's resistances without clarifying what is being challenged, she runs the risk of the person perceiving the therapist to be criticizing him rather than challenging his defenses. Separating the patient from his defenses prior to challenge is critical.

Related to this, challenge only resistances that are actively operating. For example, if the therapist challenges passivity when the person is detaching, the end result can be flattening out or misalliance.

Premature Challenge

At a low rise in the transference, use only pressure to mobilize the unconscious feelings, unconscious therapeutic alliance, and defenses. When these defenses crystallize in the room, then you can clarify the damage they cause and challenge them.

Premature challenge occurs when the therapist challenges at low rise, before the unconscious therapeutic alliance is mobilized. The effects are a reduction of the rise in complex transference feelings and unconscious therapeutic alliance: the patient flattens out. The solution is accurate detection of the degree of rise and exclusive use of pressure interventions until you are confident resistance is moving into the transference. (See chapters 8 and 10.)

Dropping of Pressure at Mid Rise in the Transference

Feeding the therapeutic alliance with pressure and encouragement shows the patient that you are comfortable with her unconscious feelings. If you drop the pressure, the patient will become more anxious and thus more defensive.

Issues with the Passage of the Complex Transference Feelings

Several problems can arise regarding the passage of complex transference feelings.

Bypassing the Rage in the Transference

When the rage is trying to pass in the transference, focus on the rage and help the person experience it as deeply as possible. Bypassing this would frustrate the patient and the alliance.

Premature Portraying of Rage: Somatic Pathway Not Activated

Mobilize transference feelings until the patient experiences them viscerally prior to focusing on the portrait of what the rage wants to do. When the somatic pathway of rage is firing, heat and energy move upward through the body with a violent urge. As this happens, an equal drop in anxiety and a rise in unconscious therapeutic alliance occur. This does not happen with a primarily cognitive process at low rise. Portraying rage at too low a rise in complex transference feelings can also induce compliance where the patient will begin to repeatedly portray too early to prevent feeling the rage and guilt.

Passage of Guilt and Love

When the rage is felt, a sense of satisfaction is attached to it. As you do with other feelings, help the person experience this satisfaction and relief to facilitate the passage of the guilt about the rage. Some of the key technical problems arising when helping the patient experience the guilt include the following:

- *Avoiding the body:* If the therapist or patient moves away from the dead body on the floor, the passage of guilt is thwarted. Help the patient to mentally approach the damaged or dead body, keep focused on the eyes, and touch and engage to contact the loving feelings beneath the rage.

- *Failing to detect the passage of guilt:* If you miss the evidence that guilt is trying to pass, you may inadvertently keep pressing for rage: this focus may distract from and block access to the guilt. Use your empathic responses to sense when guilt and other emotions are being experienced.

- *Interrupting the passage of guilt:* Many ISTDP sessions contain partial passages of guilt that can easily be interrupted if the therapist talks excessively or makes distracting comments.

- *Missing the loving feelings:* In some cases, when the rage is felt, the patient may see or recall positive images of the loved one. He may place these images and emotions side-by-side with this dead body as a means of feeling the guilt about the rage. This product of the unconscious therapeutic alliance should not be interrupted. (See chapter 15, p. 246.)

Failure to Recognize the Unconscious Therapeutic Alliance

Because these patients are resistant, the unconscious therapeutic alliance is initially only partly activated. If you miss or misread it, you may inadvertently bypass, block, or argue with the unconscious therapeutic alliance. Try to recognize negation, whispers from the alliance, linkages, and imagery showing up in proportion to the degree that the complex transference feelings were experienced.

Issues with Recapping

When recapping after unlocking, some common technical issues include the following:

- *Insufficient amount of recapping:* With insufficient quantity or completeness of recapping, the unconscious therapeutic alliance may not be fueled adequately or the resistance may more quickly reestablish itself. Repeatedly recap tying together the corners of the triangle of conflict (feelings and impulses-anxiety-defense) and the triangle of person (past-current-transference). Recapping is important for symptom reduction in patients with depression and panic, for example, and to truly educate the alliance and strengthen its capacity for further exploration of the unconscious.

- *Missing elements in recapitulation:* Review all the elements of the complex feelings, anxiety, and defense, thus bringing the patient's entire narrative into a clearer light.

- *Dropping pressure during recapitulation:* As long as resistance is active, constantly feed the unconscious therapeutic alliance with pressure in order to cement the connection between your unconscious and the unconscious of the patient. Pressure is constant encouragement from you to the patient to battle resistance, to be present with you, and to identify and work through very difficult emotions: such pressure is the engine to the therapeutic alliance.

COUNTERTRANSFERENCE WITH THE MODERATELY RESISTANT PATIENT

In contrast to that of the low resistance patient, the moderately resistant patient's unconscious feelings and defenses may activate your own unprocessed unconscious feelings, anxiety, and defenses. If this happens, the defenses can interrupt the rise in the transference feelings and the subsequent development of the unconscious therapeutic alliance. To resolve this, feel the feelings that are triggered while reviewing your tapes or during the session. The intensity of emotions triggered by these cases is relatively mild compared with those triggered by more complex cases: reaching through resistance requires us to overcome at least some of our own resistances to being engaged with others (Abbass 2004).

OUTCOMES

Moderately resistant patients tend to respond very well to ISTDP. In a published case series I found that these patients all stopped medications and returned to work in a short treatment course of a few months. They did not have symptomatic relapses (Abbass 2002a).

Moderately resistant cases have murderous rage and guilt in the unconscious, creating major resistances and a tendency toward self-punitive resistance of guilt. These patients have good anxiety tolerance with striated muscle anxiety and isolation of affect. The defenses are more dystonic than syntonic. These people require pressure and limited challenge to unlock the unconscious. Understanding metapsychology of the unconscious helps us to activate, recognize, and work with the unconscious therapeutic alliance. These cases all tend to do well with short courses of ISTDP.

CHAPTER 14

The Highly Resistant Patient: The Fortified Castle

Highly resistant patients are the most common group of patients referred to outpatient psychiatric practices, constituting nearly half of all referred patients (Abbass, 2002a). They present with a broad range of symptom and character problems but with little or no cognitive-perceptual disruption. These patients alternate between somatic symptoms, anxiety, depression, major interpersonal disturbances, and self-destructive behavior problems. They meet diagnostic criteria for one or more personality disorders. Some are so resistant that they do not have any symptoms. These "lost souls" fumble through life, not recognizing the destruction they are leaving behind. They often present in crisis when their life is ending, realizing they had not lived, loved, or allowed themselves to be loved.

Underlying this collection of problems is a person who has experienced trauma between the ages of two and five, resulting in primitive rage, guilt about the rage, and intense grief. These emotions are mobilized in any relationship where there is potential emotional closeness with the risk of loss or trauma. Openness and vulnerability in relationships is nearly impossible as a result of this set of defenses.

The unconscious of these patients contains layers of increasingly intense rage, guilt and grief with correspondingly intense anxiety and defenses. At the base, related to the earliest attachment trauma, is primitive murderous rage that provokes cognitive-perceptual disruption and primitive defenses (Davanloo 2005). (See fig. 14.1.)

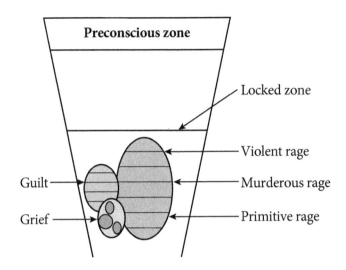

Figure 14.1 Structure of the unconscious in highly resistant patients

These patients have prominent resistances against emotional closeness. Due to the massive rage and guilt, these patients have major resistance of guilt (punitive superego). (See chapter 3.) Thus, they have long-standing self-defeating, self-sabotaging behaviors including the erection of barriers and various character defenses that undermine therapy.

A highly resistant patient is like a person stuck in a prison deep under a castle ruled by a punitive king. The castle has guards at the gates. The king, guards, and prisoner are all aspects of the same patient. Many people have tried to reach the captive, but with each attempt the king has become more punitive and the guards have pushed the people away. The prisoner becomes more and more discouraged and considers death a viable option.

However we may feel about these parts, we must reach through to the person in the dungeon and help him face and disarm his king and guards.

TREATMENT PHASES IN HIGHLY RESISTANT PATIENTS

Highly resistant patients' treatment course includes extended trial therapy, repeated unlocking of the unconscious, working through, and termination. (See table 14.1.)

Table 14.1 Treatment process for highly resistant patients

Phase	Task
Trial therapy	Initial evaluation, psychodiagnosis, and turning the patient against his resistance with small breakthroughs; unlocking the unconscious using pressure, challenge, and head-on collision
Repeated unlocking	Repeated major unlocking to optimize the unconscious therapeutic alliance
Working through	Mobilization and experience of residual rage, guilt, and grief
Termination	Closure of the therapy relationship over three to ten sessions

TRIAL THERAPY

Here we will review elements of a typical trial therapy with highly resistant patients underscoring the central dynamic sequence (Davanloo 2001). (See fig. 13.2.)

Phase 1: Inquiry

Highly resistant patients may come with many initial barriers to engagement and with any of the four fronts of the system operating. (See chapter 6.) Inquire into the nature and degree of problems when you see no obvious evidence of activated anxiety, defense, or feelings. If the patient comes with feelings, explore the feelings so you can psychodiagnose the patient and mobilize the unconscious. If she comes with a high degree of activated unconscious anxiety or defense, focus on them to psychodiagnose the patient and mobilize the unconscious.

We will review some of the inquiry phase with the case of the sixty-two-year-old accountant described in chapters 9–11. The patient is sitting quite relaxed without evidence of feelings, anxiety, or defense activated, so I conduct an inquiry.

Th: Can you tell me the problems that you're experiencing?

Pt: I think the big one was sort of an anxiety and panic attack and the whole feeling of despondency. Just the, the uselessness of it all.

Th: Your mood is down?

Pt: Well, it was.

Th: How about at this point?

Pt: I'm somewhat better now.

Th: What problems are you experiencing at this point?

Pt: Still a question of despondency.

Th: Somewhat down.

Pt: Somewhat down, it comes and it goes. Sometimes I feel pretty good, but I still have that feeling of, you know, "can I really get out from under it all?"

Th: Sort of weighted down?

Pt: Yeah.

Th: And so your energy is not great, you mean?

Pt: I'm, I'm tired a lot, and I fall asleep during the day quite a bit.

Th: Uh-huh.

Pt: And I wake up feeling tired; although I had a good night's sleep, I feel tired.

Th: When did that all start?

Phase 2: Pressure and Psychodiagnostic Evaluation

Pressure applied to these patients may be in any of the formats reviewed. (See chapter 9.) This pressure reaches through to the person stuck underneath the resistance; it is a clear statement that you want to know who he is and what crimes he has committed so that he can be freed from the dungeon. Thus, always sustain pressure as long as any resistance is an operation.

As described in chapter 9 with pressure to feelings about being fired from a contract, the sixty-two-year-old accountant responded with intellectual defenses, the turning of anger inward, and crystalliza-tion of defenses in the transference. Thus, we confirmed he was highly resistant. (See chapters 9–11.)

Phases 3 and 4: Challenge Leading to Transference Resistance

Highly resistant patients respond to pressure with crystallization of resistances in the transference, high avoidance, rumination, emo-tional detachment, distancing, and character defenses. Their defenses are *syntonic*; the patient does not see the defenses or their destructive effect. These patients do not know they are killing off opportunities by pushing people away and adopting other self-punishing conducts.

Now that these defenses are crystallizing into the therapy relation-ship, they pose a threat to the therapy bond. Now is the time to clarify the defenses that make up this wall to help the patient identify her resistance, separate herself from it, and then turn against it. This work should only be done at *mid to high rise* (chapter 8) in the transference feelings when the defenses are creating a wall in the treatment process.

With this pressure and challenge further crystallization of resistance occurs and subsequently further work is necessary to undo this resistance. This therapeutic effort leads to first breakthroughs of grief about having been victimized by this defensive structure. This grief further turns the patient against the defenses making them more dystonic. These events are small breakthroughs of emotions that can bring linkages to past key relationships and insight into the sources of the patient's suffering. (See chapter 11.)

At this high rise in complex transference feelings and resistance the head-on collision with resistances becomes important. (See chapter 11.) Now the resistances are heavily crystallized in the transference, doing their best to stop the uprising of the unconscious therapeutic alliance and to prevent the person from leaving the dungeon. This is a state of intrapsychic crisis.

The head-on collision points out the destructive nature of the resistance, the potential of the alliance and the benefits for the person, and the limits of what the therapist can do. It reminds the patient that he is the prime mover and provides a lot of encouragement to do something about the resistance. (See chapter 11.)

Phase 5: Unlocking the Unconscious

At this state of high tension between the unconscious therapeutic alliance and the resistance, head-on collision can trigger an unlocking of the unconscious with passage of the complex transference feelings, dropping of anxiety and resistance, and activation of the unconscious therapeutic alliance. With highly resistant patients, this unlocking of the unconscious will only be a partial unlocking with limited experience of rage and guilt and clear linkage to the past trauma. Extensive recapitulation of the process, linking together all the phenomena, should be done to strengthen the unconscious therapeutic alliance since resistance is still present in this partially unlocked state.

Remainder of Trial Therapy after Unlocking the Unconscious

After the unconscious therapeutic alliance is partially mobilized, do an extensive recapitulation of the process. Recapping fuels the unconscious therapeutic alliance, which you can then follow to gain a deep understanding of the patient's problems and history. The patient may feel some complex feelings and grief about her own story. The therapist's role is to help her feel her emotions and understand herself with compassion. A psychiatric and medical history can then follow. This work is followed by a phase of consolidation with extensive and repeated recapitulation of what you have learned. Treatment can be planned and the trial therapy is concluded over three to five hours.

We will now illustrate these phenomena and processes with a trial therapy with a highly resistant patient.

Vignette: Trial Therapy with a Highly Resistant Patient

This is a case of a middle-aged man with a longstanding pattern of emotional detachment and distancing behaviors. He had tried medication and psychotherapy several times over thirty years.

Phases 1 and 2: Clarification of Problem Areas and Pressure

The man arrives with some unconscious anxiety and feelings about having been referred to me. We evaluate the front of the system.

Pt: Hi, I feel like I've been sent to the principal's office.

Th: Like you've been sent to the principal's office.

Pt: Yeah, for misbehavior. [*Shows tension: clenches hands and sighs.*]

Th: How do you mean?

Pt: No, it just struck me. It's just that it doesn't seem I made much progress with the other therapist.

Th: Mm-hmm.

Pt: But I still want the help; she's cured me of that.

Th: Which difficulties do you see at this point in time that you want to go after?

Pt: Ah, depression.

Th: That's one thing, but what you're saying also is when you're coming in you're anxious; did you notice that? And you mentioned about being in the principal's office, too.

Pt: Yeah.

Th: How did you feel about that when you're coming in? [*Pressure to identify feelings.*]

Pt: Fear that I might be cut off, that there's no help for me. [*Intellectualization.*]

Th: So certain thoughts then, right? [*Clarification of thoughts versus feelings.*]

Pt: Yeah.

Th: What are the emotions that are attached to these thoughts in there that make you tense up in your body? What are those feelings that are activated? [*Pressure to identify feelings.*]

Pt: Mostly fear. [*Intellectualization.*]

Th: You mean anxiety in the form of worry in your thoughts and tension in your body? [*Clarification.*]

Pt: Yeah.

Th: Okay, anxiety. What other feelings do you have besides that, the other emotions that are activated here with me just from coming in . . . the feelings that you have that are tightening you up? [*Pressure to identify feelings.*]

Pt: That I'm incurable. [*Intellectualization.*]

Th: The emotions toward me, the emotions that are activated toward me. You know you have these thoughts about not being treated or being put out or this kind of thing that's in your mind, right? [*Clarification.*]

Pt: Yes.

Th: So what feelings do you feel toward me that cause you to tighten up? [*Pressure to identify feelings.*]

Pt: It's adversarial. [*Intellectual response.*]

Th: A series of thoughts, right? What are the emotions that tighten you up? [*Pressure to identify feelings.*]

Pt: Yes.

Th: You're aware of those thoughts, right? And your body tightens up and gets anxious. So what are the emotions bound into that, that produce that tension in you? [*Pressure to identify feelings.*]

Pt: I feel less than worthy. I don't deserve to be here. [*Self-critical rumination.*]

Th: This is another set of thoughts that you get secondary to the first set? [*Clarification.*]

Pt: Yeah.

Th: Okay, the first thing is you're having an initial set of thoughts and feelings, right? And then it goes to some negative thoughts on you. Is that the pathway? [*Clarification.*]

Pt: It's all about me.

Th: It goes back inward, negative? [*Clarification of self-hate.*]

Pt: Absolutely.

Th: Okay, what are the feelings mobilized first toward me before you go negative at yourself?

Pt: The emotion is that you can hurt me. [*Intellectualization.*]

Initial Responses

Notice that the patient exhibits intellectualization and striated muscle anxiety. Thus, the therapist can explore feelings at this point without worrying about the patient's anxiety. I keep focusing on underlying feelings to see whether he is capable of tolerating a direct move to the unconscious or whether some work with his defenses and anxiety pathways is required first.

Th: These are again ideas you're having, right? The ideas that tighten you up.

Pt: Yes.

Th: So what are the emotions inside? [*Pressure.*]

Pt: See, that's where we run into trouble. [*Intellectualization.*]

Th: So identifying and experiencing the emotions, you find that hard to do? [*Clarification.*]

Pt: Extremely.

Th: You tend more to get some tension and get critical of yourself? Is that the pathway? [*Clarification.*]

Pt: Yeah, I told the other doctor before that the minute we discuss feelings, I have no clue what she is talking about. [*Absence of striated muscle signals.*]

Trouble with Emotions

This man has major difficulties identifying emotions. Instead he intellectualizes and experiences self-punitive rumination. He primarily worries about what others think, an obsessive type of projection, and he criticizes himself. So I will now pressure to understand his problems and turn him against his defenses.

Th: The thing is that you find it hard to feel without thinking.

Pt: Oh, absolutely.

Th: To relax your mind and feel something. To be spontaneously going with the feeling. So in what way do you find that a problem for you apart from the fact that you find it a challenge in the sessions? [Pressure to see the defenses and turn against them.]

Pt: Well, it hides my feelings from me. I've been doing it for so long that I'm actually hiding from me. [Syntonic system.]

Th: From your own emotion? In what way does that hurt you?

Pt: Uh, well, I live like a bear. I live in a cave. I don't go out. I don't socialize. [Self-deprivation and isolation: signs of resistance of guilt.]

Th: You mean you don't go around people very much?

Pt: Not anymore, no.

Th: And that's partly because of the emotional issue?

Pt: Yeah, I don't want the contact. I'm afraid of the contact. [Anxiety and avoidance.]

Th: So what are you afraid of? Of the feelings that are going to come up or what?

Pt: Yeah, somehow I feel less a person because I don't feel worthy. All my life I've had a self-worth problem because from an early age I was told I wasn't worth anything. [Self-devaluation.]

Th: You mean it's a self-defeating thinking pattern you have?

Pt: Oh, absolutely.

Th: So there's a self-destructive thinking pattern that you've adapted since you were very small? [Clarification of self-destructiveness.]

Pt: And action pattern.

Th: And self-destructive actions, what actions do you do?

Pt: Well, I live like a pig. [Self-deprivation.]

Th: In your house, you mean?

Pt: I've got about six months' of newspapers just piled up beside the couch. [*Self-neglect.*]

Th: It makes you feel bad the way you're living, is that what you mean?

Pt: No, I feel I deserve it. [*Self-hatred: sign of a severe resistance of guilt.*]

Resistance of Guilt (Punitive Superego) and Syntonicity

We see extensive data for major resistance of guilt. (See punitive superego, chapter 2.) The patient cannot differentiate himself from the defenses. They feel right to him. The therapist must turn him against this punitive force, like asking the frightened person in the dungeon to revolt against the punitive king and force him to stop this abuse!

Th: So in one way you don't like it. But on one hand you feel you deserve something negative. But at the same time you're here; you don't like having the negative toward yourself, right? [*Differentiation of the patient from his resistance.*]

Pt: I don't like being put in that position.

Th: But on the other hand, there's part of you that does think that that's the way it should be, the negative toward you, you should live in a . . . [*Resistance.*]

Pt: I deserve it, yeah.

Th: That you deserve something bad, so there's something that says you deserve something bad, but the rest of you says "but I don't want something bad." [*Differentiation of the patient from his resistance.*]

Pt: And that's the realization I'm coming to now. [*Increased differentiation of the patient from his resistance.*]

Th: And it's a fight. [*Between frightened prisoner and punitive king: patient versus resistance.*]

Pt: And I'm losing.

Separating Patient from Resistance

This is a good example of separating the patient from his own resistances. Saying, "Be good to yourself," or pointing the resistance out only once is not enough. The highly resistant patient's major resistances are like a web that must be cut away piece by piece to help him free himself. (See fig. 14.2.)

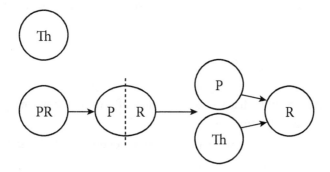

Figure 14.2 Separating patient from resistance
Th: therapist, P: patient, R: resistance

> *Th:* The thing is that when you're coming here you've been working to undo this notion that you deserve negatives, that you deserve some bad things. To override that. [*Pressure to task.*]
>
> *Pt:* Yeah.
>
> *Th:* To replace it with that you deserve the good things. That's what you're working on? [*Clarification of the task of that moment, pressure to self-compassion.*]
>
> *Pt:* But apparently I'm too smart for my own good.
>
> *Th:* Is there some reason for that, are there some crimes you did that you feel you deserve a bad thing? [*Rhetorical question to the unconscious: speaking to the prisoner.*]
>
> *Pt:* No, no.
>
> *Th:* I mean emotional crimes or something?
>
> *Pt:* Yeah, uh.
>
> *Th:* Whom did you hurt?

Rhetorical Questions to the Unconscious

As soon as possible talk to the unconscious and begin to align with the prisoner stuck underneath versus the punitive king. Directly questioning and confronting the self-destructive resistance is a very powerful intervention. It threatens the punitive king, giving the prisoner hope for freedom.

> *Pt:* Lots of people. I hurt people by not returning their affection. I mean I didn't love my mother enough. I wanted my father's affection too much.

Th: You mean you kept them away; you mean you kept your parents at a distance?

Pt: No. I was kept at a distance. It's a strange dichotomy. My mother smothered me.

Th: Okay, you're saying that there are some ways you hurt your relationships, that you didn't return affection. Whom did you not return affection to?

Pt: Probably my mother. I didn't tell her enough that I loved her.

Th: You didn't give her enough love?

Pt: Yeah.

Th: So you didn't give her all the affection you wanted to give her—you withheld.

Pt: Yes.

Th: What happened eventually with your mother?

Pt: She died.

Th: So she died and you didn't give her the affection you wanted to give her in her life?

Breakthrough of Painful Feeling about His Resistance

Confronting his punitive system mobilizes grief and guilt about withholding from his mother. This makes this man's defenses more dystonic, weakening the hold the punitive king has over the prisoner.

Pt: Pretty much, yeah. [*Becomes teary-eyed.*]

Th: How do you feel about that, about not giving her the affection you wanted to give her?

Pt: I feel like a piece of crap.

Th: There is a painful feeling in there. [*Slowing of the process to empathize with the patient's emerging grief.*]

Pt: Yeah, I was afraid of the love. [*Blinks away tears.*]

Th: Uh-huh, but there's a painful feeling in you right now when you think about withholding affection when you wanted to give it. At the same time, you kept her at a distance. It's a painful feeling. [*Pressure to grief and guilt.*]

Pt: Yeah, well, it's a dichotomy. She could be smothering. [*Diversification away from this grief and guilt.*]

Th: But right now, first there's a painful feeling that you wanted to give that but you didn't. [*Pressure to grief and guilt.*]

Pt: I wanted to be a better son.

Th: You regret that now, that you wanted to give her more affection. That's a painful feeling right now though. If you just let that be, there's an actual feeling in you right now, painful. [*Pressure to grief and guilt.*]

Pt: Yeah, but I'm scrambling to bury it.

Backlash from the Punitive King

As soon as the prisoner feels an emotion, the punitive king moves to punish him. So I press and challenge the resistance.

Th: If you don't let a wall stay around you anymore, there's something in you that doesn't want any walls anymore like that. [*Challenge and pressure to the prisoner to fight the king and reach back to me.*]

Pt: I think I've come that far, yeah. At first I wasn't too sure about it.

Th: There's a painful feeling that tries to come. You don't want to hold that in anymore. [*Pressure to grief and guilt.*]

Pt: [*Becomes more teary.*] But that's the other painful part, is that I don't think I have anybody to share that with. [*Grief about self-imposed isolation.*]

Th: But, this is a painful thing, too, not having the people close to you right now to share your affections with. [*Pressure to grief and guilt.*]

Pt: Or trust.

Th: Either way you want someone close, but you keep a distance and then the feelings all stay in you and then all this old sadness is stuck in there. [*Recap: feelings-defenses.*]

Pt: Yeah.

Th: It's painful. It's a sad thing. [*Pressure to grief and guilt.*]

Power of This Small Breakthrough

This was a breakthrough of painful feeling, a feeling I also felt for him. No antidote for defensive irritability in the resistant patient is greater than the breakthrough of feeling where both you and the patient feel empathy for him. This is a huge event for this detached man. But how will the punitive king and the guards react to this? Remember, the prisoner is being punished for having committed murders and other atrocities.

> *Pt*: Now I'm fighting with myself because I was feeling sorry for myself. But then all my upbringing, all my reserves are going "what do you mean feel sorry for yourself, you don't deserve to feel sorry for yourself!" [*Voice of the punitive king.*]

Interlocking Chain of Head-On Collision

I move to a chain of head-on collisions with this destructive system and its crushing effect on the patient and the process.

> *Th*: Something in you says you don't get to feel some sadness for what you wanted and what you also wanted to give but didn't give. You don't get to let yourself feel the guilt about that or the sadness about that. [*Head-on collision: self-punitive effects.*]

> *Pt*: Yeah.

> *Th*: Something says "don't feel that positive feeling. Don't feel that for yourself. You don't deserve to feel good for yourself. You don't deserve to feel that!" [*Head-on collision: self-punitive.*]

> *Pt*: I don't want to risk feeling that. [*Fear of the punitive king.*]

> *Th*: But, these are ways of not experiencing a feeling right now. Something in you wanted a different relationship with your mother, wanted a different relationship with your father, wanted a different relationship with other people, too, but some part of you has held in those feelings and said not to let anyone get close to you anymore. [*Head-on collision: drive for love, impact of resistances.*]

> *Pt*: Well, I have a friend now that I talk to but I try not to burden him.

> *Th*: Mm-hmm. The problem is there's something in there that says put up a wall and keep the feelings all blocked up inside and don't let anyone else get to know those feelings. [*Head-on collision: resistance against emotional closeness and self-destructiveness.*]

> *Pt*: Well, in my family that was a weakness.

> *Th*: Mm-hmm. For whatever the reason, it's still there; it's part of you that you took in. You bought it. You bought that. [*Head-on collision: the internal cause of his difficulties.*]

> *Pt*: Oh, absolutely.

Th: And you said, I'm not letting anyone close to me; I'm keeping all these people away. I'm keeping all the feelings on myself, which is a self-destructive way of hurting yourself. [*Head-on collision: resistance against emotional closeness, self-destructiveness.*]

Pt: Yeah, I see.

Th: But, how do you feel about that because you're a very bright person? We're sitting here talking. That's been something that's been hurting yourself for a long time now and you don't want to live the rest of your life like that, do you? [*Head-on collision: self-defeat, rhetorical question to the unconscious, pressure to unconscious therapeutic alliance.*]

Pt: No.

Th: See there's a painful feeling in there, about this barrier, this wall, but you're holding that back right now here with me. [*Head-on collision: pressure to be present with feelings.*]

Pt: It probably comes down to self-image.

Th: It's still a painful feeling right now, though, that you've been holding back. You've been holding this for too long. [*Head-on collision: pressure to be present with feelings.*]

Pt: Yeah, but I really, honestly, don't know what to do about it. [*Unconscious therapeutic alliance: negation.*]

Th: There's a painful feeling in your eyes; there's tears in there that want to come out. You're holding those back though. You fight them off here when we're talking. [*Head-on collision: pressure to feel grief, emotional barrier.*]

Pt: Oh, absolutely.

High Rise: Head-On Collision

The complex transference feelings, resistance, and unconscious therapeutic alliance are all activated now. These resistances are crystallizing in the transference blocking the process. I now continue this chain of head-on collisions.

Th: But if you keep this wall, it ends up hurting the opportunity in this minute here with me, doesn't it? [*Head-on collision: damage of the resistance.*] It hurts the opportunity you have here in this time you have with me; doesn't it? [*Head-on collision: partnership and potential of alliance.*] Another hour goes by in your life that you kept things in, you kept people out, and you kept these feelings buried in you. [*Head-on collision: nature and impact of resistance.*]. But that's not why you came here, is it? [*Head-on collision: pressure to do good for himself.*] To keep people out and to bury your feelings?

Pt: No.

Th: So let's see what are we going to do, as soon as the sadness, the painful feeling and the guilt want to come . . . [*Head-on collision: pressure to do his best.*]

Pt: I shut down. [*Whisper from the unconscious therapeutic alliance, collaboration with me in the head-on collision.*]

Th: You go detached with me. [*Head-on collision: resistance against emotional closeness.*] That means that you hurt what you're trying to do here with me. [*Head-on collision: destructive effects.*] It hurts this opportunity here with me, and it keeps me outside, and I can't be of use to you. [*Head-on collision: deactivation of the notion of therapist omnipotence.*] So what are we going to do about this, about this barrier here with me, this detachment here with me? [*Head-on collision: high pressure.*] You see it there right now because these feelings want to come, and you put that wall right back up. [*Head-on collision: barrier.*]

Pt: Yes.

Th: So let's see what we can do about this wall. [*Head-on collision: pressure to task, partnership.*]

Flushing Out the Guards

This intense series of head-on collisions mobilizes the center of the self-destructive organization of the unconscious. The king will alert the guards to act and throw me out, the same as he has done every other time someone has tried to get close to him.

Pt: [*Adopts a sarcastic and mischievous appearance.*] Well, you said the magic words. I don't know if it's silly or not, it's when you start using phrases like "here with me"—that strikes me as somewhat formulaic. [*Critical position meant to induce an argument.*]

Th: Formulaic. But it's you and me here.

Pt: And the other thing is how do I feel? If I knew how I felt, I wouldn't be here. I mean how do I get . . . [*Defensiveness, attempt to provoke an argument.*]

Th: Let me phrase it another way. Right now something in you wants to put up some kind of barrier here with me [*by making an argument*].

Pt: Oh, absolutely! [*Smiles and looks relieved.*]

Benefit of Direct Identification of Resistance

It is so important to note that resistant patients are extremely relieved when you place a spotlight on the resistances rather than failing to recognize or failing to react to the resistance. Hope and the unconscious therapeutic alliance go up immediately when defenses are accurately identified.

Th: You had that painful feeling. There's a guilt feeling. There's a craving of closeness that you have within you; these are your emotions that you have.

Pt: Yes.

Th: At the same time they want to come, part of you wants to pull back and move away and distance yourself here with me. That's what's happening. I don't know how else to say it, but why do you want to do that to yourself? [*Head-on collision: asking alliance to take upper hand.*] Why do you have a need to put a barrier around yourself, to hurt yourself anymore, to make yourself have to be in a cave, to keep these feelings buried? Why? What crime did you do? This is what I'm saying: "What crime did you do that you have to isolate yourself?" [*Talking to the king, guards, and prisoner: the essence of a head-on collision.*]

Pt: Nothing!

Th: So what are we going to do about this wall and barrier that's coming up here, see because you're still backing away from me? [*Head-on collision: pressure, challenge.*]

Pt: Yeah, I don't trust you.

Resistance against Emotional Closeness

The concept of trust is often taken to mean a stop sign for therapists. In this case the word *trust* refers to resistance against emotional closeness. So instead of becoming supportive, we should address this as resistance against emotional closeness.

Th: Is it that, or just that you don't want to be open with me? [*Clarification.*]

Pt: I don't trust myself and I don't trust you.

Th: But is it an issue of trust or does it have to do with these feelings that are painful and part of you just wants to push them away by finding some way not to be open?

Pt: It's probably both but more the trust thing.

Th: But is it really trust, or does it have to do with the feelings that are painful so your mind finds some way that you don't feel pain? It puts a wall back up and then you don't feel pain; you don't feel these emotions.

Pt: It's a little confusing, but I don't trust you to tell you what I actually feel because you're going to use it against me.

Handling Obsessive Projection

This projection that I am a threat can be worked with as a tactic to keep a distance from me. Fixed projections in fragile patients require more extensive work to replace projection with isolation of affect. (See chapters 16–17.)

Th: Again, this doesn't help us see what the feelings are though.

Pt: No, it doesn't.

Th: See, you've already established what the feelings are. You've already told me what they are. You've already experienced a little bit of it, so we don't disagree about anything.

Pt: No.

Th: Those are the feelings you have in there. The question is what do we have to do so that every opportunity in your life has what you want in it? Has the opportunity to be open, to not be afraid and avoid people, to not be isolated? A life that has that for you: options for you to open up if you want to—how do we make it so that your life is yours? You know what I mean, for you. How do we do that? What do we do? [*High pressure and challenge.*]

Pt: My life is already mine, but I'm self-destructive. [*Unconscious therapeutic alliance: whisper with deep insight.*]

Whisper from the Unconscious Therapeutic Alliance

For a moment the unconscious therapeutic alliance has become dominant and the patient can say exactly what is going on. This is a "whisper" from the unconscious therapeutic alliance (Abbass 2012). Now anticipating that the punitive king will rail against this disclosure, I move rapidly to bring pressure and recapping to shore up the unconscious therapeutic alliance against the expected onslaught from the punitive king and guards: the resistance.

Th: Well, how do we remove that? That's what I'm saying. How do we remove that destructive barrier? Because as soon as the feelings come, you see the guard wants to come back up and you push me out. I'm pushed away, and then you're stuck in there alone trying to wrestle with these emotions and wrestle with this part of you that shuts down. [Punitive king.] Do you understand? [Head-on collision: barrier, task, positive intention, limits of the therapist, end result of resistance.]

Pt: Yes, yes.

Th: So what are we going to do about that so you don't do that anymore, to override this system of shutting down and detaching? [Head-on collision: pressure and challenge.]

Pt: I think it's got to do with if I'm going to fail, I'm going to fail with what I'm comfortable. I always have the thought that I didn't try hard enough. I could have done it. I wanted to but I didn't want to. I'm defeated before I start. [Masochism.]

Th: Yeah, so not trying. This is one way of self-defeating is you don't make a . . .

Pt: True effort, yeah.

Th: You don't try anymore. You gave up trying. Is that what you mean?

Pt: Well, I try but in a way that I know is going to fail. But I know that I've caused the failure. [Masochism.]

Th: Okay, but see, that's a self-defeating system then!

Pt: Self-destructive, yeah! [Smiles with relief, sits forward very engaged.]

Th: Yeah, so why do you have this? What crimes did you do that you have to hurt yourself and what can we do about it here at this point so we weaken that self-destructiveness? [Rhetorical question to the unconscious.]

Th: How can we weaken that system and cause that system to stop hurting you? How can we do that? How do we put our forces together to do that? [*Pressure to partnership, task.*] This barrier wants to stay up here as a way to keep those feelings pushed away, so how do we address that part? [*Pressure to closeness.*]

Pt: I've got to learn my own self-worth, I just . . . [*Unconscious therapeutic alliance.*]

Th: You have something in there that says not to value yourself. That's a self-destructive system, too!

Pt: Yeah, I mean, I've only just realized within the last, say six months that I'm fairly bright, and that was a head turner.

Th: Really!

Pt: But I come from a family who are just as bright as I am, just as verbal as I am, just as closed off as I am. I mean, we got four alcoholics in my family. When I was in college, I didn't know I was drunk till I came home and got sober. I was drinking a liter a day, but when I left college, then I found narcotics and I was abusing those.

Th: So at different times there have been different kinds of medical crutches or alcohol.

Pt: Oh, absolutely!

Th: So this is part of a self-destructive system that is some kind of an external crutch, leaning on something? [*Pressure on self-destructive system.*]

Pt: Yeah.

Th: But then you don't have your own power. Is that what you mean?

Pt: Yeah, maybe I just had a revelation and I don't know if it's what you said or it's "what did I do to deserve this?" [*Unconscious therapeutic alliance.*]

Second Communication from the Unconscious Therapeutic Alliance

This extensive work of reaching through the resistance, with all the effort that I could muster, brings a major communication from the unconscious as the alliance takes an upward position over the resistance. I recap to bolster the patient in his courageous challenge to his own self-punitive king.

Th: Yes, this is the question. The feelings want to come up. These are your natural feelings when you sit with another person, here with me. These emotions come up about all the disappointments and guilt about the old emotions and old relationships. These all come up. They're all there on the surface, trying to break through, but you start getting critical of yourself and start hurting yourself in some way to deal with whatever these feelings are. This part of your mind says don't let someone else get close to you because you didn't let your mother, your father, or other people close to you. So you don't have anyone close to you now because there's too much guilt about that. [*Global recap with pressure.*]

Th: Do you know what I mean? But, what can we do about this? Because there's still some kind of barrier here, but you're saying there's some kind of revelation. What is the revelation that you're getting in your mind?

Pt: Maybe I'm not as bad as I thought it was.

Freedom?

For a brief moment the prisoner steps out of his cell. Will his punitive king allow this?

Th: But how do you feel when you say that?

Pt: A little lightheaded. [*Laughs.*]

Th: Did you say you feel light or did you feel lightheaded? [*Clarification.*]

Pt: Both.

Th: You felt a bit of an uplifting when you said this. That "maybe I'm not so bad," right? You said maybe I'm not so bad, which is a good feeling for you, right? Some positive to you, right? You felt a bit lighter with that. [*Clarification.*]

Pt: Isn't it ironic that now that it's out there I realize that I'm not that bad a person?

Th: How do you feel when you recognize that? You're saying you deserve the good things when you say that, aren't you? You don't deserve the bad things. You don't deserve to live in a situation that's not good. You don't deserve to be in a cave. You don't deserve to put yourself down. This is what you're saying, right?

Temporary Relief

As the prisoner smells nice fresh air after being underground for years, the king and the guards revolt. The major resistance of guilt moves.

Pt: Yeah, when you put it that way, then I fall back on the family mantra of, "Well, what do you deserve? You don't deserve anything." [*Voice of the punitive king.*]

Th: So again you have that voice in your head from somewhere in the past.

Pt: Yeah.

Th: Putting you down again.

Pt: Oh, all the time.

Th: So what are we going to do about that because that puts a barrier up again here with me? [*Pressure.*] That puts you down as you're sitting talking to me. How do we get these out of here, out of your mind? How do we remove the barrier that still tries to come up here between you and me? [*Pressure.*]

Be Relentless

As I described, the resistance doesn't just give up and go away after one or even a dozen interventions. It will keep returning until the alliance can be in a dominant position. Our never giving up or taking a defeated position is essential. I performed a head-on collision with this resistance.

Pt: Now I feel a tension. [*Avoids eye contact.*]

Th: You're detaching from me, too. You feel that?

Pt: Yes, yes.

Th: Here's the situation: you're going away from me now. Something is saying to put a wall up with me and don't let me get too close, you know, for whatever reason. [*Head-on collision: barrier.*]

Th: So what will we do about that? The wall is trying to form as much as you're trying not to form a wall, but part of you is putting the wall up with me. Do you see that? [*Head-on collision: barrier.*]

Pt: And it's not even with you; it's with me.

Th: Well, the truth is, it's also between you and me.

Pt: Yeah.

Th: It's between yourself and you but it's between you and me because I'm on the outside. Totally on the outside here when you detach. What can we do about this barrier here between you and me? See if you don't go detached from me . . . [*Head-on collision: undoing omnipotence, barrier, and pressure.*]

Pt: And that's when you lose me, I, that's . . .

Th: If you don't go detached . . . [*Head-on collision: challenge.*]

Pt: If I knew how to touch those feelings or let other people see them . . . [*Attempt to begin an argument.*]

Th: I didn't say anything about feelings; I just said about detachment. Let's see what we can do with the barrier between us, to remove this barrier between you and yourself and between you and me because the risk is that I stay on the outside. I don't get to be helpful to you. [*Head-on collision: consequences.*] Do you follow me? And that would make another sad moment for you. [*Head-on collision: consequences.*]

Pt: But how . . . what do I? See, that's the . . . I'm looking for a direction. I know I shouldn't be. I'm intellectualizing because I'm looking for clues to how to respond. [*Mobilization of the unconscious therapeutic alliance, battling the resistances of passivity and helplessness.*]

Th: How to respond to the detachment?

Pt: Yes.

Th: So let's see what we can do about the detachment if you don't back away from me. [*Head-on collision: pressure and challenge.*]

Pt: I feel uncomfortable because you're asking me right now for something I don't think I can give.

Th: To not be detached from me?

Pt: Detached from anybody . . . even myself.

Th: Right, but this is our objective though, right? So you don't have to be detached and to find out why you did this detachment to begin with. This is what our goal is? [*Head-on collision: task.*]

Pt: Yeah.

Th: Here's the situation: if you don't go detached now, we can sort out why you ever became detached to start with. [*Head-on collision: task, pressure, and potential benefit.*]

Pt: But that's the frightening part: if I overcome the detachment then how do I control the attachments? [*Unconscious therapeutic alliance bringing dynamically relevant content.*]

Th: See, there's still a barrier. Let's see what we can do about the barrier here if you don't go detached and if you don't avoid me. [*Pressure and challenge.*]

Pt: Okay. [*Becomes detached and thinks to himself.*]

Th: Are you thinking a lot right now?

Pt: I'm battling not to think, but it's definitely happening.

Th: So part of the detachment from me then is just the thinking. So if you try not to think, are you starting to wait for me to do something else? [*Clarification of passivity.*] Does the thought come to your mind that "he knows what to do next"?

Pt: Yes! [*Displays excitement and relief that the therapist sees what is happening.*]

Th: Okay, so another aspect that keeps you at a distance then is a passive position.

Pt: Yes, I sit and wait for you to show me what to do.

Th: Okay, when you're waiting, though, you're not in yourself. You're kind of looking outside to me. But I can't do more than what I'm doing. Is that part of the self-destructive system, this passivity? [*Head-on collision: passivity and undoing of the notion of the omnipotent therapist.*]

Pt: It's . . .

Th: The passive waiting, passive like a waiting position.

Pt: Have you ever played games with somebody who knows the rules to a tee? They know all the rules and how to use the rules? That's me!

Th: So here with your emotional system and yourself, are you an expert on it?

Pt: No. I have made a special effort not to know it. [*Unconscious therapeutic alliance.*]

Th: But here's what I see happening. Everything I understand I've fed back to you. I don't have any other tools in the kit except that you're telling me that when you try to open up more, the passivity comes. That's another barrier that comes. You start to wait and look externally but waiting becomes an interruption that hurts you again. It hurts what we're trying to do here. Do you see that? [*Head-on collision: passive, helpless position, undoing of notion of omnipotence.*]

Pt: No.

Th: You see how you can be hurt if you're waiting for me to do something I can't do? [*Head-on collision: deactivation of the notion of omnipotence.*] Passivity is a way to block off what you feel, so if you don't go passive, if you don't wait for me, if you don't go detached because if you go detached the same thing happens. [*Head-on collision: challenge to every resistance.*]

Pt: [*Begins to ruminate.*]

Th: If you don't think, that interrupts the process, too, because you're not with me. You're inside your own mind. You're not here with me. [*Challenge.*]

Interlocking Chain of Head-On Collisions

The previous segment reflects the technique of creating an interlocking chain of head-on collisions where each form of operating syntonic defense is clarified, challenged, and pressured in a strong and concerted fashion. As another set of defenses activates, these defenses are then handled similarly. (See chapter 13.)

Pt: I'm looking for a hint.

Th: But see again I . . .

Pt: I know you don't do hints.

Th: I can try, but it doesn't do anything. [*Head-on collision: undoing of notion of omnipotence.*] What can we do about the passive waiting that you have? [*Head-on collision: pressure.*] That's a system that you've adapted in your life. If we interrupt it, if you stop it. [*Head-on collision: challenge.*]

Pt: It sucks big time, doesn't it?

Th: The passive waiting.

Pt: Yeah.

Th: It must have left you waiting for a long time. If you don't have that, if you don't do that, if you don't avoid me, if you don't think . . . [*Head-on collision: pressure and challenge to all resistance in the transference.*]

Emergence of Fear

Now with all this work to interrupt defenses and to mobilize the unconscious, the patient becomes visibly afraid.

Th: I see you've gone quiet now. It's like a nonverbal barrier.

Pt: I'm afraid.

Th: Your body is anxious again?

Pt: It's odd; I don't feel tense, but I know intellectually I'm afraid.

Th: Is it a sensation in your body of fear?

Pt: A little tightening up around my eyes, around my head, and my head aching.

Th: So when you're saying fear, you mean some anxious thoughts more than in your body?

Pt: I wouldn't mind getting up and leaving right now.

Handling Fear in a Resistant Patient

The patient is experiencing fear. He has no striated muscle anxiety. I pressed and challenged to interrupt this fearful state rather than to become supportive. This therapeutic activity boosts the unconscious therapeutic alliance through adding further pressure to mobilize the complex transference feelings and reduce the anxiety.

Th: So as soon as we're getting to the point that you're more open, the thought comes to go away, to go back into your cave again. [*Head-on collision: clarification of defense.*]

Pt: Yeah.

Th: What can we do about this? There's something that's frightening you about being open. Something frightens you about being open here with me. What are we going to do about that? There's something that you're afraid of; you're afraid to just sit here and be yourself. What can we do about this if you don't go away from me? [*Head-on collision: high pressure to be present.*]

Fear as a Resistance to Closeness

I opted to challenge the patient's fear as another obstacle to closeness and the therapeutic success. This action is a part of the interlocking head-on collision.

Pt: I'm not worth it.

Self-Devaluation

When we counter fear, the punitive king uses another route of self-destructiveness: self-devaluation. The resistance just takes another form. Different guards come to push me out. The closer you are to removing the king and freeing the prisoner, the more vicious the guards become, in this case mobilizing fear, detachment, self-devaluation, argumentation, passivity, and helplessness.

Th: If you don't attack yourself like that—because that self-attack becomes another way not to be here with me.

Pt: But am I worth it? [*Questioning of the statement from the king.*]

Th: That is another way to put yourself down.

Pt: I'm not . . .

Th: Worthy of being open?

Pt: Or being loved.

Th: So what can we do about that idea?

Pt: Well, sex is out of the question.

Th: That goes with it, too, though, sex and intimacy?

Pt: Yeah.

Th: Right, they're all in the same basket.

Pt: I suck at that [sexual function].

Th: There are barriers interrupting all the way around. How do we stop those destructive mechanisms right now here with me so we can sort out why you ever put them here in the first place? [*Head-on collision: task and goal.*] What's at the root of this—if you don't go away from me—if you don't go detached from me? [*Head-on collision: high pressure.*]

Power of Mirroring

Here we see the importance of constant communication about every aspect of the patient: reaching to the prisoner, countering his fear, challenging the guards, and both questioning and discrediting the punitive king. Ultimately, this process is an example of accurate mirroring of the patient.

Pt: No, I'm thinking. I can give you all the intellectual answers, like I wasn't loved enough; I didn't have my father's love.

Th: Let's see what we can do about the barrier here with me though, too; if you don't go detached from me. You have some feelings trying to come up just while we're sitting here talking. [*Challenge and pressure.*]

Pt: Yeah.

Th: What emotions are inside you there when you're here with me as we talk? [*Pressure.*]

Pt: You haven't earned my trust yet. I don't trust you.

Using Empathic Responses

Now I feel anger in my chest; I'm picking this anger up by empathic attunement. The patient moves back to the tactic and projection of mistrust. At this point, I opt to bypass these defenses entirely because I am confident from my internal, somatic experience that he is in some contact with feelings. This means that the complex transference feelings are being experienced on some level and that the unconscious therapeutic alliance is close to taking an upward position over the resistance.

Th: But there's some kind of feeling coming, isn't there? In your chest.

Pt: A little anger.

Th: How do you experience that in your body? Is it anger that you feel in your body? You see, if we remove the barrier between us then we get to see what actually is going on inside you that caused you to close up in your life. Right? That's what we can do. We can sort out why you ever closed up to start with and stop you from doing that in the future. [*Head-on collision: task and potential benefit.*] Right? But here's the problem, part of you is still trying to close yourself down and to keep away from me so if you don't keep away from me, if you're just here . . . [*Head-on collision: high pressure to be present, challenge to detachment.*]

Further Head-On Collision

Here I provide further elements of head-on collision addressing the remaining resistance, and I emphatically call the prisoner to rise up with me and defeat the king.

Pt: That's another coping mechanism. Since that meekness didn't work, now I'm going to the attack. [*Reference to devaluation, criticism, argumentativeness.*]

Th: This is another way to put up a barrier with me.

Pt: Yes!

Th: Okay, if you don't put a barrier up with me . . . [*Challenge.*]

Pt: Well, we're running out of barriers, aren't we? [*Unconscious therapeutic alliance.*]

Th: If we do run out then that's good, right? [*Brief smiles from both therapist and patient.*]

Pt: Yes, yes, oh, absolutely! [*Sits forward in his seat, highly engaged.*]

Th: So here with me you are saying there are many different ways over the years you've kept people at a distance. One way is going on the attack; another is attacking yourself. A bunch of destructive thoughts come. There's the passive waiting. There's isolation. These things have hurt you. How do you feel about that? How do you feel about that when I just said it?

Breakthrough of Grief

This is a compressed, summary head-on collision as part of the interlocking chain of head-on collisions. I sense some sadness passing here. This is a self-compassionate response for what his king has done to him by having vicious guards.

Pt: A little relieved.

Th: Is there some sadness, too, when I said that?

Pt: Not yet.

Th: If you're here with me, you don't feel that's a sad story?

Pt: I've passed over that now. I'm already in my cocoon again.

Th: You felt some sadness again.

Pt: Yeah.

Th: For a second as soon as the sadness came. It's here. It's something we both feel about it, right? As soon as that feeling came . . .

Power of Transparency

One feature of ISTDP is the transparent position we take with the patient. The patient's unconscious and the therapist's are interconnected from the beginning of the session. He knows what I feel about him throughout the session. At this point I'm pressing him to know I feel sad for him: this is a powerful empathic intervention that stems simply from caring about another human and helping him escape his own destructive system.

Pt: I ran and hid.

Th: You went away from it again.

Pt: Yeah.

Th: How does the sadness feel? If you think about it, how painful is it if you think about it? You've kept these barriers in your life to keep people out.

Pt: What a waste . . .

Th: And for no good reason that we know about—no crime committed.

Pt: No murders. No dead bodies. Nothing like that. [*Unconscious therapeutic alliance: negation.*] And it is a waste 'cause I've had a fairly good life even in a cocoon. I mean, I've been around the world. I got to go to college. I had some really good jobs and I knew some really good people.

Th: So this is a painful feeling, too, that this thinking and behavior has hurt you for so long like this. [*Pressure to self-compassion and grief.*]

Pt: I'm dealing with that right now. I know it's painful, but I can't feel it.

Th: It's in your eyes, though. I can see it. [*Pressure to grief.*]

Pt: But I'm . . .

Th: So if you don't fight it, there's a painful feeling for yourself right there.

Pt: I'm trying to feel it and part of me is fighting not to feel it. [*Resistance and alliance.*]

Th: If you just feel it and let it be, there's a painful feeling that wants to come out of you. [*Pressure to grief.*]

Pt: All those missed opportunities. Yeah, I'm really good at self-sabotage. It's like it's a self-fulfilling thing. [*Becomes teary-eyed.*]

Th: But there's a painful feeling in you; just let it move out of you. You've been holding onto that too long. You've hurt yourself for too long. [*Pressure to grief.*]

Backlash but Weaker

This moment of self-caring and grief could spell defeat for the king and his guards. In a desperate move, the king fires back.

Pt: But how do I know I don't deserve it? [*A softer position with himself now compared to a few minutes earlier.*]

Th: So this is again the barrier that wants to return.

Pt: Oh yeah.

Th: Uh-huh.

Pt: And feeling sorry for oneself is forbidden. [*The king's statement.*]

Don't Relent

At this point you can become discouraged, thinking something is wrong. Keep reaching to the prisoner beneath the resistance, empowering him to turn against the king and the guards. Research and experience show that each move toward underlying feelings and against the resistance mobilizes the unconscious therapeutic alliance. The principle of ISTDP is to meet resistance with pressure, challenge, and head-on collision, which all increase the complex transference feelings and unconscious therapeutic alliance until they dominate the resistance.

Th: That's another barrier.

Pt: That's another barrier.

Th: Okay, what are we going to do about that self-destructive system that wants to operate here with you and me? You and I decided we're going to get to the bottom of this system from where it started and undo it. At the same time, part of you wants to defeat what we're trying to do. It wants to interrupt what you're trying to do here with me. Do you follow me? [*Head-on collision: task, partnership, barrier, and self-defeat.*]

Pt: Yeah, but isn't it a pity, and it's destructive as well? [*Unconscious therapeutic alliance.*]

Th: It's a painful feeling you have.

Pt: It's guilt. [*Unconscious therapeutic alliance.*]

Th: You've done this even without knowing you've been doing it over the years. You've hurt yourself. You've kept people out. You hurt yourself and didn't even do it on purpose. That's a painful thing. [*Head-on collision: pressure to hate the resistance.*]

High Rate of Intervention

Forty minutes into the interview I have used a very high number of interventions, and all were required to help the patient battle his resistance. One study of trial therapies found an average of 165.5 interventions per hour, 97 of which were pressure interventions (Abbass, Joffres, and Ogrodniczuk 2008).

> Pt: How do I know I didn't do it on purpose? [*A much softer stance toward himself now.*]
>
> Th: Did you? What crime did you do?
>
> Pt: I wasn't good enough as a person, as a son. No one loved me, so why should I love myself?
>
> Th: So what can we do about this remaining barrier here with me? There's a distance still here between us. What if you don't go away from me?

Pressure to Be Together with Me

My constant pressure to "be with me" reassures the prisoner that I'm not afraid of whatever he may face. Pressure to be with me means I will not leave him when he is most afraid. I will accept him completely as a person, a human being hurt by events of life.

> Pt: I'm just realizing there's a fear of pushing myself on other people when I'm not wanted. I saw my father do it to my mother all the time. [*Unconscious therapeutic alliance.*]
>
> Th: Pushing yourself on people when they don't want it?
>
> Pt: Yeah, a form of mental or emotional rape, I saw my dad do that to my mom.

Unconscious Therapeutic Alliance

Now we see a major communication from the unconscious therapeutic alliance. The meaning of this does not become clear until later in this session.

> Th: How does that work? How do you do that?
>
> Pt: Forcing your emotions on them to their detriment.
>
> Th: Mm-hmm.
>
> Pt: "To hell with you; I'm getting mine. Screw you." [*Shows sadness in his eyes.*]

Th: So how do you feel right now when you said that?

Pt: Sad.

Th: That's a painful one, too. If you don't avoid, there's a painful feeling again about that. This is where you learned these distancing behaviors back then. If you don't avoid them, there's a sadness that this happened to you, that you had to learn that and take it in. [*Pressure to grief.*]

Pt: [*Detaches from the grief.*]

Th: See, you're thinking rather than letting the sadness come out. If you don't think, just . . .

Pt: No, I'm starting to get a little angry about my parents, about how their dysfunction made me dysfunctional. Their only job on the face of this earth was to love their children. [*A major statement from the unconscious therapeutic alliance, in service of the child he was.*]

Th: Mm-hmm.

Pt: And all they did was screw us all up. What a waste of humanity. [*Unconscious therapeutic alliance.*]

Th: Is there something you're seeing very clearly in your mind right now when you think of them hurting you? [*Question to the unconscious therapeutic alliance.*]

Pt: I'm thinking what my life would have been like if I were healthy. [*Detachment seems to be occurring and resistance is still in operation.*]

Th: Mm-hmm, but see, there still seems to be some barrier here with me. This is still there.

Pt: Oh, you're going to get barrier for a while!

Th: The question is what can we do about that? How much longer do you want to have that barrier around you? [*Appeal to the unconscious therapeutic alliance to take the lead.*]

Pt: Right now I feel threatened.

Fear

The patient looks somewhat afraid again and is in some degree of a projective stance. Because the unconscious therapeutic alliance is present here, I do a head-on collision with the resistance to deactivate the transference.

Th: See, again, the thing is you're trying to put this barrier down.

Pt: Yes.

Th: And at the same time . . .

Pt: I feel threatened by putting it down . . .

Th: And part of you wants to put it back up.

Pt: Yes.

Th: So what are we going to do? This is how it's worked out every time over the years. The feelings come up from your life from way back when you were small. They start to come up inside you when you're with someone. These feelings rise and then you close up with the person. And closing up makes more pain and more suffering and more guilt for you over the years, doesn't it? [*Head-on collision: residual resistances.*]

First Breakthrough to the Unconscious

More grief passes now, a direct immediate product of this head-on collision that mobilized the unconscious therapeutic alliance higher than the resistance.

Pt: But, now I'm afraid these feelings will be uncontrollable.

Th: What feelings are coming up as we talk here, you and me?

Pt: Sadness. [*Weeps quietly.*]

Th: A lot of it.

Pt: What a messed-up existence. I mean what did I ever do to deserve it besides being born? [*Major statement from unconscious therapeutic alliance.*]

Pt: I want to be loved and I want to love, but I'm scared to death of them. [*Unconscious therapeutic alliance does his own recapitulation.*]

Th: What are you afraid of right now?

Pt: Letting go.

Th: What feelings are you afraid are going to come up?

Pt: The sadness.

Th: That's very painful. [*I move more slowly here.*] Here with me these feelings come up naturally. You have a lot of sadness in there and feelings about your parents, but the barrier forms when the feelings try to break through. [*Recap.*]

Pt: Yes.

Th: The feelings peek through, and then you pull back. So what can we do so that door remains open? How do we push the door back so that access to your emotions is there and then you can work through these feelings? What can we do so that you can have people as close as you want and your caring for yourself is top priority? [*Recap with high pressure to unconscious therapeutic alliance.*]

Pt: My immediate response is that I don't know, but I think I'm afraid to know.

Th: Mm-hmm.

Pt: Or I don't want to know. How do I share emotions . . . ? [*Sadness emerging.*]

Th: There's a painful feeling right there, isn't there again?

Pt: I feel a little lost. I have so much to give, but I don't know how to give it. [*Weeps.*]

Th: But that's a painful feeling. You've held back all of yourself over the years.

Pt: Not to everybody, actually no. With my nephews I do nothing but give them open love and support.

Th: So you saved space for them.

Pt: Yeah.

Th: How did you do that?

Pt: I made that choice.

Th: Mm-hmm.

Pt: I knew the pain I went through by always being at the end of criticism, not only from my parents but also from my relatives.

Linkage to the Past

The unconscious therapeutic alliance is clearly in the upper position here and bringing a linkage to the past with his relatives.

Pt: I was ten years old when I was kicked out of my aunt and uncle's house for dirtying a towel. I washed my hands and I did it improperly, so there was dirty water still on the towel. I was never invited back again, and I never heard the end of it.

Th: They kicked you out? How did they kick you out?

Pt: They said "Just don't come back." They went on for about half an hour about the dirty towel.

Th: The two of them?

Pt: Yeah.

Rage

The somatic pathway of rage is activating as he speaks about this memory. Now I press to help him experience the somatic pathway of the rage. Extensive research shows that the more intensely he can experience the feelings, the greater his somatic anxiety will reduce and the greater the unconscious therapeutic alliance will rise above the resistance (Town, Abbass, and Bernier 2013; Johansson, Town, and Abbass 2014).

Th: And how do you feel toward them when you say that? [*Pressure to experience rage.*]

Pt: Pissed.

Th: How much anger is in your body right now? [*Pressure to experience rage.*]

Pt: A lot.

Th: Do you remember feeling that anger?

Pt: No, I felt shame and remorse then.

Th: How much anger do you feel now though? [*Pressure to experience rage.*]

Pt: A lot!

Th: Is your body charged up with this anger? [*Pressure to experience rage.*]

Pt: Yeah.

Th: How much do you feel the power of this anger in your body when you're going through this? [*Pressure to experience rage.*] If you don't go away from me and don't go detached from me . . . [*Challenge.*]

Pt: No, I'm trying to connect to it [the rage].

Th: Your body has some anger in it right now, right? [*Pressure to experience rage.*]

Pt: I feel emotionally angry. I don't feel tight or anything like that. [*Drop in anxiety as the somatic pathway of rage displaces the anxiety.*]

Th: No, there's just anger.

Pt: Yeah.

Portrait

With the drop in tension and the presence of concomitant rage, I press for a portrait of this rage. To portray it when he is not in some contact with the rage would be a cognitive exercise that could increase his anxiety and defensiveness.

Th: Now, if you're an adult and you face up to those people, what do you want to say and do right now with this anger inside you? [*Pressure.*]

Pt: I'd say "I'm ten fucking years old."

Th: What physically do you feel like doing with this energy? [*Pressure to portray.*]

Pt: Yell at them; I don't hit. [*Unconscious therapeutic alliance: negation.*]

Th: And does your body want to hit out? I'm talking about this feeling in your body. What does it want to do?

Pt: [I would call them] "stunted old crocks."

Th: With the energy in your chest and body, you feel that. What does the energy want to do if you were an uncivilized guy? You know, if you were an aggressive person. How does the aggression want to go when you have that anger in you? How would you physically go at those guys? [*Pressure to portray.*]

Pt: Oh, hit the uncle with a straight arm.

Th: Like straight this way?

Pt: Yes. [*Puts arm straight out to the side.*]

Th: Push aside the uncle?

Pt: Yeah.

Th: But, what about the aunt? What does she get?

Pt: A smack upside of the head.

Th: With what?

Pt: An open hand.

Th: And then what? He gets pushed aside. She gets slapped. Does that get the anger out of your chest?

Pt: No, they've got to understand what they did.

Th: What does it take to get the rest of this out of your body?

Pt: Telling them I'm a ten-year-old freaking kid. I don't normally have towels at home that are clean. So, yeah, I leave some soap scum on the towel. Big deal. *I'm here to be loved!*

Self-Love

This is perhaps the strongest self-loving statement yet from the prisoner who has now clearly moved out of the dungeon.

Pt: And nurtured.

Th: It's a very painful feeling there.

Pt: How can they be so shallow?

Th: There's a painful feeling in there now, too.

Pt: Yeah, I was young. I had needs.

Th: You wanted love from them. You didn't want that rejection.

Pt: Not necessarily love but just plain acceptance.

Th: Acceptance, but how do you feel when this painful feeling about them is there about them putting you out? But also there's a rage due to the pain and a desire to smack her and push him. How do you feel if you actually smacked her and pushed him? How do you feel about that if you did that? [*Pressure to experience guilt.*]

Pt: I feel bad. No one deserves that kind of treatment—even them. [*Guilt.*] I mean that's something I've always believed: violence is a defeat. [*Another communication from the unconscious therapeutic alliance; becomes teary-eyed.*]

Th: It's painful for you to have a violent feeling in you. [*Underscoring of guilt.*] It puts guilt in you to have that rage in you.

Pt: Yeah, because I wasn't able to resolve it.

Th: I mean the guilt about if you did it, how guilty you'd feel.

Pt: Oh, absolutely, yeah.

Recapitulation

Now follows a collaborative recapitulation that strengthens the unconscious therapeutic alliance to further examine why this man was thrown in the dungeon to begin with.

Th: Your body had a charge in it because you were hurt emotionally by what they were doing. Emotionally it hurt you. But this urge generated guilt in you.

Pt: No one deserves to be struck. Where did that come from? [*Unconscious therapeutic alliance is speaking to him.*]

Th: Where did that come from in your mind?

Pt: I don't know if that's an intellectual or an emotional response but I'm going to have to think about that.

Th: See, that came from somewhere inside you. [*Communication with unconscious therapeutic alliance.*] Someplace inside you know that's wrong. Violence is wrong, and just having the feeling is like a crime.

Pt: Yeah.

Th: You feel like you committed a crime back at age ten. You felt enraged inside yourself but you didn't do violence.

Pt: Yeah.

Th: You didn't even feel the rage consciously at the time; you just got ashamed.

Pt: No. Just totally ashamed. [*Rage turned into self-hatred, punishment, and the dungeon.*]

Th: You turned it all on yourself, right? But also underneath you have a painful feeling about being put out and rejected, right?

Pt: See I'm not comfortable now with this talk of violence. I mean when the other therapist did it, I wasn't comfortable.

Th: When you say uncomfortable, does that mean that it brings some painful feeling to have had anger inside in the past? Is that what you mean?

Guilt

At this point any defense that moves is due to underlying mobilized guilt. I'm pressing him here to feel guilt rather than to go to anxiety and fear.

Pt: Yeah, but then I feel like you're trying to not agitate but incite me and that anger is probably one of the most frightening of emotions.

Th: Is it that, or is it that when you have anger about life in the past there's guilt that inhibits your body and pushes the anger back on itself? You feel bad as if you had hurt people just by talking about it. The violent rage feels so real in a way. It's painful to have anger toward people you liked or you wanted to have good things from. That's a painful feeling.

Pt: Yeah.

Handling Residual Projection

In the previous passages, we see another transient emergence of projection with the patient's perception that I was provoking him. Now that the unconscious therapeutic alliance is mobilized, the patient is better able to see his defenses, and simple clarification and pressure to feel the guilt undo the projection immediately.

Th: See, there's a painful feeling about having anger, about being hurt even though you were hurt. It's what happened. That's what happened.

Pt: But having an angry response . . .

Th: Inside your body . . .

Pt: Yes, it's fine. But to actually revert to violence is not fine.

Th: Sure.

Pt: And, there's no emotional confusion there.

Th: That's why even having a feeling brings the guilt as if you are actually doing violence—so for this reason your body doesn't want to feel the anger, right?

Pt: The anger shuts down. And, maybe that's the frightening part because I can't think clearly at that moment.

Th: You can't think.

Pt: Like everything shuts down and I can't even respond superficially; everything shuts down.

Th: When there are strong, strong feelings, you can't think.

Pt: Yes.

Th: So here's the situation. Your body has always inhibited the strong feelings by going either weak or tense. Then detaching and going away is a way for you not to feel any strong feelings. That's another whole system.

Highly Resistant versus Fragile

We must consider that on a basic level this man is not fragile, but when the strong deeper zones of his unconscious are mobilized, he will freeze and become panicked, afraid, and confused. This early trauma generates primitive murderous rage and guilt that in turn activate cognitive-perceptual disruption and primitive defenses. This is the pattern of highly resistant patients with early trauma. (See figs. 3.1, 3.2, and 14.1.)

The patient then related a story of being a nightclub bouncer and hockey player and how these roles allowed him to control his aggression and other people's aggression.

Pt: Wow. [*Unconscious therapeutic alliance is giving insight.*] And the same way with being a bouncer, you're always in charge. Maybe that's why I liked hockey and that's why I like bouncing—because you're always in charge.

Th: So you actually get to calm people down and stop the aggression.

Pt: Yeah. Actually, I was pretty famous for that.

Th: So all these people you were keeping at peace, who were all these people representing in your life emotionally? [*Question to the unconscious therapeutic alliance.*]

Pt: Drunk, stupid people.

Th: So who was that who you knew in your life? [*Question to the unconscious therapeutic alliance.*]

Pt: My father. [*Unconscious therapeutic alliance: clear linkage.*]

Th: Your father. Keeping him at peace. Keeping him away.

Pt: Yeah.

Th: Keeping him away from whom? From your brothers?

Pt: My mother.

Th: From your mother. So you're in control now but back then you weren't.

Pt: Not as a child, no, but I'd still step in when I was a child.

Th: Between them, your parents.

Pt: Yeah.

Th: How did you do that?

Pt: You divert his attention by doing something stupid. You start yelling at him, and that would interrupt him.

Th: So you provoked him to distract him from your mother. Do you remember a time when you did that?

Pt: Apparently quite a few times. I didn't realize that before, but it's too buried to give you a specific incident. [*Unconscious therapeutic alliance: negation—just give him a few seconds.*]

Pt: Ah yes. The one that comes right to mind is when I was young, we were living in an apartment. The people downstairs were the

Smiths and my father accused my mother of fooling around with John.

Th: So he accused her of fooling around with John downstairs. What did she do? What did she say?

Pt: At first she tried joking and stuff like that, but after a while she would . . . Wow, I haven't thought about that for a while. She'd cry. [*Cries.*]

Th: Uh-huh, it's a painful memory—seeing her cry.

Unconscious Therapeutic Alliance Operations

Clearly the unconscious therapeutic alliance is in operation. Now I follow it, and the patient brings emotion-laden memories that are so relevant to his own self-development. Notice my activity level is much lower here as I'm following the unconscious therapeutic alliance and summarizing and consolidating. Notice that I no longer challenge since the resistance has stopped.

Here we see the origins of this man's tendency to argue and provoke argument, which was his contribution to the misalliance with the previous therapist.

Pt: Yeah, and I'm too small to do anything about it.

Th: So you'd step in?

Pt: I'd step in; that's the thing I can't remember. I'd try to distract him.

Th: Like what did you do?

Pt: Oh, I just stood there and said "Leave her the hell alone."

Th: And then what would he do?

Pt: He started in on me: "Who do you think you are?"

Th: Uh-huh.

Th: So he starts putting you down.

Pt: Oh yeah, and threatening to throw me out.

Th: To get rid of you? Throw you out of the house?

The patient does not respond, so I continue.

Th: So at that point when you see him yelling at your mother, telling her she's having an affair, she just starts crying. You step in. You start to provoke him and get him away from her.

Pt: Yeah.

Th: He starts saying you're nothing. And what happens then?

Pt: We start yelling at each other.

Th: And he's yelling at you, and you're yelling at him.

Pt: Oh, it was interchangeable. We all did it. It was us against him.

Pt: And then Mom would break it up.

Th: So then she gets in between you and him.

Pt: Wow. I haven't thought of that for a while. [*Unconscious therapeutic alliance bringing insight after insight.*]

Th: What happens then? She breaks it up, protects you, and gets back between you and him because you're a kid. And then what? So she's the bouncer. First you're the bouncer, and then she's the bouncer.

Pt: Yeah, that's tense.

Th: Tense. What emotions are there in you when I'm here talking about it?

Pt: A little rage. A little hate. [*Becomes teary-eyed.*]

Th: Some sadness, too?

Pt: A lot of it. [*Exhibits sadness.*]

Th: Is the sadness the most powerful or the rage right now? This is a painful early life situation.

Collaboration with the Unconscious Therapeutic Alliance

Notice here a different position that I have with the patient. With the unconscious therapeutic alliance dominant, I ask the unconscious therapeutic alliance what is happening without worrying that the resistance will try to mislead or sabotage our efforts.

Pt: How can you be that mean to a human being? [*Unconscious therapeutic alliance asking questions he knows the answer to.*] I mean, I realize why he did it; he was in pain himself. But why am I forgiving him? Well, I did forgive him when he died. [*Unconscious therapeutic alliance answering his own question.*]

Th: Is there a rage left there or more pain or both when you remember now? What's on the surface there inside your body and in your mind?

Pt: I feel like an idiot because I still love him.

Th: You still love him?

Pt: I loved him then and I love him now.

Th: So it's very painful when he's pushing you away like that then, isn't it? [*Linking of his distancing defenses to what his father did to him.*]

Pt: And when all I wanted was his recognition and his love. Yeah.

Th: How painful is it when you remember him pushing you away, putting you down, and yelling at you? That's a painful memory.

Pt: A painful memory, yeah.

Th: Very painful, him pushing you away. So he pushed you away.

Pt: He never laid a hand on me.

Th: But emotionally he pushed you away.

Pt: Oh, absolutely.

Th: Uh-huh, the same thing that you do, he did.

Pt: And continue to do.

Unconscious Therapeutic Alliance Is Dominant: Everything Makes Sense

This memory helps us understand the patient's character patterns of arguing, distancing, and pushing people away. It also explains why he has always been argumentative, as if to provoke the father and be punished by the father. This *repetition compulsion* is driven by his complex feelings for the father and mother.

Th: How do you feel that he did that, that he pushed you away like that; he crushed your affection for him?

Pt: He crushed my life, and I still love the son of a bitch.

Th: But see, there's a painful feeling inside you there, right?

Pt: Yeah, I'm angry.

Th: Is it that or is it pain?

Pt: Well, the pain's always there, but I've never dwelled on the actual situations. I learned at an early, early, early age to never show your emotions because that's when you lose.

Fear of Openness

Here this man highlights how risky vulnerability was in his house. Now is a key time to do a thorough recapitulation and analysis of the process.

Th: But here's what happened. It's a painful feeling in you when you remember him pushing you away. But the way you dealt with this painful feeling is to push other people away so that you don't feel this old pain from way back in those days, right? See here with me, if you had kept the barrier up with me today, we wouldn't have seen this painful feeling from when you're age five or whatever you are. You would have instead kept me out, right? [*Linking of feelings and defenses in the transference to the past.*]

Pt: Yes, and that shows my willingness to deal with it. [*Unconscious therapeutic alliance.*]

Th: Exactly, this is a part of you that says "no more. I'm not going to push out people anymore. I'm going to deal with what I have to. I'm going to feel what I have to. So I don't have to put a barrier up every time I turn around. I'm not going to limit my life." You know you're tired of living like you're back in that house. You're tired of living like you can't have anyone in your house. The same way you couldn't have people in when you lived in his house. You know what I'm saying? Isn't that what you're telling me? [*Underscoring of the unconscious therapeutic alliance.*]

Pt: Yeah.

Th: You're saying that you are tired of that. At the same time, there's something in you that says keep a distance. Don't let the feelings come out. Don't open up with someone because all these old painful feelings and anger will come up.

Pt: How do you control the anger when you let it loose? [*Unconscious therapeutic alliance asking a question he can answer.*]

Th: The guilt comes up.

Pt: Yeah, how do I control these feelings and . . . That's a self-answering question. You don't control them, you just experience them. [*Becomes teary with grief over understanding what he has done to himself.*] Oh jeez.

Th: I think you see right now that this hasn't been anything to be afraid of. This has been pain and disappointment, frustration.

The Status of the Castle

This recapitulation mobilizes the unconscious therapeutic alliance even more. This passage of guilt and grief for having hurt himself further weakens the resistance of guilt. The punitive king and the guards are retired and the patient is now freely examining the crimes that caused him to build the castle and throw himself in the dungeon. The unconscious therapeutic alliance now sheds light on major traumatic experiences from his childhood.

Pt: Now there's one in there that's not coming out today.

Th: A memory?

Pt: Memories. God, it's ugly. When I was really young, I shared a bedroom with my father and mother and you could hear him forcing himself on my mother. Right there in the room. It was marital rape or whatever you want to call it. And I still loved that man.

Th: And you remember him raping her in the nighttime when you were half asleep?

Pt: I could hear it.

Th: Yeah, you remember hearing it though?

Pt: Yeah. "No, Donnie, no." That's my dad's name.

Th: So she was saying no, no.

Pt: Yeah.

Th: And then what? Did you hear them struggling?

Pt: Forcing, and then I turned it off; I tuned it out. [*Reference to dissociation.*]

Th: What did you hear after the "no"?

Pt: I don't remember because I tuned it out.

Th: You remember the "no, Donnie, no," though?

Pt: Yeah.

Th: So how did you know there was rape happening after that? Was there a physical struggle that you'd hear?

Pt: A bit of one, and then you'd hear him finish. Now I feel light-headed. [*Rise in anxiety.*]

Th: This is a memory from how old roughly?

Pt: In school, grade one.

Th: So put it this way. You're in the middle of that situation and that was something you disconnected and tuned out from because it was too horrendous a memory at the time. There was too much emotion in it, right?

Pt: Yeah.

Th: So when you remember it, for a second you get a little bit of that mental fuzziness. Right? You tuned it out. [*Recap to reduce anxiety.*]

Pt: I'm still lightheaded.

Primitive Emotions: Primitive Anxiety and Defense

This memory with very intense rage causes cognitive-perceptual disruption. This high anxiety is a typical reaction to the first mobilizations of primitive murderous rage and guilt. Similarly, these intense feelings account for some of the transient projection (fear) we saw earlier in this session. Now we understand where the anxiety and defenses were coming from; we can also now see why the patient was defending so much and why he had misalliance and argued with the previous therapist. Now I recap and try to help him tolerate the anxiety mobilized by this content.

Th: Okay, you get a bit of lightheadedness when you remember that, right? So when your brother and you are in bed and your parents are in the same room in a bed, you hear the struggle. You hear the "no," then you hear a physical struggle and you know that she's . . .

Pt: Resisting. [*Use of isolation of affect; reduction in anxiety.*]

Th: She's resisting and then next he's finished the rape. But when that was happening you were tuning out; you were disconnecting from those emotions.

Pt: Oh, absolutely.

Th: When you're remembering that, though, you see it a bit in your mind, right? Because you're conjuring up a memory of it in your mind.

Pt: I just remember the darkness. I'm lying in the darkness.

Th: So it's dark. It's basically black.

Pt: It's always dark, yeah.

Th: So basically you're really hearing it when you remember.

Pt: Yes.

Th: Even though we're sitting in the light now, you're hearing it and you're in the dark, in your mind. When we're talking here, you remember being in the dark listening to this. That's what you remember.

Pt: Yeah, but now I'm trying to tune out the whole thing.

Suppression versus Dissociation

Note at this point I felt that "tuning out" referred more to the suppression that highly resistant patients use than dissociation as an unconscious process used more by fragile patients. I take this tuning out as an indicator to press further.

Th: Tuning out the memory of it?

Pt: And what we're discussing, yeah.

Th: Let's put it another way. The split second before the fuzziness happened, you must have had some emotions come in attached to this memory and sound, right? Emotions about the time came up strong inside you.

Pt: I didn't know what was going on, but I knew it was wrong.

Th: You knew it was wrong that she was being forced to do something.

Pt: Yes.

Th: Right. What kind of emotions does that bring up inside you when you remember that now in your body, in that second before it got a little too strong when we talked here?

Pt: Fear. But, I don't know what I'm afraid of. [*Unconscious therapeutic alliance: negation.*] I was too scared to move in the bed.

Th: Yeah, but right now as we're talking and we're sitting here, you and I, what do you feel remembering that? [*Grounding of patient in the present moment to prevent cognitive-perceptual disruption.*] What do you feel if you happen to walk in the room and see this right now?

Pt: Violence would be called for. [*Stronger position of patient.*]

Th: Violence would be called for, yeah. So your body is trying to activate a violent feeling, right? A natural violent reaction, right? It's trying to activate that when you remember, right? [*Pressure, attempt to hold him with the feeling.*]

Pt: No, I'm tuning out too fast. I'm battling myself to stay tuned in.

Recapitulation

At this point I move to a global recapitulation of the links between feelings-anxiety-defense and the past-transference-current.

Th: You see how it goes, right? The feelings are strong so your mind will disconnect so you don't have the feeling and you lose the memory with it. So your mind tries to push the feeling and the memory away so you don't have the feeling. That's what it tries to do. [*Recap: feelings-anxiety-defense.*]

Pt: Yes.

Th: What you're saying is you loved your father, but this was wrong. This was hurtful. This produced a violent feeling in your body, and all this is happening, and you're in bed, and you're five, and it's dark, and you're frightened. But now as we are sitting here in adult times looking back on that, those feelings try to come up. As they do, the memory tries to go away so you don't have the feelings. But see, it's really important because these are the same feelings that come up when you're sitting opened up with somebody. You're sitting open with me. Do you see that? [*Recap: two triangles.*]

Pt: Yeah.

Th: As soon as you open up with me, these are the feelings that come up.

Pt: But I'm afraid of the violence.

Th: You're afraid of the feeling in your body. [*Recap: feelings-anxiety.*]

Pt: There seems to be a fear . . .

Th: You're afraid of the feeling, but that's why you close up partly, right? It's fear of the feeling. [*Recap: feelings-anxiety.*]

Pt: Oh, absolutely.

Th: Okay, you close up for different reasons: one is because there's old pain; one is because there's old anger; one is because there's old guilt and old disappointments and sadness. These are the reasons you close up in the moment here and with everybody else. [*Recap: impulses and feelings-defense, past-transference-current relationships.*]

Pt: It's mostly pain avoidance.

Th: Sure. These are the reasons why you've had to close up with anybody over the years. It's because every time you open up like you have with me, these emotions start percolating up through: sadness comes in waves; guilt comes in waves; anger in the past comes up in waves; guilt comes in more waves. The emotions get you anxious—they tighten you up—and they bind up your body. That causes you to back up away from the feelings, causes you to bring defenses. One defense is attacking yourself emotionally; another is distancing, pushing people away actively. [*Recap: two triangles.*]

Pt: Intellectual attack.

Th: Yeah, to intellectually push people away or intellectually push yourself away. One of the two. We see where all of this comes from. You see where all this comes from, all these behaviors, these mechanisms?

Pt: Yeah.

Th: It's identical to what you saw, isn't it?

Pt: Now I'm distant. I'm sorry. I just don't want to remember it.

Unconscious Therapeutic Alliance Keeps the Memory

Now the unconscious therapeutic alliance uses negation to say he is still thinking about that memory and wants to examine it. With anxiety still high, I use elements of recap and head-on collision to mobilize the complex transference feelings and reduce the anxiety.

Th: What you're saying is you remember it, but you don't want to remember it. It's coming up, but you don't want to remember it.

Pt: Yeah.

Th: Okay. You've told me when it comes to some of these memories, part of you tries to remember and wants to remember these experiences to go through the feelings so they don't result in barriers with people today, right?

Pt: Yeah.

Th: Part of you wants to get rid of the old barriers, okay, and that's what brings you in, right? To get rid of these old barriers so that your life is opened up in whatever direction you want it to go. At the same time you have fear of the old emotions or this old pain and guilt that says "don't let this guy get close," and "don't let anyone get close to you." You know, hurt yourself and make yourself feel bad. It's to do something negative against yourself. [*Global recap.*]

Pt: No, I'm still there, I just . . . [*Continuation of experience of the trauma.*]

Pressure to Feel Guilt

At this point and with the help of the recap, the memory and emotions are still in the patient's mind and he wants to explore them as much as possible. The main source of suffering is the guilt about the rage toward the father he loved. I will ask him about the rage and then move to the guilt to reduce any residual symptoms related to the rage and guilt.

Th: Okay, here's what is happening. I don't think you can help that the feelings and memory are there. Here's what you said before you got anxious. You said you had a violent feeling. How bad would you have felt if you had hurt your father right then? How bad would that have been for you, or how good would you have felt for a moment if you had hurt him?

Pt: My immediate reaction is that I would have felt good.

Th: How good would it feel? [*Pressure to satisfaction at hurting father.*] How does that good feeling feel to hurt him?

Pt: It's not even so much the blow. It's just the physical hurt it would cause him.

Th: Yeah, how good does that feel for you to do it? [*Pressure to satisfaction at hurting father.*]

Pt: It doesn't feel good at all. [*Unconscious therapeutic alliance: negation.*] It's immediate relief, but it's not a good feeling.

Th: How terrible is it to hurt your father if you had really hurt him at the time equally to how he was hurting your mother? [*Pressure to feel guilt.*] How bad do you feel if you see your father's eyes after you really put a bad beating on him for what he did? How does that feel, seeing his eyes there? [*Pressure to feel guilt.*]

PA: I don't even imagine beating him.

Th: How painful is it to imagine that? [*Pressure to feel guilt.*]

Pt: I'm feeling my mom's pain, her powerlessness.

Th: You mean your father would be that powerless after you beat him? If you could put your father into that position, how do you feel?

Pt: Yeah, my dad was only about five feet tall.

Th: How would you feel if you had really hurt him at that time and really damaged him and put him into a helpless position? [*Pressure to feel guilt.*]

Pt: It probably would have ruined him. He was even almost as messed up as I am.

Th: So you would have wrecked his life, damaged him emotionally. [*Pressure to feel guilt.*]

Pt: Emotionally, yeah.

Th: And physically, too.

Pt: Yeah.

Th: So how do you feel if you damaged your father that bad? [*Pressure to feel guilt.*]

Pt: Bad. I didn't want to hurt him. I wanted him to love me. [*Tearful with some passage of guilt.*]

Th: It's a very painful feeling to have hatred and love at the same time.

Pressure to Guilt: Global Healing

Here we see the powerful healing effect of pressure to feel guilt about rage toward a loved one. This process removes residual symptoms, reduces self-destructiveness through helping the patient to see that he is a loving person who was hurt. He is not a destructive person who should be punished. This process removes paranoia and the need to be punished, to distance others, and to attack himself—even one of these events in therapy has a strong effect on projection. He now knows that he is "here to be loved." We now move to extensive recapitulation on the process.

Th: You understand your father but you hate what he did. You hate that he pushed you away. You hate that he hurt your mother. But at the same time you wanted him to love you. [*Recap: complex feelings.*]

Pt: Yeah.

Th: You have all these very mixed feelings toward your father. Very complex feelings. And then we've got to ask ourselves, is this the crime you did? When we talked about the crime earlier, is having rage toward somebody you love and having guilt about that rage a crime? Is that the crime? [*Global recap, emphasis on self-punishment for crimes.*]

Pt: I think I feel guilty about ignoring my mom. All she ever wanted was someone to love her.

Th: There's guilt about that, too.

Pt: Way more, yeah.

Th: At least those two parts then, but see, there's also that guilt about the anger part. You have that mixture of feelings: anger, guilt about the anger, and then all the pain and sadness.

Pt: I think listening to him assault her cured me of real anger.

Th: It cured you? What do you mean?

Pt: I can be angry.

Th: Mm-hmm, but it's like a distancing maneuver.

Pt: Yes.

Th: But you couldn't feel anger anymore after that, is that what you mean? You couldn't experience it anymore?

Pt: It was a form of rape to me—to raise your hand to someone in anger.

Unconscious Therapeutic Alliance: Everything Makes Sense

Recall earlier in the session the patient said emotional closeness was linked to "a form of mental or emotional rape." Following this understanding, we continue this global recap and consolidate what has been learned.

Th: You mean it's tied to rape.

Pt: Yes.

Th: So that makes a lot of sense then, too. Doesn't it?

Pt: Yeah, forcing my emotions on you is a form of rape.

Th: Yes, it's as if feeling your emotions is the same as raping somebody.

Pt: Yeah, I'm forcing myself on them.

Th: Yeah, but we can see where that came from, right?

Pt: Yes! [*Unconscious therapeutic alliance with intense relief at understanding all these connections.*]

Th: Because the feelings you had about rapes caused you to mix the two. And if feeling your anger about a rape is the same as doing a rape, then you have all the guilt and you feel like you did a crime—and then you close up and keep a distance with people as if you're going to hurt people.

Pt: Or I'm going to get raped.

Th: Someone's going to get it.

Pt: By giving out emotions, you give power to other people. Giving away power opens yourself up to rape. Where the hell did that come from? [*Hears his own unconscious therapeutic alliance talking to him and is surprised by this.*]

Th: It comes from people using power against others?

Pt: Yeah, if giving anything away leaves me vulnerable, I'm not going to be open.

Th: Okay, that's the hurt part. That's the sadness and the painful feelings that caused you to close up in the past. But then there's also the guilt about being closed up in the past, about how it's hurt you or someone else.

Pt: And not doing anything about it.

Th: And then the other side is the anger and guilt about the past that's caused you to close up. So there are different mechanisms and emotions underneath. When we came in, we set a task here today to sort out what the barrier is about, right? We wanted to find out why this naturally comes up, the tension, the barrier, and the walls that come up here with me. Why there's a guilt system. Why there's a self-critical system. You know what I'm saying?

Pt: No, I'm sorry; I have to stop. There's just too much. [*Is overcome with a very painful wave of feeling, weeps.*]

Th: There's a very painful realization there.

I paused for a moment to allow the grief.

Th: So if we sum it up, you detach from people for different reasons, old pain, old guilt, old disappointment, old anger, and guilt about the anger.

Pt: Yes.

Th: Then you have guilt about the distancing you've done.

Pt: Yes.

Th: Equal guilt, sadness, anger, and disappointed cravings. Add that together and here's what you get, when you sit with someone like me: the tension comes up, anxiety comes up, distancing starts to happen, and you get self-critical as if you did something wrong just by sitting talking to me. Even though you didn't do anything wrong, you had feelings of the past.

Pt: So how am I sitting now? Am I here?

Th: Do you feel like you're open right now here with me?

Pt: Yes.

Th: So do I. Here's what we know: when you feel some of these emotions, you don't need to close up anymore, right? You've been closed up about feelings that were from when you were small and you weren't conscious of why or what was happening. You were just stuck with the distancing.

Pt: I remember the feelings now, but I don't want to. I'm afraid that when I walk out that door, the minute I get to the front steps, I'm going to forget about them.

Th: Then what's going to come up, more sadness? More guilt? More of everything to some degree? So these emotions are going to try to come up.

Pt: For a while until I bury them again. I'm very good at that. [*Asks about the treatment process from here.*]

Th: Yeah, but put it this way: what if you give them a little bit of air, you let some of the feelings out? Do you think that what we did here today was helpful? When you look at it now? Do you think that if you get to spend more time on what we did here today, that will free you up in the future so you don't have to be distant with anybody if you don't want to?

Pt: To answer your question, I've made more progress today than I have in thirty years.

Th: In thirty years?

Pt: Thirty years of trying psychologists and psychiatrists and counselors and, I mean, I started in my twenties asking for help and no one ever got it.

He went on to summarize his many treatment efforts, including times he had "outsmarted" therapists, laughed at therapists, argued with therapists, and walked out of sessions sensing the treatment could not reach him.

Defensive Anger

Some resistant patients use angry behavior as a defense to distance themselves from you and push you away. Misunderstanding this as rage and focusing on it can lead to misalliance. The patient offered this comment to learners at the end of the interview.

Pt: Everything's distancing with me; all my reactions are to push people away.

Th: Apart from the feelings you have?

Pt: Yes, okay.

Th: Apart from the actual you underneath.

Pt: Ninety-nine percent of what I say is bullshit except when it gets down to the moment of a feeling.

Th: Yeah.

Pt: I think the emotion is only there a second, and then it's gone.

Th: Then at that point you're already backing away.

Pt: Yes.

Th: So the whole key is interrupting the backing away of any sort. That's the whole key. That's all we did here today.

Pt: Yeah. I actually care about people, but I've felt I had to keep a certain amount of distance to avoid these feelings.

TREATMENT COURSE AFTER TRIAL THERAPY

Highly resistant patients typically need twenty to forty one-hour sessions. The symptoms are usually reduced or removed within the first three to eight sessions. The later sessions involve mobilization and the experiencing of deeper zones of the unconscious and optimization of the unconscious therapeutic alliance.

PHASE OF REPEATED UNLOCKING

With the breakthroughs in the trial therapy, the unconscious therapeutic alliance is gaining strength, allowing partial and major unlocking of the unconscious. These breakthroughs further boost the unconscious therapeutic alliance. Thereafter, deeper and deeper zones of the unconscious complex feelings may be experienced. The emotions will move from violent rage to murderous rage to primitive murderous rage and guilt at these deeper levels. At each of these levels, the pain of the trauma is also increasingly intense. As described in the previous case, deeper zones of rage and guilt can mobilize more primitive defenses such as repression to smooth muscle anxiety, depression, conversion, cognitive-perceptual disruption, and projective defenses (fig. 14.1). You may need to build capacity to tolerate this anxiety so the patient can safely experience these feelings. (See chapter 15.) A typical vignette illustrating major unlocking of the unconscious in this treatment phase follows.

Vignette: Repeated Unlocking with a highly resistant patient

This is session thirteen of a woman with a history of dysthymic disorder and choking panic attacks. She has already had several unlockings. Walking up the hallway to the office, I can feel rise of heated anger in my chest reflecting the patient's activated feelings. She sits in the chair, very tense with hands clenching and sighing.

Pt: My husband again said he is going to leave me. Every day he is threatening this.

Th: How do you feel toward him?

Pt: I just feel like killing him. [*Presses hands together at fingertips in a strangling position.*]

Th: So how do you experience the murderous rage in you?

Pt: [*Sighs.*] I got anxious instead: I was gasping a bit. [*Unconscious therapeutic alliance: insight and prediction that the rage will take the form of strangling.*]

Th: If we look at it now, how do you experience this rage?

Pt: Right now I have powerful arms and I just feel like killing him. [*Shows strong arms but displays some tension in chest.*]

Th: How do you fully experience this rage? [*Pressure.*]

Pt: At the time I got anxious, but now it's just rage.

Th: Are you feeling this fully? If you don't shut any of it down . . . [*Pressure, challenge.*]

Pt: It's flowing in my chest and arms—I just feel like strangling him. [*Moves hands animatedly, displays no tension.*]

Th: How would it go on him if you don't hold back? [*Pressure to portray.*]

Pt: I would strangle [*holds hands in choking position*]—just keep strangling, strangling until he can't breathe. It feels like I'm doing it right now. [*Holds hands in this position.*]

Th: Is he dead then?

Pt: Then I feel sad. [*Passage of guilt; weeps heavily.*]

Major Unlocking

This woman has experienced the somatic pathway of rage on a high level for a few minutes. She kept engaged with the image of her husband and felt guilt about this rage over the threatened separation. Now the unconscious therapeutic alliance becomes dominant over resistance.

Th: What do you see looking in his eyes?

Pt: White. I see his eyes. But not his eyes. I see blue eyes. [*Weeps heavily.*]

I pause while she is weeping.

Th: You see blue eyes?

Pt: I see my father's eyes. [*Cries heavily.*]

Th: You see your father's eyes.

Pt: [*Cries heavily with guilt.*]

Major Unlocking and Projective Identification

By this point in therapy, the patient has had several unlockings of the unconscious. The unconscious therapeutic alliance was easily mobilized, bringing a major unlocking of the unconscious with a prolonged passage of rage, a clearing out of anxiety and resistance, and a visual transfer to the father with the passage of guilt. Note that this rage was to strangle the husband and father, but she had for years been experiencing choking panic attacks as if she is being choked. This symptom is *projective identification and symptom formation* (Davanloo 2005), where she felt what the victim of the rage would feel. A product of nonexperienced guilt, this symptom stopped after the first unlocking where she felt a rage to strangle and guilt about the rage. For moderately or highly resistant patients who have panic disorder, a single unlocking like this usually completely stops this symptom. This phenomenon is commonly observed when working in the deeper zones of the unconscious in resistant and fragile patients.

WORKING THROUGH

In the phase of working through, pockets of grief mobilize other pockets of rage and guilt about the rage. The past is put into context. Losses are grieved. Empathy toward family members increases. Reunion with family members may take place as well. If the family members are deceased, then an emotional reunification may occur on an imaginary level.

Without some cleaning out of guilt about rage, *self-forgiveness* and genuine *forgiveness of others* is impossible: self-punishment demands that all positive feelings toward others be repressed. Forgiveness of oneself for the rage enables forgiveness of others for harm done. This process changes the entire perception of others (Davanloo 2005).

Vignette: Working Through with a Highly Resistant Young Woman

This is the thirty-fifth session of a highly resistant woman who had over fifty unlockings going to earlier and more intense layers of rage and guilt. In the recent sessions, intense grief and guilt about the damage her defensive system caused was emerging.

Pt: Last week was our national holiday and I called home. I felt really good because for the first time, I had a very nice long conversation with my mom. She sounded so sweet toward me. I have never had that before. [*Weeps.*]

Th: That's a very painful feeling.

She feels grief for a minute.

Pt: I always thought my mom hated me, but now I know that was not true.

Th: How do you feel about that?

Pt: It's so painful. I'm so regretful. [*Weeps.*]

Pt: How could I ever have so much intense rage toward people whom I actually love? [*Weeps heavily with guilt and grief.*]

Pt: I can't believe I would react that way. [*Weeps more.*]

This session is followed a few weeks later with a very nice, in-person visit with her mother. She had never had such a pleasant experience with her mother. The following session she has a final mobilization of intense rage toward the mother.

Pt: I feel so much rage now flowing through me. I feel like I'm floating.

Th: Floating.

Pt: Yes, I'm not on the ground, and my jaw is so full of rage. I want to bite. [*Makes biting motions.*]

Th: How do you bite her?

Pt: Right on her neck so tight . . . tearing into it. [*Clamps jaw in session.*]

Th: Your arms?

Pt: No arms. Jaw. [*Makes biting motions.*]

Th: Then what happens?

Pt: I feel so sad again. I really hurt my mom. She is so young (in the image). [*Heavy passage of guilt, unconscious therapeutic alliance at a very high level.*]

Unconscious Therapeutic Alliance and Early Childhood Rage

In this passage the patient was experiencing feelings from her infancy when she was separated from her parents. She is visually seeing the mother at this very early age. The passages of love for the mother in recent weeks had enabled a mobilization of this early primitive rage. This is her last passage of unconscious rage and guilt.

TERMINATION

The phase of termination may be three to five or more one-hour sessions. In this phase typically some grief occurs about the end of the treatment relationship. This grief may mobilize some other feelings of rage, guilt, and grief related to the past separations and other trauma. This is a phase of saying goodbye to the therapist. Coupled with this some further pockets of grief may be mobilized. Often the highly resistant patient will have more work to do after this relatively short treatment course. The therapist and patient anticipate the remaining work needed and how any future adversity will be managed. Over several months in follow up, further pockets of painful feeling and rage and guilt may be experienced.

Vignette: Termination with a Highly Resistant Young Woman

In the final session with the patient above we reviewed her thoughts about her forty-session treatment course.

Pt: The most important thing that we have accomplished together is removing that furnace. That furnace of rage that I have had for so many years has disappeared. It completely went off after the last session when we talked about my mom. And I'm very aware of that. It's so sad I had that furnace for so long. [*Weeps with grief.*]

She experiences grief for a moment.

Pt: Carrying around all these feelings had been such a burden on me. But I feel like I've unloaded all the bags from the past. I'm free now.

Health

At this point and with so many unlockings, the patient has no resistance in operation. Grief flows easily, without obstruction. Love and empathy for the family members replaces distancing and disdain. This is a typical outcome when the process goes to the deep zones of the unconscious, something achievable with ISTDP in up to forty sessions with many highly resistant patients.

CHALLENGES IN WORKING WITH THE HIGHLY RESISTANT PATIENT

Therapists can have the difficulties seen with the moderately resistant patient, including inadequate psychodiagnostic phase, premature challenge, dropping of pressure at mid rise, inadequate mobilization of the transference feelings prior to portraying, and missing the unconscious therapeutic alliance. In addition, following are other challenges of working with highly resistant patients:

1. *Finding the front of the system:* Highly resistant patients may arrive for therapy very confused about their own problems, and often knowing where to focus is difficult. In these cases, search for and examine syntonic resistances. The therapist may be confused about this process or may assume that the patient understands his own resistances: this misunderstanding can lead to confusion in the patient and even misalliance.

2. *Ventilation and regression:* When highly resistant patients externalize and ventilate, the therapist may mistake regressive weeping and temper tantrums for passage of emotions. Explosive discharge or other regressive phenomena may look

like emotions but are actually defensive operations. The management of regressive defenses depends on the cause. If caused by too much anxiety mediated by muscle tension, reduce anxiety by recapping. If caused by the patient's habitual character defenses, acquaint the patient with the behaviors and their consequences.

3. *Lack of challenge:* When the resistant patient crystallizes her defense in the transference, clarify and challenge these resistances. Further pressure in this situation only increases the resistance more or has no effect. Clarification and challenge are required to mobilize complex transference feelings and the unconscious therapeutic alliance.

4. *Problems with head-on collision:* When a high rise in the complex transference feelings exists, step up the level of challenge to match. Now head-on collision is required. Examples of difficulties with head-on collision include the following:

   - *Missing elements of head-on collision:* Bring in all active elements of the resistance, alliance, and transference pattern of relating. Deactivate the transference and undo the omnipotence in cases when they are present. If one provides a head-on collision but does not undo the notion of omnipotence, then the patient can interpret this to mean "You're doing everything wrong and I know how to fix it for you." Include all the relevant elements of head-on collisions to avoid confusion and misalliance.

   - *Premature head-on collision:* Use a comprehensive head-on collision only when the resistance is well crystallized in the transference and the unconscious alliance is mobilized to a significant degree. Doing such a head-on collision prior to this will cause the complex feelings and the unconscious therapeutic alliance to drop. A very heavy intervention requires a high-level alliance and strongly activated complex feelings near breakthrough. Prior to this the system doesn't contain enough energy for the patient to benefit from a head-on collision.

- *Wrong type of head-on collision:* Head-on collisions are tailored for different degrees of rise in the complex feelings. For example, a short-range head-on collision when there is heavy crystallization of resistance in the transference is unlikely to be helpful. Conversely a major head-on collision at a low or medium rise in transference can cause the patient to flatten out.

- *Bypassing the head-on collision entirely:* Patients with high resistance and with crystallization require a head-on collision to break through to the unconscious. If the therapist fails to provide a head-on collision, the person is stuck with the resistance, and the alliance and unconscious complex feelings are frustrated.

- *Becoming supportive and dropping the pressure:* When high mobilization of the unconscious complex feelings, resistance, and alliance exist, maintaining pressure as described above is critical. Again, pressure is the lifeline to the person stuck underneath the resistance. Thus, maintaining contact with the person when providing such a heavy intervention as head-on collision is crucial.

- *Inadequate separation of the patient from his own resistance:* If you try to approach the unconscious without a solid alliance where the patient sees the price of the resistance, he will resist and his unconscious will close. In addition, the patient may misinterpret your efforts as punitive or critical, leading to misalliance and even dropout.

- *Transference activation:* Under high pressure and challenge, the transference may become activated. At this point the therapist is filling the roles of a punitive parent or neglecting parent or some other punitive character of the person's past. This is a complementary type of countertransference pattern akin to projective identification with both parties participating. Recognizing when this is happening and deactivating the transference is crucial. The deactivation process is a typical component of the head-on collision for this very reason.

Here is an example:

Pt: [*Highly detached; avoids eyes, closes hands, remains silent, and sits in an overt defiant position at high rise in the transference.*]

Th: So what are we going to do about it? [*Pressure to partnership.*]

Pt: [*No response; still sits in defiant posture.*]

Th: Because as long as this major wall and barrier stay here, this process is defeated, and it goes beyond anything I can do about it. [*Undoing of omnipotence, deactivation of the transference.*] So what do you want to do about it? [*Pressure to the will.*]

Pt: [*Gazes upward.*] What do you want me to do? [*Defiance, passive comment.*]

Th: Right now you are maintaining a major wall and barrier here, and part of you says "there is no way I'm going to take the wall down." [*Defiance.*] But if you continue that way, who are you defying and defeating? [*Deactivation of the resistance of defiance.*] My life goes on after this meeting, but what happens if we don't break through this? Who are you defeating? [*Clarification that the resistance will not defeat the therapist.*]

Pt: [*Pauses for a moment.*] Myself. [*Sighs and sits forward.*] And I don't want to do that.

Th: So what are we going to do about this? [*Pressure to partnership and task.*]

COUNTERTRANSFERENCE

Highly resistant patients have very powerful unconscious resistances that destroy relationships. Within the first minute the patient is in the office, the therapist's unconscious knows the patient's unconscious and vice versa. Any intense primitive emotions mobilized within the therapist's unconscious can generate unconscious anxiety and defenses, which can lead the therapist to shut down the process. Moreover, these emotions can lead to primitive defenses including devaluation of the patient or self (Abbass 2004). Countertransference must be addressed through supervision or therapy if it keeps interrupting treatment success.

OUTCOMES

ISTDP was specifically developed for the highly resistant patient (Davanloo 1995d). In published studies of patients with personality disorders, most of these patients are highly resistant or have high resistance with repression. Outcomes in these studies favored ISTDP over controls, and treatment effects were large and sustained (Winston, et al. 1994; Abbass, Sheldon, et al. 2008). ISTDP should be a first line treatment consideration for these populations. In the sample from my first six years of ISTDP study, 60.8 to 85.3 percent of these patients reported gains, 8.8 to 11.5 percent did not respond, and 5.9 to 15.4 percent dropped out. Of these patients, 70 to 85 percent had symptom and interpersonal problem improvement. Over 80 percent returned to work after an average of three months of therapy (Abbass 2002a).

Highly resistant patients have endured early attachment trauma resulting in primitive rage and guilt in the unconscious. These result in major resistance and self-defeating resistance of guilt. The process of treating highly resistant patients includes turning them against their resistances, challenge, and head-on collision to enable small and then larger breakthroughs to the unconscious. Then the unconscious therapeutic alliance takes a dominant position allowing access to and experience of underlying intense complex feelings. This is followed by repeated unlockings, working through, and termination. The majority of these patients experience sustained gains in the hands of a moderately trained ISTDP therapist.

CHAPTER 15

High Resistance with Repression: The Paralyzed Prisoner

A pproximately half of highly resistant patients repress their unconscious emotions at some level of rise in feelings. Rather than use isolation of affect and striated muscle tension, these patients have smooth muscle response, conversion, or depression to repress emotions out of consciousness. This incapacitating problem needs to be handled properly by the therapist to avoid worsening physical symptoms, depression, or suicidality (Davanloo 1995b, c; Abbass and Bechard 2007).

Laden with massive guilt about primitive rage toward loved ones, these patients are paralyzed and suffering in a dungeon under a castle ruled by a punitive king. This vicious king would quickly stop any move out of the dungeon and cripple the prisoner for even daring to ask for help. So weakened under this tyranny, the prisoner doesn't even need guards to keep people out: if anyone enters the castle, the punishment would be so paralyzing, she could not escape. After a while no one wants to witness this self-imposed misery and she is left to suffer in isolation. Death to escape this misery becomes a calming and soothing idea.

A strong, firm, and persistent reach from you is required before the patient will dare to make a move: she is terrified of further torment from the punitive king.

This self-punitive system explains the suicide risk when severely depressed people are artificially energized by psychiatric medications: the paralysis of depression can actually prevent suicide, so there is serious risk of putting energy in the system when this self-destructive system is still operating unchallenged.

TREATMENT CONSIDERATIONS

These patients require a detailed assessment of capacity followed by systematic work to build capacities including anxiety tolerance, self-reflective capacity, positive self-regard, and capacity to feel all the emotions. The paralyzed prisoner needs to be educated, see his dungeon and castle, care for himself, and become energized to revolt and break free of this destructive setting.

TREATMENT PHASES

Treatment of these patients requires detailed psychodiagnostic evaluation, building of capacities with the graded format, repeated unlocking, working through, and termination. (See table 15.1.)

Table 15.1 Phases of treatment in patients with high resistance with repression

Phase	Task
Initial process	Initial evaluation, psychodiagnostic evaluation to detect thresholds to and manifestations of repression
Graded format	Multidimensional structural work to build capacity to tolerate anxiety and to overcome repression and self-punitive defenses
Repeated unlocking	First breakthroughs, partial unlockings, and major unlockings to optimize the unconscious therapeutic alliance
Working through	Mobilization and experience of residual grief, rage, guilt, and consolidation
Termination	Closure of the therapy relationship over three to five sessions

TYPICAL PRESENTATIONS

Patients with repression can present in multiple physical (chapter 2) and psychiatric ways. This pattern is frequently seen in medical, surgical, and emergency department patients (Abbass, Lovas, and Purdy 2008). Some typical presenting problems are shown in table 15.2.

Table 15.2 Common presentations in resistant patients with repression

Major depression
Physical exhaustion
Irritable bowel syndrome
Hypertension
Bladder spasm or interstitial cystitis
Conversion disorder
Migraine headache
Gastroesophageal reflux disease
Reactive airway disease: asthma

INITIAL EVALUATION

Barriers to engage are common with these patients. (See chapters 6–7.) Hopelessness, low self-worth, and suicidal ideation, among other issues, can lead to lack of meaningful engagement. These barriers all need to be addressed before psychodiagnosis can be performed. A complete lack of signals is a worrisome sign that the patient may in fact be hiding suicidal intent. (See chapter 7.) Thus, a thorough history needs to be taken in cases of severe depression. Go through the checklist for "Why No Signals?" so you can be certain where the psychopathological dynamic forces are going. (See chapter 7.) If you cannot determine the cause of lack of signals, you should consider that psychotherapy may be contraindicated since your efforts could worsen symptoms because of repressive mechanisms. If you can see some partial signals and have a clear picture of the causes of limiting signals (such as sedative medication), you can proceed with psychodiagnostic evaluation.

CASE VIGNETTE: BARRIERS TO ENGAGE IN A MAJOR DEPRESSION CASE

A man arrives at the third session of treatment after having a crisis with his brother that spiraled his mood downward.

Pt: Doctor, I just came in to say I've decided to end my life. I kept my appointment because I made the appointment. [*Zero unconscious anxiety, zero defenses visible.*]

Th: So what does that mean in terms of you and me and what we are hoping to do? Can we look at how you are feeling with me? [*Pressure to attachment with me and to his will.*]

Pt: There isn't any hope for me at this point.

Th: Can we look into that? What does that mean about us here? [*The obvious issue is that if he is dead, treatment ends.*]

Pt: [*Clasps hands together.*]

Th: Because we have seen you have a destructive system and keep shutting down and walling off yourself. Let's see what we can do about this. [*Recap and high pressure, reaching to the person beneath.*]

Pt: [*Sighs.*]

Th: And you are anxious here, too. What feelings are coming up here with me?

Pt: I'll tell you what happened two days ago. My brother and I got into an argument and I was so enraged, I walked out of the house and slammed the door so hard that I broke a window in the house. When I saw that, I . . .

Th: So you saw a massive rage in yourself that day.

Pt: Yes. [*Sighs.*]

Decision Making

I decided that reaching to this person under the resistance and applying high pressure for him to join me in battling his self-destructive system was a psychotherapeutic emergency. Based on his lack of signals, I was prepared to admit him into the hospital unless I could see a response from his unconscious. He needed this high pressure, my expression of caring about him, to face the massive rage and guilt stirred by that conflict. He responded by giving up the suicidal plan as evidenced by striated muscle unconscious anxiety and engagement with me.

PSYCHODIAGNOSIS

Patients with high resistance with repression have a threshold at which they repress rage inward toward themselves instead of feeling the feelings. As a result, they go flat, lose tone, and become physically unwell, weak, or more depressed. Patients with severe repression go flat at low rise in complex transference feelings; those with moderate repression do so at mid rise in complex transference feelings while those with mild repression do so at high rise in complex transference feelings. (See fig. 15.1.) Thus, we need to carefully evaluate not only the *presence of thresholds* but also *how high the thresholds are* and *what happens above the threshold*. (See chapter 6.)

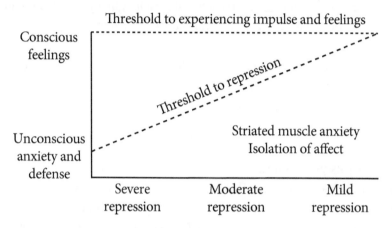

Figure 15.1 High resistance with repression

CASE VIGNETTE: PSYCHODIAGNOSTIC EVALUATION

This is a man with severe irritable bowel syndrome with no sign of striated muscle tension.

Th: Can you tell me about a time you experienced this diarrhea. [*Pressure to be specific, structuring the interview.*]

Pt: It comes out of the blue. There is no warning. [*Suggestion that he does not see emotional linkage.*]

Th: Can you describe a specific time this happened so we can see how that works? [*Pressure to be specific.*]

Pt: It happened when I missed the first session.

Th: Can you tell me about that? How did you feel when you missed the session? [*Pressure to identify feelings.*]

Pt: I called you, then got cramps and later diarrhea.

Th: When you called me, how did you feel? [*Pressure to identify feelings.*]

Pt: I thought I was an idiot for missing the appointment.

Th: You mean you were angry, but at whom? [*Pressure to identify anger toward therapist.*]

Pt: At me. [*Self-attack.*]

Th: So you mean you were angry with yourself? Is that what happens at times? [*Clarification of defense.*]

Pt: Yes, I guess it does.

Th: Because in your approach to tell me about that you became angry with yourself? [*Repeat of clarification of defense.*]

Pt: Yes, I did.

Th: Can we look into that? How that happens here? [*Pressure to task and patient's will.*]

Pt: Sure, I think we have to.

Initial Status

At this point I hear gastrointestinal gurgling sounds and see no striated muscle anxiety. This suggests that his anxiety is being repressed into the smooth muscle of his gastrointestinal tract (Abbass and Bechard 2007): the patient looks relaxed but his gastrointestinal tract is in spasm. I knew by his history that he was not actively suicidal, and I determined that the gastrointestinal tract was taking the brunt of his repression. We could then use this evaluation to monitor response to the interview.

Th: What is happening now?

Pt: Heartburn. [*Points to his chest.*]

Th: Did you just get heartburn? Anything else?

Pt: I can hear my stomach gurgling.

Th: So you can hear it gurgling. Is this what happens sometimes when you have strong feelings and anger, that you get heartburn and cramps? [*Recap: feelings-anxiety.*]

Pt: Yes, it must be.

Th: Because in your approach to talking about anger you got heartburn and cramps here. So is that where the anger goes? [*Repeat of recap.*]

Pt: Must be, because it just happened.

Confirmation of the Finding

These responses suggest that he represses emotions to the smooth muscle. To confirm this finding and assess how high his threshold is, we explore another focus.

Th: Can you tell me about another time this happened? [*Pressure.*]

Pt: Yes, when I'm angry with my brother, I don't say anything. I ignore him.

Th: Can you tell me about a time that happened? [*Repeat of pressure.*]

Pt: Yes, just the other day he did something to irritate me . . . and that is coming back again . . . the heartburn. [*Again, the patient appears totally relaxed with no striated muscle response.*]

Th: So again, when you speak of anger, your stomach reacts with acid and cramps. [*Recap: feelings-anxiety.*]

Assessment

Through this psychodiagnostic evaluation, I confirmed that this man had repression because his anxiety did not go into the striated muscle but rather into the smooth muscle of his bowel. This was occurring at a low rise in complex feelings, so he had severe repression. He had little ability to isolate affect or intellectualize about his emotions. Since we had passed the threshold for repression, mobilizing the unconscious would worsen his gastrointestinal symptoms. Hence, he needed the graded format of ISTDP to first build capacity to tolerate unconscious anxiety (Davanloo 1995b; Whittemore 1996; Abbass and Bechard 2007).

THE GRADED FORMAT OF ISTDP

Davanloo (1995b) developed the graded format of ISTDP to build capacity in patients in whom the standard, unremitting format would exacerbate symptoms. Highly resistant patients with repression are unable to distinguish between feelings, anxiety, and defenses. The graded format increases their ability to self-observe and isolate affect, overcoming the repression of affect, thus allowing them to differentiate between feeling, anxiety, and defense. Isolation of affect and self-reflection eventually replace repression and somatization of affect.

This change causes the remarkable neurobiological transition where the unconscious anxiety shifts into striated muscle, improving the patient's capacity to tolerate anxiety and experience underlying feelings. (See chapter 2.)

In contrast with the unremitting standard format of ISTDP, the graded format involves cycles of pressure alternating with recapitulation. When the anxiety approaches the threshold to repression, reduce it by recapping on the links between emotion, anxiety, and defense, as well as the link between the patient's past and present relationships and the transference. (See fig. 15.2.)

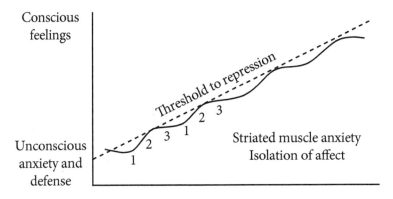

1. Pressure to feelings or to defenses
2. Rise in complex transference feelings and anxiety
3. Intellectual recap to bring isolation of affect

Figure 15.2: The graded format

GRADED FORMAT TECHNICAL ISSUES

Following are the main technical considerations of the graded format with highly resistant patients with repression.

When to Raise Pressure

In patients with repression it is both safe and warranted to increase pressure when some anxiety is visible in the striated muscle and when the patient can self-reflect and isolate affect. These are indicators you are below the threshold to repression.

How to Raise Pressure

Any efforts you make to connect with the patient, to encourage her to be present with you, to identify her underlying feelings, and to battle against defenses constitutes pressure. The patient is uplifted by your efforts to encourage her. At the same time she is irritated by the encouragement because you imply that she must change for her own benefit. Multiple ways of delivering pressure were reviewed in chapter 9.

Working with the Front of the System

Find the front of the system where it interfaces with you and the therapy process. For example, in the vignette of the man with severe irritable bowel syndrome, when the patient became angry with himself, the focus was on self-directed anger. When he developed heartburn and cramps, we recapped to overcome repression. If he had gone flat and depressed, the focus would have been on overcoming repression to the state of depression. With each of your efforts, try to replace repression with isolation of affect and self-reflection.

When to Lower Pressure

How do you know when the pressure is too high and must be reduced? What are the signals of being above the threshold? Specifically, there will be a lack of striated muscle anxiety and isolation of affect: the discharge pathway of anxiety will shift to smooth muscle. The patient will not be aware that emotions were just repressed, but instead she will regress into depression or physical manifestations of repression.

How to Lower Pressure

The vignette of the man with severe irritable bowel syndrome also illustrates how to lower pressure.

- *Stop current focus:* Temporarily stop the current focus and change to another area of focus. For example, change from pressure on feeling to exploring the content of a recent incident.
- *Recapitulate:* Review the process in partnership with the patient, clarifying what has just occurred and linking feelings to anxiety and defenses observed in those moments. This helps the patient see that he had feelings that were repressed.

- *Change stations:* Shift the focus to another corner of the triangle of person, for example from the transference (T) to his current life (C). Then ask for specific examples of this conflict at other times. Alternating between exploring in the T and C in the graded format is typical.

- *Review the experience of anxiety:* Examine the physical and mental experience of the anxiety to promote the ability to observe and describe his internal physical cues. Such *isolation of affect* and *self-reflection* cause anxiety to manifest as striated muscle tension.

Managing Extreme Anxiety

What do you do when the patient's anxiety goes high above threshold? For example, what if the patient experiences panic or severe cramps in the abdomen? These events call for direct efforts to immediately reduce anxiety. The techniques described in the previous section can reduce anxiety. In addition, consider the following:

- *Take an assertive stance:* Take a verbally assertive and active stance; otherwise, the patient may fill your silence with his projections, making conscious anxiety increase.

- *Handle hyperventilation:* If the patient is hyperventilating, tell her to stop breathing for a few moments. Otherwise, she will breathe herself into a confused state.

- *Go to the transference:* Focus on the feelings that were mobilized in the transference. After all, what you had been doing or not doing mobilized this anxiety. Focusing for a moment on the patient's feelings with you shows him you are not afraid of his feelings. It also can mobilize the complex transference feelings that may reduce his anxiety level.

- *Keep talking: be present:* If the patient is confused, she may not hear or see you very well. Help her ground herself. Patients will tell you that during these times they focused on your voice or your face to calm down. (See chapter 16.)

- *Develop your copilot:* Ask the patient to monitor and tell you the first cues he notices the next time he becomes highly anxious. This will help develop the patient as a copilot in the process.

- *Recap afterward:* Recap liberally after this event. Repeat the insights gained because the patient will tend to repress and forget what she was learning. Recapping repeatedly this time will reduce her anxiety the next time because she will remember how the two of you got through the previous session. You are safe to move on again when you start seeing signals of striated muscle anxiety.

Optimization

The degree of rise in the unconscious feelings and anxiety, as with behavioral exposure, has an optimal intensity the patient can bear and master without untoward effects. Help the patient bear the highest possible levels of affect. However, make sure the level of affect is well tolerated so that she will want to do further exposure work and gain more mastery.

In figure 15.3 we see that working in the *therapeutic window* near the threshold of anxiety tolerance maximizes the work being done (1). If the rise is too low, anxiety tolerance will not improve and capacity to overcome repression will develop more slowly than necessary (2). If anxiety is above the threshold, the patient will suffer the adverse effects of repression (3). Thus, aim to mobilize affect in the therapeutic window near but not above the threshold to repression.

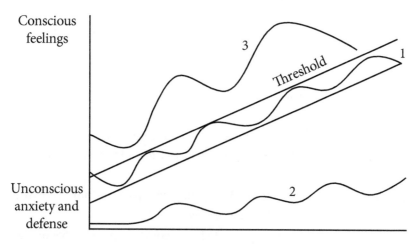

Figure 15.3 Optimization of graded format

One Foot in the Transference

Whether reviewing current incidents outside the office or the moment in the office, watch closely for repression. Always focus on the moment in the office to help the patient see that this is how he handles complex feelings with all people, past and present, and with you. This moment-to-moment real-time study of the process builds capacity to tolerate complex feelings and anxiety.

CASE VIGNETTES FROM THE FOURTH ONE-HOUR SESSION

The patient with severe irritable bowel syndrome returns for his fourth session.

Th: When you were coming, you were anxious and had some reflux symptoms? [*Pressure.*]

Pt: Yes, I was thinking about this issue of anger and I was upset with my brother the other day. [*Has a partial sigh indicating some striated anxiety.*]

Th: So you had some strong feelings you came to speak about, and your stomach reacted. Do you have any cramps or heartburn now? [*Recap: feelings-anxiety.*]

Pt: No, not now. [*Slightly clenches hands: striated anxiety.*]

Th: Can we look into the feelings you have coming in today? [*Pressure to identify feelings.*]

Pt: I was at his place, and we were talking about growing up. He seemed to think life in the family was pretty good back then, and I felt annoyed at him.

Th: How do you experience your anger? [*Pressure to experience rage.*]

Pt: I got nauseated and had diarrhea afterward. [*No longer has any striated signals.*]

Th: So the anger again went to your stomach? [*Recap: feelings-anxiety.*] Why didn't you get to feel the anger? What were you afraid of? [*Pressure.*]

Pt: I don't know. [*Burps.*] I'm getting cramps again now. [*Points to abdomen: smooth muscle anxiety.*]

Th: So right now the anger we focus on goes to cramps. Is that process happening again? [*Recapitulation: link anger and anxiety.*]

Pt: Yes.

Go to the Transference

This is a key moment to study the process that just took place. The complex transference feelings were rising but became instantly repressed.

Th: When we focus on the feelings now, the emotions go to your stomach rather than being felt. [*Recap: feelings-anxiety.*] Can we look at how you are feeling here with me when we speak? [*Pressure to identify feelings.*]

Pt: With you? I don't have any feelings toward you. I feel irritated at myself. My stomach still feels bad. [*No striated signal: smooth muscle anxiety.*]

Th: So again, when the emotions rise, anger turns inward on you, as if shutting down the anger to hold it inward and keep it from anyone else. [*Recap: anger-defense.*]

Span across to Guilt

If the patient can intellectually tell you he felt anger, then he may be intellectually able to see he had guilt about the anger that led to the instant repression. Jumping to focus on positive feelings and guilt with the person is a great antidote for repression, projection, and other defenses—it can be very effective even if it is only done on the cognitive level.

Th: How would you feel had you been angry in some way with your brother or here with me? [*Pressure alluding to guilt.*]

Pt: It would feel pretty bad. He has had a pretty tough time for the past five years since Mom died and his marriage was in trouble, too. He has the same thing I do with the bowel and anxiety. [*Empathic response, albeit intellectual.*]

Th: So there is positive feeling as well. Is this why the anger turns inward on yourself? To protect him . . . [*Recap: feelings-defense.*]

Pt: To beat up me . . . I feel always like I should be punished for some reason . . . or that someone will punish me. [*Insight into the pattern.*]

Th: This is very important. You have love at the base but anger as well. When the anger comes, it is shut down into depression, anxiety, and some kind of guilt system. As if you had harmed someone you care about . . . [*Recap: two triangles.*]

Pt: So I direct it at myself. [*Copilot helping out with the recap.*]

Th: Do you think?

Pt: Seems that way to me. It makes sense, but I don't want that anymore. [*Looks stronger and calmer and has striated signals back with better body tone, clenches hands.*]

Th: Let's see what we can do about it. [*Pressure.*]

Pt: What do I do? [*Displays some passivity.*]

Th: Let's see. Are you waiting for me? [*Clarification of passivity, pressure.*]

Pt: I'm not sure what to do. [*Displays some tension, sighs.*]

Th: How do you feel toward me right now? [*Pressure to identify feelings.*]

Pt: Frustrated.

Th: How do you feel this frustration inside? [*Pressure to experience rage.*]

Pt: I don't. It is toward me, really.

Th: So back at you again. Back to the mixed feelings again? Let's see how we can address that to stop it. Because the feelings go in a few directions . . . to your stomach, to anxiety, to depression, to avoidance, and to a passive position. All back on yourself—as if to protect the other person. [*Recapitulation and pressure.*]

Pt: That is what I'm doing, and I don't like it really . . .

Improved Capacity

By this point in the session we see decreased depressive process and smooth muscle anxiety. Now he has increased energy, some striated muscle discharge, and some isolation of affect. These are typical symptom changes seen by the fourth hour of therapy when this treatment is going well. This shift surprises physicians who have seen the patient suffer the same health complaints for years despite the best medical care. The patient now has a moderate capacity to tolerate anxiety. Because of his moderate use of repression, he can have smooth muscle and depressive responses but at a higher level of complex feelings than before. He can now think and talk about his emotions without his symptoms worsening. He is closer to being able to experience his emotions, the ultimate goal of the therapy.

Changes in the Early Phase of Treatment

The graded format increases the threshold at which the patient can isolate affect and hold anxiety in striated muscle. Once repression and smooth muscle anxiety discharge stop, the therapy looks increasingly like the standard format of ISTDP, mobilizing the unconscious feelings with unlockings of the unconscious. The patient becomes able to tolerate enough rise in complex transference feelings for the unconscious therapeutic alliance to dominate the resistance, allowing first breakthrough or partial unlocking of the unconscious (Davanloo 1995c). These changes may occur in one session or gradually accrue over several sessions, depending on how high the threshold is for repression.

CASE VIGNETTES FROM THE EIGHTH ONE-HOUR SESSION

The eighth session with the man with severe irritable bowel syndrome begins.

Pt: I have been feeling better . . . the diarrhea has stopped for a few weeks now, but I've been noticing that I don't like my sister-in-law very much. [*Striated anxiety: clenches hand and sighs.*]

Th: Can you tell me more about that? First, why your diarrhea has stopped.

Pt: I'm not sure exactly [*sighs*], but something is different. I am thinking about the feelings more and not letting them get to me . . . the anger and anxiety we talk about. [*Anxiety in striated muscle, isolating affect: structural change.*]

Unconscious Changes

This session shows a common response to the graded format. The therapy changes patients at an unconscious level so they report feeling better and being more aware of emotion. But they are unable to explain why they are better or what has changed. However, we can see that anxiety now goes into the striated muscle and resistance is now in the form of isolation of affect. He is now using different brain regions with good benefit (Abbass, Nowoweiski, et al. 2014).

Th: Can we look into what happened with your sister-in-law? A specific situation you noticed. [*Pressure to be specific.*]

Pt: Yes, my nephew. John's gerbil died and she wanted to flush it down the toilet . . . my nephew was so upset and crying.

Th: How did you feel? [*Pressure to identify feelings.*]

Pt: I told her to be sensitive and consider the effects on John . . . and she did. [*Sighs again.*]

Th: She had a good response to that?

Pt: Yes, she did actually. She was surprised I said anything, and she thanked me for it later. What I said was measured and calm. I was a bit surprised! [*Appears proud and smiles.*]

Th: So you felt good about that and good with her, too? [*Clarification and pressure to experience positive feelings.*]

Pt: Yes, but when she was saying that, it tore my heart out and I felt enraged. [*Sighs; emergence of next component of the complex transference feelings.*]

Th: How do you physically experience the rage when you think of it now? [*Pressure to experience rage.*]

Pt: It just . . . [*Moves hands from lower abdomen to upper body in sweeping motion, indicating somatic pathway of rage is activating.*]

Th: How does that feel now? [*Pressure to experience rage.*]

Pt: It's in my gut and chest . . . moving up . . . a heat. [*Drop in tension, patient is energized with some degree of somatic pathway of rage activated.*]

Th: How does that feel? [*Pressure to experience rage.*]

Pt: Like I want to poke, to point. [*Gestures in a strong fashion.*]

Th: How does it want to go if it is not stoppable? [*Pressure to portray rage.*]

Pt: It wants to zap out like a laser beam! [*Speaks forcefully and expressively.*] And it would zap her into the wall.

Th: Then what happens? [*Pressure to portray rage.*]

Pt: Then she is stopped . . . and I feel bad. [*Becomes teary-eyed.*]

Th: It's a painful feeling . . . [*Resonating with his emotion.*]

Pt: Yes. [*Weeps quietly with some mixture of grief and guilt.*]

Partial Unlocking of the Unconscious

Since anxiety and resistance are temporarily absent, pressure and challenge are not indicated. I simply highlight the painful aspect of this emotion and do not interrupt the process by talking. After the wave of painful feeling passes, we recap again.

Th: In that moment there were strong complex feelings all at once. You identified with John and his loss, and this mobilized sadness and rage with a body experience in it. But this rage had guilt attached to it. [Recap: triangle of conflict.]

Pt: Yes. But I didn't get diarrhea or cramps that time, and I said something, and it worked out well, really.

Th: Yes, you were conscious of the feelings but didn't get to quite experience them until now. And when you did feel them, the anxiety and tension dropped and the feelings were felt. But they were mixed and strong. Before, it would have been running to the washroom, having a panic attack, becoming more depressed, but for sure not talking about it. [Recap: triangle of conflict.]

Pt: That is for sure.

Th: But we have a question about these feelings. Do you have any thoughts what this all meant to you and why you felt so strongly? [Question to the unconscious therapeutic alliance.]

Pt: I do. [Wells up with wave of sadness and tears.] . . . My mom. [Unconscious therapeutic alliance brings link to a past figure with whom there is unresolved emotion.]

Th: There is a very painful feeling . . . [Resonating with and highlighting of feeling.]

Pt: [Weeps.] My father and mother divorced when I was five years old. All I remember after that was how I was not allowed to talk about my father, and I rarely got to see him. My mother wouldn't allow it. It was like he died.

Th: There is a lot of painful feeling there.

Pt: [Displays more grief.]

First Unlockings

First breakthroughs or partial unlockings seen when using the graded format include grief related primarily to the past. Relatively little rage and guilt are experienced in these early breakthroughs; rather, grief is predominant.

This session illustrates a partial unlocking of the unconscious. There is no transfer of the image to a past figure with whom the patient has unresolved feelings. Rather, a clear link to that person develops, which may come as a surprise to the patient. Then we can examine the feelings around the original figure. In this example, he felt empathy for his nephew, who was being deprived of the chance to mourn his loss with no acknowledgment of his right to grieve. We could then understand the link to the patient's feelings about his experience with his mother and the broken bond with his father.

Recapitulation

After this unlocking and with each rise in emotion with the graded format, having an extensive phase of consolidation is essential. This consolidation lays out for the patient the links between anxiety, feeling, and defense (triangle of conflict), in the past, present, and therapeutic relationships (triangle of person). This systematic, repeated review helps the patient understand the therapy and himself. This consolidation weakens repression and cements isolation of affect, thus creating unconscious character change. Such recapping after breakthrough is important with all patients, but especially so with fragile patients and those with repression (Davanloo 2001). Here is an example:

Th: So we see here you have a lot of very mixed feelings about your mother and father that were stirred up with this breakup and more recently with your nephew. [*Recap: two triangles.*]

Pt: Yes.

Th: And those feelings included pain, rage, and guilt about the rage—guilt about the rage as if you did violence to people you care about. [*Recap: complex feelings.*]

Pt: I see.

Th: And do you see where the rage and guilt went? To your stomach and depression and back on yourself in general. [*Recap: self-attack.*]

Pt: I beat myself up.

Th: Yes, as if your rage is a real action that requires you to suffer and be punished. So it kept going back on you. But what we see here is that you can feel this rage in your body and some guilt about it. When this happens . . . [*Recap: self-punishment relieved by feeling guilt.*]

Pt: I feel relief. It's a relief. [*Displays a bit of sadness.*]

Th: You've been suffering for years for things you didn't do. So how about if we keep moving to clean up the old guilt and rage from the past to stop them from contaminating the present and hurting you? [*Pressure to task ahead.*]

Pt: Please, let's do that.

GUIDELINES FOR RECAPPING

Here are some basic guidelines for recapping.

1. Patients with *more symptoms* require more repeated and extensive recapping to replace symptoms with isolation of affect and striated muscle anxiety.

2. Those with *cognitive-perceptual disruption and smooth muscle* anxiety (versus striated muscle anxiety) at lower levels of rise in anxiety require more repeated and more extensive recapping.

3. Recaps at the *end of sessions* usually include more elaborate global reviews to cover all aspects and to project the upcoming therapeutic work.

4. Shorter or fewer recaps should be used with the phase of pressure in patients with *good striated signaling*. Otherwise recapping would drop the pressure and delay the breakthrough. Use recaps when and as needed based on presence or lack of signals.

5. All available elements, including materials from previous sessions that come to your mind, should be used in global recaps. Help the patient to understand processes in greater depth, session to session.

IMPACT OF THE FIRST UNLOCKING OF THE UNCONSCIOUS

With the breakthrough of the complex transference feelings in the case of the man with severe irritable bowel syndrome above, the patient has faced his own frightening feelings and impulses. This markedly reduces his fear of his own impulses, brings global symptom reduction, and creates character changes. He now knows to an extent that he didn't kill anyone and need not repress his emotions. Thus, the repressive mechanism is significantly reduced with a single unlocking (Davanloo 1995c).

MAJOR UNLOCKING: PASSAGES OF GUILT

In-depth treatment of patients with high resistance with repression necessitates the capacity to experience all of the unresolved unconscious feelings and impulses. Guilt about rage toward loved ones must be experienced to remove the need to self-destruct. To access this guilt, the patient must have a high tolerance of anxiety and complex feelings of love and rage: the resistance of repression must be overcome and self-love must increase.

Following are key vignettes from a fifth treatment session with a man with a history of depression, panic, irritable bowel syndrome, and longstanding self-defeating character patterns. This man had definite evidence of a pervasive self-punitive system manifesting as a combination of symptoms and character problems.

In the first four sessions a similar process to that already described took place, and he had some partial unlockings. He came into this session reporting gains, medication reductions, and positive feelings toward the therapist.

Th: How do you feel about that when you're coming in to tell me that? [*Pressure to experience positive feeling.*]

Pt: Relieved.

Th: Some positive feeling?

Pt: Yeah.

Th: How does that feel? [*Pressure to experience positive feeling.*]

Pt: Good, good.

Th: So a positive feeling.

Pt: Yeah. I've been here before, and that's what worries me. I'm going into the future worry again. [*Sighs: punitive king moves.*]

Positive Feeling Must Be Punished

As with other patients of this type, this man's psychic structure is like a paralyzed prisoner deep in a dungeon ruled by a punitive king. Positive feelings about progress are causing alarm in the castle, and the punitive king is retaliating. He needs to self-punish because of guilt about the rage that is being stirred by the positive feelings toward the therapist.

Th: The first part you have is a positive feeling though. [*Pressure to experience positive feeling.*]

Pt: Yes. [*Clasps hands, takes partial sigh.*]

Th: What does that feel like in your body when you feel a positive feeling here with me? What do you notice compared to other feelings? [*Pressure to experience positive feeling.*]

Pt: Oh, relaxation here. [*Points to stomach.*]

Th: Your stomach relaxes itself.

Pt: So my body is not as tense.

Th: So with the positive feeling, your body seems to relax. [*Recap.*] Is there anything that tells you that it's a positive feeling as opposed to just a relaxed state? How do you know you feel a good feeling in your body compared to these other feelings we focused on? [*Pressure to experience positive feeling.*]

Pt: Yes.

Th: Okay, there's a positive feeling and there's something else: is there some anxiousness at the same time as the positive feeling, some anxiety?

Pt: Yeah, it's more like, "This is not going to last."

The Punitive King Retaliates

At this point the patient has limited capacity to tolerate positive feelings and rage. As I apply pressure for him to experience this positive feeling with me, the unconscious anxiety and the need to self-punish increase. This finding can explain how some of these patients worsen with supportive care. Now we focus on this process and the underlying feelings to mobilize the unconscious.

Th: Okay, what other feelings are in there at the same time as your positive feeling here with me? What mixed emotions stir up in there? [*Pressure to identify feelings.*]

Pt: You know, I think the underlying, irrational fear of not having had success or what I believe to be success with treatment in the past. [*Tension in hands, intellectual response.*]

Th: What other emotions are within you that tighten you up alongside the positive feeling? How else are you feeling inside your body? [*Pressure to identify negative feelings.*]

Pt: Well, the anxiety. [*Takes a partial sigh.*]

Th: What emotions do you feel toward me with the positive feeling? How else do you feel at the same time? [*Pressure to identify negative feelings.*]

Pt: Um, cautious.

Th: This is a component of anxiety. [*Clarification.*]

Pt: I suspect so, yes.

Th: How do you feel toward me besides the positive feeling? [*Pressure to identify negative feelings.*]

Pt: Um, well, again, I think it's probably more the sensation of anxiety I'm feeling.

Th: So can we reach below that? [*Pressure to task.*]

Pt: If I can get below that. [*Sighs.*]

Th: Something frightens you about the positive feeling. Is that what it is? You're frightened somehow about the positive feeling, and the fear makes your body anxious. [*Recap: feelings-anxiety.*]

Pt: Yeah, it closes me down and makes me think that this is not going to last. [*Unconscious therapeutic alliance is rising: whisper from alliance.*]

Th: So what can we do about this? Let's see what's under that, what drives the anxiety. [*Pressure.*]

Pt: I would say that it would have to be shame and guilt. [*Whisper from the unconscious therapeutic alliance.*]

Th: But guilt about what right now? [*Rhetorical question to the unconscious.*]

Pt: Well, about my whole belief system, you know, and the willingness to feel the positive feelings is overshadowed by all this crap that I feel. [*Whisper from the unconscious therapeutic alliance: need to self-punish.*]

Bolstering the Unconscious Therapeutic Alliance

At this point in treatment, the unconscious therapeutic alliance is a young force requiring continuous boosting through recaps and various forms of pressure to mobilize the complex transference feelings. Sensing a lag in the patient's energy, I provide a recap.

Th: How else do you feel here toward me below the anxiety? What is churning around under there? Because we already established that there is a system of mixed emotions producing anger that turns in toward your body. It goes back in when you've got a positive feeling toward somebody. It then shuts you down. The anger turns toward you as if you did a crime: remember that from before? [*Recap, pressure to remember what we know.*]

Pt: Yes.

Th: So what emotions are in there today, here with me? How do you feel toward me below the tension? [*Pressure to identify feelings.*]

Pt: Well, below the tension.

Th: Under the tension in the muscles, what builds into that? What emotions are built into that right now? [*Pressure to identify feelings.*]

Pt: [*Sighs deeply.*] Well, I guess a fear that I'm not going to be able— that this is not going to be . . .

Th: This is the anxiety again, right? This anxiety, worry, tension and nervousness all inhibit and shut you down. [*Short recap and pressure.*]

Pt: Right.

Th: So what emotions are in you that cause self-doubt, anxiety, and shut down of yourself? [*Pressure to identify feelings.*]

Pt: I'm scared to step out.

Fear of the Punitive King

The prisoner is literally afraid to step out of the dungeon: he knows well how severely he will be punished if he dares stand up to the king. He must pay for all the vicious murders he committed. Keep recapping and pressing to bolster his capacity to face his own self-destructive system.

Th: But that's the anxiety again, right? So how do you feel toward me? What emotions are here toward me below all that? [*Pressure to feeling in the transference.*]

Pt: I wonder if I'm not sure I understand. Everything I try to do I've got to understand in my head. [*Request for a recap.*]

Th: In your body, what emotions do you feel here besides the positive feeling at the same time? Because you're blocking yourself and attacking yourself. The anger turning inward is happening. That's what we know happens. [*Recap: triangle of conflict.*]

Pt: Well, I can tell you in terms of sensations, my back is as tight as hell. [*Striated muscle anxiety.*]

Th: So what emotions do you feel (the anger and guilt) toward me before you pull it back on you? We've seen this anxiety as a container of anger and guilt and positive feelings all stuck in at the same time—jamming you down. Do you remember that? Your body jams the anger down: the anger wants to come up and your body jams it down. [*Recap: triangle of conflict, pressure to remember.*]

Battling Repression

Ongoing pressure and recapitulation serve several purposes. First, they overcome the forces of repression, or simply put, help him remember what we have learned. Second, the rise in complex transference feelings desensitizes him to complex feelings: this improves his anxiety tolerance. Finally, the pressure and recapitulation increase the power of the unconscious therapeutic alliance versus the resistance by mobilizing the complex transference feelings.

Th: So how do you feel these feelings if you don't let it [resistance] jam yourself down? [*Pressure to identify feelings.*]

Pt: It's still in there. [*Unconscious therapeutic alliance saying the resistance is still in operation.*]

Th: So how do you feel toward me? You've got a good feeling with me. How else do you feel toward me at the same moment? If you pull all the feelings together. [*Pressure to identify negative feelings.*]

Pt: At the moment I feel positive and worried.

Th: How does that feel in your body? [*Pressure to experience positive feeling.*]

Pt: It feels calming, you know; it feels positive.

Th: Is there something good inside your body? A good warm feeling of some sort that tells you there's a positive feeling? [*Pressure to experience positive feeling.*]

Pt: No. It's kind of mixed with anxiety. It's there, but it's so crushed by the anxiety.

Th: We see the anxiety crushing down positives, and the anger and everything gets stuck in the same moment, see? [*Recap: triangle of conflict.*]

Pt: Yes.

Th: Let's see how we can activate the emotions and push them through the anxiety. Let the emotions rise; don't let them get blocked. How do you feel whatever is in you here today toward me? [*Combination recap and pressure: short recap and pressure.*]

Pt: Well, excited, you know, if I can make progress.

Th: That's a part of the positive feeling.

Pt: Yes. Maybe there is a breakthrough here. I just allowed myself to feel excited about making progress.

First Breakthrough to the Unconscious

Here we see a partial passage of the complex transference feelings with a predominance of positive feeling and excitement; this means the beat-down prisoner is activated and taking a step out of the dungeon. The constant pressure and recaps have mobilized the complex transference feelings and unconscious therapeutic alliance with a partial experience of them, mostly on a preconscious level. With this event, we listen for a communication from the unconscious therapeutic alliance in the form of a linkage or memory. I respond with a recapitulation.

Th: How does that feel?

Pt: That loosens my stomach up again.

Th: See, something happens when you feel a good feeling, something changes in your body.

Th: And that shift is important. It's almost like one counters the other: the anger counters the positive, the positive counters the anger. Anxiety tries to block both of those down. [*Recap: triangle of conflict.*]

Pt: That's right. The anger deals with the past, and the positive is shut down by fear of the future.

Th: Is there something that just came to your mind about anger in the past?

Pt: Well, these very negative belief systems that I have. I'm believing now that I've created most of those as opposed to someone else who may have had a part of it. Certainly not my intention, but that is what has happened. [*Whisper from the unconscious therapeutic alliance, deep understanding and start of linking.*]

Th: That you have taken that in from others.

Pt: I have taken all that and crashed it in on myself.

Th: So where did the anger in the past come from that turned into a crashing anger toward yourself? [*Question to the unconscious therapeutic alliance.*]

Pt: Just the anger that I was feeling toward my parents and my sister.

Th: So are you thinking about the past with them? [*Question to the unconscious therapeutic alliance.*]

Unconscious Therapeutic Alliance versus Resistance

The unconscious therapeutic alliance has become activated with a linkage to past complex feelings that led to a self-punitive system. I followed this with a global recap, with pressure to encourage the unconscious therapeutic alliance to bring forth a clear linked event. The patient was able to link complex feelings toward both his mother and his sister in relationship to abuse perpetrated by his cousin who lived in the house. Upon linking this, he became anxious, and the focus was on feelings in the transference.

Th: Yes, but what's under there that you're tensing about? We are looking to help you get out from under there. [*Pressure, calling to prisoner stuck underneath.*]

Pt: Well, it's frustration with myself for not being able to identify the Goddamn . . . [*Punitive king, self-attack.*]

Th: Frustrated with whom? Who's asking you to see the feelings? [*Pressure to identify feelings.*]

Pt: You are.

Th: So how do you feel toward me? [*Pressure to identify feelings.*]

Pt: Um, frustrated with myself. [*The punitive king still in operation.*]

Th: Yeah, but how do you feel toward me? [*Pressure to identify feelings.*]

Pt: I can't—I'm not getting to see it. [*Resistance of repression is working.*]

Th: But what are you feeling inside? [*Pressure to identify feelings.*]

Pt: Everything I say is either anxious or fear, and it is that second level; I don't understand what this first level of feelings is. [*Unconscious therapeutic alliance trying to operate.*]

Th: How do you feel toward me? [*Pressure to identify feelings.*]

Pt: Frustrated as hell. [*Clenches hands, appears tense.*]

Th: What do you feel in your body right there that tells you you're frustrated? [*Pressure to experience rage.*]

Pt: It's a tightness.

Th: Okay, tightness would be some of the tension of anxiety. [*Differentiation of anxiety from rage.*]

Pt: Yeah, yes.

Th: But, what about the feeling of anger in your body? [*Pressure to experience rage.*]

Pt: Well, it would have to originate with anger.

Bracing: Combining Pressure and Recap

This man does not appear to have much energy, despite his words. He is at the threshold of repression. Pressure intermingled with constant reflection on body cues and thoughts will bolster his ability to self-reflect while starting to feel emotions. This dual therapeutic focus, which I call *bracing*, activates both the brain's self-reflective regions (including the dorsolateral prefrontal cortex) and limbic structures related to emotions (including the amygdala). Patients with severe repression and fragility have limited capacity to pair these activities. This dual focus builds capacity to experience feelings in a conscious, mindful fashion. (See fig. 15.4.) This self-reflective activity promotes isolation of affect that in turn activates striated muscle anxiety; anxiety is converted from cognitive-perceptual disruption and smooth muscle anxiety to striated muscle anxiety. (See chapter 2.) As you will see, I was detecting that he was losing momentum and going flat. When a threshold has been exceeded, he will need more recapitulation.

Th: What happens, though, is it goes to anger on your body and nervous tension in your body—so how do you feel the frustration and anger with me first before it pulled back on you? How do you experience it first in your body before it converts back to anger on you? [*Bracing: experience of rage.*]

Pt: Um, just a quick sensation of anger, I guess.

Th: Can you describe that, because it seems like there's still a lot of tension in your body right now. [*Bracing: anxiety.*]

Pt: There is a feeling that wants to push out of my chest. [*Somatic pathway of rage.*] It's a pushing out as opposed to a pulling in.

Th: Okay, you feel a rage expanding out to some degree? [*Bracing: experience of rage.*]

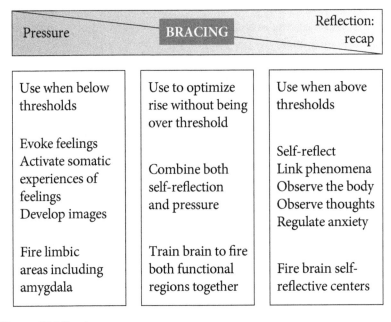

Pressure	BRACING	Reflection: recap
Use when below thresholds Evoke feelings Activate somatic experiences of feelings Develop images Fire limbic areas including amygdala	Use to optimize rise without being over threshold Combine both self-reflection and pressure Train brain to fire both functional regions together	Use when above thresholds Self-reflect Link phenomena Observe the body Observe thoughts Regulate anxiety Fire brain self-reflective centers

Figure 15.4 Bracing

> *Pt:* Well, trying to expand, and the way it expands is it comes up to my chest. [*Self-reflective response to bracing: description of the somatic pathway of rage.*]
>
> *Th:* Right, and then we see the anxiety attempts to push it back down. The rage is clamped back down toward your stomach, and it tries to pull itself up. Remember that? So when you feel this anger or rage moving up the body, can you let that move up through that tightness, through the tension, and not let it get clamped? If you don't let it get clamped down and let it move all the way up, how do you feel that rage? [*Bracing: experience of rage.*]
>
> *Pt:* Um, weakness, weakness in my arms. [*Motor conversion.*]
>
> *Th:* Do you see what happened there? That's shutting off the anger, and your arms go weak, right? [*Recap: rage and the defense of conversion.*]
>
> *Pt:* Again in my legs here.
>
> *Th:* Weak or strong?
>
> *Pt:* Weak. [*Motor conversion.*]

Th: Okay, what's happening is you're losing your body motor power at the same time the anger wants to come. Do you see how it goes? [*Recap: feeling-defense.*]

Pt: Yes.

Th: That would keep you glued in the chair. [*Recap: the defense of conversion.*]

Pt: Right.

Conversion: Pressure Through or Recap?

The patient developed motor conversion at this rise in complex feelings as if to prevent violent acting out, due to the activated intense rage and guilt. Thus, I try to press through this conversion. If the patient cannot tolerate the pressure, he will flatten out and I will do more recapping. If he can tolerate it, a significant breakthrough will occur since we are at a high rise in the complex feelings.

Th: But how do you feel this anger move up as it gets in your whole body? No weakness and no shutting down of tension and not turning toward yourself. What do you feel going up? [*Pressure to experience rage with some challenge.*]

Pt: I feel hyper. You know I just feel . . . [*Moves arms around.*]

Th: Can you feel some of that, and let yourself feel that in your arms and your legs, your whole body with no weakness? How do you experience this anger as it charges up? Is there energy? [*Pressure to experience rage.*]

Pt: Yeah.

Th: Okay, can you describe the energy component in your body? [*Bracing.*] What does that feel like? [*Pressure to experience rage versus anxiety.*]

Pt: Well, here it feels like pushing up. [*Rubs chest.*]

Th: And your arms? It comes and goes in your arms, does it? [*Bracing: experience of rage.*]

Pt: Right, yes.

Th: They have some power and then they don't have power. [*Conversion coming and going.*]

Pt: Yes. When I get the weakness, it starts here [top of left arm]. When I feel the strength, it's here [bottom of left arm] and from here [legs].

Somatic Pathway of Rage versus Conversion

Transient conversion is very common in patients with repression. Here he describes the somatic pathway of rage starting in the feet and going upward. After it gets to the top of the chest, it activates the hand and then the arm with an urge to grab and do some form of violence (See chapter 5.)

Th: So when you get the strong part of that anger, your energy's flowing out of you. Can you feel that pretty well right now in your arms? [Bracing: experience of rage.]

Pt: Yeah, a little.

Th: Are they weak or not too weak? [Bracing: focus on body experiences.]

Pt: Not weak but they're not strong. The sensation is more in the back of my arms than it was, so there is more strength.

Th: Do your hands have some power in them? [Bracing: experience of rage.]

Pt: Yeah, some.

Th: Okay, there is some energy flowing around. [Bracing: experience of rage.]

Pt: Yes.

Th: The legs, are they strong or weak or in the middle? [Bracing: focus on body experiences.]

Pt: The sensation is here in my legs so there's strength; they're stronger than they were.

Th: Could you move yourself if you wanted to? [Bracing: experience of rage.]

Pt: Yes.

Guided Experiencing of Emotions

Bracing, with its emotionally activated study of body responses, is starting to yield dividends. First, he is tolerating a high rise in complex feelings. Second, this focus on the rage toward me reassures the patient I am confident in both his capacity and the safety of his experiencing it: this reduces his conscious anxiety. With this much somatic activation, I now shift to pressure to the portrait of the rage.

Th: How much aggressive energy is in this piece of anger compared to the other ones you told me before? What physically would come out of the arms and legs in terms of your thoughts? What would someone come at me like if the anger came out uncontrolled? How does it come in an image in your mind with the arms? [*Stack of pressures to activate and portray the rage.*]

Pt: Well, for example, if someone were to walk through that door with a knife, you know, I would act first not last. You know, I would take the fight to him as opposed to him taking it to me.

Th: Okay.

Pt: The legs and arms attack. [*Moves legs as if kneeing someone and swings arms.*]

Th: You feel all that energy to move right now, right?

Pt: Yes.

Temporary Use of Third Parties

This is displacement of the rage toward me onto another person, but it is helping the patient access and express the aggression in his body. Now that he is experiencing the impulse I focus on what rage *he* had protected me from.

Th: If all that anger was coming in my direction and you couldn't stop it, what would the picture look like? Can you tell me how the rage would go through the arms and legs if they went in a blind attack and you couldn't stop? Does it want your arms to attack? [*Pressure to portray rage.*]

Pt: It's an arm and leg thing. [*Is poised to move both aggressively.*]

Th: What do the arms do? [*Pressure to portray rage.*]

Pt: Go. Grab. [*Aims hands forward toward my neck.*]

Th: Grab. [*Bracing: aggressive impulse.*]

Pt: Yeah, the goal is to get control of the neck. [*Moves his arms.*]

Th: This is to get control of the neck? [*Bracing: aggressive impulse.*]

Pt: But if I want control of you, I'm going like this. [*Simulates headlock.*]

Th: Okay, your arms go round the neck, and what do they do next? What do your legs want to do? [*Bracing: aggressive impulse.*]

Pt: Twist my body and twist the body.

Th: You twisted me? [*Bracing: aggressive impulse.*]

Pt: That's correct.

Th: What does it take to release the whole thing? What happens next? [*Pressure to portray rage.*]

Pt: Uh, well, until there is quiet. Until you're quiet and the situation is safe.

Th: Okay, so I'm quiet. I can't talk.

Pt: Right, if you were down and out from whatever beating I put on you.

Th: What kind of beating wants to come out of your hands and feet or legs? What kind of beating wants to come? What do you see me looking like when you pull me down there? What type of beating is it? [*Pressure to portray rage.*]

Pt: It's legs, knees, yeah. [*Moves knees and arms.*]

Th: Kneeing me when I'm down there? [*Pressure to portray rage.*]

Pt: To me, it's all designed to get control as opposed to wreak violence on you or wreak harm. [*Unconscious therapeutic alliance: negation.*]

Th: Uh-huh. How do you feel now?

Pt: Alert. [*Exhilarating effect of emotional experiencing.*]

Th: Quite awake, right.

Pt: Yes, just still some rage.

Th: But see, what does it take to get that all out? [*Pressure to portray rage.*]

Pt: Break your neck. Kill you.

Th: So if I'm dead there with a broken neck, how does that feel? If you could see the eyes down there, how is it to look at the eyes?

Pt: It would be hard.

Th: It's painful. [*Pressure to feel guilt.*]

Pt: Yes. [*Looks sad.*]

Unconscious Therapeutic Alliance

With combinations of bracing and pressure, the rage has been experienced and the focus is on the unconscious therapeutic alliance to come and link the process to a past person through an image or linkage. The somatic pathway was mobilized in a gradual fashion up to a moderate level of rage. This is sufficient for the unconscious therapeutic alliance to transfer the image to a past person. The next vignette takes place a few minutes later and the process is slower than the text depicts. The focus is on the attachment feelings and guilt about this rage.

Th: How do the eyes look?

Pt: Just glassy. Shocked.

Th: What kind of color?

Pt: I see blue. [*Unconscious therapeutic alliance: image transfer.*]

Th: How do you feel when you see the dead blue eyes? Whose eyes are these? [*Question to the unconscious therapeutic alliance.*]

Pt: Not yours . . . it's my mother.

Th: Your mother's eyes? How do you feel with your mother dead down there? [*Facilitation of guilt.*]

Pt: Very sad.

Th: It's a painful feeling. [*Facilitation of guilt.*]

Pt: Yeah, just total guilt.

Th: It's a painful feeling when you see her eyes there. [*The eyes relate to the bond with the mother.*]

Pt: Yes. [*Closes eyes and turns head away, fighting off guilt.*]

Th: What would you say to her? [*Facilitation of guilt.*]

Pt: I'm sorry. I have so much anger; each time that a little bit comes out, it terrifies me. [*Anxious response.*]

Th: But how much terror would you have if you just murdered her? [*Facilitation of the experience of guilt.*]

Pt: Oh my God.

Facilitate the Passage of Guilt

The healing process of ISTDP is the removal of guilt as a source of self-destruction. The way out of the dungeon is through the tombs of the unconscious and through the guilt to the love underneath. To assist in this journey I press for the patient to be close to the body of the dead mother.

Pt: I just lie in a fetal position next to her, facing her.

Th: Curled up. Curled up with her.

Pt: Yes.

Th: She's dead there.

Pt: Just a tremendous feeling of remorse.

Th: What does she say to you before she dies there? [*Facilitation of guilt.*]

Pt: I'm sorry.

Th: She'd be sorry to you. [*Facilitation of guilt.*]

Pt: [*Nods head.*]

Th: There's no anger in her.

Pt: No.

Th: How painful is it for her to leave you like that? [*Facilitation of guilt, reference to the loving bond.*]

Pt: Just overwhelming. I get the weakness. You know my whole body is weak. It needs to curl up. I'm in shock. [*Motor conversion.*]

Th: If we look at it then, there's a lot of guilt, love, and painful feeling in you buried with this rage, and it generates the anxiety, and it goes to rage toward you. And then it jams you down when you have feelings that could trigger it. The feelings come up and the anxiety jams it down as if you did that in reality. [*Recap: triangle of conflict.*]

Somatization of the Guilt

Because of repression, the patient developed somatic symptoms rather than feel the guilt about the rage. Now I will press for him to feel the guilt. This work ties together all the complex feelings and improves his capacity to tolerate anxiety. It also strengthens the unconscious therapeutic alliance to bring deeper feelings.

Th: But how bad would it have been if you had really killed your mother. [*Facilitation of the experience of guilt.*]

Pt: I would have been completely devastated. I would never have talked again, probably.

Th: You wouldn't talk again.

Pt: No, I would just completely shut down. I'd be totally incapacitated. It's kind of what I'm feeling right now. [*The paralyzed murderer in the dungeon.*]

Th: Yeah. That's what I'm wondering. How much guilt do you have and how does that guilt feel? How does that guilt feel about having this rage in you? [*Pressure to experience guilt.*]

Pt: It feels overwhelming. [*Struggles to fight off pain, weeps quietly.*]

Th: Painful feelings.

The Punitive King Responds

The job of the punitive king is to make sure the prisoner never gets free from punishment. Thus, the patient must never be allowed to feel the guilt about the rage and must be punished for even daring to try to free himself. It's no wonder that the best standard treatments do not solve the problems of these patients: the punitive system must undermine any success to atone for vicious murders.

Pt: Painful. If I have anger, it's at the bloody guilt, you know, because I created it.

Th: But you can see her eyes looking at you. The blue eyes. It's a painful feeling to see her eyes. The pain wants to come out, and you are holding the pain back in. [Focus on the eyes and attachment.]

Pt: It's anger. [Rubs chest.]

Th: There's anger there, too?

Pt: Yeah, at myself. [Self-attack.]

Th: With whom?

Th: Who is it toward first?

Pt: It's a result of these people from the past, primarily my mother.

Th: So how does the rage want to go?

Pt: It's a result of myself.

Th: So how does the rage feel toward her?

Pt: Oh, it's not. I can't get to it.

Bolstering the Prisoner versus the Punitive King

The prisoner is struggling under the self-punitive resistance even though he had a partial experience of the complex feelings linked to the mother. The punitive king, sensing defeat, moved to choke him off and throw him back in the dungeon: the guilt about the rage toward the mother was repressed into somatization. Now I provide a solid recap to fuel him to battle his own self-punitive system.

Th: Then let's see how we can get to it, because you see how it works, right? Here with me, these feelings move partly up and your body clamps down. But when you feel it, you see that there's rage but at the same time there's a positive feeling and guilt as if you did harm. But when you see the image, it's her that you see actually. It doesn't have to do with me, but it stirs up with me. [*Recap of the two triangles.*]

Pt: Yeah.

Th: And as it stirs up, you get anxious as if it's going to go on me, and then you pull back on to yourself to protect me. [*Recap triangle of conflict.*]

Pt: Yes.

Th: When you have her image in mind, some rage moves back into yourself. So how do you feel toward her? See, you felt the rage as if it was me; but it's not me, right? So how do you feel the rage toward her when you think about her at some point in the past or present or recent time? [*Pressure seeking clear link from the unconscious therapeutic alliance.*]

Pt: Yes, and how does it feel? [*Unconscious therapeutic alliance pressures himself.*]

Th: Is there a point where you had the most rage toward her in your life that you can think of right now? [*Pressure.*]

Pt: I don't. It's not rage. [*Unconscious therapeutic alliance: negation.*] I think of a situation where I went to put my arms around her as a young boy, and I was told to go away.

Th: Do you remember that? How do you feel toward her? [*Pressure to rage.*]

Pt: Well, it's, it's angry. [*Moves arms with power.*]

Th: Is it in your hands again? [*Combination reflection and pressure.*]

Pt: Yeah, yeah.

Th: So it's the same thing as what you already felt? When she rejects you at that moment? [*Pressure focusing on the incident.*]

Pt: The sensation is not a strength. [*Unconscious therapeutic alliance: negation.*]

Th: You don't have strong hands? [*Combination reflection and pressure.*]

Pt: Well, it's closing my hands and . . . [*Clenches fists.*]

Th: It *is* strength.

Pt: Yeah.

Th: The rage has arms and legs; it has force. Do you feel some of it in your arms compared to the way you felt with me? [*Bracing: experience of rage.*]

Pt: Yeah. Back here. [*Rubs back of left arm.*] The strength is back.

Keep Pressing

Here you see the technique of continued pressure and bracing to override repression and internalization of rage. A recap followed closely by high pressure helps the somatic pathway to fire.

Th: What does this one want to do physically, if you went berserk with her? [*Pressure to portray rage.*]

Pt: Well, that's it. [*Squeezes hands closed, gripping.*]

Th: Grabbing then. [*Pressure to portray rage.*]

Pt: And it's not going around the neck because I want her attention.

Th: Yeah, but what about the berserk rage, if it couldn't be controlled by you, what does it want to do? [*Pressure to portray rage.*]

Pt: Well, it shakes. It can scream. [*Shakes arms.*]

Th: If you went berserk on her, it grabs and shakes her, and then what? [*Pressure to portray rage.*]

Pt: Screaming in terms of what kind of attention I want.

Th: What else does it want to do in your body, in your arms, in your legs? What do they want to do, you know, if the berserk rage goes out, where does it want to go? [*Pressure to portray rage.*]

Pt: [*Nods head.*]

Th: What does the rage want to do to her? [*Pressure to portray rage.*]

Pt: Oh. [*Drop in energy for a moment; drops hands.*]

Th: You already felt a wave of it; now it's pulled back. Has it?

Pt: [*Nods head.*]

Th: Okay, the rage went up, right? Then the anxiety came up and pushed it down. Right? And then you get pulled back and that guilt pulls you back. It's like restraining yourself. [*Recap: triangle of conflict.*]

Pt: Yes, that's right.

Th: Okay, just what you felt a minute ago, how does that rage go? If you attacked viciously on her back, then similar to what you felt with me, how does it go on her? [*Pressure to portray rage.*]

Pt: Well, it would just be grabbing. [*Clutches hands again.*] Wrestling to the ground.

Th: So you pull her on the floor. Where do you see that in the house?

Pt: The kitchen.

Th: In the kitchen. So she's pulled on the floor, and then what does the rage do next? [*Pressure to portray.*]

Pt: Just . . . [*Swings arm.*]

Th: Punching.

Pt: Beating on her shoulders and back. On the upper torso. [*Recall his back was "tight as hell"; moves arms in punching motion.*]

Th: And if the whole thing goes berserk, then what else? [*Pressure to portray.*]

Pt: Just continue beating in a rage. I'd just continue until peace, until she's gone.

Th: She's finally gone, beaten. Then she's dead there in the kitchen. You were young then—how old then?

Pt: Yeah, she's in her thirties.

Th: She's young. She's down there dead on the floor in the kitchen.

Pt: Yes.

Facilitating Guilt

Now the somatic pathway of rage has passed at a moderately high level for a few minutes. Guilt is now in the preconscious zone and ready to be experienced. At this early treatment phase and with resistances still in place, pressure to keep the feelings mobilized will help the patient feel this guilt.

Th: How does it feel when you're standing over her dead body? [*Pressure to feel guilt.*]

Pt: Just, just terrible. Remorse and fear. [*Painful appearance.*] In the fetal position. [*Curls up his body.*]

Th: Can you see her eyes when you're in that position lying beside her? If you can see her eyes . . . [*Pressure to feel guilt.*]

Pt: Again, it's shock. It's just shock.

Th: How do you feel when you see your mother's shocked, dead eyes looking at you? [*Pressure to feel guilt.*]

Pt: Oh, nauseated. [*Repression to smooth muscle.*]

Pressure to Experience Guilt

Again we see somatic symptoms trying to block access to the guilt. Pressure to experience the love for the mother and guilt will override these symptoms and produce a major therapeutic event.

Th: It's a very painful feeling coming up. [*Facilitation of the experience of guilt.*]

Pt: Oh yeah.

Th: It's a very painful thing to see when you're that small. [*Facilitation of the experience of guilt.*]

Pt: Oh, I just shut down. I can't feel anything.

Th: What do you do with her? [*Facilitation of the experience of guilt.*]

Pt: I'd just lie there. I'd just be a shaky mess.

Th: What would you say to her when she's dying away? [*Facilitation of the experience of guilt.*]

Pt: I'm so sorry. [*Increasing painful feeling.*]

I slow the process here.

Th: What would she say back to you with her eyes? [*Underscoring of the attachment to facilitate the experience of guilt.*]

Pt: God bless you.

Th: God bless you in your life.

Pt: [*Nods head.*]

Th: After you murdered her, she is blessing you. [*Love from the mother.*]

Pt: [*Nods head.*]

Th: She wants a good life for you. [*Love from the mother.*]

Pt: [*Removes glasses, begins to weep but holds back.*]

Th: It's a very painful feeling that's been in there a long time. Don't let yourself fight that. Let it just come out. [*Facilitation of the experience of guilt, process is slow, and I feel painful feeling for him.*]

Pt: [*Starts to cry but holds stomach and is in some physical pain.*]

Th: Let it come out of your eyes [as opposed to your body]. It's a very painful thing to see. [*Pressure to feel guilt.*]

Pt: Oh, it's buried down here at the moment. [*Rubs stomach.*]

Th: There's love on the bottom of all this, both ways between you both. [*Recap complex feelings.*]

Pt: [*Nods head.*] That's what makes it so hard.

Th: Yeah.

Pt: [*Cries some more.*] I just want to hug her.

Th: Hug her.

Pt: [*Cries heavily for several minutes. Displays no signs of any somatic symptoms now.*]

Love—Enabling Passages of Guilt—Heals

Again we see that the experience of love for the mother, enabling the passage of guilt about the rage, resolves the need for the patient to punish himself with somatic symptoms. In this early treatment phase he required sustained pressure to allow passage of guilt and removal of symptoms. Now we do a comprehensive recapitulation and review of the process. This repeated review is critical to prevent symptoms returning after a breakthrough like this.

Th: That's a very complex set of feelings from way back then. They put you in a major conflict with yourself. [*Recap: complex feelings.*]

Pt: Yeah.

Th: You have a system there as if you did this and then all anger has to be pushed back down into yourself after that. Your body has to get shut off as if you're going to murder somebody. [*Recap: punitive king.*]

Pt: Yes.

Th: But even when we're talking about feelings from many years ago, these are activated here with the positive feeling with me, right? Do you see what I mean? [*Recap: attachment and bond.*]

Pt: Yes.

Th: It was also activated when you felt irritation with me along with the positive feeling, right? [*Recap: complexity of feelings.*]

Pt: Yes.

Th: And those feelings activate anxiety because when the old rage comes up, the positive feelings and guilt push it back. These all tend to go to your stomach or just toward yourself as if you did some crime. [*Recap: repression due to guilt.*]

Pt: Yes.

Th: It's like you're being haunted by all this. Her dead body says "How dare you enjoy your life when you murdered me!" But when we look at it, that's actually not what she would say anyway. [*Recap: love between his mother and him, punitive king.*]

Pt: No, and that just adds to the shame and guilt.

Th: When you get down to it, it's a loving feeling under there and a lot of disappointment and pain. [*Recap: core of loving attachment.*]

Pt: Yeah, but the rage just created guilt and shame on me. [*Unconscious therapeutic alliance contributing to the recap.*]

Th: Yes, as if you did this.

Pt: But to me, I felt this anger and it is as if I did it. I mean all of the angry feelings or thoughts I have buried then—it's as if I did it. They didn't go off somewhere; they were buried by the guilt. [*Unconscious therapeutic alliance: excellent understanding of process.*]

Th: Yeah, and it feels like an actual action. When you're getting close to these feelings, your anxiety goes up as if it's going to be an action. [*Recap: feelings-anxiety.*]

Pt: Yes.

Th: This has been in essence what has made your body go weak, anxious, tired, depressed, and made you direct rage toward yourself. The shutdown is a last-minute effort so that the rage doesn't come up. [*Recap: conversion explained.*]

Pt: Yeah.

Th: It's as if you've got to protect everybody from this rage, even though it's an internal emotion that's years old. But the rage gets triggered and feels like you're going to act on it in this moment. Do you know what I mean? [*Recap: triangle of person.*]

Pt: Yeah, there's just so much in there that my fear is to let go of a piece of it, that I'll unravel and all the rage is going to come out at once.

Anxiety Reduction through Experience

This experience of intense emotions has a massive effect on anxiety as well as depression. The patient now knows he will not become violent if he feels emotions. He knows we are a solid working team: he is ready for further, even more intense, breakthroughs.

Pt: But this is reassuring that it's not going to go unraveling. There's a whole lot more of that crap down there. [*Forecast of the bloody road ahead for us.*]

Th: Yeah, well, this is one piece of that system, you know. [*"I'm ready to go there with you."*]

Impact of This Session

This graded work leading to unlocking the unconscious has a powerful effect on this man's mood and somatic symptoms. His anxiety tolerance improved markedly and repression was largely overcome. The subsequent sessions were full of deeper emotional experiences related to past trauma.

OPTIMIZATION OF THE UNCONSCIOUS THERAPEUTIC ALLIANCE: REPEATED UNLOCKING

With repeated unlocking of the unconscious, the unconscious therapeutic alliance can become dominant over the resistance, allowing in-depth passages of primitive rage and guilt: these can result in major character change.

We continue this same case with the eighth session. The patient arrived with positive changes and symptom reduction, planning a visit to estranged family members. He is smiling widely on coming in, stating, "It's a great day out there today." The focus is on the positive feelings with me.

Positive Feelings toward the Therapist

Note that he has much greater capacity to tolerate pressure without the need for much recapping or bracing interventions. He can now operate as a resistant patient without repression.

Th: What's it feel like coming in with that positive feeling?

Pt: Well, it's such a feeling of relief and gratefulness.

Th: Uh-huh.

Pt: But again, as soon as I say that, I'm watching over my shoulder. [*Expectation that the punitive king will retaliate.*]

Status of the Castle

By this point in time this man has had several partial unlockings of the unconscious and has been steadily improving. He is out of the dungeon but still in the castle. Now, a primitive load of feelings is emerging leading to fear of retaliation from the now-weakened king. This anxiety about a backlash is common when working to the deeper zones of the unconscious where primitive rage and guilt reside.

Th: You feel that inside, this positive feeling? [*Pressure to experience positive feeling.*]

Pt: Yes.

Th: The positive and gratitude, is it a bodily feeling of positive that you notice? [*Pressure to experience positive feeling.*]

Pt: Yeah, it certainly is an absence of anxiety. Just safe. A comfortable feeling.

Th: So how do you feel about having that good feeling with me? [*Pressure to experience positive feeling.*]

Pt: Well, again, now it feels good, but I'm looking over my shoulder. [*Clenches hands and sighs.*]

Th: So what feelings do you feel toward me besides the positive feeling? What do you feel toward me in your body that gets triggered with the positive feeling? [*Pressure to identify feelings.*]

Pt: Well, I guess I'm not sure it's a feeling toward you. It's a feeling toward myself. It's a fear that I will have no control over the other [*punitive king*] coming back.

Th: So this anxiety moved in.

Pt: Yes.

Th: Let's see what emotions get stirred up when you feel a good feeling toward me. How else do you feel here with me in your body under the tension? [*Pressure to identify feelings.*]

Pt: I guess underlying the anxiety is probably fearfulness.

Th: What's below that, below the anxiety? [*Pressure to identify feelings.*]

Pt: I guess that's what I would refer to as the fear of the future. [*Sighs.*]

NATURE OF INTERVENTIONS

At this point he has unconscious anxiety in the striated muscle and can isolate affect. He has structural changes that enable a more direct mobilization of the unconscious. Now he can tolerate and benefit from more pressure and requires less recapping and bracing.

Th: On its own that's anxiety, but what emotions fuel that right now? [*Clarification and pressure.*] What other feelings are in you here with me right now? How else do you feel toward me besides the positive, because you have tension in your chest? [*Stack of pressures to feeling.*]

Pt: [*Nods head.*] Yeah, I feel the tension.

Th: What feelings do you feel toward me that are getting clamped? [*Pressure to identify feelings.*]

Pt: In terms of negative feelings?

Th: Whatever's in there that you're tensing down. [*Bracing.*]

Pt: Well, I don't know how to describe it other than the fear. [*Unconscious therapeutic alliance: negation, pressure to feelings.*]

Th: See what feeling moves up into your arms and then you get tense and shut your arms down? [*Bracing: experience of rage.*] The same process we have seen before. [*Pressure to remember previously learned material.*] What feelings do you feel there now that you're holding down? How else do you feel toward me besides the positive feeling? [*Stack of pressures to feelings.*]

Continue to Feed the Unconscious Therapeutic Alliance

I continue to intersperse short recaps with pressures. The use of stacks of pressure mobilizes the triple factors of complex transference feelings, unconscious therapeutic alliance, and transference component of resistance. A heavy load of feelings is emerging so the patient needs heavy sustained pressure. Notice that challenge is of little use; the main intervention is pressure—reaching through to the person beneath the remaining resistance.

Pt: Well, there's a feeling of that strength here. [*Rubs top of left arm.*] Although it's not a tendency to go like that. [*Makes grabbing motion with both hands toward my neck; unconscious therapeutic alliance: negation.*] It's more a normal feeling of strength as opposed to a weakness.

Th: Uh-huh, but you have some energy into your arms like that. Your arms want to move in some way. So you mean some of the rage is in the arms. [*Pressure to experience rage.*]

Pt: Yeah, perhaps so, but it's not, you know, it's not to the intensity that it was before. [*Unconscious therapeutic alliance: negation, call for more pressure.*]

Th: Okay, can you let yourself feel whatever is there fully without it getting clamped or shut down? How do you just feel the whole thing in your arm? How can you experience that feeling? [*Pressure to experience rage.*]

Pt: Well, a tendency to do that again. [*Makes grabbing motion toward my neck.*]

Th: How does the anger feel in your arms? [*Pressure to experience rage.*]

Pt: The tension is lower than it was moments ago. [*Drop in tension as somatic pathway of rage is activated.*]

Th: Okay, you feel some of that rage in your arms, and it wants to go like that. [*Grabs out; pressure to experience rage.*]

Pt: Yeah, in the arms and the legs, too. [*Moves arms freely.*]

Th: How does the anger feel in your legs? [*Pressure to experience rage.*]

Pt: Just sort of poised to jump. [*Moves his legs, prepared to pounce, shows no tension in arms.*]

Markers of Somatic Pathway of Rage

With all interventions I'm looking for body reactions of a drop in muscle tension (reduced hand clenching and sighing) coupled with an energized, freed-up urge to move. The greater degree of somatic rage and drop in anxiety, the greater the strength of the unconscious therapeutic alliance will be. When these changes occur, I will press to portray the rage.

Th: Poised to pounce. You feel that your arms want to go, your legs want to pounce. So what physically do they feel like doing right now here if you didn't stop them and pull them back? [*Pressure to portray the rage.*]

Pt: Physically go after you on the neck. [*Thrusts hands forward toward my neck.*]

Th: So face on, on my neck with the hands squeezing. So how do they squeeze on my neck? [*Pressure to portray the rage.*]

Pt: Just— [*Puts hands out in front as if to squeeze.*]

Th: Tight on there. [*Pressure to portray the rage.*]

Pt: Yeah.

Th: And then what's happening to me? What does the whole rage do if it's holding on? [*Pressure to portray the rage.*]

Unconscious Therapeutic Alliance

At this point the somatic rage has been experienced for three to four minutes. It is inevitable that the unconscious therapeutic alliance will become activated.

Pt: I'm seeing my sister. [*Unconscious therapeutic alliance: image transfer.*]

Th: You mean your sister is there?

Pt: Once I try to imagine doing that to you, it's not you; it's my sister.

Th: What image is there with her?

Pt: Shock.

Th: Your hands are on her neck?

Pt: Yes.

Th: How do they do that, just squeezing from the front face on or . . . ? [*Pressure to portray the rage.*]

Pt: More shaking and choking. [*Holds hands in shaking/choking fashion.*]

Th: Shaking and choking together.

Pt: Yes.

Th: And her neck, what about her neck? [*Pressure to portray the rage.*]

Pt: Well, no, more on the shoulders.

Th: Some part of you didn't want to go on the neck, you mean?

Pt: [*Nods head.*] Yeah.

Th: How do you feel when you strangle her and your arms are there and she's strangled?

Pt: The tension is back in my chest again. Rather than dealing with it, it's causing me to pull it in.

Th: So the total rage goes on her throat and . . .

Pt: Causes me to back off.

Th: So how do you feel when you see that?

Decision Point: Guilt versus Rage

At this point the unconscious therapeutic alliance is at a very high level with this major unlocking of the unconscious transferring the image to the sister as soon as his hands reached my neck. Some of the rage was felt, but some of the feelings have been repressed into temporary weakness. Now I will, as always, follow the lead of the unconscious therapeutic alliance and see what wants to come first, guilt or more rage.

> Pt: The tension comes back in my chest, so there's a real conflict over this. [*Unconscious therapeutic alliance.*]
>
> Th: If this whole rage goes onto her neck strangling her and then she's down there—
>
> Pt: Yeah.
>
> Th: Is the rage still in you when she's dead there?
>
> Pt: No, it's more a weakness. [*Conversion.*]
>
> Th: What do you see looking at her?
>
> Pt: Well, it changes between wanting to continue to attack and wanting to stop.
>
> Th: Do you feel some of that rage still?
>
> Pt: Yeah.
>
> Th: So how physically would you attack her with this rage if this whole rage went berserk onto her body? How does it come out of you? [*Pressure to portray rage.*]
>
> Pt: It's in the leg. [*Presses his leg on the floor in front of his body.*]
>
> Th: And your leg wants to do what? [*Pressure to portray rage.*]
>
> Pt: Just crush her face and just basically crush her mouth.
>
> Th: What else does it want to do? [*Pressure to portray rage.*]
>
> Pt: It's still crushing.
>
> Th: Crushing her head.
>
> Pt: Yeah. [*Suddenly moves leg forward on the floor.*]
>
> Th: What happened?
>
> Pt: Her head just detached, oh.
>
> Th: You mean it just went off at the neck?
>
> Pt: Yeah.
>
> Th: Is the rage still in you or is it gone now?
>
> Pt: It's shock. Her head is rolling away.

Primitive Murderous Rage

This is a long passage of primitive murderous rage over several minutes. Guilt about such a rage will be heavy. My task now is to help the guilt pass as fully as possible by focusing on the loving bond, the eyes, and the closeness.

Th: How do you feel when you see her eyes?

Pt: Just terrified.

Th: Terrified eyes—her eyes look terrified?

Pt: Her eyes are just sort of staring with shock and disbelief.

Th: So what do you do with her head, her eyes? It's a very painful feeling.

Pt: [*Begins to weep heavily.*] I want to pick it [the head] up and hug it, oh, God.

Th: Are you holding her dead body?

Pt: Oh, trying to put the head back on.

Pt: Oh, she's back together again. It's just a mutual hugging, just trying to protect her.

Th: Her body's a dead body there you mean or . . . ?

Pt: No, she's alive again.

Trust the Unconscious Therapeutic Alliance

The previous passage may seem confusing. How did the body become alive again? After many years of doing this work I have learned to trust the unconscious therapeutic alliance and how it operates. In this case the unconscious therapeutic alliance is bringing an image of loving mutual affection side by side with one of horrific primitive rage. This will greatly facilitate the passage of guilt, and that is the prime task of the unconscious therapeutic alliance.

Th: She's alive and you're trying to protect her, and then there's the dead body. [*Keeping both images in view.*]

Pt: Protect her from the rage.

Th: And then there's the dead body and her head is off. [*Keeping both images in view.*]

Pt: It's terrifying.

Th: They're both there: hugging her, loving her, and murdering her. [*Maintenance of both images in view.*]

Pt: [*Cries with heavy, hard wave of guilt for a few minutes.*]

Pt: [*Closes his eyes and looks away from the image on the floor.*] Oh God, it's just terrifying when I open my eyes and see that image [on the floor].

Th: It's a very painful feeling.

Guilt: The Most Painful Emotion

The passage of guilt after the passage of primitive rage is extremely painful, physically and emotionally. This man is trying to not see the image by looking away, but the unconscious therapeutic alliance will project the image everywhere, even inside his eyelids, so he cannot escape it.

Pt: Oh, I'm seeing the same image even with my eyes closed now.

Th: It's very painful.

Pt: [*Hard wave of guilt for a few minutes.*]

Pt: Oh, it's just so confusing; it's just back and forth, back and forth. [*Refers to both the loving image and the murdered image.*]

Th: There's love in there.

Pt: [*Another hard passage of guilt for a few minutes.*]

What Do We Do Next?

How do we know what to do next in therapy sessions? I hope these passages illustrate that this decision is always dictated by the unconscious therapeutic alliance. Prior to this, our sole task is mobilizing the complex transference feelings to usher in the unconscious therapeutic alliance so it can lead the process—then we are a facilitating witness to a wonderful healing process.

Pt: Oh, it's changed now to my cousin, oh God.

Th: Your cousin is there? How does he come in your mind?

Pt: He replaced her in the image on the floor with my foot on his neck. [*Powerful somatic rage focused in his leg.*]

Th: So he's alive, and your foot's on his neck?

Pt: Yeah, just begging me to stop.

Th: He's begging you, looking up, begging you. You feel that rage in your leg again?

Pt: Uh-huh.

Th: And crushing still. [*My leg is out forward and pressing hard on the floor.*]

Pt: Standing up and crushing down on the neck. He's choking.

Th: He's choking and can't breathe.

Pt: Putting more pressure on it trying to break the neck off. [*Leg gives way suddenly.*] Oh God, kicking the head away from the body, oh, kicking the head.

Th: What does he look like now after that?

Pt: His head is over in the corner and his body is in another place.

Th: What do his eyes look like? [*Pressure to experience guilt.*]

Pt: His eyes are just begging, but they're not begging for forgiveness, they're just begging for me to stop. [*Sees projected hostility in the cousin's eyes.*]

Th: Uh-huh, what do you do with his eyes?

Pt: He seems to be recognizing how he hurt me.

Th: What about his head that's off over there? [*Pressure to experience guilt.*]

Pt: Yeah, the eyes have gone more from begging to stop to begging for forgiveness.

Th: For you to forgive him. How do you feel then? You murdered him and then he wants you to forgive him. [*Pressure to experience guilt.*]

Pt: Really confused.

Th: You forgive him when he does that?

Pt: It goes back and forth between forgiveness and sympathy and rage and kicking again.

Th: If you keep looking in his eyes, how do you feel?

Pt: It's sort of a feeling of satisfaction.

Th: There's a satisfied feeling, a good feeling, then, to get this off you and do that to him.

Pt: Oh yeah.

Th: Do you feel that satisfaction feeling? [*Pressure to feel the satisfaction.*]

Pt: No, not for very long. It's a feeling of guilt.

Satisfaction about Rage and the Experience of Guilt

Rage has a feeling of satisfaction as part of the experience. Helping the patient feel this satisfaction about the primitive murder helps him feel the guilt; there is greater guilt when he can see the rage was enjoyable and satisfying.

A minute passes.

Pt: I can feel it right now. [*Becomes teary-eyed.*]

Th: If you look at the eyes of your cousin, how do you feel to see them? It's very painful. [*Facilitation of the experience of guilt.*]

Pt: [*Cries intensely with passage of guilt.*]

Chain Reaction in the Unconscious

When the unconscious is well mobilized, cycles of rage leading to guilt leading to rage begin. The positive feelings attached to the guilt free up a passage of rage that in turn frees up a passage of love and guilt. What follows in this session is a series of decapitations and reattaching the head back on the body with passage of guilt.

Th: What else does this rage want to do?

Pt: [*Presses his leg down heavily on the floor.*] Just crush the neck again till I get the head off again.

Th: Crushing it, and then what?

Pt: Oh, he's trying to get it back on.

Th: And what about his body there on the floor, is the head off now?

Pt: No, it's back on, but he's just lying there in a fetal position.

Th: His head is on again somehow.

Pt: Yeah.

Th: So it's basically on and off, on and off.

Pt: Yeah.

Th: It's on and off, back and forth, over and over, really. More torture and then more terror.

Pt: Yeah, it's just sort of like the, oh God, it's resembling the feeling he had after he abused me and then he had to do it again—so it's just going back and forth. [*Repeated abuse from this cousin who lived in the house.*]

Th: So is it for each of those times of abuse? The same primitive rage each time?

Pt: [*Nods head.*]

Th: So how many mutilated, dead bodies are in there?

Pt: Oh my God. There is a whole room full. Dozens maybe.

Intense Passage of Guilt

Now the tombs of the unconscious have opened widely with literally stacks of decapitated images of his cousin and sister.

Th: Yeah, but if you look at how you feel toward him, his neck coming off by your foot, seeing it pop off.

Pt: Oh, I just want to put it back on.

Th: If you put it back on . . .

Pt: Oh God, and kick it off again. I can see his eyes blaming me. [*Projection of his own guilt.*]

Th: That's the guilt, very painful mixed feelings.

Pt: Oh my God.

Th: It's as complex as it can be.

Pt: [*Passage of intense guilt for a few minutes, inability to speak.*] I just get remorse, and then I just get angry, oh God.

Th: They're both there, very painful. And then the rage and then the guilt and satisfaction and positive and then the circle goes back again to the rage, guilt, pain, positive feeling.

Pt: [*Passage of intense guilt for a few minutes.*]

Recapitulation

When these major waves of guilt cease, we recap what we have learned together.

Th: But do you see what triggered this today?

Pt: Positive feeling.

Th: Yeah, positive feeling you felt coming in here with me triggered this volume of rage and guilt. [*Recap: chain reaction of positive feeling, rage, and guilt.*]

Pt: [*Passage of intense guilt for a few minutes.*]

Th: Where did that pain just come from, right there?

Pt: Guilt.

Th: Guilt. It's as if you aren't allowed to have a positive feeling. [*Recap: guilt.*]

Pt: Yeah.

Th: These dead bodies are reaching up to you and saying, "Look at what you did to me. Look at what you did to me." [*Recap: self-punitive king.*]

Pt: Yeah. [*Weeps heavily, likely mix of grief and guilt.*]

Th: As soon as the positive comes, you have to suffer. You can see this now as clear as anything. [*Recap: need to suffer.*]

Pt: Yeah.

Th: And then the guilt turns into fear that you're going to get hunted by these dead bodies. [*Recap: self-punishment.*]

Pt: Yeah.

Th: You're looking over your shoulder and there's another dead body and another one. [*Recap: anxiety about success.*]

Pt: Yeah. [*Cries heavily again.*]

Th: The heart of this each time now has been positive feelings that are disappointed. And then disappointment produced the pain and then that pain produces the rage, and the rage, because of the positive feeling to start with, produces the guilt about the rage. This causes that instant turning inward on yourself. [*Recap: triangle of conflict.*]

Pt: Yes.

Th: And then the head goes off, but then the loving feeling comes and the head goes back on and then the guilt comes. It's like trying to repair it but at the same trying to destroy. [*Recap: complex feelings.*]

Pt: [*Nods head.*] Because it's just the terrible guilt.

Th: You describe that there are some days you feel pretty good and the good days are going to bring up the rage and guilt because you feel good; the guilt is going to try to make a symptom in your body, anxiety or something. You know what I mean? [*Recap: need to suffer.*]

Pt: It's all very clear right now. I feel a lot of relief.

REMAINING TREATMENT PROCESSES

After capacity building, the process moves through similar phases as the highly resistant patient, including repeated unlocking of the unconscious, working through, and termination. Treatment tends to be somewhat longer here than with highly resistant patients without repression because of the time needed to build capacity. The total course ranges from twenty to fifty sessions. Shorter courses from five to ten sessions are usually adequate for symptom reduction, but the patient has a greater risk of relapse after such short courses, as character changes are limited.

CHALLENGES OF WORKING WITH THE HIGHLY RESISTANT PATIENT WITH REPRESSION

Common problems in addition to those described for moderate and highly resistant patients include the following.

Failure to Recognize Being Above Threshold

If the therapist misses that the process is above threshold, the patient can become fatigued or develop other symptoms due to major repression of impulses and feelings. Monitoring the level of striated muscle anxiety and the capacity to isolate affect is critical to be sure the process is below threshold.

Not Enough Pressure

Conversely, if the rise in the complex transference feelings is too low, inadequate amount of exposure to the emotions will occur and capacity building will be delayed. Insufficient pressure can also result in increased regressive defenses, patient frustration, delayed response to treatment, and loss of hope in the patient. Working as near as possible to the threshold of repression is crucial. (See fig. 15.3.)

Failure to Detect Breakthrough

With highly resistant patients with repression, the breakthrough of feelings and impulses looks different than when feelings break through defenses in other groups of resistant patients. In these cases, impulse and feeling are essentially breaking through repression as opposed to breaking through major defenses in the transferences. Thus, the therapist may miss the complex transference feelings that are actually being experienced. If this happens, the unconscious therapeutic alliance may be missed and blocked by therapist activity. Mirror experiences in your body and the markers of low level unconscious therapeutic alliance (whispers, negation, links) (chapter 4) are often the only signs that the complex transference feelings have been experienced on a low level.

Inadequate Recapping

As described above, inadequate amounts of focused recapping can result in a delay in symptom reduction.

Risk of Worsening

Patients with repression suffer from worsening symptoms if the therapist fails to recognize the signals of unconscious anxiety or repression. Thus, do not work with these patients until you have a good understanding of this metapsychology and can monitor the signaling system of the unconscious.

High resistance patients with repression have also had severe early attachment trauma but they do not have operational character defenses—instead they suffer the somatic and depressive effects of major repression. They require capacity building through the graded format in order to bring dominance of the unconscious therapeutic alliance over the resistance prior to repeated unlockings, working through, and termination.

CHAPTER 16

Fragile Character Structure: Terror in the Dungeon

The most recent group of patients ISTDP has been developed for are patients with fragile character structure (Davanloo 2005). They are a complex group of patients requiring advanced therapeutic skills in order to safely and effectively deliver the treatment. Following is an introduction to the metapsychology and process with a case example of a patient with mild fragile character structure.

METAPSYCHOLOGY OF PATIENTS WITH FRAGILE CHARACTER STRUCTURE

Patients with fragile character structure have suffered repeated early attachment disruption and failure to form healthy attachments. These events produce massive painful feelings, craving of attachments, primitive rage, guilt, and self-destructive systems. This disorder is caused by a failure to develop an integrated cohesive self, compounded by severe *superego pathology: major resistance of guilt.* Temperamental factors, including sensitivity to emotions, possibly hereditary factors, and some neurobiological factors may predispose to fragile character structure.

The intense repressed feelings trigger primitive defenses and massive anxiety with cognitive and perceptual disruption. Cognitive-perceptual disruption takes the forms of some combination of visual blurring, disturbance of hearing, mental confusion, change in level of consciousness, and hallucination. Cognitive-perceptual disruption is sometimes a *defense* against homicidal or suicidal impulses. Owing to repression, memory functioning is poor. For example, at the end of a therapy session, mild to moderately fragile patients may not remember what happened twenty minutes earlier.

Since these patients have limited access to isolation of affect, they use primarily primitive defenses such as projection, projective identification, and splitting. They may also have behaviors that include temper tantrums, explosive discharge of affect, poor impulse control, and self-injurious behavior. They experience extremely high levels of fear and distress and are prone to substance abuse and addiction. They have major projection and secondary defiance (e.g., projecting that the therapist is controlling and then defying them). They may have spontaneous breakthroughs of rage that are not connected to any unconscious issue.

These patients frequently experience *projective identification and symptom formation*, a term Davanloo (2005) used to describe the process whereby the patient feels rage in a violent fantasy toward an attachment figure and then identifies with that person's body. As a result, psychosomatic symptoms will exactly match the injuries the patient unconsciously imagined inflicting (e.g., he wanted to crush someone's chest and then he feels crushing chest pain). The patient may also experience chronic pain or weakness in the part of his body that would have inflicted these injuries (e.g., he wanted to stomp his victim to death and then he suffers weakness in his legs). This defense unconsciously punishes the patient and protects others from his rage. Projective identification and symptom formation are driven by unconscious guilt (Davanloo 2005).

These patients have had few, if any, good relationships through which to internalize higher-level defenses like isolation of affect. Projective mechanisms and primitive defenses create severe interpersonal problems, including countertransference responses in therapists. Interestingly, clinical case research has shown that any positive affectionate bond in life will prevent the development of fragility or borderline organization; in many cases, this first bond is with a therapist.

Terrified in the Dungeon

These patients are like a terrified person in a torture chamber deep below a castle ruled by a sadistic and vicious king. There may be several torturers taking turns on the victim. She is so weakened and paralyzed by fear that guards are not needed to push people out. You are welcome inside to witness her self-torture. If she tries to mend her bones and become strong enough to escape, further torture is delivered to break her again. The punitive king, the torturers, and the victim are all aspects of the same single patient although she may project any of these facets onto you or others.

A consistent and confident voice is required to reach through this resistance and help generate hope for healing and freedom.

SPECTRUM OF PATIENTS WITH FRAGILE CHARACTER STRUCTURE

This spectrum denotes how high a rise in anxiety the patient can tolerate before experiencing cognitive-perceptual disruption or primitive defenses. Below this threshold the patient may experience striated muscle unconscious anxiety and isolation of affect. At this threshold, muscle tension ceases and ability to isolate affect wavers. Above this threshold, there is no striated muscle anxiety and the patient cannot isolate affect. Patients with mild fragility have cognitive-perceptual disruption or primitive defenses at a high rise in the transference. Hence, they present as having low anxiety tolerance. When anxiety rises above the threshold of tolerance it can be brought down with less than five minutes of recapping and other techniques to reduce anxiety.

Those with moderate fragility experience cognitive-perceptual disruption or primitive defense at mid rise in the transference. Thus, they have more obvious emotional intolerance, becoming easily flustered and overwhelmed. When they are above threshold, bringing the anxiety down with anxiety-reducing techniques typically takes from five to thirty minutes.

Patients with severe fragile character structure or *borderline organization* are even more impaired. Although not the same as borderline personality disorder, patients with severe fragility typically do meet criteria for that condition. They lack an integrated self, and projection, projective identification, and splitting are primary defenses against experiencing anxiety. At a very low rise in the transference, these patients are either using primitive defenses or experiencing cognitive-perceptual disruption. If anxiety can be brought below threshold, it typically takes over thirty minutes to do so. This group of patients will be reviewed in detail in chapter 17.

Fragile patients have a threshold to cognitive-perceptual disruption and primitive defenses that defines their degree of fragility. They also can have repression and may have episodes of major depression, smooth muscle anxiety (e.g., migraines, irritable bowel syndrome), or motor conversion with weakness. The spectrum of fragile patients can be represented as in figure 16.1. This figure describes a threshold and the various pathological mechanisms occurring above it. These phenomena are not necessarily hierarchical, but the order of thresholds from cognitive-perceptual disruption to primitive defenses is most typical in my experience. Some severely fragile cases do not have active unconscious anxiety in any format. Many mildly to moderately fragile patients have a layer in which they can have smooth muscle anxiety, depression, or conversion under the mechanism of repression.

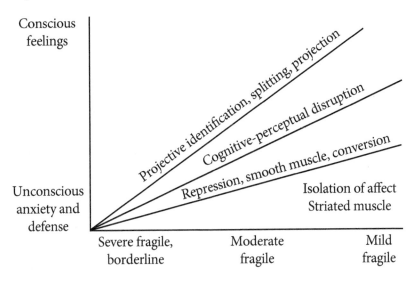

Figure 16.1: Spectrum of patients with fragile character structure

TREATMENT PHASES IN PATIENTS WITH MILD TO MODERATE FRAGILE CHARACTER STRUCTURE

Treatment of fragile patients goes from initial evaluation and trial therapy to capacity building through the graded format to repeated unlocking to working through and finally to termination. These steps are outlined in table 16.1. In general the process of capacity building in mildly to moderately fragile patients parallels that of patients with high resistance with repression.

Table 16.1 Treatment phases with mild to moderate fragile character structure

Phase	Task
Initial evaluation and trial therapy	Management of barriers to engagement, detection of the rotating fronts, psycho-diagnosis, evaluation of thresholds and determination of pace of treatment
Graded format	Build capacity to tolerate anxiety and to overcome projection, cognitive-perceptual disruption, self-attack, and repression; building of capacity to bear complex feelings
Repeated unlocking	Experience of repressed pain, rage, guilt, and craving of attachment
Working through	Mobilization and experience of residual grief, rage, and guilt. Consolidation of gains.
Termination	Closure of the therapy relationship over ten to twenty sessions

PHASE 1: INITIAL EVALUATION

The initial evaluation includes assessing barriers to engagement, detecting the front of the system, and performing psychodiagnostic assessment.

Step 1. Barriers to Engagement

Common barriers to engagement include absence of internal problem, suicidal ideation, being forced to attend, substance use, and other behavioral problems. (See chapter 6.)

Step 2. Front of the System

Fragile patients typically have high anxiety at the forefront with somatic symptoms and cognitive-perceptual disruption. They may arrive using projection or projective identification and appear agitated or afraid. They may also be self-attacking or have repression with exhaustion and depressive features. The front often rotates rapidly in this population, transitioning from between one front and another within minutes. (See chapter 6.)

Step 3. Psychodiagnosis

To determine the presence and severity of fragility, use pressure to mobilize the complex transference feelings and unconscious anxiety.

When striated muscle anxiety stops and the patient cannot isolate affect, he will go flat: at this point anxiety goes into cognitive-perceptual disruption or the patient uses projection, splitting, or projective identification and you will have located the tolerance threshold. Verify the level of any threshold by going above and below it a few times. (See fig. 16.2.)

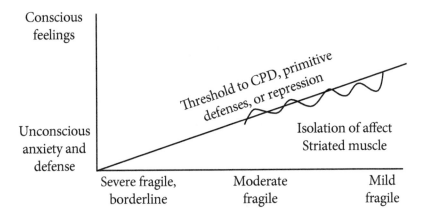

Figure 16.2 Psychodiagnostic evaluation in fragile patients

The degree of fragility can be noted by how high a rise in the transference is needed to reach threshold and by how long it takes to bring the anxiety down to below threshold. Severely fragile patients, reviewed in chapter 17, may have no unconscious anxiety and instead use only primitive defenses even at low rise in the transference.

CASE VIGNETTE: FRAGILE CHARACTER STRUCTURE: FORTY-FIVE-YEAR-OLD BUSINESSMAN

I will illustrate these processes with a patient with mild to moderate fragile character structure by using the case of a forty-five-year-old married businessman who has panic, suspiciousness, irritable bowel syndrome, depression, and interpersonal problems.

In this trial therapy, note the rapid rotation of defensive fronts, sometimes changing within seconds, and that multiple rotating means of self-torment exist. In the first psychodiagnostic segment numerous different fronts have to be addressed.

Start of Trial Therapy: Initial Evaluation and Psychodiagnosis

The patient looks quite anxious with fidgeting, quick-moving gestures, and some signs of muscle tension with hand clenching and a sigh. The front of the system was anxiety and fearfulness in the transference. I did not detect any obvious barriers to initial engagement.

Th: I notice you're anxious coming in. What does that feel like physically when you feel that? [*Exploration of anxiety.*]

Pt: Well, I'm anxious, and I feel a little bit nauseous [*points to stomach*], and I'm a little forgetful, too. [*Allusion to cognitive-perceptual disruption.*]

Th: You are a little forgetful?

Pt: Yeah.

Th: So do you have any physical symptoms right now, apart from that nausea? [*Exploration of anxiety.*]

Pt: No physical symptoms to speak of, no.

Th: So why are you anxious right now? [*Pressure.*]

Pt: Oh, because it has . . . Why I'm anxious with you? Is because you're a new person I'm referring . . . talking a lot about my problems to. I don't really know you and I'm a little bit nervous about that. [*Nonfluent speech, projection of what threat the therapist may represent.*]

Th: What feelings create the nervousness that you have here with me? [*Pressure to feelings beneath the projection.*]

Pt: Oh, I think it's because of . . . I think it's just . . . what feelings are inside me? [*Nonfluent speech due to anxiety.*]

Th: Yeah. How do you feel here with me and my being a new person? How does that make you feel that makes you nervous? [*Pressure to identify feelings.*]

Pt: Well, I guess it's some of the topics I have to raise, and I often wonder where all this is going to go to. I think if I say that, I'm starting to move toward the peak of a pyramid right now. [*Intellectual rumination.*]

Detect Thresholds

In this first minute, the patient has some striated anxiety signal and some intellectual rumination. His thought flow and verbal responses are not fluid and coherent. To find his threshold to cognitive-perceptual disruption, I will use pressure to mobilize the complex transference feelings and at the same time interrupt the intellectualization, primarily by clarification.

As with any patient, high pressure and interruption of defenses applied to the fragile patient can only result in one of three main responses: *feel* the complex transference feelings; become tense and *defend*; or *go flat* as anxiety crosses a threshold to repression, projection, or cognitive-perceptual disruption.

> Pt: Consultations and stuff like that and just fear of the future I think. [*Intellectual rumination.*]
>
> Th: Well, what feelings do you have toward me that makes you nervous here with me though? How do you feel toward me that makes you nervous? [*Pressure to identify feelings.*]
>
> Pt: I guess it's because I don't know you very well. [*Intellectual.*]
>
> Th: What feelings do you have inside? Are these thoughts you have? [*Clarification of intellectual defense.*]
>
> Pt: Yeah.
>
> Th: What feelings do you have that get you tensed up? [*Pressure to identify feelings.*]
>
> Pt: Fear basically.
>
> Th: What emotions do you have inside? [*Pressure to identify feelings.*]
>
> Pt: That is mostly fear right now.
>
> Th: You mean nervousness?

Focus on Feelings beneath the Projection

Fear refers to an external threat whereas anxiety and nervousness refer to internal threats. Here I'm pressing to what is inside him that he is afraid of. This interrupts projection from operating and distorting the process.

> Pt: Nervousness, yeah.
>
> Th: Okay, what causes the nervousness? How do you feel that gets you nervous? [*Pressure to identify feelings.*]
>
> Pt: Um, how I feel is . . . [*Sighs.*]
>
> Th: Emotionally here with me. Because see, you're sighing, and there is tension. [*Identification of the anxiety.*]

Pt: Yes, that's right.

Th: What feelings do you have here with me that you're getting tensed up about? [*Pressure to identify feelings.*]

Pt: Okay, the feelings I have with you. I guess the thing is that I don't know your background. [*Projection.*]

Th: But what emotions create the tension though? What feelings do you have toward me? [*Interruption of projection and pressure to feeling.*]

Blocking Projection

The patient is attempting to project some negative attributes onto me. I use a unique format of pressure here that pushes his projections into himself. I ask, "What are the feelings beneath your anxiety and thoughts?" which means "What is going on *inside* you?" By asking these questions, I block his projections. I let him know I'm here to help him understand what makes him so anxious. If he can tolerate the anxiety associated with this intensive procedure, blocking of projection can rapidly build his emotional capacities and provide ready access to his unconscious feelings and impulses. Close monitoring of anxiety and defensive responses is very important when using this approach.

Pt: The feelings are, this is, uh. [*Nonfluent speech due to anxiety.*]

Th: The emotions.

Pt: Emotions are something that . . .

Th: You have trouble identifying them? [*Clarification of the problem.*]

Pt: I do, you see, this is one of the big things. Yeah, that's what happens. I try to organize my thoughts, but that's one of the big things. I can't express that. It sounds strange but it's one of those things. What happens is I get confused. [*Forecast of cognitive-perceptual disruption.*]

Th: You have trouble getting hold of your emotions, you mean? [*Clarification.*]

Pt: Yeah, that's it, how to express them properly.

Th: How about if we first try to figure out what's going on that creates this nervousness and tension within you? [*Recap, pressure to task.*]

Pt: Right.

Th: Okay, let's see how you feel here toward me that you're nervous about? [*Pressure to identify feelings.*]

Interruption of Rumination Combined with Pressure

By getting this consensus on the process and the therapeutic task, we develop a greater conscious therapeutic alliance. This prevents a misalliance based on projection and a failure to understand what we should do and why we should do it.

Pt: [*Sighs; rumination.*] You know the thing is that . . .

Th: But you see again, this is a thought that's going to come. [*Blocking of rumination.*]

Pt: It is a thought though.

Th: But what do you feel inside, emotions? [*Pressure to identify feelings.*]

Pt: The feelings—I don't—I can't see—I don't know I . . . [*Nonfluent speech due to anxiety.*]

Th: Let's see how we can figure that out. Okay? [*Pressure to partnership and task.*]

Pt: Okay.

Th: How do you feel here toward me? [*Pressure to identify feelings.*]

Pt: I feel that you're a stranger but . . . again that's a thought. [*Self-correction, attempt to find feeling versus thoughts.*]

Th: How do you feel emotions inside here? [*Pressure to identify feelings.*]

Pt: I feel like I want to run away at times. [*Fear.*]

Th: But that's the tension, anxiety?

Pt: Exactly.

Th: But how do you feel that gets you nervous? [*Pressure to identify feelings.*]

Pt: It just, I'm just scared. I'm scared the feelings are—I don't know what the feelings are, believe it or not, it's . . .

Th: You have trouble identifying them? [*Clarification of problem with emotions.*]

Pt: I have immense trouble to identify them.

Th: So let's see. Do you want us to try to make some steps toward that? [*Clarification of his will.*]

Pt: Yes, absolutely, yes.

Th: So let's see how you feel here toward me under the tension. Besides tense, how do you feel toward me? [*Pressure to identify feelings.*]

Pt: How I feel toward you; well, I guess I sort of look into people's background and I know you're an academic. [*Projection.*]

Th: But these are thoughts again. [*Blocking.*]

Pt: I see what you're saying; I see what you're saying. I know ... [*Rubs head, acknowledging he is finding thoughts but no feelings.*]

Th: But seeing it is part of the solution. But the other part is what can we do about it because what's happening is you're thinking. But how do you feel that gets you nervous? [*Clarification of defense and pressure.*]

Pt: Well, feelings are things like love and hate and fear?

Th: Yeah, but how do you feel here toward me? [*Pressure to identify feelings.*]

Pt: Borderlines on hate, I guess.

Misalliance Risk

Now I clarify this statement to be clear that a fixed hostile projection is not in place. At no time in the treatment process should a patient actually be angry with you: there should rather be complex feelings that mobilize the unconscious therapeutic alliance. Otherwise, you have a misalliance that must be corrected.

Th: But do you feel something inside that you say is hate? [*Pressure to identify feelings.*]

Pt: No, it's one [a feeling] of not knowing what [kind of a threat] you are, that's all. [*Questioning of his projection.*]

Th: These are more thoughts again, right? [*Patient removes glasses and rubs face, becoming somewhat confused.*]

Pt: Um. Okay. I cannot express it. Believe it or not, I don't know.

Th: So let's see what we can do because ...

Pt: Yeah.

Th: Because tension has obviously been a stress for you. It's been bothering you, has it? [*Recap: nature of the problem.*]

Pt: Oh, that's right. It's part of what goes on, yeah.

Th: So let's see how you feel here toward me that makes you nervous. [*Pressure to identify feelings.*]

Pt: Okay. I feel ... [*Ruminating.*]

Th: The thoughts are going to come again. You see, you're operating from your thoughts. [*Recap: rumination.*] But, what are your gut feelings here toward me? [*Pressure to identify feelings.*]

Pt: [*Sighs.*] I don't know. All I keep doing is analyzing you and I just think of your statements and I think of your background. [*Projection.*]

Th: That becomes a way that you avoid your feelings then, by analyzing the other person or me. What do we do about that? [*Clarification of the process of projection.*]

Pt: Yeah, but . . .

Th: Because if you do that, we won't find out what's causing this nervousness. [*Clarification of the problem of projection.*]

Pt: Yeah, okay.

Th: So let's see what we can do about this thinking that you're doing. [*Pressure against rumination.*]

Pt: Okay, all right. If I was to totally block the analysis, all right. [*Turns head away.*]

Th: Let's see.

Pt: And looking at just the way I feel about you right now . . . I think.

Th: You see, there's a thought again. [*Blocking of rumination.*]

Pt: They are thoughts. [*Clenches left hand into fist.*]

Th: Let's see how you feel toward me. [*Pressure to identify feelings.*]

Pt: I think you're . . . [*Looks at left fist.*]

Th: These are thoughts again. [*Blocking of rumination.*]

Declaration of Feelings

Now the patient is looking at his fist. He obviously has some feelings but is keeping them to himself. A few minutes later he declares a feeling.

Pt: I don't even know what. I'm okay, I'm okay, but I'm getting a little frustrated—but that's not . . .

Th: Frustrated with whom? [*Pressure.*]

Pt: With you, but . . .

Th: You say you're "getting" frustrated. [*Blocking of tactical defense of speaking of the future.*]

Pt: Yeah.

Th: But you don't feel that yet in you? [*Blocking of tactical defense.*]

Pt: Yeah, I feel a little bit frustrated because . . . [*Rationalization.*]

Th: See, you're feeling "a bit" and "frustrated." [*Blocking of tactical defense of minimizing.*]

Pt: Yeah, because I'm trying to reach in to see . . .

Th: See, when you're saying frustrated, frustrated with whom?

Pt: Frustrated with myself because I can't . . . [*Self-attack.*]

Th: But, see what I was asking is how do you feel toward me. [*Clarification of self-attack.*]

Pt: You're asking a very simple question, and I should be able to answer this.

Th: But what you're saying though is that you hear me asking you a question that you're finding hard. [*Clarification.*]

Pt: I am.

Th: But how do you feel toward the question? [*Pressure.*]

Pt: I feel, I feel that it's a simple question, and it's just something I should be able to answer.

Turning Anger Inward

As I try to reach to the person stuck in the torture chamber, he attacks himself; this is a mild version of self-torture, never letting himself free. This turning anger inward is very common in fragile patients. So I ask, "How did you feel first with me before you turned the anger inward?" This blocks his defense of self-attack while helping him feel the feelings toward me.

Th: Yeah, but is that what you do with any anger? You let it go in at you? [*Clarification of self-attack.*]

Pt: I usually keep it in.

Th: How do you do that? What do you do to yourself? [*Clarification of the damage when turning rage inward.*]

Pt: Well, what I'm saying is that sometimes I burst out.

Th: How much does that hurt you when you do that? [*Pressure to see destructive effects of temper outburst.*]

Pt: Well, it hurts me a lot.

Th: So that becomes one way that you hurt yourself then is that you burst out?

Pt: Yeah.

Th: How else do you do that because we see here that you get a lot of tension when you talk about frustration? [*Bracing: anxiety and feelings.*]

Pt: Yeah, I do.

Th: So let's see underneath this tension why you're doing that to yourself. Let's see how you feel here toward me if you don't do that. [*Bracing: anxiety and feelings.*]

Short Recapitulation

I examine this process intellectually to help him self-observe and isolate affect instead of going flat and turning anger inward. This self-reflective work, isolating affect, makes the anxiety go into striated muscle away from cognitive-perceptual disruption.

Th: Let's see how you experience the emotions you feel here toward me. [*Pressure to experience feelings.*]

Pt: Okay, let's try our best. My feelings toward you are . . . [*Rumination.*]

Th: That's a thought again.

Pt: The thought. My feelings are one of . . . [*Rumination.*]

Th: These are still descriptions of thoughts.

Pt: Exactly. [*Turns eyes away and detaches from the therapist.*]

Th: Now you see your eyes are going away from me. [*Clarification of resistances in the transference.*]

Pt: Yes, they are.

Th: Because as you think, you're going in and withdrawing from me. You're closing yourself in. [*Clarification of defense.*]

Pt: Yes.

Th: But that blocks the feelings off, too. [*Destructive effects of defense.*]

Pt: Yes, it does.

Th: So let's see what we can do about the detaching. [*Pressure to be present.*]

Pt: Okay.

Th: Let's see how you feel here toward me. [*Pressure to identify feelings.*]

Pt: How do I feel inside? I'm, I feel sad. No, no, it's not sad, I just . . . [*Turns eyes away again.*]

Th: Now see, your eyes are away from me. [*Clarification of defense.*]

Pt: I know, because I don't know how to answer that question. [*Speaks in a helpless manner.*]

Th: Yeah, but isn't that a helpless position to take when you have these feelings. Do you go helpless when you get nervous? Is that what happens? [*Clarification of the helpless defense.*]

Pt: It does happen, yeah.

Th: Okay, let's see what we can do about the helplessness. [*Pressure to battle helplessness.*]

Pt: All right.

Th: So we'll see how we can figure that out and get to the bottom of why that's happening to you, too. [*Clarification of task.*]

Pt: Okay, certainly.

Th: Let's see how you feel here toward me. [*Pressure to identify feelings.*]

Pt: You did it again and I'm just . . .

Th: You mean I'm asking how you feel?

Pt: Yes, the bottom line is, it's a very fundamental question. A simple question that you're asking, and you're trying to pull it out of me.

Deactivation of Projection Alternates with Self-Attack

Here this man states I'm "trying to pull" something out of him, a projection. I clarify this to interrupt it. He then flips to self-attack. Thus, he goes from self-abuse to projecting an abuser onto me in a few seconds.

Th: But, it's not for me to pull out though. If you and I together want to get to the bottom of this nervousness, right. [*Deactivation of the projection that I'm trying to do something against his will.*]

Pt: No, you're right. It isn't up to you. It's something that I should be able to express. [*Reverts to self-attacking.*]

Th: I'm not saying, "You should be able." [*Deactivation of the self-attack.*] But what do you want us to do? Is it to get to the bottom of what's happening? [*Pressure to the will.*]

Pt: Yes.

Th: Why you're detached from these things. Why you have trouble identifying things. Why you suffer from tension and nausea. Is that what you want us to do? [*Pressure to the will.*]

Pt: Yes.

Th: How do you feel here toward me? [*Pressure to identify feelings.*]

Pt: I feel . . . [*Turns eyes away.*]

Th: And your eyes went away when I asked you how you felt; you closed up again, see? [*Identification of the defense.*]

Pt: Yeah, but I can't. [*Reverts to helpless position.*]

Th: But if you don't go helpless though . . . [*Challenge to helpless position.*]

Pt: All right. I'm not going to go helpless. [*Sits more upright, grips his legs.*]

Th: But see, your hands are gripping your legs. Did you notice that? They're turning into fists almost. Did you notice? [*Identification of nonverbal cues of rage.*]

Pt: Yes, but . . . [*Begins to weep.*]

Th: So let's see how you feel here toward me inside. [*Pressure to identify feelings.*]

Pt: I'm going to cry . . .

Cognitive-Perceptual Disruption

The patient is now struggling to maintain his thought process. He is staring blankly at me. My pointing out his hands becoming fists means I told him that I see he has violence inside him and this markedly increased his anxiety. I now move to reduce anxiety.

Th: Did you just get all constricted in your throat there? [*Exploration of body cues.*]

Pt: Yes. [*Barely audible.*]

Th: Can you describe what happened in your body there for a second? [*Intellectual review to bring down anxiety.*]

Pt: I just . . . I just felt all lost.

Th: Maybe ten seconds ago, what happened? Can you tell me what happened? [*Exploration of phenomena.*]

Pt: I just totally felt . . . everything's fully blacked out . . . I almost.

Th: Tell me what you noticed there. What did you experience in your head? [*Exploration of phenomena.*]

Pt: It was like a dark thing. Just a darkness that goes up through my mind. I envisioned this dark object that comes up, and it quickly came up and grabbed hold of me, and then I started to cry.

Th: So you had a vision of something black? [*Exploration of phenomena.*]

Pt: Yeah. It was a black form, a black liquid. It went forward on my head, and it was just like I blacked out and I just saw the blackness and then—I don't know why I started crying. [*Cognitive-perceptual disruption.*]

Th: Okay, you said blacked out. Did your thoughts become jumbled? [*Exploration of phenomena.*]

Pt: Very much, it just became all scrambled.

Th: How long did it last—a second or two? [*Exploration of phenomena.*]

Pt: Seconds.

Th: Okay, for a second you got that, and then your thoughts were hard to sort out with that coming up. Your thoughts blanked out. [*Recap.*]

Recapitulation

Here the patient had transient cognitive-perceptual disruption where he completely blanked out as if terrified of torture. He experienced blackness going over his head, and then he disrupted. Now I'm helping him observe the process intellectually at a fairly high rise in complex feelings. He was close to experiencing the complex transference feelings, but he aborted the feelings with cognitive-perceptual disruption. We have found a threshold at mid to high rise in the complex transference feelings. Now we focus once again on that moment to see if he can tolerate the anxiety enough to see the emotions. We do this also to verify how high the threshold is.

Th: Can you remember back a few minutes before this sensation started?

Pt: Yes I can.

Th: Okay, we were talking and I pointed out that your hands turned into fists. Do you remember?

Pt: Yes.

Th: Now what did it mean to you when I said that your hands turned into fists?

Pt: It was almost like it was squeezing out.

Th: Did you feel something in your body apart from the thing in the back of your head? [*Pressure to notice emotions.*]

Pt: I felt, well I . . . [*Makes a sweeping upward motion from his stomach to the top of his chest, the somatic pathway of rage.*]

Th: So what was in your chest? [*Pressure to notice emotions.*]

Pt: Okay, it was my chest. [*Acknowledges there was some impulse there.*]

Th: What was there? [*Pressure to notice emotions.*]

Pt: Like hurt. Like a pain. It was like something pressed down upon it (referring to the anger in his chest), and then I felt a tingling up the back of my neck, and then I had a vision of this darkness that came up and also my thinking went lost.

Th: It just cut across your thoughts right then . . .

Pt: That's it.

Th: Okay, let me ask you intellectually. A couple of minutes ago, was there a brief moment that you felt some frustration in your body? [*Pressure to identify the experience of rage.*]

Pt: Yes.

Th: Is that what you have in your body here? [*Pressure to experience rage.*]

Pt: Yes.

Th: Okay, now who is that frustration with if I ask you at that very moment? [*Pressure to express the anger toward the therapist.*]

Pt: It was with me.

Th: Are you sure? [*Pressure.*]

Pt: I'm absolutely sure because you're asking such a fundamental question.

Th: Yes, but you are frustrated with the question then? [*Pressure.*]

Pt: Exactly.

Th: Now who asked the question? [*Pressure to express the anger toward the therapist.*]

Pt: You did.

Th: So how did you feel toward me? [*Pressure to identify feelings.*]

Pt: I felt, why did you . . . okay, that's a thought. [*Counters his own defense.*]

Th: So tell me your thoughts. [*Encouragement to isolate affect versus to experience cognitive-perceptual disruption.*]

Pt: Okay, the thought was the fact that you keep driving at it and driving at it and then . . .

Th: How do you feel about that? [*Pressure to identify feelings.*]

Pt: I just got worked up in the sense of frustrated and tense.

Th: Frustrated with whom? [*Pressure to identify negative feelings toward the therapist.*]

Pt: With myself.

Self-Attack

We see here the powerful self-directing of rage because of the punitive king: he is not going to easily be freed from self-induced torture. He clearly has to punish himself, project this punishment on me, and fear me or dissociate. He can also repress rage into depression and into his stomach with nausea or irritable bowel syndrome. And notice how rapidly he can shift between projection, self-attack, cognitive-perceptual disruption, and repression: all these mechanisms must be understood and overcome to mobilize his unconscious. Such rapid rotation of defenses is typical of patients with fragile character structure and makes them complex to treat. I recap to bring isolation of affect at this high rise in the transference to help this man see his defenses and tolerate the anxiety.

Th: But is that what happens with frustration within yourself? When you get frustrated with someone else do you get anxious and tense and have this experience in your head? [*Recap: feelings-anxiety-defense.*]

Pt: Yeah, it blacks out.

Th: You even become confused. [*Recap.*]

Pt: Yes.

Brief Move to Current Relationship Experience

It is clear this patient cannot tolerate a direct rapid move to his unconscious; he needs the graded format to build capacity. Part of the graded format of ISTDP is movement from the transference to current relationships and back again drawing parallels. This will happen naturally or you can ask how these things work in other current relationships.

Th: But this happens very fast when you have anger toward another person, doesn't it? You get tense, you get anxious, and your body may become nauseated. You get these sensations. [*Recap.*]

Pt: Yeah, and then I just lose control. I do silly things. I could run out of the house or run out of a meeting.

Th: If you get real anxious, you would run out? Is that what you mean?

Pt: Anxious, yeah. Anxious or if I just can't figure out what is happening. [*Reference to when he cognitively disrupts.*] If I have an argument with my wife, then all of a sudden—boom. I get confused and I have to run out.

Th: If you got into an argument with her, you might have this thing happening in your head?

Pt: Yeah, and it just blacks out.

Th: Then you go out of the house?

Pt: Yeah, I run away.

Recapitulation

We are recapping and reviewing exactly how the patient handles complex feelings in current situations. This recapping aims to cement isolation of affect, reduce the anxiety, and clarify our task together.

Th: And here with me it seems you get very anxious when you have any frustration or anger with someone. Is that what happens: you get real frightened of them? [*Recap: feelings-anxiety-projection.*]

Recap to Avert Projection

Here I'm linking rage with anxiety and projection. I do this because I can sense that the patient is still near to projection despite our intellectual review process and growing conscious alliance. Now we will try to slowly mobilize the feelings again.

Pt: Yeah.

Th: And here with me you felt a bit of it [anger] though. [*Bracing: experience of rage.*]

Pt: Yeah.

Th: Now, you felt something in your body that told you—you felt anger in your body or frustration? [*Bracing: experience of rage.*]

Pt: Frustration. This is the way I would see it because I was trying to reach in and trying to find out what the hell . . .

Th: So who is that frustration aimed at concerning the question originally? [*Pressure to recognize the anger in the transference.*]

Pt: It would have to be with me. [*Self-attack.*]

Rotating Fronts: Splitting

Why isn't he disrupting right now? He's not disrupting because he switched to turning the rage in on himself. He's doing a type of splitting where he's all bad and I'm all good. This primitive defense prevents any anxiety and temporarily allows him to not use repression or cognitive-perceptual disruption. When I interrupt this splitting we will expect cognitive-perceptual disruption or some other defense to activate under his need for self-torment.

Th: But if I didn't ask you the question, would you have frustration? [*Pressure.*]

Pt: Definitely not. Okay, in that sense it would be you because you initiated the conversation. [*Rubs his eyes, tending to stare.*]

Th: Then the frustration is first with me?

Pt: Okay, in a sense, yes. Because if it was initiated by you, you were the catalyst that set it off.

Recap: Near Threshold

The patient looks at this point like he is near cognitive disruption again. I do a recap to try to help him isolate affect, and then apply pressure to help him identify and feel the feelings.

Th: We're looking into what's under this anxiety together. What's under this tension? When we focus on that, there are some feelings in you: one is frustration and then you get that frustration or anger in your body. [*Recap.*] Did you know what it felt like compared to this tension? What did you feel in your body that told you it was anger? Did you notice the difference? [*Bracing: experience of rage.*]

Pt: Yeah, I did.

Th: Behind the nervousness. [*Bracing: experience of rage.*]

Pt: Yeah, I did.

Th: By the time the fists started, did you notice? [*Pressure, testing his tolerance of the word "fist."*]

Pt: Yeah, I did. At the end it's like, it's almost like I want to run away. [*Projection and idea to run away.*]

Th: See, what was the sensation in your body that made you nervous when you have anger? What did it feel like in your body that made you nervous right then? [*Bracing: anxiety and rage.*]

Pt: The anger felt like pain. It was like a pushing, a pressure.

Th: Where was the pressure at? [*Bracing: experience of rage.*]

Pt: On the chest and it was almost like swelling from the stomach upward. [*Description of the somatic pathway of rage.*]

Th: It swelled up and then it went into your chest? [*Bracing: experience of rage.*]

Pt: Yes, and then I envisioned it sneaking up through my spine.

Th: Then this is a piece of anger in your chest. Is that correct? [*Bracing: experience of rage.*]

Pt: Yes, that's correct.

Th: Now what were you nervous about having anger in your chest? [*Pressure to portray.*]

Can the Patient Tolerate This Feeling?

This man finally declared after a gradual rise in feelings that he had anger with me. The use of bracing, coupling self-reflection with pressure to feeling, appears to be yielding dividends. Can he tolerate the experience of this feeling or is he going to cognitively disrupt, project, self-attack, or go to repression again? Further focus on the rage will clarify whether he has a threshold at high rise in the complex transference feelings that will prevent breakthrough.

Th: Now why were you nervous about having anger in your chest? What were you afraid it was going to do, you know, in terms of your thoughts? I'm asking you intellectually. [*Pressure to portray.*]

Use of Portrayal

Here I'm asking the patient to try to isolate affect to prevent cognitive disruption. I'm asking him to portray the rage in an intellectual fashion to help him see and be aware of his impulse. In this way, portrayal is used as a vehicle to build anxiety tolerance and the ability to isolate affect. If he has enough anxiety tolerance, then this gentle move to intellectualize about it will enable a small first breakthrough to the unconscious. If not, then he will disrupt and we will confirm a threshold that we will need to raise with further graded work.

Notice I'm emphasizing that he has positive feelings with me by asking what he is afraid of doing and what he holds back to protect me from. These questions reflect the positive feelings toward me and reduce any conscious anxiety about his rage doing harm.

> *Th:* What were you afraid the anger was going to be like if it came out here? [*Pressure to intellectually portray.*]
>
> *Pt:* I'd run away. [*Projection; looks afraid.*]
>
> *Th:* You'd run away to protect whom?
>
> *Pt:* To get away from you. Just to take off and get away. [*Becomes tearful and looks afraid: above threshold with projection.*]

Threshold

Now the patient appears afraid and has experienced *instant projection*, a rapid onset projective stance seen in most fragile patients. In this second his rage is not a threat to me; rather, I am a threat to him. This is projection of the punitive king and torturers onto me. I am cast in the role of the person punishing him for his rage. The process is so swift that the move from self-attack, through to high anxiety with cognitive-perceptual disruption, through to projection is almost invisible. This rapid shifting is one reason that video-recording study of second-to-second processes is central to teaching and supervision of the care of fragile patients.

We have confirmed that he has a threshold that must be worked on to build his capacity. This threshold is at a mid- to high rise in the transference, meaning he is mild to moderately fragile and will require graded format to bring structural changes in anxiety and defense to remove this fragility.

Fragile versus Resistant Patients

Here we can see the difference between fragile patients and highly resistant patients: highly resistant patients tend not to project the punishing guilt onto others; rather, they punish themselves. They also maintain cognitive functioning in general unless deeper zones of rage and guilt are being mobilized during a course of therapy.

PHASE 2: GRADED FORMAT—BRINGING STRUCTURAL CHANGES

Once psychodiagnosis reveals that the patient has a threshold to cognitive-perceptual disruption or projection, you and the patient can now move to bring structural changes in unconscious defenses toward isolation of affect and in anxiety toward striated muscle anxiety. To restructure the patient's fragility, a graded exposure to a rise in complex transference feelings and anxiety is now required.

As described in chapter 15, graded work includes cycles of pressure bringing a rise in complex transference feelings followed by recapitulation to augment the ability to tolerate this rise in anxiety-producing affect. (See fig. 16.3.)

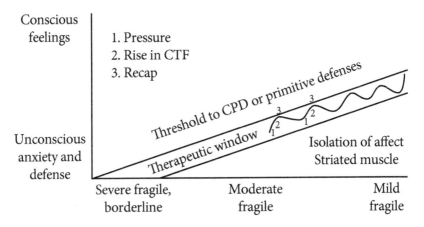

Figure 16.3 Graded format with patients with fragile character structure
CPD: cognitive-perceptual disruption, CTF: complex transference feelings

Therapeutic Window

In graded work, fragile patients can work within a *therapeutic window* of rise in complex transference feelings while anxiety is in the striated muscle. If the level of complex transference feelings is too low, it may prolong treatment. If the level of complex transference feelings is too high, projection will dominate, and the therapist and others will be seen as attackers or abusers. Initially the therapeutic window is small and staying under the threshold to projection and repression is difficult. As the patient develops an intellectual understanding of her defenses, the therapeutic window continues to enlarge. (See fig. 16.3.)

Undoing Instant Repression of Rage and Guilt

In fragile patients, instant repression of complex feelings is common. Restructure instant repression by examining situations that mobilize mixed feelings and trigger repression. Then help the patient see how anger gets turned inward to activate depression, self-harm, anxiety, and somatization. This understanding overcomes instant repression by the use of self-reflection and isolation of affect. Use the graded format to both build a higher capacity to tolerate complex transference feelings and prevent untoward effects of repression.

Major Resistance of Guilt

To help turn the patient against any remaining self-destructiveness, examine the link between the mixed feelings and the self-destructive behaviors. Focusing on the self-destructive system could not be successful while the defenses of major fragmentation and projective identification were still operating, but now the patient can self-reflect and challenge these mechanisms. If work on self-destructiveness were done while primitive defenses were still operating, the patient, through projection, would equate the therapist with an abuser, leading to reduction in the therapeutic alliance and acting out. Under these circumstances, the patient may become compliant with the projection on the therapist while becoming more depressed or self-destructive.

Working on the Rotating Front of the System

Fragile patients will rotate from repression to projection to cognitive-perceptual disruption to self-attacks to acting out against projections. Some will also rotate to behavior problems like drug use, eating disorders, and self-harm. Work with each of these systems as they move to the front of the process. Use the work at that level to increase the capacity to tolerate feelings and anxiety. (See fig. 16.4.)

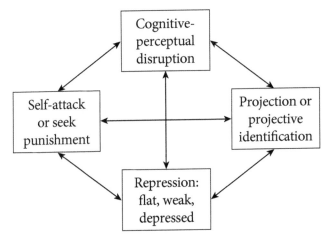

Figure 16.4 Rotating front of the system

Therapeutic Alliance over the Treatment Course

The therapist's work on projections mobilizes the complex transference feelings and the unconscious therapeutic alliance. Therefore, the patient's hope rises, acting out decreases, symptoms remit and functioning improves, and the patient can see light at the end of the tunnel. These changes can occur even before any significant breakthroughs to the unconscious. The later signs related to the development of the unconscious therapeutic alliance include insights, linkages, and images of the unconscious. (See table 16.2.)

Table 16.2. Development of the therapeutic alliance with patients with fragile character structure

Early treatment phases: conscious and early unconscious therapeutic alliance develops
1. Acting out, such as binge eating and self-harm, is reduced.
2. Patient is cautiously hopeful and less depressed.
3. Primitive defenses are reduced: patients' best defenses come forward.
4. Avoidant behaviors are reversed without a primary behavioral focus.
5. Conscious anxiety is low.
6. Somatization and regressive weepiness or tantrums are absent.
7. Defiance/compliance with the therapist is not prominent.

Later Phases: unconscious therapeutic alliance dominates
1. Whispers—statements of clear insight into internal dynamics are made.
2. Linkages to traumatic events are made.
3. Visual imagery related to traumatic events.
4. Mental images of the primitive emotions in the unconscious emerge.

Case Vignette: Trial Therapy with the Forty-Five-Year-Old Businessman

We will now review some of these concepts with the same fragile patient from the previous vignette. This is the continuation of the trial therapy at the eighteen-minute mark.

Moving to a Current Incident

I move the process out of the transference into a current situation since we have evidence he cannot tolerate that high a rise in the transference yet. This movement in and out of the transference and from one situation to another is one hallmark of the graded format.

Th: So does this anxiety and blanking out happen in other situations like with family and friends when you feel angry? [*Move to a current relationship.*]

Pt: Family and friends and coworkers at times.

Th: What makes you feel nervous about being so angry with them? Can you tell me of a time when you had the anger with another person? [*Pressure to specific incident.*]

Pt: It could be a coworker. Okay, with my manager, I get sarcastic with her.

Th: That's how you deal with it, you mean? [*Clarification of action versus feeling.*]

Pt: Yeah. I get sarcastic, then I just, like I have all these reasons in my mind why I'm angry, and all of a sudden I'll start getting a little bit sarcastic. And then I'll blank out, and then I get frustrated, and that's it. [*Description of projection and cognitive disruption.*]

Th: You walk out of the office?

Pt: I walk out, yeah.

Th: Okay. Something is happening in the very second you're in the middle of a conflict. When you got angry with someone, you get acutely anxious. If we can figure out why, it would make a big difference, don't you think? [*Recap: clarification of task and potential benefit.*]

Pt: Understood.

Th: So in that moment with her, is that a particular time you're thinking of? [*Pressure to specific incident.*]

Pt: That's a particular time, yeah.

Th: What happened at that time?

Pt: All I know is that I just got tense, and I don't know why. Okay. Thinking back to what happened, I didn't go in her office. I just leaned against the door and started talking to her. She's a busy person and I tried to get my point across, and then it's as if I want to drive the point home. I just get a bit sarcastic.

Th: Okay. Was there anger in your body again? [*Bracing: experience of rage.*]

Pt: Yes, there was. [*Looks activated and might display some degree of anger coming up in the chest.*]

Th: How did that feel at that time with her? [*Pressure to experience rage.*]

Pt: You know, I can remember physically bouncing against the doorframe. I was grabbing the doorframe.

Th: With your hands?

Pt: With my hands and swinging it.

Th: Did you have anger inside your body? [*Bracing: experience of rage.*]

Pt: Well, yeah. I didn't when I started and then all of a sudden I could feel it.

Th: It started to move up in you. [*Bracing: experience of rage.*]

Pt: Yeah, it started to move up.

Th: Okay, in your chest and started to move up. [*Bracing.*] Then what were you afraid the anger was going to do? [*Pressure to portray the rage.*]

Portraying

At this point I moved quickly to portray the rage before any repression, cognitive-perceptual disruption, or projection could move. A small portion of the somatic pathway was activated and the goal is to help him isolate affect without disruption through this degree of feeling. I move fast at these points to grab a picture of it before it disappears.

Pt: My fear of the anger was that I would . . . I never imagined . . . I don't hit, I don't.

Th: In terms of your thoughts in your head, what were you afraid you would do? [*Clarification of the difference between thoughts and actions.*]

Portraying with a Fragile Patient

I quell his anxiety about acting out by asking him to isolate affect, to intellectualize about the impulse. Asking him about his fear lets him know that I am aware he holds back the rage to protect people: that is, he is a protector, not a perpetrator. I let him know that I know he is a caring person with guilt about his rage. The question is, can he tolerate the feelings or will some defense move in?

Pt: Exactly.

Th: Now you have a thought like a fear that something is going to come out of you—fear that your body is going to do something with that anger. [*Recap and clarification.*]

Pt: Yeah.

Th: What were you afraid your body wanted to do when you had anger in it? What were you afraid the anger wanted to do? In your imagination. [*Pressure to intellectually portray.*]

Pt: Okay, in my imagination, I want to throw myself out the window. Of all the silly things.

Rapid Self-Attack

Twenty seconds before, the patient had anger toward the boss. We focused on what his anger wanted to do to the boss, and the next moment he's throwing himself out the window. Isn't that striking? These processes are very rapid. This is why these patients are complicated to work with. They end up on antipsychotic medications because these responses are so quick that they frighten clinicians. When he cognitively disrupts, I stop, do a recap, and bring the anxiety down until I see some tension and intellectualizing. Then we press for feelings again.

So the process is pressure on, pressure off, talk about it, then repeat. Either we mobilize the unconscious or we talk about the process until we can mobilize the unconscious again. Alternate between these two interventions that involve self-reflective and limbic brain regions. When the patient is tense and defending, you are mobilizing the unconscious. When he's flat and confused or scared, talk about the process until tension and intellectualization return. We continue here with a collaborative recap of all we know so far. Each recap becomes richer as the structure of his psychic system is revealed.

Th: Who was the anger with? [*Pressure to identify the target of the anger.*]

Pt: Myself.

Th: And who was it with first? [*Pressure.*]

Pt: With her because . . .

Th: That flip happened again, didn't it? [*Recap: self-attack.*]

Pt: Yeah.

Th: What I mean by the flipping is that first the anger is with her and then anger flips back on yourself and then you toss yourself out the window. [*Recap self-attack.*]

Pt: That's right.

Th: Do you follow me?

Pt: I follow you.

Th: It's like a split second here. The anger comes up and gets onto you directly. [*Recap.*]

Pt: Yes.

Th: Flips in on yourself. [*Recap.*]

Pt: Yeah, it does, and then I get frustrated because I can't get my point across and the anger wells up and . . .

Th: And then it gets flipped on you . . . [*Recap.*]

Pt: That's right, and then I walk away, or I do something. That's the way I handle it.

Th: Okay, so different ways you go. You might walk away. You might say something. You might have some sarcasm, but inside your body it's like you're reacting to the fear and the feelings. Do you follow me? [*Recap.*]

Pt: I do follow you in that sense, but it's almost as if I couldn't be honest with my feelings. I couldn't just sit there and have a normal conversation. [*Recap of his own.*]

Resuming Pressure

His anxiety has now reduced with signs of striated muscle anxiety (sighing) and he is now isolating affect. We are now below threshold, so we have evidence that we can safely resume pressure.

Th: What were you so frightened you were going to do to her? [*Pressure to intellectually portray.*]

Pt: [*Sighs.*] I didn't want to hurt her. [*Unconscious therapeutic alliance: negation.*]

Th: You didn't obviously but . . .

Negation

"I didn't want to hurt her," is a negation of what he is about to say: he wanted to hurt her. This statement is an early sign of the unconscious therapeutic alliance rising, revealing his feelings and urges.

Th: What about this anger? What did *it* want, if you weren't controlling it? [*Pressure to portray, separation of rage from himself.*]

Pt: It just. Okay, in my thoughts what it wanted to do—my anger just wanted to . . .

Th: Physically what did it want to do? [*Pressure to portray.*]

Pt: It just really wanted to yell, and I wanted to yell, and I wanted to scream. [*Good tone in his body, activated and energized with some sign of somatic rage rising.*]

Th: What physically did your body want to do? [*Pressure to portray.*]

Pt: It physically didn't want to. [*Negation.*] I just wanted to grab something. I wanted to break something. I just wanted to . . .

Th: Who was the anger with though? [*Pressure to portray.*]

Pt: With her.

Th: So how did you want to grab and break? [*Pressure to portray.*]

Pt: I, I wanted to break, to kick a garbage can.

Th: Who's the anger with? [*Pressure to portray.*]

Pt: Anger with her.

Th: You understand what you're doing?

Pt: Yeah, I see. I've diverted the anger away from her to an object. [*Recap of his own.*]

Signs of Improving Capacities

A half hour into the session and after numerous interventions, the patient's capacities to tolerate anxiety and understand the process have improved. His tension is rising. He is isolating affect and intellectualizing at a higher rise in the complex transference feelings. He has enough striated anxiety that pressure can continue. He is becoming activated and feeling some anger.

Th: But see, we're not talking about you because we know what you did with it. [*Underscoring of his positive feelings.*]

Pt: Right.

Th: We're talking about the energy you had in your chest. [*Separation of the anger from himself.*]

Pt: Right.

Facilitating Early Portrayal with Fragile Patients

One way to facilitate portrayal of rage in highly anxious or low-capacity patients is to focus on the rage as an external force that he actually restrains to protect you.

Th: What did *it* want to do? [*Pressure to portray.*]

Pt: It wanted to make me run away. [*Anxiety.*]

Th: What did the anger want to do if it's out of you and you're not restraining it like you always do? What did it want to do? [*Pressure to portray.*]

Pt: That's what the energy actually wanted to do.

Th: That's the anxiety.

Pt: That is the anxiety.

Th: First the anger. [*Pressure to portray.*]

Pt: Okay, the anger wanted me to break something. It wanted me to attract attention.

Th: But the anger was with her though, right? [*Pressure to place the rage on the target.*]

Pt: Yes, initially.

Th: So how would it have gone after her physically? [*Pressure to portray.*]

Pt: I suppose it would have . . . in my mind, I probably would have grabbed her and made her listen. [*Grabs hands forward.*]

Somatic Pathway of Rage

This steady supportive pressure yields results. Now the somatic pathway of rage is partly activated. The patient is moving his arms in a grabbing fashion and anxiety has dropped.

Th: You would have grabbed her? [*Pressure to portray.*]

Pt: On her arms.

Th: Grabbed her arms? [*Pressure to portray.*]

Pt: Yeah.

Th: And then what? [*Pressure to portray.*]

Pt: And then maybe shake, but I couldn't envision anything else other than that. [*Unconscious therapeutic alliance: negation.*]

Passage of Complex Transference Feelings

This is also negation as a part of the unconscious therapeutic alliance. The patient is saying he *can envision* more rage beyond the grabbing. Here he is experiencing some of the somatic pathway of rage with energy going to his arms and a drop in anxiety. Now I focus on the content of the impulse.

Th: Can you see that in your head? [*Pressure to portray.*]

Pt: Yes, I can.

Th: Grabbing her and shaking her? [*Pressure to portray.*]

Pt: Right.

Th: And then what? [*Pressure to portray.*]

Pt: And then I'd be yelling in her face, making my point, and that's what I'm doing.

Th: What else? What did the anger want to do? [*Pressure to portray.*]

Pt: The anger wanted to go away, I think. No, the anger just wanted to stay.

Th: And do what with her? [*Pressure to portray.*]

Pt: Just grab her by the arms and shake her. I did it only with one hand for some reason or other. [*Unconscious therapeutic alliance: revealing a link to past trauma.*]

Th: What's your other arm doing when you're shaking and grabbing? [*Pressure to portray.*]

Pt: It's grabbing onto something else.

Th: Like what? [*Pressure to portray.*]

Pt: A chair. Doing something like that. [*Grabs arm of chair and is quite animated.*] If I was to physically get up and just make her listen . . .

Th: Did the anger want to grab a chair though? [*Pressure to portray.*]

Pt: It's diverting in the fact that it's only a physical object as opposed to her. I wanted to grab her. I wanted to grab her arm. I wanted to squeeze it. I wanted to.

Th: So the anger wanted you to grab and squeeze. [*Pressure to portray.*]

Pt: Yeah, in other words, physically hurt her and cause physical pain. But that's not the way I am. [*Appearance of guilt; becomes tearful.*]

Th: No, but that's a distressing thought for you. [*Underscoring of guilt.*]

Pt: Yes. [*Weeps.*]

Th: To even think about it. [*Underscoring of guilt.*]

Pt: Yes.

Th: It's a very upsetting thing. [*Underscoring of guilt.*]

Pt: Yeah. [*Cries, wipes tears away.*]

Ushering in the Unconscious Therapeutic Alliance

This patient has had a passage of a small amount of rage and guilt about the rage. Thus, he has now experienced the complex transference feelings in relation to this current figure, his boss. Now we expect a drop in anxiety and a drop in resistance: the unconscious therapeutic alliance can now take a stronger position with this reduced resistance. This is a first breakthrough to the unconscious.

Pt: It's something my uncle battled all the time with wife abuse. It's something I could never do. I never would do it. I never will do it.

Th: But see, right now you have a painful feeling to think about if you grabbed this woman and shook her. That's painful . . . [*Underscoring of guilt.*]

Pt: That's painful. A shocker. She's scared, and I don't like to do things like that.

Th: This is a painful feeling as if you just did it. [*Recap.*]

Pt: Yes. [*Becomes tearful with feeling of grief and guilt.*] Yeah, it is. It is. I just want people to be happy. I just want to get along. To cooperate. To have conversations in a normal way. That's all. [*Craving of loving relationships; weeps.*]

Th: Yes, there are a lot of mixed feelings—a lot of cravings. There are several things happening at once there.

Extensive Recapitulation

With this small passage of complex feelings, the anxiety and defenses are lowered. We now do an extensive collaborative recapitulation linking all the phenomena together. This gives strength to the unconscious therapeutic alliance and we can see if it is powerful enough to bring a linkage to the past. Notice with each item of recapitulation, I wait for a response from the patient that confirms what I'm saying is correct and we are in agreement.

Th: There are several things at once that are happening here.

Pt: [*Nods yes.*]

Th: First of all with her, there are mixed feelings. First, you wanted to get your point across. Second, you didn't like what she was doing. It stirred up this anger in your chest that had aggression in it. [*Recap: feelings.*]

Pt: That's right.

Th: And you got anxious and tense, and then you got out of the office as if you have to protect her from the feeling. Do you follow me? [*Recap: feelings-defense.*]

Pt: I follow you.

Th: So you felt some part of this anger, and then there's guilt attached to it as if feeling it is the same as doing it. [*Recap: guilt.*]

Pt: Yes, as if I physically did it.

Th: So you're anxious here as if you did something violent right here in the room. [*Recap: feelings-anxiety.*]

Pt: That's right. Which of course is all in my mind. It's not as if I physically acted it out.

Th: But what you see happens in that very moment is sometimes your mind might go blank. You might get very tense or you might go out of the room or you might do some defense like sarcasm as a way to kind of quell it. [*Recap: cognitive-perceptual disruption and defense.*]

Pt: That's right.

Th: So inside you then, mixed feelings were there with her. Do you follow me? [*Recap: complex feelings.*]

Pt: That's right they were.

Th: A complex bunch of feelings.

Pt: Very complex feelings toward her.

Th: But where they go is the anger goes in yourself. Do you follow me? [*Recap: self-attack.*]

Pt: I follow you. I divert it inside of me.

Th: Yeah, as if you have to protect her just from a feeling. [*Recap: feelings-defense.*]

Pt: That's right. So then I start concentrating within myself, and, like you say, the feelings come inside. I have a sense I want to run away and that's what happens.

Th: So this is a very important thing that seems to happen here because when you were here earlier this frustration built up in your body and you had the same response. There was a built-up anger in your chest. [*Recap: link current to transference.*]

Pt: Yes.

Th: And when that came, you had some force in you, and then you got anxious as if you were going to blast out but then you blast in. [*Recap: self-attack.*]

Pt: Yeah.

Th: You see how quickly?

Pt: Yeah, it's quick to change.

Th: As if you're frightened that if you feel anger you might do something. [*Recap: feelings-anxiety.*]

Pt: Yeah.

Th: Even though you just sit there and we talk about it.

Pt: That's right. Yeah, that's right.

Speaking to the Unconscious Therapeutic Alliance

All this collaborative recapping gives strength to the unconscious therapeutic alliance and lowers the resistance. Now I ask the unconscious therapeutic alliance where these emotions and patterns come from.

Th: So we have a question. What is it about this anger and the fear of anger? Where does it come from? Where do you get that from in your experience of life? [*Question to the unconscious therapeutic alliance.*]

Pt: Oh, the fear of acting out how I feel? Childhood. My father was a strictly religious man and my mother was very reserved, and, you know, emotions were never acknowledged in the family.

Th: Uh-huh.

Pt: You know, usually if you had a sad face they said to "smarten up." The bottom line is that it came from my parents.

Th: What did you experience with your parents, this anger and this guilt and this blocking? [*Pressure to identify feelings.*]

Pt: They'd always, usually, it wasn't predominant, but sometimes they'd hit me. [*Tactical defense: minimizing.*]

Th: You'd get hit by them?

Pt: Yeah, that's right.

Th: You remember a time that you really got it? [*Pressure to specific incident.*]

Pt: Yeah, oh yeah, with the belt. Every kid got hit with the belt. [*Tactical defense: generalization.*]

Deciding How to Handle Residual Defenses

Note that some anxiety and tactical defenses are still present since this was only a partial mobilization of the unconscious therapeutic alliance and the resistance is still in operation. With pressure to specific events and feelings I will see whether we need to handle these tactical defenses or whether we can simply ignore them.

Th: Do you remember a time when you got it with the belt? [*Pressure to specific incident.*]

Pt: Yeah, yeah I do.

Th: When was that? [*Pressure to specific incident.*]

Pt: All right, I just remember once I broke a lamp and I lied about it and I got whacked with a belt that time.

Th: What happened that day? [*Exploration of incident.*]

Pt: Well, I hid in the closet. My father came home and dragged me out and whacked me.

Th: You were hiding knowing you were going to get it, you mean?

Pt: Yeah, that's right, yeah.

Th: So you had already run away. [*Identification of parallel to the transference reaction.*]

Pt: That's right. I knew what I did was wrong, and I knew I was going to get it when he got home.

Th: How did he drag you out?

Pt: Well, he just reached in and grabbed me. [*Makes a grabbing motion with his arm.*]

Th: He grabbed you by the arm?

Pt: Yeah, by the arm. [*Looks amazed at the obvious link to the impulse he had with his boss.*]

Th: He pulled your arm?

Pt: Yeah.

Th: And pulled you out of the closet and then—

Pt: That's right and then he, you know, he'd take down your pants and whack you on the rear end.

Th: With a belt? What part of the belt?

Pt: It was just the leather part, but what he always did was he always folded it in half.

Th: So he doubled it.

Pt: Yeah, so it's doubled. That's what he does. It's just the leather part. That's all.

Th: And he's hitting you.

Link to Boss

Recall that this man's rage toward his boss wanted him to grab and do something else with the other hand. The meaning of this is now clear: he is both the battering father and the victim. He projected one and then the other onto his boss; then he would throw himself out the window to his death.

Pt: Yeah.

Th: Let's see how you felt toward him when you think about that now? [*Pressure to identify feelings.*]

Pt: Well, when I think about that now, in a mature way I'd say, well, this was a different time, the 1950s, and this is what went on. [*Tactic: rationalizing.*]

Th: Yeah.

Pt: But going back into detail, if you really want to get at it, I feel pissed off at him, angry that why couldn't he just . . . [*Rise of some* somatic anger in his body that I can sense by mirror process, drop in tension.]

Th: Well, how do you experience that anger in your body now? [*Pressure to experience rage.*]

Pt: Well, how I feel that anger—I'm just starting to get more tense now.

Th: How does the anger feel itself? [*Pressure to experience rage, separating rage from anxiety.*]

Pt: I'm sort of trying to keep that away. I don't really express those feelings of anger toward him because over the years I've rationalized it. I rationalize.

Focus on the Lasting Impact of Trauma

This is a linkage to a past trauma. The violence produced rage and guilt in the patient, and these feelings were transferred onto his boss and me. Because of the guilt, he shuts down to protect me while tormenting himself. This is evidence that partial mobilization of the unconscious therapeutic alliance over the resistance has occurred. The task now is to help him experience these complex feelings, if he is capable. I recap here to bring down anxiety and reduce residual defenses in advance of what will be a difficult area of focus.

Th: I see you still have tension about this. [*Recap: feelings-anxiety.*]

Pt: Unless I deal with this.

Th: When you come in the door, you have tension with a stranger. [*Recap: anxiety in the transference.*]

Pt: That's right.

Th: So we can see, if you want, what this is about. Why are you anxious in this situation with me? You know what I mean? [*Recap: task to understand transference.*]

Pt: Yeah.

Th: Why's that happening to you? And we're seeing that you have mixed feelings in you that get stirred up here and get stirred up with your boss and back there with your father. And when you go back there, you're tense. [*Recap: two triangles.*]

Pt: Yes.

Impact of Recapitulation

This process fuels the unconscious therapeutic alliance and brings rise in the complex transference feelings through pressure on the patient's residual defenses and pressure to override his anxiety and feel the feelings. Now we focus on the feelings.

> Th: I wonder how do you feel this anger toward him when he's beating you with this belt? How do you feel that anger when you think about that? [*Pressure to experience rage.*]
>
> Pt: All I remember is I just wondered, I always wondered after, if I always wanted to run away. My feeling is that I wanted to be away from him. [*Projection and escape.*]

Parallel to the Transference

Remember in the transference with me, when we focused on his rage toward me he became afraid and said he wanted "to run away" to "get away from" me. It's obvious now what was being transferred and projected.

> Th: But how did you feel? [*Pressure to identify feelings.*]
>
> Pt: My feeling was inside.
>
> Th: But how does the anger feel toward him when you think about him belting you? [*Pressure to experience rage.*]
>
> Pt: It was, I felt . . .
>
> Th: In your chest. How does that anger feel? Remember you felt it just a few minutes ago? [*Reminder that he felt it with the boss, pressure to identify feeling.*]
>
> Pt: Yeah, I did.
>
> Th: How does it feel now thinking about him? [*Pressure to identify feelings.*]
>
> Pt: Thinking about him. I just . . . when he was doing it, I just, I didn't want it to happen and I felt, inwardly, I just got tense and I . . . [*Loss of fluency in speech.*]
>
> Th: That's anxiety.
>
> Pt: Anxious: that's what happened.
>
> Th: But how did you feel toward him when he did that? [*Pressure to identify feelings.*]
>
> Pt: It felt . . . [*Sighs.*]

Th: How does the anger feel toward him? [*Pressure to experience rage.*]

Pt: I didn't feel anger. I didn't feel. I just couldn't. [*Unconscious therapeutic alliance: negation.*]

Th: But how do you feel that anger inside now? [*Pressure to experience rage.*]

Threshold to Cognitive-Perceptual Disruption

Now the patient's muscle tone is dropping, he looks afraid, and his thoughts are becoming less coherent. Also his speech is becoming less fluent. We are at threshold. The king and torturers move in, paralyzing him.

Pt: See now my mind's almost . . . like it's blocking off and I . . . [*Loss of fluency due to anxiety.*]

Th: Are you having that happen now?

Pt: Yeah, it's almost like now I'm having a veil come across my vision. [*Perceptual disruption.*]

Th: Where is it? [*Cognitive exploration of symptoms to reduce anxiety.*]

Pt: It's, it's . . .

Th: Up the neck again?

Pt: No, it came from up here [*touches head*] and it was like . . .

Th: Where did it—?

Pt: It was like a clear sheet right in front of my eyes. [*Cries due to high anxiety.*]

Recapitulation

This man had cognitive-perceptual disruption again, so his anxiety went too high and we are above threshold. Rather than guess at his maximal capacity, we use pressure to assess his actual capacity. Otherwise, therapy and his suffering will last longer than necessary. Always work at the highest level of anxiety the patient can manage. Now is the time to recap and bring down the anxiety.

Pt: It's almost as if it did. I just all of a sudden focused in on you, your face.

Th: Okay, for a second here again when you talked about how you felt there, your anxiety went up again. [*Recap: triangle of conflict.*]

Pt: Right. [*Cries a few tears from anxiety.*]

Th: First of all it went into the muscles in your body where you had this tension. What also happened is it rose up a bit more almost as if it was going to interrupt your thoughts like it did before. Do you get me? [*Recap: anxiety formats.*]

Pt: I do get you.

Th: Almost as high but not quite as high as before. Is that right? [*Recap: anxiety levels.*]

Pt: That's right.

Th: Okay.

Pt: And this time was almost like the anxiety took a shortcut and it was like, of all things, a clear sheet over my vision, and I concentrated on your mouth.

Th: That's fine. Was it a bit like a screen, like a screen door? [*Exploration of anxiety phenomena.*]

Pt: Yeah, something like that. Actually, it was like a plastic sheet. That's what it was like. That's what it was and it was also as if all of a sudden I'm looking at what you're asking and now I'm concentrating on you, your mouth.

Th: Which is fine because your anxiety went back down when you did that, right?

Pt: Exactly.

Th: Let me know if that happens again, okay. And we'll do the same to bring the anxiety down.

Pt: All right.

Comonitoring of Anxiety: Cementing the Conscious Alliance

The patient noted that he started to concentrate on my face. I took this as a positive event that he had used a focus on me to calm himself down. Showing fragile patients that you can help them calm down when they are distressed is crucial. This experience of anxiety reduction builds their confidence in you and the therapy process: they know they will never be too anxious and they know that, together, the therapy team can deal with whatever shows up. I also asked him to tell me when the anxiety goes too high again. Thus, we are both monitoring the process and as a team will regulate it.

Here we examined this man's experience of the anxiety to bring down the anxiety by intellectualizing about it. This use of isolation of affect causes the anxiety to drop and tend to go into the striated muscle. Now we do further recapping to link past-current-transference and feeling-anxiety-defense.

> *Th:* Here's what you're telling me. Back there with your father you had some feelings that create anxiety today when you think about them. And it has something to do with anger and other feelings from back then. [*Recap: two triangles.*]
>
> *Pt:* Yeah.
>
> *Th:* When we talk about it now, you get the nervousness now. When you're in the situation with this woman and there's anger you get some nervousness there. [*Recap: triangle of person.*]
>
> *Pt:* Yes.
>
> *Th:* When we focused on anger here you get nervousness here. You follow me? [*Recap: feelings-anxiety.*]
>
> *Pt:* I do follow you.
>
> *Th:* So in a sense, these feelings that you have from someplace in your past generate anxiety, and the anxiety can cause some of these responses that we see. [*Recap: two triangles.*]
>
> *Pt:* That's right.
>
> *Th:* It can affect your body certain ways. [*Recap: anxiety.*]
>
> *Pt:* Yeah.
>
> *Th:* It can affect the vision at certain times if it's at a peak. [*Recap: anxiety.*]
>
> *Pt:* That's right, if you really push the right buttons; yeah, you're right. I say you, but within me I push the right buttons, and it's almost like trying to distract myself from the core question. [*Self-correction of a tendency to project hostility that "I pushed buttons."*]
>
> *Th:* Okay, how far back in your life do these visual and these blanking phenomena go?
>
> *Pt:* It goes back to when I was a kid.

Monitoring Capacity

With this recap I am looking for signs that the patient's capacity is increasing: these indications include striated muscle tension, isolation of affect, intellectualization, ability to recap the triangles, and ability to describe and understand the process. Seeing markers of striated muscle tension and isolation of affect means we are back below threshold and can then use pressure again. The interview proceeds to history taking and some exploration of his childhood. We plan follow-up meetings, and I ask how he feels at the end of the interview. Here is his response:

> Pt: It's almost like I'm feeling that I'm in a garden, of all things, sitting talking to you the way people should talk.
>
> Th: So you have a good feeling.
>
> Pt: Yeah, I do.
>
> Th: We've gone through a hard piece of work.
>
> Pt: Yeah, we did.
>
> Th: Felt some of these things.
>
> Pt: Yes.
>
> Th: And you've come out of it more comfortable.
>
> Pt: That's right, I do.
>
> Th: So what about if we do have a series of meetings then?
>
> Pt: Certainly.

Summary of Trial Therapy

This patient had mild to moderate fragility that required graded work. In this session he was able to have some small experiences of feelings. However, with anxiety and resistances present throughout the session, the experiences were difficult to incorporate consciously. This trial set the stage for more sessions to build capacity, enabling greater breakthroughs to the unconscious.

PHASE 3: FIRST BREAKTHROUGHS AND UNLOCKINGS

Unlocking of the unconscious in patients with fragile character structure occurs first in the form of grief over the negative impact of projection, past losses, and trauma. Later partial unlockings progress with some experience of rage with some guilt and grief, followed by major unlockings of rage and guilt about the rage when anxiety tolerance is higher.

Later in therapy during repeated unlocking of the unconscious, these patients experience clear linkages and imagery as a product of the unconscious therapeutic alliance. For example, the dead body of the boss turns into the image of the mother. They may experience body image distortions, such as seeing themselves in the mirror appearing like a wild animal because of the intensity of their unconscious rage. At the core, fragile patients have primitive murderous rage with a wish to torture their traumatizers. This rage causes massive guilt in the patients' unconscious, since they also wanted a positive bond with these same people. Additionally, the grief of the trauma is very intense due to the intensity of the trauma.

Vignette: Graded Work to First Unlockings

We now begin the third treatment session with this same patient to further examine the capacity building graded format and first breakthroughs to the unconscious.

He begins the session proudly describing his understanding of the process and where he wants to focus.

Pt: Last time we were talking, and we came to some pretty good resolutions on some issues. Just briefly, in the session we were trying to recount what feelings I actually experienced. We focused on the fact that I had trouble with authority figures. I went through this incident in my life with my boss, and I couldn't experience anger correctly and we went through the process what would happen if—we went right through the process and what I thought was the anger came up and went to my fingertips, grabbing the boss, and it felt like a resolution, and I felt peace.

Th: Um-hmm.

Pt: Then we talked about my childhood, and I talked about my father and beatings and everything like that—how I couldn't get away— and again it was that feeling of anger, but there was no resolution to that. It was the more you squirmed, the more you got hurt; therefore, you just had to keep it inside. Then we went back to dealing with what I call *people of senior rank*, whether it's a director, manager, or even a medical doctor. The problem is that I have a tendency that when I get angry, this blackness would come up when I feel the anger; it's almost like a switch goes off and that leads to anxiety, and that's where I get confused and feel guilt.

Th: Mm-hmm.

Pt: We ended on a note that what I wanted to do was try to figure out why these feelings that happened in the past, with my father beating me, keep mixing into present-day reality with other authority figures. It's rather unrealistic.

Th: Mm-hmm.

Pt: And the second problem I wanted to resolve was expressing the anger freely without activating that switch (anxiety). And that's where we sort of left off. [*Laughs.*] Did you want me to continue on? [*Looks proud.*]

Capacity to Self-Reflect and Understand Process

We see the patient is able to isolate affect and describe his two triangles. To set the stage for the session, he has done his own recap of the process. Most fragile patients cannot do this at the beginning of early sessions and are very anxious, afraid, and confused, so we can help them by beginning with a summary recap. In this case, this man is showing signs of improved capacity and has done his own recap. He understands the road map and can lead the journey today. This is a marker that he is ready for further mobilization of the unconscious. On a dynamic level, he sees the way out of the dungeon and castle and wants to achieve this. He looks very pleased and I focus on his positive feelings with me.

Th: How did you feel about all that right now with what you described and everything. How do you feel with me? [*Pressure to experience positive feeling.*]

Pt: Well, I feel really good with you.

Th: Uh-huh.

Pt: Like I could, yeah, I could really relax with you.

Th: It's a positive feeling. [*Pressure to experience positive feeling.*]

Pt: Very positive, yeah. You know this is one time I feel like I can feel some sort of synergy between you and I.

Th: Mm-hmm.

Pt: Yeah, it feels good. Put it that way; it really does feel good.

Th: Mm-hmm. What's that like for you to feel that way here with me? [*Pressure to experience positive feeling.*]

Pt: It feels like I can talk. I can articulate myself a lot better. I don't feel like you're in judgment or anything like that. [*Inactive projection.*]

Th: Do you have a sensation of a positive feeling? Do you feel that inside you, that kind of feeling? [*Pressure to experience positive feeling.*]

Pt: It feels—I just feel loose on the shoulders actually. It feels loose up here and it just feels loose. [*Touches shoulders.*]

Th: Looseness.

Pt: Yeah, looseness as if I don't feel tense, which is probably a pseudonormal state that I'm in at times.

Th: Uh-huh.

Pt: The muscular tension—I don't feel that at all. [*Unconscious therapeutic alliance: negation; clenches hands.*]

Th: Uh-huh.

Pt: [*Sighs.*]

Response to Focus on Positive Feelings

Here I focus on the positive feeling with me, which mobilizes all the attachment feelings, anxiety, and defenses in the same way focusing on avoided rage will. One of the common misperceptions of ISTDP is that we selectively focus on rage, but we are actually interested in helping the patient feel all his avoided feelings and impulses including guilt-activating positive feelings. This focus on positive feelings is mobilizing rage and guilt in his unconscious as indicated by a rise in unconscious anxiety with a sigh.

This patient's mind goes to a current incident with complex feelings. He describes an incident of conflict at the workplace where he tried to be assertive but ended up with cognitive-perceptual disruption.

Pt: On the way to her office I got overly emotional. I wouldn't let her complete her sentences. I'd interrupt her and my voice was elevated. I asked if there was anything else to say about this and she said no, and I went back to my cubicle. About fifteen minutes later she came back and said to me "What was that all about?" and I said, "I just lost it." [*Lost control of his temper, anxiety.*]

Th: Okay. Do you want us to look into that?

Pt: Yeah, because there is something odd. She said, she said it was as if she wasn't even there, and that's the way I was approaching it.

She says she's never come across anybody like that who would express like that as if she wasn't even there. It's like I was yelling at a different person but not her as a human being but as a manager.

Analysis and Decision Point

Here the patient describes the process of projection that took place alternating with cognitive-perceptual disruption, resulting in a minor but disruptive outburst. While doing this he is isolating affect with me and he is tense. So now we will press to what underlying feelings were being mobilized. If he were cognitively disrupting while recalling the situation, I would recap down—but he is not, so I will press up. The main pressure is to experience the feelings toward the boss as he talks about the incident.

Pt: It's funny that she made the distinction

Th: Okay, how do you feel right now? [*Pressure to identify feelings.*]

Pt: Anxious because now I'm starting to feel . . . believe it or not, re-enacting that event. Now it's coming back, you know.

Th: So you were talking about that feeling on your way to the office. [*Bracing: identifying feelings.*]

Pt: That's right.

Th: You had a scenario in your mind. Which scenario was that? [*Exploration of his projection.*]

Pt: The scenario was, "I bet you she's not going to listen" so in other words . . .

Facilitating the Experience of Rage

At the point where this man is tolerating the unconscious anxiety and isolating affect, I press to help him experience the feelings. Through pressure to keep remembering the incident and pressure to feelings, my goal is to help him keep the feelings going upward and help him tolerate the feelings. I will also provide short recaps to underscore the body reactions, the thoughts, and the overall process. I also use bracing, where the emotions are both activated and reflected upon simultaneously. (See chapter 15.)

Th: She was going to reject what you said. How did you feel toward her on the way to the office? How do you feel toward her? [*Recap, pressure to feeling.*]

Pt: I felt anger.

Th: Like a strong anger? [*Bracing: experience of rage.*]

Pt: A strong anger.

Th: How does that feel in your body right now? [*Bracing: experience of rage.*]

Pt: Right now I'm starting to hurt right down here in my stomach.

Th: It's low down right now? [*Bracing: experience of rage.*]

Pt: Yeah, and I'm just starting to get a little pain.

Th: How does it feel if it goes farther up? Moves up over that. [*Bracing: experience of rage.*]

Pt: Yeah, now it's up here. [*Points to his chest.*]

Th: Around the chest? [*Bracing: experience of rage.*]

Pt: Around the chest, yeah.

Th: How does it feel when it moves? [*Bracing: experience of rage.*]

Pt: Well, it—now my neck's starting to hurt a little bit. It just starts going up. Just thinking about me going up the stairs to go up to her office and these thoughts were cascading in my mind.

Th: It was all her rejecting your ideas and not listening to you. [*Reminder of the trigger of the feelings.*]

Pt: That's correct.

Bracing with Fragile Patients

Fragile patients benefit from the technique of bracing, as do highly resistant patients with repression. (See chapter 15.) Bracing is particularly useful near the threshold to cognitive-perceptual disruption when pressure alone could shoot anxiety too high. It allows a close titration of the dosage of exposure to the complex feelings. Bracing engages the brain regions responsible for reflecting on body sensations and emotions while activating underlying complex feelings.

Th: That was the whole main thing.

Pt: That was about it. I just had a feeling that—yeah, it was rejection of my ideas and yeah, it was.

Th: So how does that type of anger feel as it moves up further on your body? [*Bracing: experience of rage.*]

Pt: Well, now it's hurting; chest is a little bit tight. [*Striated muscle anxiety.*]

Th: So there's tension. [*Bracing: anxiety about the rage.*]

Pt: There's tension.

Th: That's the anxiety and the muscle tension. [*Bracing: anxiety about rage.*]

Pt: Okay, that's the tension, yeah.

Th: You remember the anger? How that felt before when you were here? [*Reminder of a past session where he felt some somatic pathway.*]

Pt: The way it felt. You mean when we continued the process?

Th: Yeah.

Pt: I felt what happened, the anger would go up. I always felt in the neck, right, and that's where I made the breakthrough before of it going down my arm.

Th: Uh-huh, right.

Pt: And then I found what happened after it came out the fingertips; it never went to that point. I don't remember completing it. I was kind of hoping that sort of thing would have happened and that would have been the completion of the feeling.

Th: That you would have felt it all, right?

Pt: Yeah.

Th: Now, has it gone up there? [*Points to chest.*] Can you feel it now? How do you experience it now? [*Bracing: experience of rage.*]

Pt: You know, I bet you if we went through role playing and I was to think about the anger, it might go up there.

Th: It was like a real put-down from her in your mind that was going to come, wasn't it? [*Reminder of the trigger of the feelings to combat repression of the memory.*]

Projection versus the Complex Transference Feelings

What is the difference between using projection versus the complex transference feelings? In isolating affect about this patient's projection, we are mobilizing all his complex transference feelings with the boss and me. Thus, we are mobilizing love, pain, rage, guilt, and craving of attachment related to past attachment trauma. In contrast, projection is a split where all he would feel is rage in response to the projection: the unconscious attachment feelings are blocked off and inaccessible at that time and you are the enemy.

We need to get the patient to the point where he can hold complex feelings in his mind, isolate affect, self-reflect, and have striated muscle anxiety about these feelings before we can break through to the unconscious. This central monitoring tool is a key feature of this method rendering it an efficient method with an extremely broad range of patients. We see here he is making gains in this direction.

Pt: A put-down from her.

Th: From her, that's what you were expecting. [*Reminder of the trigger of the feelings.*]

Pt: That's what I was anticipating. A put-down.

Th: How did that whole rage feel on the way to her office? [*Pressure to experience rage.*]

Pt: It just felt like I . . . just almost felt like I was burning a bit. I remember actually, I was going up the stairs and I remember going through the door.

Th: Yeah.

Pt: I have a key card and I remember swiping it, and it didn't work because I went too fast. [*Clear recall of the situation.*]

Th: Okay, you're tense and there's energy. [*Clarification, short recap.*]

Pt: Yeah.

Th: And then it built up to this kind of high point suddenly.

Pt: Yeah.

Th: But when we look back, you had different feelings with her and that increased the anxiety, right? [*Recap: feelings-anxiety.*]

Pt: [*Nods.*]

Th: And one of them at least was anger, and some of them were other feelings, but how does that anger feel when you think about it now in your body? [*Bracing: experience of rage.*]

Pt: Well, thinking about the anger now, it feels like I can feel it going. Talking to you about it in a different way. [*Puts hand up to his shoulder.*]

Th: In your shoulders? [*Bracing: experience of rage.*]

Pt: Yes, in my shoulders is what's happening. It's actually come out of my stomach; it's come up here now, now it's . . . [*Points to shoulder.*]

Th: To your shoulders? [*Further bracing.*]

Pt: Yeah, yeah.

Th: So how do your shoulders feel? [*Further bracing.*]

Pt: Yeah, they're starting to feel.

Th: In your arms now? [*Further bracing.*]

Using Mirror Processes

Mirror processes, where you detect the somatic feelings of the patient, are an invaluable guide. They will tell you how high the rise in feelings is and what it feels like. You can also detect some of the anxiety experiences as you are trying to tune in to the patient's emotional process. Use this empathic response as a gauge when ushering up the complex feelings.

Pt: Yeah, well, no, it's only here [*points to top of shoulders*], no, not quite down to the arms.

Th: Okay, yeah.

Pt: So that's the feeling I have thinking about it. [*Loses muscle tone and slows down.*]

Th: It only just made it to your upper body? [*Bracing: experience of rage.*]

Pt: Yeah, it's only the upper part. You see that's it and I got angry and I . . .

Th: Okay, is that as far as it went do you think, or did it go farther actually? [*Bracing: experience of rage.*] See what we're really looking at now is the feeling that you had that didn't quite make it to consciousness, right? [*Recap: feelings-defense.*]

Pt: Right.

Th: It actually turned into anxiety that wiped out this whole experience. That's what we're looking at. [*Recap: feelings-anxiety.*]

Pt: Right.

Th: See, the anger came up but the anxiety overrode it and you didn't get to feel it—and you went into defense mode, right? [*Recap: triangle of conflict.*]

Pt: Right.

Th: So first here we're letting it move through you, and it's moving to your arms. [*Bracing: experience of rage.*]

Pt: Yeah. [*Removes glasses.*]

Th: When you think about this put-down from her, how does that feel in the rest of your arms? You know what I mean? How far is it in your arms? [*Bracing: experience of rage.*]

Working with Thresholds

Throughout the above segment, the patient was increasingly anxious. Little anxiety was present in his striated muscles, so he was tending to go to cognitive-perceptual disruption. I was helping him to not repress the memory and not disrupt and dissociate away from the focus. Here I was bracing, since I was detecting that he was having trouble holding focus and was at the threshold.

Pressure, bracing, and recap are used at different levels of rise. Recapping and other interventions used to reduce anxiety are used when well above the threshold. Bracing is used near or at the threshold. Finally, pressure is reserved for when the anxiety is clearly below the threshold and manifest as striated muscle tension.

Th: In your arm there now? [*Bracing: experience of rage.*]

Pt: Actually, it feels like something going down this little finger only [on left side] on this side for some reason. [*This is the bottom of the somatic pathway of rage as it starts in the small finger of the hand and then goes to the rest of the hand. (See chapter 5.)*]

Th: And so if you let it move further and hold that in you a little bit more—if really the put-down occurred as badly as you thought it would. [*Bracing: experience of rage.*]

Pt: Yeah, and I go in there and I, okay, I'm mad. I'm coming through the door and I really have things to say and I want to say these things. Yeah, I can feel the energy start to come down here. [*Becomes more animated, points to arm.*]

Th: Down from part of your neck? [*Bracing: experience of rage.*]

Pt: Yeah, I am actually.

Th: Both of your arms? [*Further bracing.*]

Pt: Now it's both of them.

Th: So is the anxiety going down yet, or is it still up? [*Bracing: anxiety versus rage.*]

Pt: No, I feel like it's a mixture in there. I know it is.

Th: It's a mix of the two right now. [*Bracing: anxiety versus rage.*]

Pt: Yeah, I've got to concentrate on it. I have to. I've got to think about the anger and not this anxiety. It's like I'm flipping. [*Looks somewhat confused.*]

Th: The two are together though, right? [*Bracing: anxiety versus rage.*]

Pt: The two are together, yeah. This way it's like I'm seeing a conflict. It's like . . .

Th: Anger and then holding it with anxiety. [*Bracing: anxiety versus rage.*]

Pt: Yeah, holding it with anxiety, and that's where I sort of get confused.

Th: Are you getting any of the confusion at all now? Are you thinking clearly enough right now or is your thinking on the edge of confusion? [*Monitoring for cognitive-perceptual disruption.*]

Pt: It's on the edge of confusion. My head is unclear. [*Cognitive-perceptual disruption.*]

Threshold to Cognitive-Perceptual Disruption

Here I'm looking for markers of striated anxiety and isolation of affect where I can press up, or cognitive-perceptual disruption and projection where we have to stop and recap. Without clear evidence of whether we're working above or below the threshold, I use bracing, which combines both of these interventions. Now we are clearly above threshold. I recap to bring down the anxiety and bring back isolation of affect.

Th: Okay, here's what's happening. You're reviewing a strong anger about ideas and thoughts about being put down. The anxiety when it's on a low level will affect your body with tension mostly. [*Recap: feelings and anxiety channels.*]

Pt: Right.

Th: And as it goes up, it can start to interrupt your thoughts in some ways. [*Recap: cognitive-perceptual disruption.*]

Pt: Right.

Th: We've seen there are feelings underlying the anxiety. One is the anger. The anger moves up gradually and then moves down into the arms where you've got some energy in the arms. [*Recap: somatic pathway of rage.*]

Pt: Yes.

Th: And that can make your anxiety go up higher. [*Recap: anxiety.*]

Pt: Right.

Th: The anxiety can go up and try to interrupt your thoughts, which makes the feeling go away. [Recap: defensive function of cognitive-perceptual disruption.]

Pt: Yes.

Th: You see, the anxiety pushes all the feelings back to the unconscious. Right? [Recap: repression.]

Pt: Yes, I see what you're saying there.

Th: The anger gets activated and then repressed down.

Pt: That's right and then the anxiety takes over . . . in the unconscious [Sighs deeply: striated anxiety returning.]

Th: Yes, in the unconscious.

Pt: But why does that sort of thing happen? Why, it has to be some pattern of thought I guess. [Request for pressure.]

Th: Yeah.

Pt: It's something I've patterned into myself. This is the way to handle it. [Sighs.]

Resume Pressure

Now this man is completely back. How do I know? We see two nice sighs. He intellectualizes asking, "Why does this sort of thing happen?" The sigh and intellectualization are signs we are back below threshold. When asking me why, he is asking for me to resume pressure.

Following this we focus on how he felt aggression with his boss and had a small amount of guilt about this. He linked this to the past with his father, and when we focused on the past with his father, again he had cognitive-perceptual disruption. I do some recapping to bring down anxiety and bring back isolation of affect.

Pt: Just, it's just like we did it. I felt, I felt it spike up and then I got confused and my mind went hazy trying to think back.

Th: When you were thinking about anger and where it came from and people you relate it to and guilt about the anger, your anxiety went up. [Recap: feelings-anxiety.]

Pt: Yeah.

Th: And your anxiety went up again.

Pt: That's exactly it. It's like flashes.

Th: You mean you were having some flashes? Were you thinking of things?

Pt: Thinking of things like what's causing that. I was thinking back about why do I even think that people are bad. [*Projection.*] People are generally good. Why do I go around thinking the worst of people, that they're going to do that? Why do I do it . . . childhood, you're asking the question. It's almost what is happening is I'm getting confused.

Move into the Transference

The patient is attempting to not use projection, and this is causing a rise in anxiety in the form of cognitive-perceptual disruption. This is a good sign that projection is weakening as a destructive force in the treatment. At this point, I opted to leave the current incident and focus into the transference as a component of graded format and to bring further rise in the complex transference feelings and the unconscious therapeutic alliance.

Th: Let me ask it another way. When I asked about the past, your anxiety went up, okay?

Pt: Yes, it did.

Th: How did you feel about me asking it? [*Pressure to identify feelings.*]

Pt: How did I feel? Jeez, this is a thought, but my feeling was one of where I didn't want you to do it, but then again I wanted you to do it.

Complex Feelings

Here he is declaring complex feelings in the transference. He is cognitively intact enough to focus on these complex feelings since his mind is relatively clear and he has some tension. We start with a collaborative recap of the process again.

Th: So you had two . . .

Pt: Two complete thoughts . . .

Th: Two thoughts and two feelings. [*Recap: complex feelings.*]

Pt: And two feelings, yeah, with you.

Th: Okay, you had a mixed feeling with me in a split second. [*Recap: complex feelings.*]

Pt: That's right.

Th: It caused the anxiety to go up. [*Recap: anxiety.*]

Pt: Exactly.

Th: So there were two aspects. One that you want me to ask about that so we can look at it, but the other is that at the same time you don't want me to ask. [*Recap: complex feelings.*]

Pt: Exactly.

Th: Both.

Pt: A negative and a positive feeling.

Th: Exactly—the two feelings like we've seen with her, right? [*Linking of current to therapeutic relationships.*]

Pt: Yeah.

Th: Those feelings you have inside you quickly tracked to anxiety. [*Recap: feelings-anxiety.*]

Pt: Yes, it fast tracked, yes. [*Sighs.*]

Th: Yeah, so you had mixed thoughts here with me and the mixed thoughts brought mixed feelings and the mixed feelings produce anxiety. [*Recap: triangle of conflict.*]

Pt: Anxiety.

Th: Anxiety, exactly. Is the anxiety still up?

Pt: I'm just trying to think about why I'm . . . Well, it is up, but when I rub my head, I'm just thinking. Trying to think why . . .

Th: Why do I react this way?

Pt: You know what? There's a moment of feeling sorry for myself. What I was actually doing was asking myself "Why am I like this?" [*Self-attack, but he caught it.*]

Recapitulation on Self-Directed Rage

At this point rage is turning inward so we address it by recapping. This is another rapid rotation of the front of the system, but this time it comes back with less force. With whatever front comes, our job is to read and respond with combinations of recapping, bracing, and pressure.

Th: Did you just get mad at yourself?

Pt: Yes, I did.

Th: So that's the other point. Remember that phenomenon? When you have that frustration or anger with another person it might go in at yourself. [*Recap: self-attack.*]

Pt: That's right, I internalize it.

Th: So first, if we follow this, you had some kind of positive feeling with me and also some kind of negative feeling with me—but the negative feeling turned in on yourself. [*Recap: complex feelings, self-attack.*]

Pt: Yes, it did.

Th: The anger turned inward on you. [*Recap: self-attack.*]

Pt: That's right.

Th: The anger was first, originally, with me because I'm asking a hard question. [*Recap: self-attack.*]

Pt: Yeah, you are.

Th: So, when I asked the hard question you got mixed feelings about it. [*Recap: complex feelings.*]

Pt: Yeah.

Th: But that produces anger turning inward on you or anxiety. [*Recap: self-attack.*]

Pt: Yeah, that is it. [*Sighs: shift to striated muscle anxiety, back below threshold.*]

Th: Okay, what about if we can try to identify those mixed feelings you had with me? [*Pressure.*]

Pt: Sure.

Th: Because that seemed to spike the anxiety up.

Pt: Yes.

Th: Sure, did you get enough of a sense of those feelings? [*Pressure to experience complex feelings.*]

Pt: Yeah, I did, but do we have time this session?

Th: We have fifteen more minutes.

Pt: Yeah, sure. Just could you provoke me one more time, just to give me some more? [*Request for pressure.*]

Th: You mean for me to ask you how you felt with me at that second? [*Clarification of the difference between provocation and pressure.*] You had the positive feeling and the negative feeling.

Pt: Right.

Th: The two. Maybe can you describe those? [*Bracing: complex feelings.*]

Pt: When I went through that positive feeling, it was one where we're in a good groove. I want to continue on that good feeling I had before with you. [*Smiles widely and I respond with a smile.*]

Th: Right.

Pt: The other feeling was because this is difficult work.

Th: Yes.

Pt: I don't want to go there, I mean, I'm happy with the positive groove. I want to keep on with the positive feeling—not this part where I'm going to have to struggle with these thoughts. My anxiety level just went up. [*Self-reflection, rise in anxiety.*]

Th: So here's what the negative feeling had to do with: I was asking if you wanted to do something, which is look into something painful. [*Recap: complex feelings.*]

Pt: Yeah.

Resuming Pressure

Now the patient is cognitively clearer and anxiety is in striated muscle. He is also directly asking me to pressure to the underlying feelings again. We are back below threshold, and I resume pressure.

Th: Which I'm doing again, actually, by the way. [*Activation of complex feelings by broadcasting this work.*]

Pt: You are.

Th: I'm asking you about how you feel.

Pt: You are.

Th: So can you describe the feelings? What those feelings felt like? The positive feeling and whatever you want to call the negative feeling, whatever you noticed within yourself? [*Bracing: experience of complex feelings.*]

Pt: Sure. Okay, I started with the positive feeling, but I have to admit, the negative feeling had come through stronger.

Th: Okay.

Pt: And right now, even thinking about it, my neck's killing me and my stomach is actually feeling tense. [*Reference to abdominal wall muscle tension.*]

Th: Tension?

Pt: Well, yeah, my neck's killing me right now. [*Projective identification, which will be discussed later.*]

Th: Did you get any experience of the negative feeling? Do you have any experience of that inside you there? [*Bracing: experience of rage.*]

Pt: Yes, I do.

Th: What do you notice there with the frustration or anger part? [*Bracing: experience of rage.*]

Pt: Yeah, I just feel . . . I feel it just going up. [*Gestures with arms moving up the body, smiles widely, holding the positive feeling with the anger.*]

Th: Going up!

Pt: Coming up! Yeah, and actually it's coming through my neck.

Th: Is it going through that zone of your neck or just going up to it? [*Bracing: experience of rage.*]

Pt: No, it isn't, only up to it because you haven't pushed me far enough. Because I know if you push me far enough, I know it will reach a certain point and then that's where I lose concentration and then I'm really in trouble. [*Reference to the threshold.*]

Th: So we want it to go up and hold it there before you lose concentration right? [*Bracing: rage versus anxiety.*]

Pt: That's right, we want to see it before I lose it.

Th: Yeah. You want to activate it and then hold it. [*Bracing: underscoring the emotional task.*]

Toward an Integrated Conscious Experience

Each of these interventions contains pressure to experience the rage as part of the complex transference feelings coupled with self-reflection on the experience of the feeling. The positive feeling is sustaining throughout this segment and keeping his anxiety low. This activation of the complex transference feelings keeps his anxiety relatively low since the positive feeling reduces anxiety about acting out the rage. Here we continue to usher in the somatic rage while holding the positive feeling.

Th: Okay, did it get to your shoulders now? [*Bracing: experience of rage.*]

Pt: No, it didn't.

Th: To your chest? [*Further bracing.*]

Pt: Just stomach and chest down here [*Points to lower chest.*]

Th: Lower chest. [*Further bracing.*]

Pt: But actually up in the neck now. This is what's happening.

Th: It's tight there? [*Further bracing.*]

Pt: It's tight there on the back of my neck, and I don't know why. [*Unconscious therapeutic alliance: negation.*] And the stomach is feeling nausea right now.

Decision to Press or Recap

The patient reports nausea, which suggests the feelings are being repressed into the smooth muscle. The decision now is to either recap or to press up and help the feelings pass through. I decide based on how much he can isolate affect, how much anxiety is in striated muscle, and whether there are signs of the unconscious therapeutic alliance at the moment. The unconscious therapeutic alliance is activating bringing the negation about his *neck killing* him and *not knowing why his neck is tight*: we will see later these are directly related to unconscious content of his aggressive impulses. Here I decided to recap.

Th: First there's the frustration component or whatever you're going to call it, anger or whatever. [*Recap: feelings.*]

Pt: Right.

Th: But it got in your stomach and it got the tension on your neck. [*Recap: anxiety.*]

Pt: Right.

Th: There's positive feeling, and then there's frustration or anger and the two of them are together. [*Recap: complex feelings.*]

Pt: Right.

Th: And you pulled anger right in by this nausea and tension and this anxiety. [*Recap: feelings-anxiety.*]

Pt: Yeah.

Th: That keeps the anger down as if you're afraid of feeling it in your body. [*Recap: feeling-anxiety.*] What are your thoughts on how we can figure this out?

Pt: My thought is that I've got to try to explore these feelings. I want to go through this idea of positive feeling and negative feeling and why—thinking about me sitting with you—I'm having such a difficult time talking about the feelings. Like why you ask a simple question about the past and all of a sudden I get so anxious when I connect with you.

Self-Directed Rage: Recap

Here we recapped to bring isolation of affect to override the repression to smooth muscle. Now the patient moves to self-criticism, and I recap on that. Again we see rapid rotation between defensive systems that must all be addressed in turn. Notice these recaps become shorter as his capacity grows.

Th: Are you putting yourself down a bit? [*Clarification of self-criticism.*]

Pt: Yeah, I see your point.

Th: So first with me, I was the one asking you the hard question, right?

Pt: Right, right, right.

Th: That's part of why you got these feelings, the positive feeling and the irritation, right? [*Recap: complex feelings.*]

Pt: Yeah.

Th: So the anger part—did you feel it at all flash through you in your body? [*Bracing: experience of rage.*]

Pt: You know, when I think about it, at one point I did actually.

Th: A split second, was it? [*Bracing: experience of rage.*]

Pt: A split second of it, yeah.

Th: Did it loosen up the anxiety in any way? [*Bracing: anxiety versus rage.*]

Pt: Part of it's the feeling of anger, yeah; you're right about that.

Th: It kind of holds. [*Bracing: experience of rage.*]

Pt: Jeez, I just started to realize that, okay. I'm getting into new territory. Maybe I didn't recognize these feelings and stuff like that, but yeah.

Combinations of Self-Reflection and Pressure: Bracing

Notice I continue to use bracing interventions, holding a reflective focus on the body or thoughts while nudging the patient toward higher levels of complex feelings. Such work mobilizes a dosage of complex feelings toward the therapist that can be fine tuned to the patient's capacity. When he is clearly below the threshold, we resume pressure and when clearly above the threshold we use recap; in between we combine these two with bracing. (See fig. 15.4.)

Th: Then did it get to the shoulders? [*Bracing: experience of rage.*]

Pt: No, it just went right by.

Th: It bypassed the shoulders? [*Bracing: experience of rage.*]

Pt: It's certainly frustrating here [*points to neck*], but I won't allow it to go down past the shoulders.

Th: It's not in your upper arms? It's in your upper arms a little bit? [*Further bracing.*]

Pt: The anger?

Th: Yeah, is it not? [*Further bracing.*]

Pt: You know what I'm doing right now? I'm thinking about it. [*Positive response to bracing: self-reflection about the feelings.*] You ask me these questions and I'm getting frustrated. And okay, I feel it up here. [*Rubs shoulder.*]

Th: Only here? [*Bracing: experience of rage.*]

Pt: Thinking about you and your asking me these hard questions.

Th: Only your left shoulder? [*Bracing: experience of rage.*]

Pt: Both of them actually, equally. And my neck's just really tight. Yeah, it's definitely there. I can feel it in the shoulders, and I keep reacting in my mind. I want to keep up this focus and you're going to keep asking me hard questions. [*Request for continued bracing.*]

Th: Yeah, and you've got a couple of feelings about it. [*Recap.*]

Pt: Yeah.

Th: One of them is this feeling of anger . . .

Pt: That's it.

Th: And then the other is the positive feeling. [*Bracing: keeping positive feeling and rage in focus.*]

Pt: Yeah. Because you're going to keep on asking me these hard questions.

Portraying the Impulse

Here each of my communications has elements of pressure for the patient to feel the complex feelings in the moment. We are also doing a detailed study of his body responses of anxiety and somatic pathway, while continually cementing the alliance and positive feelings. Anxiety is kept low, and we are monitoring every part of his psychic system that moves. This bracing activity improves his self-reflective capacity to isolate affect, the conscious therapeutic alliance, the complex transference feelings, and the unconscious therapeutic alliance. With evidence of somatic pathway activation and his anxiety being at a good level, I now move to ask him to portray the impulse.

> *Th:* Tell me your thoughts. Do you feel it enough to describe that anger part? [*Pressure to portray.*]
>
> *Pt:* Yeah, I actually know what it feels like. I know we were talking energy before but it's almost like . . . it's almost like your human self, forming. It's like you're becoming extremely aware of your human physiology. [*Positive response to bracing: somatic experiencing.*]

Experiencing Sensations in the Body

It is amazing when fragile patients experience the somatic pathway of rage consciously for the first time. They report acute awareness of the whole body. Prior to this event, they appear to have never experienced their bodies.

> *Th:* You're aware of your body.
>
> *Pt:* You're very aware of your body, and that's something I never really thought of before.
>
> *Th:* And you have some energy at the shoulder level. [*Bracing: experience of rage.*]
>
> *Pt:* Yeah, that's right. I can feel the muscles. I feel like I'm aware of my body.
>
> *Th:* How much would you say in your thoughts that aggression has in it compared to with the manager incident? [*Bracing: experience of rage while linking current event to the transference.*]
>
> *Pt:* Oh, with this one I have to admit that I'm trying my best to think negative thoughts about you. So I have to admit, this one is lower.
>
> *Th:* Is there enough energy to do anything if it was uncontrolled by you? [*Pressure to portray.*]
>
> *Pt:* If it was uncontrolled by me?
>
> *Th:* What would it want to do if it was totally uncontrolled by you? If the third person is there again? [*Pressure, invitation to use another person to act out the rage in his fantasy.*]

Pt: Yeah, I can envision that person. [*Throws up both fists.*] Again the fists.

Th: Grabbing?

Pt: Grabbing and doing this, of all things, and getting up and standing up in a threatening way. [*Bangs his hands on his legs and pushes himself up in an aggressive posture, smiling while doing so with the simultaneous positive feelings.*]

Th: Over me?

Pt: Over you. And then I see you go like this again. [*Demonstrate my backing away frightened.*] It must have been a shock, but you're like "Jeez what buttons did I push?" That's what I envision.

Th: So intimidation and a threat.

Pt: A threat.

Th: Anything else? Would that expel it all if I was threatened and afraid? [*Pressure to portray.*]

Pt: Yeah, it would. Then it's almost like that guy has gotten your attention. Every fiber in your body's listening to him.

Th: Out of fear.

Pt: Yeah, out of fear, I guess, and undivided attention. Jeez, this sounds terrible, but now you're going to hear this person out. This person wants you to listen to him.

Move the Impulse Back to the Patient

Now the patient has felt this feeling to an extent and he is calm. Now I bring the rage back to him and me so he can experience it more with him as the agent. Note now I can use pressures without the need for bracing or recapping, a sign of improving capacity.

Th: That would be you, right? [*Pressure to own the rage.*]

Pt: Okay, yeah, let's go back to me. But I'm never going to act that way.

Th: But you know what I mean.

Pt: Yeah, I see what you're saying.

Th: So it would be intimidation of me for you to frighten me, and then I'm forced to attend to you.

Pt: Right.

Th: Forced to attend to you out of fear, right?

Pt: Exactly, you're right. You're forced to listen to me. When I get up and I'm towering over you, you're forced to listen to me. Anything that comes out of my mouth, you're forced to listen to.

Th: But how would you have felt if you had done that? [*Pressure to experience guilt.*]

Pt: I would have felt like shit if I actually went through that because that's not treating you with respect. It's not treating you as a fellow human being. I wouldn't do it to you. I couldn't. I would never do that to you. [*Weeps.*]

Th: This is a painful feeling—the idea of frightening me.

Pt: Threatening people or frightening people. Look now, you see that's something. Now why is that happening? Jeez, I can do so much just playacting with that, but I can't do it myself. And why the hell do I get like that? It doesn't make sense.

Breakthrough with Mix of Feelings and Regressive Defenses

Here we see some regressive defenses appearing as anxiety increased with the focus on this man's aggression and guilt. Now you can see why I used a third person to do the rage: owning the rage shoots his anxiety very high. With the complex transference feelings experienced, I am watching for the unconscious therapeutic alliance.

Th: You have a painful feeling in you about the idea of striking and threatening and intimidation.

Pt: Yeah, but I would never do that. I'm not going to hurt you. [*Cries, quite distressed, and pleads that he won't hurt me.*]

Th: Maybe we can take a look at it, right, because it is as if you did it. [*Recap: guilt.*]

Pt: Yeah. I'm not going to hurt you. [*Cries uncontrollably.*] Jesus Christ, I don't believe this. Okay, I'm sorry. [*Buries head in hands.*]

Th: There's something in this that's very important to you. [*Question to the unconscious therapeutic alliance.*]

Pt: What is it?

Th: I don't know. What is it you're thinking about? [*Question to the unconscious therapeutic alliance.*]

Pt: I don't want to hurt you! I'm not going to hurt you! [*Pleads and appears desperate.*]

Unconscious Therapeutic Alliance

At this moment the unconscious therapeutic alliance is gaining power. On a preconscious level I am not me. He is pleading to someone else that he will not hurt him.

Th: Let's take a look at it for a second.

Pt: I'm not going to hurt you, and I won't hurt anybody. But why is this coming? [*Unconscious therapeutic alliance speaks to himself.*]

Th: Where is all this pain coming from? [*Question to the unconscious therapeutic alliance.*]

Pt: I'm envisioning oceans and darkness and life rafts and ships sinking. I don't know. Complete blackness. What is it coming from? From something dark. [*Unconscious therapeutic alliance: negation and imagery.*]

Th: Let me ask another way. Who are you thinking about when you think about this intimidation?

Pt: My father. But why? What has he done? And I cannot . . . But I've never scared him . . . I've never had the strength. I'm just . . . I'm too young. [*Unconscious therapeutic alliance.*]

Th: Yeah, but when you think about it, at some time you wanted to.

Pt: Yeah, maybe somewhere I wanted to. I've never done this. Maybe I wanted to. I don't know. Why am I thinking of my father? [*Unconscious therapeutic alliance.*]

Th: Mm-hmm.

Pt: What did he do? What had he done in the past? [*Unconscious therapeutic alliance.*]

Recapitulation

From here we recap, linking feelings-anxiety-defense and past-current-transference relationships. With this recap the patient has transient cognitive-perceptual disruption as all defenses, including projection and repression, had been interrupted.

Summary

In this session we saw graded work to build the patient's capacity to tolerate a rise in complex transference feelings and the unconscious therapeutic alliance. We saw some structural changes in unconscious anxiety and defense where he could tolerate more rise without cognitive-perceptual disruption. (See fig. 16.5.) Ultimately the complex transference feelings were experienced enough to bring the unconscious therapeutic alliance up above the resistance. Clearly this is a major event, a first partial unlocking of the unconscious. The unconscious therapeutic alliance gained power in this session, bringing images of darkness, oceans, ships sinking, and his father. For now, we don't know what this means.

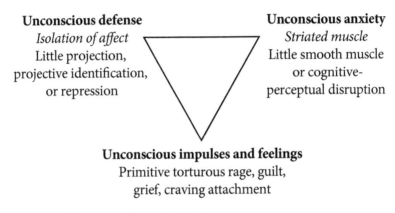

Unconscious defense
Isolation of affect
Little projection,
projective identification,
or repression

Unconscious anxiety
Striated muscle
Little smooth muscle
or cognitive-
perceptual disruption

Unconscious impulses and feelings
Primitive torturous rage, guilt,
grief, craving attachment

Figure 16.5 Changes with graded format

PHASE 3: SEVENTH TREATMENT SESSION—STRUCTURAL CHANGE AND UNLOCKING

We now review aspects of the seventh treatment session to illustrate further structural change and the technique of unlocking the unconscious. Note that this man can now tolerate pressure without much need for bracing or recapping.

Positive Feelings and Initial Focus

At the start of this session the patient reported that he was calmer in dealing with people. An incident happened where his wife was upset, but instead of becoming frightened and running out of the house, he helped calm her and comfort her. He felt very positive about this.

Pt: [*Sits with good tone in his body with hands clenching and no sign of projection or cognitive-perceptual disruption.*] This time I just kept thinking about you, and I thought, yeah, he's really actually a cool guy. I'm not going to get worked up in going to see him. [*Lack of projection.*]

Th: So when you were coming in this time you had a positive feeling with me then. Is that right? [*Pressure to experience positive feeling.*]

Pt: I did, I had a very positive feeling. I felt good and I said, yeah, I'm going to see him. And I started sort of chuckling to myself. I sort of thought humorously of you more than anything else.

Th: So how does the positive feeling feel when you feel that right now? [*Pressure to experience positive feeling.*]

Pt: It feels good, you know. It feels like I don't have a weight on my shoulders.

Th: Do you feel kind of a warm feeling? [*Pressure to experience positive feeling.*]

Pt: Yeah, I do.

Th: You do feel that inside you? [*Pressure to experience positive feeling.*]

Pressure to Experience the Positive Feeling

In this moment I am actually feeling this same way about the patient and using my empathic response to guide me. I am pressing for him to feel this positive feeling because it will be a catalyst bringing up any unresolved attachment trauma feelings as described in session three (see Vignette: Graded Work to First Unlockings).

Pt: Yeah, I do feel warm. It's like I don't have any tension, and I'm not worked up thinking that, you know, you're going to be critical of me or anything like that. [*Description of the absence of projection.*]

Th: Uh-huh.

Pt: I don't know how this ever happened. [*Negation.*]

Changes That Are Unconscious to the Patient

Fragile patients typically report they make gains, but they are unable to say why they are improved. As they do improve, they develop striated muscle anxiety and isolation of affect as opposed to repression, projection, and cognitive-perceptual disruption. These changes take place on an unconscious level so patients cannot consciously notice them at first.

Th: This is a positive feeling with me, right? [*Pressure to experience positive feeling.*]

Pt: Oh yeah, very much so. [*Sighs.*]

Th: So situations are bothering you less; you're finding things easier to deal with.

Pt: I'm finding things easier to deal with; that's right.

Th: And there is a positive feeling with me that you're aware of? That you notice? [*Pressure to experience positive feeling.*]

Pt: Yeah, there is. [*Sighs.*]

Th: So then how do you feel about the fact that we've done a hard piece of work and there are gains coming for you? [*Pressure to experience positive feeling.*]

Pt: I feel positive about it, but there are always these questions. [*Sighs.*] Last session I was in touch with the fact that I had rage toward my mother and that evolved out of her bizarre behavior.

Th: Uh-huh.

Pt: I often wondered about that issue with authority figures, but, you know, we've been down that road thinking about my father and everything like that. [*Unconscious therapeutic alliance forecasting what is to come.*]

Th: Uh-huh.

Pt: I mean, I suppose in complex ways, things do tie together, and we could probably spend a really long time trying to hook it all in.

Th: Uh-huh.

Pt: But the bottom line is that just discussing these feelings in the unconscious part connected things together and the feelings rose to the conscious part. We talked about doing that sort of thing, and consciously I thought about it and discussed it and chewed it over in my mind and that was it. [*His own understanding for the process.*]

Th: Uh-huh.

Pt: So to answer your question, it felt good. It seems like this last session we made a big breakthrough.

Th: There's a lot of positive in there.

Pt: There's a lot of positive.

Positive Feeling Mobilizes Guilt-Laden Rage

Perhaps one of the most underappreciated therapeutic factors is the catalytic effect of experiencing positive feelings in the transference. These feelings reach through to the core of the patient and his attachments and attachment longings. They also mobilize residual grief, rage, and guilt about thwarted attachment efforts and broken bonds. In short, pressure to the positive feeling in the transference can be a shortcut to major, repeated unlocking of the unconscious and in-depth changes.

At this point, I'm sensing a feeling of anger rising up and I ask about it.

> *Th:* What else is in you? What other feelings come when you have tension starting in the last few minutes? [*Pressure to identify feelings.*]
>
> *Pt:* Yeah, it's coming up here. [*Puts hand on his chest.*]
>
> *Th:* So what feelings are beneath, pressing up the tension? [*Pressure to identify feelings.*]
>
> *Pt:* Okay, it has to do with the fact that I'm thinking there's probably a hell of a lot of stuff that I'm burying. [*Unconscious therapeutic alliance heralding more feelings.*]
>
> *Th:* What else is just rising, though? How do you feel apart from the positive? [*Pressure to identify feelings.*]
>
> *Pt:* Okay, apart from the positive in all the good things that I really do feel . . .
>
> *Th:* Yeah.
>
> *Pt:* Do you ever feel evil? [*Moves hands up and down chest freely.*] We talk about anger and stuff like that.
>
> *Th:* Rage.

Pressure to Somatic Experience of Rage

Now I press to the somatic experience of the rage, helping the patient usher it upward.

> *Pt:* Rage and anger and that came up.
>
> *Th:* It's on the way up.
>
> *Pt:* It's on the way up and it's right up here (rubs left shoulder) and it's feeling—it's blocked right now.
>
> *Th:* Just in your left shoulder? [*Bracing: experience of rage.*]

Pt: Left, well, actually, the fact that I grabbed it was instinctively where I felt it first, but it's down both shoulders.

Th: How do you experience this rage that moves up into your body. How does that feel as it moves up through? [*Pressure to experience rage.*]

Pt: Okay, without it getting blocked by anxiety.

Th: Exactly.

Pt: Okay, you were talking about my positive feelings and now we're going to start talking about negativity. Things like that deep inside of me there's a ball of rage.

Th: Yeah.

Pt: Now the feeling is right here now. [*Puts hand on shoulder.*]

Th: How does it feel? [*Pressure to experience rage.*]

Pt: I feel it going. Actually, the funny thing is, I feel it up my back, which is a little bit different this time. And actually I felt it going up my neck, but it is different.

Th: Not tension, you mean?

Pt: Not tension.

Evidence of Structural Changes

Now the somatic pathway is much more mobilized than during previous sessions. Also note the complete absence of cognitive-perceptual disruption and projection. I can apply consistent pressure to mobilize the complex transference feelings. The patient looks much more neurotic as opposed to fragile now due to these structural changes. He now does his own bracing, self-reflecting, and pressuring to activate the rage; he is now a knowledgeable copilot in the process.

We will soon see that some of the neck pain and his statement that "my neck is killing me" was a product of projective identification and symptom formation (Davanloo 2005).

My task now is to supply solid pressure to help him experience the somatic pathway of rage.

Th: The rage part. [*Pressure to experience rage.*]

Pt: The rage part actually went into my neck.

Th: And then? [*Pressure to experience rage.*]

Pt: Because it's almost like I, I really do feel a little bit pissed off because . . .

Th: Without judging it or anything, see, when the rage is going up your body how does that feel? [*Pressure to experience rage.*]

Pt: It feels real fluid, but this is real anger because we were doing something positive. Now I can feel it in my arms. I feel clenching right now.

Th: Sort of in your hands?

Pt: In my hands.

Th: They want to clench.

Pt: They want to clench and I feel wanting to move around, wanting to do something.

Th: If you just let it be. [*Pressure to experience rage.*]

Pt: Okay, just let it be.

Th: Don't let yourself block it; that's the key. [*Challenge and pressure to experience rage.*]

Pt: Okay.

Th: Just let yourself feel it. [*Pressure to experience rage.*]

Pt: Okay.

Th: Don't block it. [*Challenge and pressure to experience rage.*]

Pt: Okay.

Th: How does it feel when that whole power is in you, unblocked? The whole thing. [*Pressure to experience rage.*]

Pt: When it feels unblocked, it feels like I want to get up and I want to go forward and do this. [*Makes grabbing motion with his hands toward therapist.*]

Th: Grabbing.

Pt: Yeah, grabbing. I want to grab you on the shirt is what I want to do.

Th: Do you feel that pretty good? [*Pressure to experience rage.*]

Pt: I feel that real strong feeling for some reason, yeah.

Th: How would you do that? [*Pressure to rage.*]

Pt: I would step up and I would do this. [*Makes grabbing motion, sits up tall.*]

Th: Do you feel it? [*Pressure to experience rage.*]

Pt: And I would grab you on the lapel of the shirt.

Th: Do you feel that pretty strongly though, or do you still have some tension? Is there still some anxiety there? [*Clarification of level of anxiety versus rage.*]

Pt: There's a little bit, yeah, right here. [*Points to shoulders.*]

Th: Okay, let's try to push this through. [*Pressure to experience rage.*]

Maximizing Somatic Experiencing

Here I'm pressing, as always, for the maximum experience of feeling the patient can bear. The research shows that if he can experience the somatic pathway of rage, then the guilt will pass, anxiety will drop, resistance will drop, and the unconscious therapeutic alliance will be dominant. This is the recipe for unlocking of the unconscious. Before this session his capacity was not great enough for this event. Note that I use cycles of mild pressure, holding focus on the body reactions of rage followed by higher pressure to the rage. It is a bit like dislodging a car that is stuck in the snow—first, you rock it several times and then push it out hard!

Pt: Yeah, I'm going to.

Th: Push it out. See the rage wants to be up through, if you don't clamp it down. [I *move my arms animatedly; pressure to rage, challenge to shut down.*]

Pt: Right.

Th: Don't block yourself down. [*Challenge to shut down.*]

Pt: Right.

Th: This is how we got what success we've gotten so far. [*Communication with the unconscious therapeutic alliance.*]

Pt: Yes, that's right.

Th: Because you've let this push through.

Pt: Yeah.

Th: How does that rage feel when it's pushed up through you though? If you go strong. How strong is it? [*Pressure to experience rage.*]

Mirror Experiences

Through empathic attunement I am feeling some of each of his feelings. This emotional experience in me helps me know to press up the somatic pathway, move to guilt, move to grief, and perform my other interventions. Through the same mechanism you may note some genital sensation when rage has a sexual component to harm in a sexual way. When your own physical self-awareness allows you to mirror the patient and we aren't afraid of our feelings, we can be with the patient when he goes through the hell in the unconscious. The patient is no longer alone: he is joined by you as a witness to what he went through that caused such pain and rage. Now we focus on the impulse of the rage.

> Pt: I feel it in my hands. I want to grab you. I feel it more in my head actually. [*Experience of rage: tension has dropped, arms move freely.*]
>
> Th: Uh-huh.
>
> Pt: And, the other thing is there's something that feels like there's another feeling where I want to actually cry. [*Starts to tear up.*]
>
> Th: At the same time, you mean?
>
> Pt: At the same time there's a sudden urge like that.
>
> Th: Once you grab me, you mean?
>
> Pt: Yeah, I'm just visualizing.
>
> Th: What do you see, grabbing me? And then what do you feel?
>
> Pt: Grabbing and then at the same time getting upset.
>
> Th: What do you do to me? [*Pressure to portray.*]
>
> Pt: I actually grab you by the shirt.
>
> Th: Yeah.
>
> Pt: And I'm grabbing you like this is what I'm doing, and I'm giving you a shake. [*Moves hands in grabbing motion.*]
>
> Th: Shaking me. Like boom. [*Shakes with his hands.*]

Removal of Anxiety and Resistance

At this point there is absolutely no tension. The patient has experienced the somatic pathway of rage, and guilt is now coming. Through the somatic experience of the rage, the anxiety is completely removed. Thus, the anxiety-driven resistance is removed. This means that now the unconscious therapeutic alliance is free to take an upward position over the resistance. Imagery from the unconscious is soon to arrive. All of this is evidence of major structural changes in this man at the level of unconscious anxiety and defense. He is no longer fragile.

Pt: Shaking you like that. [*Shakes his hands back and forth, confidently, with good eye contact.*]

Th: And then what do I do?

Pt: Then you're stunned or you're going to defend yourself and that's it. That's the anger.

Th: What does your whole rage want to do though? [*Pressure to portray.*]

Pt: It almost wants to leap out of my body.

Th: And do what? [*Pressure to portray.*]

Pt: The energy wants to go out and grab you, and it actually wants to do something physical. [*Moves arms in pushing motion.*]

Th: Pushing me, you mean? [*Pressure to portray.*]

Pt: Pushing you is what it wants to do.

Th: And then what? [*Pressure to portray.*]

Pt: And then I feel it going away.

Th: So you shove me back and forth a few times.

Pt: That's it, and then it goes away.

Th: And then what happens? [*Pressure to portray.*]

Pt: Then I almost feel silly. I feel like "What have I done?" and then it's just the energy going away right now. [*Resolution of the somatic rage.*]

Guilt

With the somatic rage passed, now guilt moves into consciousness.

Th: What do you do with me after you did this to me? I'm here shocked and stunned and afraid.

Pt: I stand up. I apologize, and I'm not going to run. I'm going to apologize profusely. I'm going to cry probably. I feel totally guilty like "How much of a moron can I be?" "Can you forgive me?" [*Sympathy.*]

Th: When you see my eyes and the pain in my eyes . . . [*Pressure to the eyes and bond.*]

Pt: Yes, I do.

Th: How do you feel when you see the eyes there in the image? [*Pressure to feel guilt.*]

Pt: I feel like a piece of shit. Like, what I've done to you is something terrible . . . See, right now just thinking about it makes me feel like I want to cry because I've hurt you. I've hurt a friend. I don't do things like that to a friend. [*Cries.*]

Th: This is painful.

Pt: Again, it's guilt. So what we're seeing is the anger going right to guilt. But the anger always wants to go through the hands. It always wants to grab. It wants to get physical for some reason or other. Ideally what I'd like to see the anger do is go into the head and just be there. Just deal with it in that way. [*His own solid recap.*]

Another First

Through these seven sessions the patient is aware of the patterns and somatic pathways. He is also aware that he has never in his life, until this moment, experienced anger without the contamination of the old feelings, anxiety, and defense. He is longing just to feel emotions with a person without those old blockages.

Recapitulation and Communication from the Unconscious Therapeutic Alliance

We recapitulate to empower the unconscious therapeutic alliance and let it direct the process since the anxiety and resistance are now removed.

Th: See, there's something here though. There's this pain and guilt tied into this experience, you see. [*Recap: guilt.*]

Pt: That's true.

Th: This is when you go depressed and anxious. [*Recap: symptom formation.*]

Pt: Yeah.

Th: Even before you would get confused. [*Recap: cognitive-perceptual disruption.*]

Pt: That's right, that's right.

Th: But this is the rage turning at your body, right? [*Recap: self-attack.*]

Pt: Yeah.

Th: Because of the guilt. [*Recap: self-attack.*]

Pt: That's right.

Th: There is guilt as if you just did this to me. [*Recap: guilt.*]

Pt: Yeah, I can actually mentally envision doing something like that to you; it's all so real.

Th: Yeah. So see here you have guilt, but you didn't do anything.

Pt: I didn't do anything. It's all in my mind.

Th: So this is our question: what are your thoughts about this pocket of rage that is there? [*Question to the unconscious therapeutic alliance.*]

Pt: Yeah.

Th: The guilt that is stirred up when you had the positive feeling with me. Because look at the way it goes. It wants to generate anxiety in you. [*Recap: feelings-anxiety.*]

Pt: Yes.

Th: You see, but there's a pocket of these mixed feelings inside you there. [*Recap: feelings.*]

Pt: That's right.

Th: What do you think this is related to? This wave of rage and evil, as you say? [*Question to the unconscious therapeutic alliance.*]

Pt: Yeah. It's almost like a core of the evil. It's like rivers . . . It's just like something in me that just wants . . . I want to break; I want to hit; I want to . . .

Th: Who is in your mind when you want to think about this evil rage and wanting to get violent and break? [*Question to the unconscious therapeutic alliance.*]

Pt: Right off the bat, I thought of my father instantly as soon as you said that. [*Unconscious therapeutic alliance.*]

Th: Was he in your mind? You mentioned him earlier actually.

Pt: Yeah, but I didn't consciously think about him, but, just then, first in my mind I thought of a river for some reason or other, and then I thought of my father. [*Unconscious therapeutic alliance: imagery.*]

Th: A river and your father? What do you mean?

Unconscious Therapeutic Alliance

At this point the memory systems are activated as the unconscious therapeutic alliance is activated. The resistances have ceased functioning and the patient is clear to remember and feel part of the emotional roots of his longstanding fear and self-destructive system.

> *Pt:* I don't know why that came to my mind. [*Unconscious therapeutic alliance: negation.*] It's the first thing, a dark river, brown with bits of foam on it. Why that's associated with anger I'm not sure. [*Unconscious therapeutic alliance: negation.*] You know there was something. I remember my father did something to me. I remember I was on a ferry with him one time. I was young, four years old, of all things. I can remember this. I remember him picking me up and holding me over the edge of the ferry like he was going to dump me over the edge into the water. [*Unconscious therapeutic alliance: imagery.*]

Actual Reexperiencing of the Event

With this image and memory, the patient is mentally on the ferry being held over the edge. You will see he can feel the father's sweater, and if I had asked, he could smell the salt air. He is experiencing the rage about that event now with adult capacity to feel.

> *Th:* What do you feel when you see him holding you over the rail? [*Pressure to identify feelings.*]
>
> *Pt:* It's actually a feeling of terror at that time, but what I want to do now is grab him. [*Grabs with hands.*]
>
> *Th:* You feel that? [*Pressure to portray the rage.*]
>
> *Pt:* Yeah, I feel it. I feel it with a wooly sweater that used to be knitted a long time ago, and I envision like a panic, and I'm grabbing onto his sweater like this. [*Demonstrates with his hands.*]
>
> *Th:* Yeah.
>
> *Pt:* And I want to grab onto it. That's the feeling I actually have.
>
> *Th:* To grab.
>
> *Pt:* Thinking about it, yeah, to grab onto it.
>
> *Th:* And then what does this rage want to do though? [*Pressure to portray rage.*]
>
> *Pt:* The rage is thinking as a man right now.

Th: Yeah.

Pt: That's what I'm doing, and that's the anger going right in my fingertips. [*Somatic pathway.*]

Th: To do what to him? [*Pressure to portray rage.*]

Pt: First thing is to grab him, and I'm almost playing the drama in my head that we're on the ferry and I grab him and I push *him* against the railing.

Th: Push him on the railing. [*Pressure to portray rage.*]

Pt: Push him on the railing, twirl him around, and actually *grab him on the back of the neck* and say, "How would you like this?"

Now the Symptoms Make Sense

Only after these later sessions do we understand many somatic symptoms patients have. You will recall the black liquid going over his head and the blackness before the cognitive-perceptual disruption. Recall the urge to throw himself out the window. Recall that he said his "neck is killing" him.

Th: Put him on the rail. On the edge.

Pt: Yeah, on the edge and say, "How would you like this?"

Th: And what is the rage doing to him? [*Pressure to portray rage.*]

Pt: It actually feels like, and this is hard that I'm doing this, actually grabbing him and pushing him against. The rage just feels like all physical, physical.

Th: Yeah. To do what? [*Pressure to portray rage.*]

Pt: Physical. Grabbing him on the back of the neck. [*Demonstrates with his hands.*]

Th: Yeah.

Pt: And holding him and saying, "How would you like if I dumped you in the water?" It's almost like what I'll do is grab him by the belt or something and just hold him. I know I'm not going to physically do it, though I want to bloody well lift him up. [*Shows how he would hold the father's body over the water.*]

Th: By the belt and his head is down, you mean? [*Pressure to portray rage.*]

Pt: Yeah, his head is down.

Th: Where's his head? [*Pressure to portray rage.*]

Pt: His head is dangling and he's terrorized because I'm doing this and he can't believe it.

Th: Then he's terrified.

Guilt

The somatic pathway of rage has passed now and guilt is moving in.

Pt: Yeah, but the funny thing is, he's not really even fighting back. He's sort of shouting like, "Son, don't do this to me." But, you know, the anger is going. Now I'm thinking about sympathy. Like how could I do this and there goes the guilt again. [*Cries.*]

Th: How terrified he must be, just like how you felt. [*Pressure to feel guilt.*]

Pt: Yeah. The guilt comes about right now, the eyes water up and I'm thinking I wouldn't do that to him and wondering why am I having these feelings toward him. [*Cries and wipes tears.*]

Th: There is a pain when you think about terrorizing him like that.

Pt: Yeah, there is as it would with anybody. But I hadn't thought about that.

Second Component of Impulse

Now that the patient has experienced some rage, guilt, and positive feeling for the father, he is free to experience the deeper, murderous rage.

Pt: Jeez, you know, honestly if I wanted to let go, I just feel like I had the power to let him go. If you want to ask me something . . . [*Unconscious therapeutic alliance reveals deeper rage.*]

Th: Yeah.

Pt: I had power over him. I had power over him. I'd have let go of his belt. [*Shows letting go with his hands.*]

Th: And then the darkness coming around him?

Pt: Yeah, he'd know what it was like. But this is all in my mind and it's not that it happened. It happened that he did this to me though.

Th: This terrified, this terrorized you.

Pt: Yeah it did, it really did.

Th: And this is why this rage is there, but if he's drowning down and life's going away and he's going into the blackness . . . [*Pressure to feel guilt.*]

Pt: Yeah.

Th: And you terrorized him. How do you feel that you did that? [*Pressure to feel guilt.*]

Pt: He got his own. I got him back, but it's such an ultimate thing to do. I mean, okay, I did it; he's going under the water. It's a conflict. There's still that anger that says that I got him back, then is this being tempered with remorse. Then, you know, the logic that sure enough, he's going to die. What else can you do with him? That's the ultimate as far as murdering him. [*Unconscious therapeutic alliance alluding to more intense rage underneath.*]

Th: You murdered and drowned him.

Pt: He's drowned. He will never, ever learn. He will never, ever know. There's no way that he'd ever know now, but I've murdered him in my mind. That's what I've done.

Follow the Imagery

Now we must follow the imagery to see that guilt can be experienced.

Th: When they drag up his body and he's drowned, how do you feel when you see him? When they found his dead body after you drowned him?

Pt: You know what, I don't have any feeling about it. [*Unconscious therapeutic alliance: negation.*]

Th: What do his eyes look like when you see his body come out of the water?

The Eyes

The early bond is primarily through eye contact, so we focus on the eyes of the dead father.

Pt: His eyes are open. His face is white. His hair is back with water and mud. But his eyes are open. His mouth is open, too. That's the one thing I see. I look at his body and I just sort of step back like—it sounds terrible—like I won. [*Satisfaction.*] But I shouldn't feel that way, should I? [*Rise of guilt.*]

Th: That's tough [having both feelings].

Pt: Why the eyes are open, I don't know. [*Unconscious therapeutic alliance: negation.*] That's what I see.

Th: What do you see in his eyes when you look right in his eyes? How do they look?

Pt: They're pointing upward to heaven. [*Very painful wave; chokes up with guilt.*] They're lifeless. There's not any life in them. Okay, I'm feeling guilty about this but also, there's a sense of satisfaction. A sense that I've joined things. That I've done it.

Th: There's a relief.

Pt: It's a relief.

Th: To get the rage out.

Pt: Yeah, it's almost like I've done the evil deed and that's it.

Th: But then his eyes are looking at heaven and looking at you.

Pt: Yes, okay, looking at me. I come up to the body and look at it and it's almost like, yeah, you know. It's come to conclusion. I do look at his eyes and I know in a sense that they're looking at me, and I know they're lifeless, but for some reason they're looking up into the sky and I see the blue sky reflecting in them for some reason or other. I see blue, which is actually a positive color. That's it.

Pt: I hadn't gone to that sort of conclusion before, but maybe it's something that I always wanted to do. [*Weeps heavily.*]

Th: It's very painful.

A Gift for the Father

We see that after the murder of the father, there is some love for the father, too, symbolized by giving the religious father the gift of his blue eyes gazing at heaven in his death. The patient was able to see positive feelings for the father mixed with the rage, guilt and grief. This is a good example of what is meant by the terribly complex feelings that become buried and destroy a developing child.

We now move to the phase of consolidation at the end of this one-hour session.

Th: There are a lot of painful feelings—the same as with your mother. These mixed feelings are there. [*Recap: mixed feelings.*]

Pt: It's mixed, but my logical mind's kicking in now saying who the heck would want to murder his parents. I mean, that's something that kids don't think about. But, if I want to start thinking about my mental health, perhaps it's good that I've exorcized this and just thought about killing them.

Th: If we look at it on the one hand, those feelings are there when you had a positive feeling with me, right? With the idea of victory and the positive feeling and things going well and the hard work and "you and me" and these things, right? [*Recap: positive feeling as trigger.*]

Pt: Yeah.

Th: But then what starts to happen with the positive feeling? You see what happened is the rage moves up. [*Recap: complex feelings.*]

Pt: That's right.

Th: It's like your father reached up from out of the river saying "How dare you feel positive with him when you killed me down here?" [*Recap: guilt.*]

Pt: Yeah. [*Looks a bit shocked and moved by this analogy.*]

Th: You follow me?

Pt: Yes, I do follow you.

Th: So it's like "How dare you?" He wants to drag you down into that river with him. Right beside him. But that's within you though, right? [*Recap: guilt.*]

Pt: Yeah.

Th: And the guilt is there but inside you also there was a rage because it was a terrifying experience. [*Recap: feelings.*]

Pt: Yeah.

Th: You know, for a four-year-old, that's a terrifying experience.

Pt: Yeah, yeah.

Th: It stirred up a murderous rage in you that he did that.

Pt: Yeah, it did actually; it did.

Th: But then also guilt about the rage, and then the fear that if you murdered him then you're alone with his dead body—and then the guilt about murdering him. [*Recap: rage and guilt.*]

Pt: Yes.

Th: So then where did all that go from age four? Where did all those feelings get buried in you?

Pt: Yeah, they just get buried into the subconscious.

Th: It was under the fear, wasn't it?

Pt: Yeah, terror.

Th: At that moment, terror of going into the black water. [*Recap: trauma.*]

Pt: Yes, that's it. I'm grabbing on for my life. You know, literally grabbing on.

Th: Then in a sense, what he did was generate a murderous rage in his son, wasn't it?

Pt: Yes. One of revenge that I wanted to get him back but I couldn't do that then, and I just felt really terrified after that. [*Projection.*] I didn't want him to do that to me again, but these are things that just flash through my mind when you talk about the anger. That's exactly what went through my mind and I'm having difficulty understanding why it picked that moment in my life, but it was there. [*Unconscious therapeutic alliance.*]

Collaborative Development of Narrative

Here we collaboratively build on and enrich the narrative portrait of this man's psychological development.

Pt: Normally at age four you don't really remember all that much, but I do remember that. Certain things I do remember when I was four, definitely. The public park and stuff. But that was one of the things I do remember.

Th: So the positive feelings. See, we've seen before that positive feelings trigger the rage. And then the rage has guilt tied into it and you see here with me there's guilt as if you'd grabbed me.

Pt: Yes.

Th: And terrified me, you see?

Pt: Yes.

Th: Like you were terrified really. You see, as if you did to me what he did to you.

Link to Session Three

Recall now session three where he was pleading with me "I'm not going to hurt you." He is both the father terrorizing him and himself terrorizing and murdering the father. This helps us have a clear understanding of his projective processes at work, at home, and with the therapist.

The resolution to this is clear: he must actually experience his complex feelings about the past and the present to stop needing to destroy relationships and himself.

Th: But then your mind saw this black river with foam.

Pt: Yeah.

Th: And then your father is there, and then you're over the side and then this murderous rage. So in a sense the positive feeling with me triggered off this series of feelings. [*Recap: positive feelings as trigger.*]

Pt: Yeah, yeah.

Th: The rage itself triggers off other positive feelings, and the positive feelings trigger off a rage. [*Recap: complex feelings.*]

Pt: Yeah.

Th: You see, it's like a flow.

Pt: That's right. It's almost like one can't go without the other. I am very honest; when I came in here, I was very positive. It was overwhelmingly positive toward you.

Th: Yes, is that back again now?

Pt: It's coming back again actually.

Th: So we see underneath all these things are positive feelings toward people. [*Recap: drive for attachment.*]

Pt: Yeah, yeah.

Th: But it's buried under the rage and the guilt and the pain and the defense mechanisms that block it out, right?

Repetition

Notice the major amount of repetition with restating of the linkages in several ways to tie all the phenomena together. This repetition is critical for strengthening the unconscious therapeutic alliance, for weakening the resistance, and for symptom reduction.

Pt: That's right.

Th: So we see that your natural self has been blocked under these feelings and the mechanisms that you've used over the years to cover up those feelings.

Pt: Yes, whether it could be anxiety or it could be the different personality quirks.

Th: Doing different things in a split second to hurt yourself or get at someone. You said, too, that in one second you've had these moments to get revenge on someone and you don't even know why. See here with me in one second, you see?

Pt: Yeah.

Th: These feelings come up with me, but then it's from back there in the past, you see? [*Recap: transference.*]

Pt: Yes, that's right.

Th: See, in one second you wanted to get revenge at age four. [*Recap: transference.*]

Pt: Yeah.

Th: But in the next second you could be anxious here with me and then your thought is as if you're going to get him. [*Recap: projection and transference.*]

Pt: Yeah.

Th: In a second, unconsciously it's like I'm him and you get anxious with me. [*Recap: projection.*]

Pt: That's right; that's right.

Th: As if I'm going to do that to you and then you're going to do it to me in a second, unconsciously. [*Recap: projection.*]

Pt: Yeah, that's right. I mean, that's what goes on. Like we're grappling with each other.

Th: Like the very first meetings, you remember?

Pt: Yes.

Th: You recall how the anxiety was very high when you first came in and you would even get confused. And there were strong feelings sitting under there. And we were looking to see why there was so much anxiety with me when you were coming in to talk with me. [*Recap: anxiety pathways, tying other sessions together.*]

Pt: That's right.

Th: And what we see is these old pockets of strong feelings that are sitting there create the anxiety here with me as if you're going to drown me and do these things to me. [*Recap: two triangles.*]

Pt: Yeah, I want to hit you, punch you, drown you.

Th: As if it has something to do with me, actually.

Pt: That's right.

Th: Versus that it's all feelings just making their way into the room.

Pt: Yeah.

Th: Generating anxiety in you.

Pt: Yeah.

Th: And then it's self-punishment. You would go depressed. You would go anxious and shut down. [*Recap: self-punitive.*]

Pt: Right.

Th: As if you have to protect me from something.

Pt: That's right. Yeah. I'm using you as a tool basically for all this, quite clearly.

Structural Change

Let's review this patient's increased capacities. He can now experience strong complex feelings, enabling activation of the unconscious therapeutic alliance. The unconscious therapeutic alliance enables direct access to guilt-laden rage from his childhood. Feeling the guilt reduces his need to self-defeat and self-sabotage—he sees himself as a loving person rather than a guilty criminal. Anxiety is in the form of striated muscle tension rather than cognitive-perceptual disruption, so he can maintain a clear consciousness while experiencing these feelings. Projection and projective identification are now replaced by isolation of affect, so he is no longer frightened of people. Since he no longer projects upon me, he is not afraid that I will attack him. The reductions in projection rapidly change his relationships at work and home. All of these changes enable him to experience higher levels of complex transference feelings, a process that further fuels the unconscious therapeutic alliance, yielding even greater access to the unconscious.

PHASES 3–5: MILD TO MODERATE FRAGILE CHARACTER STRUCTURE

Now the treatment process goes to repeated unlocking of the unconscious, working through, and termination. These phases in mild to moderate fragile cases are similar to those of high resistance with repression.

- *Repeated unlocking:* Repeated unlocking usually entails between twenty and on hundred unlockings of increasing intensity and going to earlier and earlier phases of life. Some of these unlockings will be in very early life phases including infancy.

- *Working through:* Working through involves experiencing many passages of guilt and grief, consolidating the understanding, reconnecting with family members, and improving current life function. Typically passages of painful feelings occur about lost time, self-harm, suffering one has caused others by suffering oneself, and lost opportunities. Guilt about having suicidal ideation will be experienced, as if one has murdered oneself and caused terrible trauma to the family this way.

- *Termination:* If the treatment is short, under forty sessions, then termination is a few sessions. If treatment goes longer with more in-depth work, then the process of termination is a few months. The concept of termination in a successful collaboration brings any unresolved rage and guilt to the surface. You can see in the previous vignette that we keep an eye on the impact of eventual successful termination as a catalyst that brings any of these unprocessed attachment feelings to the surface. The dead bodies will reach up from the grave saying, "How dare you succeed with him when you slaughtered me here!" We can then help the patient experience these old feelings and thereby pave the way for further affectionate bonding without the anchors of this guilt dragging her down.

CHALLENGES IN WORKING WITH PATIENTS WITH FRAGILE CHARACTER STRUCTURE

Therapists face multiple technical issues and challenges with regard to fragile character structure patients.

Monitoring Thresholds

Monitor the threshold to cognitive-perceptual disruption or primitive defenses closely. Missing when the process is above threshold can be a significant problem as projection can increase. The patient may become afraid of the process or go flat with repression or both.

Transference Focus and Rise in Complex Transference Feelings

To keep hope going up and anxiety low, and to fuel the developing unconscious therapeutic alliance, maintain a focus in the transference to bring rise in the complex transference feelings as much as possible. This rise further builds anxiety tolerance and desensitizes the patient to talking with you about difficult thoughts, feelings, and images.

Regressive Defenses versus Feelings

Monitor for the presence of anxiety and regressive defenses to distinguish regressive defenses, like weeping and tantrums, from actual feelings. Without this monitoring, these regressive, relationship-destroying defenses will be reinforced.

Missing the Passage of Complex Transference Feelings

First breakthroughs to the unconscious look different in these patients than with other groups of patients. All you may notice during the first breakthroughs is a rapid rise and fall in anger in your body followed by a passage of sadness about being neglected in the past. This can be subtle. Use your own body cues as well as the cues in the patient to detect when the unconscious therapeutic alliance (e.g., negation, whispers and linkages with a drop in anxiety) is beginning to operate.

The Suicidal Patient

Many patients with acute suicidal ideation are close to unconscious rage and guilt. The driving force for suicidal ideation is a rise in unconscious rage, which triggers unconscious guilt. The patient wants to kill himself to protect the people he loves from his unconscious murderous rage and to punish himself for having this rage. During this period the patient may not be using repression or other defenses excessively. Thus, what looks like a disaster may be a golden opportunity to gain a major breakthrough into the unconscious rage, guilt, and grief. However, thresholds to projection and instant repression must still be monitored and the graded format applied as required.

The Patient Who Is in Projection and Defiance

Many fragile patients move to a projective and defiant stance. At these times becoming punitive or accepting the role of the projection and then challenging a patient will increase the projection and defiance. Such therapist action can defeat the treatment. When projection happens, restructure it by bringing in higher-level defenses of self-reflection about the projections. Once the projection is undone, defiance disappears and the therapeutic alliance returns.

Countertransference, Splitting, and Boundary Issues

Intense complex feelings seen with fragile patients can mobilize intense countertransference feelings that can result in splitting, projection, and cognitive-perceptual disruption in the therapist. Under cognitive-perceptual disruption and projection, the therapist is at risk of breaching the patient's boundaries, acting out, and contributing to splitting between healthcare professionals. Because this work is emotionally so challenging for therapists, psychotherapy with fragile character structure patients should be done only with adequate training and support. Balancing the view of self and others is a key component to continued professional growth and successful therapy with these populations (Abbass 2004; Abbass, Arthey, and Nowoweiski 2013).

OUTCOMES

As a group, fragile patients tend to do reasonably well in the hands of a moderately trained ISTDP therapist (Abbass 2002a). About two-thirds of fragile patients benefit and maintain gains after treatments averaging forty sessions in completers. Dropout was seen in 15.4 percent while nonresponse and return for more treatment were each seen in 11.5 percent. Sixty-four percent returned to work from disabilities averaging four years. Longer treatments appear to provide better outcomes. Greater therapist experience also appears to improve outcomes with this challenging population. Symptom reduction was greater in fragile patients than in nonfragile patients in a recent study, but baseline symptoms were higher to begin with in the fragile group (Johansson, Town, and Abbass 2014).

Mild to moderately fragile patients have suffered early neglect, deprivation, and major trauma. They have unconscious primitive torturous murderous rage and intense guilt plus an intense craving of closeness. They have primitive defenses, repression, and cognitive-perceptual disruption, resulting in chronic personality dysfunction and symptom disturbances. They require capacity building using bracing and graded format in a process similar to the work with highly resistant patients with repression.

CHAPTER 17

Severe Fragile Character Structure: Fractured and Frightened

pproximately one-tenth of private-psychiatric-office-referred patients have severe *fragile character structure* or what is more commonly called *borderline personality disorder.* This primary disorder of self-functioning is compounded by severe resistance of guilt
or *punitive superego.* Biological factors including genetic factors and
brain injury predispose individuals to this condition.

These patients have also typically experienced massive emotional
trauma in their early attachment relationships; hence, they have repressed primitive torturous murderous rage and guilt about the rage.
They have lifelong primitive defenses including temper tantrums, poor
impulse control, projection, projective identification, splitting, dissociation, and cognitive-perceptual disruption with hallucinatory experiences (Davanloo 2001). They may have no anxiety whatsoever in cases
where psychic forces are manifested as projection, splitting, projective
identification, and repression. (See fig. 17.1.)

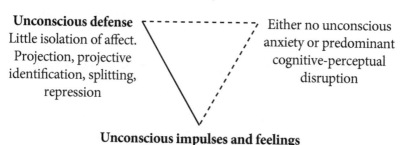

Unconscious defense
Little isolation of affect.
Projection, projective
identification, splitting,
repression

Either no unconscious
anxiety or predominant
cognitive-perceptual
disruption

Unconscious impulses and feelings
Primitive torturous rage, guilt,
grief, craving attachment

Figure 17.1 Severe fragile character structure

Under such mechanisms, these patients tend to have high levels of fear and distress and are prone to substance abuse, eating disorders and addiction (Abbass, Arthey, and Nowoweiski 2013). They have little ability to self-reflect and isolate affect. Their many behavioral problems are due to interactions with projected, split parts of the self. In addition, they may have powerful instant repression of rage and guilt. These primitive defense mechanisms occur at a very low rise in unconscious complex feelings, so they may be present throughout early treatment sessions. (See fig. 16.2.) These mechanisms create severe interpersonal problems, including countertransference responses in therapists.

On a psychic level the split parts are all players of the psyche that include torturer, victim, and punitive dictator who is demanding suffering. Part of the punishment is the process of being fractured into pieces so as to have no genuine human relationships as an integrated person. While some of the split parts may be torturers, the overall process of splitting is itself the torture. The threat of actual human contact, including with a therapist, can cause a reaction of intense self-torment manifested as combinations of cognitive-perceptual disruption, projection, splitting, self-attacks, and severe depression.

These patients are very difficult to treat, and a cautious approach is warranted in providing any form of psychotherapy: various support structures—such as peer review, team rounds, and psychiatric backup are required for your initial therapy work with this group. This chapter reviews some aspects of the advanced, modified ISTDP framework applicable with this group (Davanloo 2001). These modifications go beyond the standard graded format described in chapters 15 and 16.

TREATMENT PHASES OF SEVERE FRAGILE CHARACTER STRUCTURE

Treatment involves initial assessment, an extensive phase of multidimensional structural change including graded format, repeated unlocking, working through, and termination. Table 17.1 illustrates these phases and associated tasks.

Table 17.1 Treatment phases with severe fragile character structure

Phase	Task
Initial evaluation	Management of barriers to engagement, detection of the rotating system fronts, psychodiagnosis, evaluation of thresholds, and determination of pace of treatment. Development of conscious therapeutic alliance.
Multidimensional structural change	Psychic integration yielding first experiences of unconscious anxiety. Then graded format to build capacity to overcome projection, cognitive-perceptual disruption, self-attack, and repression. Building of capacity to bear complex feelings.
Repeated unlocking	Experience of repressed pain, primitive rage, guilt, and craving of attachment. Dominance of the unconscious therapeutic alliance.
Working through	Mobilization and experience of residual grief, rage, and guilt. Consolidation. Emergence of empathy for family members. Self-directed compassion.
Termination	Closure of the therapy relationship over ten to twenty sessions. Experience of residual emotions.

Phase 1: Initial Evaluation

Similar initial processes and issues arise with this group as with mild to moderately fragile patients.

Barriers to engagement may include serious behavioral problems such as starvation from an eating disorder or substance abuse necessitating combined treatment. In general, these types of behavioral problems are relative contraindications to ISTDP; it is wise to consider delaying treatment until medical stabilization is achieved. Chronic suicidal ideation and episodic substance use or self-harm are not a contraindication to beginning treatment: these behaviors usually settle quickly after initiation of treatment because of increased hope and decreased conscious anxiety and projection.

The *system fronts* include projection, projective identification, suicidal ideation, idealization, devaluation, repression, self-attack, and dissociation. Similar to the case in chapter 16, these mechanisms may rotate very rapidly.

Psychodiagnostic evaluation will yield little to no unconscious anxiety, little capacity to isolate affect, and the presence of only primitive defenses and repression. Unconscious anxiety and projective defenses take more than thirty minutes to bring down: the patient may be in projection throughout the first sessions.

Conscious therapeutic alliance will begin to form through the study of these various phenomena in a nonjudgmental, forthright, and supportive fashion. Through this work the patient will gain trust in you and confidence that the hard work of psychotherapy will be beneficial.

Case Vignette: Initial Evaluation

This is the middle of a trial therapy session of a young woman with severe fragile character structure. The patient displays primitive defenses and absence of striated muscle anxiety and isolation of affect.

Pt: I have major problems with people.

Th: Can you tell me about that?

Pt: Yes, once I went to my doctor for a prescription and he refused to give it to me. As soon as he said no to me, I knew he didn't care. [*Split: all caring or not at all caring, rejecting.*] I told him I wasn't going to leave his office. [*Defiance in response to the projective identification of not caring.*] Then he got his secretary and each of them took one of my arms. He was enraged, screaming. [*Projection.*] Then I went off on them, and punched her right in the face and kicked him in the crotch. They let me go after that. [*Smiles and laughs.*]

Th: That is quite a thing to have happen.

A few minutes later she describes more interpersonal problems with her boyfriend.

Pt: If my boyfriend wants to leave, sometimes I won't let him leave. When he is leaving, I'm convinced he must hate me. [*Split: all loving or all hating and rejecting.*]

Th: How does this affect you?

Pt: I just go crazy in myself. I block the door and sometimes even threaten him or threaten myself. So if he wants to go, he has to punch me. I'll do anything to make him stop.

Th: So when he's going, it switches to that he hates you. What is it like if he turns around and stays?

Pt: Then I know he loves me. [*Split: all loving.*]

Th: So is it that when he goes to you, you feel he is really loving you, but when he leaves, it is as if all of a sudden now he hates you? [*Clarification of the splitting.*]

Pt: Yes, this stuff can't be normal.

During this entire session, the patient presented with no signals of unconscious anxiety and she had no representations of an integrated multidimensional self and other. The splitting of self and other into parts created massive distress and behaviors the patient regrets.

PHASE 2: MULTIDIMENSIONAL STRUCTURAL CHANGE

This phase includes methods to bring psychic integration and graded work to build psychic capacities. This restructuring phase tends to take over twenty one-hour sessions and must be achieved before the unconscious therapeutic alliance can be activated.

Psychic Integration

Severely fragile patients use splitting, resulting in multiple personality fragments. The "presenting" personality (the patient) is frequently internally bombarded with these multiple, simultaneous split parts as she tries to engage with you. For example, severe fragile character structure patients with eating disorders often have two or more opposing ways of identifying both self and others:

>   Mode A: identify with "thin" people—hostile, driven, food restricting, independent, critical and loathing of "fat" people

>   Mode B: identify with "fat" people—passive, binge eating, dependent, laid back, critical and resentful of "thin" people

Depending on her current mode and which mode she sees others in, the patient may have a range of reactions including idealization of self and devaluation of others. She will also wonder whether you are a mode A or a mode B type: without therapeutic neutrality and awareness of your own self and your own biases (e.g., idealizing or despising thinness, seeing her as a "victim needing rescue" or "abuser needing punishment"), splitting can become amplified in treatment.

Related to this process, severely fragile patients use *instant projection*: the patient will view others as having the emotions that she herself has. She may then react to this in a complementary (afraid of your anger) or concordant (hostile toward you because of your anger) fashion. Without self-reflective capacity and ability to isolate affect, she cannot see her internal experiences.

To overcome this projection and splitting with self-reflective capacity and isolation of affect, examine how the patient sees others and himself. Then draw parallels between the self-perceptions and the projections to help him see that these are the same thing. This work allows the patient to begin to understand that, "What I see out there is really me." By recognizing inside himself what he previously projected outward, projection and projective identification are gradually overcome. This realization gives rise to grief as he begins to see the damage his projections have caused.

Battle Resistance of Guilt

As this work proceeds, help the patient continually build capacity for self-regard to balance *self-punitive* elements due to the powerful resistance of guilt: the patient must have internalized strength to battle the self-attacks that will come as she tries to exit the torture chamber.

Battle Instant Repression

Much in the same way as in chapter 15, instant repression is handled with graded work. Repression can be one of the rapidly rotating fronts to handle, or it may be more dominant during a state of depression in severely fragile patients.

Impact of Phase 2 Work

In the early phase of treatment we replace primitive processes with higher-level defenses of isolation of affect. This results in unconscious anxiety in the forms of cognitive-perceptual disruption and smooth muscle and striated muscle anxiety. Restructuring of defenses and anxiety restructures unconscious feelings. Specifically, intense underlying emotions rise more slowly so prefrontal cortex self-reflective centers can manage what would otherwise be a flood of intense affect. These changes are detectable in brain imaging studies (Abbass, Nowoweiski, et al. 2014).

THERAPIST ACTIVITY

Certain technical recommendations that apply to working with this population include the following:

- *Monitor response—verify suitability:* You need to be reasonably sure that the patient will benefit from and have no untoward effect from this therapy. If no gains occur from this type of treatment after a series of sessions, either consult a peer or do not use this approach.

- *Clarify tasks:* Make the patient aware of the current process, task, and benefits of doing the work so he can become a willing partner. Clarify this information repeatedly.

- *Maintain emotional engagement:* Be active, emotionally engaged, transparent, and distinct from what the patient projects. Maintain a general stance of positive regard for the person working hard and developing. This stance counters harsh self-attacking tendencies and prevents projections from fixing on you.

- *Conduct an intellectual examination:* Early work with these patients is primarily intellectual exploration toward building self-reflective capacity. The technique of bracing—using combinations of reflection and mild pressure interventions simultaneously—is very useful as it helps activate prefrontal cortex reflective centers in concert with some emotional activation. Help the patient see her thoughts, motives, and feelings and how all these link together in an intellectual nonjudgmental fashion.

- *Identify any feelings toward you; avoid fixed projections:* Preemptively examine projections before they fix on you. Be an ally, distinct from any projective identification. Examine projections in current situations from the start with an eye out for when they coalesce in the treatment relationship. Keep the therapeutic relationship clear by cognitively identifying any trace of feelings toward you.

- *Keep a rise in the transference:* Focus on the specific task at hand. For example, help the patient understand his difficulties, explore himself, and examine his thoughts. This focus keeps pressure up, which keeps some rise in the complex transference feelings. The rise in complex transference feelings begins to activate the unconscious therapeutic alliance. Thus, pressure keeps hope up and conscious anxiety relatively low. Working at some rise in the transference also gives a steady dose of complex feelings the patient can become desensitized to; this exposure helps build anxiety tolerance.

- *Keep moving:* Frequently change "stations." Focusing on one area or topic for too long will raise the patient's anxiety over threshold into projection. For example, move from one current incident to another current incident to the process in the office with recapping in between.

- *Use neutral validation as opposed to splitting:* Validate all aspects of the patient's experience. Do not take sides for or against any of the split parts. Your role is only to examine and acquaint the patient with the split aspects of the self. To label one part as "good" or "bad" is splitting by the therapist that may result in misalliance. Neither side is the resistance; rather the process of splitting itself is the resistance. Mirror all aspects of the patient to bring psychic integration. This basic acceptance of what is allows her to make changes later.

- *Don't challenge:* Challenge is reserved only for resistant patients who crystallize their resistances in the transference. (See chapters 10, 13, and 14.) Since severely fragile patients do not crystallize their resistances in the transference, challenge is not warranted. Challenge is highly likely to cast you in the role of some split, projected, punitive part.

- *Know yourself:* countertransference: Working with this group of patients mobilizes intense complex feelings in therapists that can result in splitting, projection, boundary violations, and other difficulties as described in chapter 16. This work requires self-knowledge, anxiety tolerance, and capacity to experience one's own feelings.

PSYCHIC INTEGRATION VIGNETTE 1: WORKING WITH PROJECTIVE IDENTIFICATIONS

The patient is a young woman with alternating anorexia and bulimia. She has both "thin" and "fat" modes described above and alternates between these split views of self and other.

Th: Can you tell me about a time you find it difficult with people?

Pt: Yes. I can't stand my boss. She acts as if she is so perfect with her skinny tight clothes. She brags that she only has a cigarette for breakfast. [*Devaluation of thin-mode boss by fat-mode patient.*]

Th: So you don't like her approach to you?

Pt: My friend and I just want to take our time there and she keeps pushing us.

Th: How do you react to her? [*Mild pressure, encouragement of self-reflection: emotions.*]

Pt: I can't stand her. She keeps bugging us to speed up at work. I like to take my time at work and relax with my friends. [*Mutual idealization of laid-back fat mode. Devaluation of thin mode.*]

Th: So this is one example. How does that affect you? [*Mild pressure, encourage self-reflection: emotions.*]

Pt: It just makes me so mad at her. [*Devaluation of projected thin mode by fat mode.*]

Th: How does that feel inside?

Pt: I just want to binge. [*Devaluation of the thin mode acted out by going to an extreme fat mode.*]

Th: It gives you an urge to binge?

Pt: Yes.

Th: So can you tell me about how it goes with the binge eating?

Pt: Yes. I get so worked up sometimes after work, I have to eat and eat. I don't even notice I'm doing it until a whole bag of chips is gone. [*Description of dissociation while bingeing.*]

Th: Then what happens?

Pt: Then I'm just disgusted with myself. I feel so fat. I think that if I don't get the food out, I may as well kill myself. So I end up either throwing up or cutting myself. [*Self-hating of her fat mode by her thin mode.*]

Th: So one way it can go is to be mad at you sometimes and feel like bingeing? [*Clarification of phenomena.*]

Pt: Yeah.

Th: And this is triggered by being mad at the boss?

Pt: Yes, I can't stand her skinniness and pushing us. [*Devaluation of the projected thin mode.*]

We continue to explore her reactions and the projections that set off the reactions.

Th: What happens after some days of bingeing? [*Exploration of sequences.*]

Pt: Then I don't eat for a day almost. Then I usually exercise at the gym a whole lot. [*Thin mode.*]

Th: What is it like with the people in the gym when you go there? [*Exploration of impact of projection.*]

Pt: I go with my friend Amanda who is a fitness instructor, skinny as a rake! I love to hang out with her at the gym. [*Idealization of thin mode by thin mode.*]

Th: What is it like to work out with the other people there? [*Exploration of impact of projection.*]

Pt: We are there laughing at all these tubby (obese) girls. We just laugh at them. [*Devaluation of fat mode by thin mode.*]

Projective Identifications

Here the patient is flipping between combinations of two projective identifications. You can see the various combinations of these two modes between self and other, all of which are problematic distortions of reality.

Th: What do you think is happening with this? It sounds like sometime you have more like an exercising thin mode and then a more laid back eating mode. Is that right? [*Use of nonjudgmental language, clarification of split parts.*]

Pt: Yes. I'm never in between.

Th: And when you are in the exercising mode how do you feel about those obese people? [*Clarification of impact of splits.*]

Pt: I can't stand them. I think, "Can't they just hide away somewhere?" [*Devaluation of fat mode by thin mode.*]

Integration

Recapitulate to integrate these split parts to bring a realistic picture of self and other.

Th: It sounds like at times you feel two different ways that seem opposed. In one mode you are relaxed and tending to binge eat more but in the other you restrict more, exercise more, and eat less. [*Clarification of splitting.*]

Pt: Yes.

Th: And one mode is critical of the other but expressed in different ways. [*Clarification of splitting.*] The thin mode is outwardly

critical of the bigger people, and the relaxed mode is quietly critical of the thin, driven people.

Pt: Yes, that's right.

Th: So one question I have is, are these all really just parts of yourself out there that you are interacting with somehow? Just different modes of you reflected in others? [Clarification of projective
identification.]

Pt: [Opens eye wide, slows, tending to cognitive-perceptual disruption.]
I think so.

Th: Because that can explain the distress you feel when you go out.
You are trying to see if a person is a "thin" or a "relaxed" person.
Then trying to see if you are in a thin or relaxed mode. Either way
could be stressful. [Clarification of the impact of splitting.]

Pt: Yeah.

Th: If they are in thin mode and you are thin mode, are you both
okay together? But the others (mode B) seem bad when you are
with a thin-mode person. And what about when you are in a
relaxed mode? What do you think about the thin people then?
[Examination of effects of splitting, pressure for integration.]

Pt: [Becomes drowsy.]

Th: What just happened? Did you get a little cloudy headed?

Pt: Yeah.

Th: Okay, when we review all these together, you become anxious.
[Recap: integration and anxiety.] So is this what happens as we
talk about these different modes?

Pt: Yes. It's okay right now.

Th: What about the relaxed-mode times? How do you feel about the
thin ones? [Exploration of reactions to splits.]

Pt: We don't like them but won't say anything about it.

Th: So there is active criticism from thin mode but more passive
criticism from relaxed mode? Do you think you are alternating between these modes and then seeing the modes in others?
[Examination of effects of splitting, pressure for integration.]

Pt: [Appears a bit cloudy headed with cognitive-perceptual disruption.]

Th: You get a bit anxious on this again?

Pt: Yes.

Th: So do you think this helps explain the turmoil in you and when you are with others—as if parts of you hate other parts of you?

Pt: Yes, I can see that.

Th: And you are either one or another mode while others are in one or another mode, like there is no in-between. [*Recap: projective identification.*]

Summary

This is an example of early work exploring split parts toward psychic integration. The process is highly cognitive and tightly focused. Each intervention is built to encourage nonjudgmental self-reflection. Recaps are built to encourage psychic integration. This work brings rise in the complex transference feelings, providing desensitization to these mixed feelings. This tacit challenge to splitting tends to result in anxiety in the form of cognitive-perceptual disruption. All this examination of split parts paves the way for further integrating and graded work to build capacity. This collaborative work also builds the conscious therapeutic alliance.

PSYCHIC INTEGRATION VIGNETTE 2: WORK WITH SELF-HATRED AND PROJECTION

A single mother with two children is the patient.

Th: What are your thoughts on how life is difficult for you?

Pt: I think everyone is laughing at me. [*Projection, no signals of anxiety.*]

Th: So you think this way? [*Encouragement to self-reflect.*]

Pt: Yes, when I'm out, I think people are always laughing at me.

Th: Is that right? [*Encouragement to self-reflect.*]

Pt: Yes. If someone is laughing, I assume it's at me.

Th: So your mind interprets that people don't like you. [*Recap, encouragement to self-reflect.*]

Pt: Yes.

Th: Is that with everyone?

Pt: No, not with my children. [*Mutual idealization, no projection of hatred.*]

Th: How do you feel about yourself? [*Exploration of self-regard.*]

Pt: Well, I hate myself.

Th: Really. Why is that? [*Encouragement to self-reflect.*]

Pt: It's been like that for years since I gained thirty kilograms.

Th: What impact does that have on you? [*Allusion to projection of hate.*]

Pt: Well, it can't be good.

Th: I wonder what it does. Do you think it is related to what you expect of others? [*Clarification of projection of hatred.*]

Pt: [*Stares, tending to cognitive-perceptual disruption.*]

Th: So there is some negative expectation in your mind. You are expecting negative and have negative in your mind, so you assume others think that, too. [*Clarification of projection.*]

Examining Projections and Self

Here we examine the parallels between the projections and internal parts of the self. The therapeutic objective is to override projective processes by seeing that parts of the patient are being projected outward; this reflective process brings psychic integration and interrupts the defense of projection. With the defense of projection interrupted, anxiety momentarily spikes in the form of cognitive-perceptual disruption.

Th: Is this happening here with me, too? [*Focus on the transference.*]

Pt: [*Stares; transient cognitive-perceptual disruption.*]

Pt: It's not as much here but more in the mall or grocery store, for example.

Th: In the mall, in public?

Pt: Yes, even if a car goes by and the people in it are laughing, it must be at me.

Th: So you assume people hate you and laugh at you.

A moment later the patient continues.

Th: You don't think the world likes you and inside yourself you hate you, too. [*Clarification of projection.*]

Pt: That's right, and I hate myself as well.

Th: So why is that there? Do you accept this thought? [*Pressure to positive self-regard.*]

Pt: I accept it because I don't know any different.

Th: So you think you don't deserve the good things?

Pt: That's right.

Th: So this is a strong force in you. What can we do about it? [*Pressure to positive self-regard.*]

Cyclic Projection of Hate and Self-Hate

This process of circular projection and the turning inward of rage is very common in severely fragile patients. Focus on these rapidly rotating fronts to replace each with isolation of affect.

Th: What does it do to you when that is in your mind? [*Clarification of impact of self-hatred.*]

Pt: I beat myself up over and over. I can't resist beating myself.

Th: What happens here in this office if you try to reject that negativity and replace it with a good feeling for you? [*Pressure to positive self-regard.*]

Pt: I don't feel it's real.

Th: When I say "what if you have a good feeling for yourself?" what happens? [*Exploration of impact of positive self-regard.*]

Pt: I reject it.

Th: It sounds like you reject the good feeling from coming in and absorb the bad you expect others to feel. [*Recap: projection.*]

Pt: Yes, that's right.

Th: When we are here to have a good feeling for you, what happens? [*Pressure to positive self-regard.*]

Pt: I don't believe it. I hate myself. [*Self-attack.*]

Splitting and Self-Punitive Behavior

Here we see the patient hold tight on the self-attacking, based on projection and harsh self-hatred. She has self-devaluation and projects this devaluation. No signals of unconscious anxiety are present, but I am constantly having the patient reflect with me through the use of recaps. Each of my statements is an intellectual probe delivered in a neutral way with no sign of judgment. My comments are all validating of her experiences. I'm holding a stance of general positive regard for her *as she was meant to be* versus these destructive splitting and self-punitive behaviors. This therapeutic stance gradually causes an internalization of positive regard and ability to nonjudgmentally see and modify these processes. This challenging process also mobilizes complex transference feelings and early elements of the unconscious therapeutic alliance.

Th: When we sit here and say you could have a good feeling for yourself, not hate yourself anymore, what happens here with me? How do you feel about that? [*Pressure to positive self-regard.*]

Pt: Hatred upon myself. [*Self-attack.*]

Th: So when I say "have a good feeling for yourself," you go to self-hatred. [*Recap: self-attack.*]

Pt: Yeah.

Th: So anger goes in on you when I put out a good feeling to you. It [the overall resistance] disagrees with what I say. [*Recap: feelings make self-hatred.*]

Pt: Yes, immediately. It's hard to stop this after many years. I can't just flip a switch and stop it. [*Sounds a bit irritated, experiences complex feelings with me.*]

Th: So if you go out and something good could happen, you erase the positive potential with a self-hate each time. [*Recap: feelings make self-hatred.*]

Pt: Yes.

Th: What can we do about that? [*Pressure to positive self-regard.*]

Pt: I have to get more positive somehow.

Th: Let's see what we can do here, now. [*Pressure to positive self-regard.*]

Pt: Okay.

Th: When I say "have a positive feeling about yourself," what happens? What are the steps? [*Examination of impact of positive self-regard.*]

Pt: It's a bunch of bad thoughts.

Th: Do you get any feelings? [*Pressure to identify feelings.*]

Pt: No. None.

Th: Do you have a positive feeling about what I'm saying, even for a second? [*Pressure to experience positive feeling.*]

Pt: There is a bit of hope we can fix this, but my head says "forget it."

Th: What is the positive feeling stirring up? [*Pressure to experience positive feeling.*]

Pt: Calmer inside my body. A relaxed body.

Focusing on Positive Self-Regard

The efforts we just saw, including pressure to positive self-regard, yield some benefits in the form of a momentary state of calmness. These brief experiences, caused by active examination, collaboration, and pressure to self-caring, fuel the conscious therapeutic alliance. As these patients have harsh self-punitive systems because of guilt, we can expect a backlash of anxiety and projection. The patient's punishing dictator, her punitive superego, demands suffering for all the crimes she has done. Some of this suffering is the process of projection, and some of it is direct self-attacking.

> Th: How do you feel about having that for a moment? [*Pressure to positive feeling.*]
>
> Pt: Good. It's very foreign to feel this way.
>
> Th: How do you feel about this? What would it be like to always have a piece of good feeling for you? [*Pressure to positive self-regard.*]
>
> Pt: That would be great. [*Looks sad.*]
>
> Th: There's a bit of sadness about the fact that you haven't had a good feeling about you come in from anyone in a long time.
>
> Pt: Most definitely. [*Sniffs away tears.*]
>
> Th: Because you didn't do any terrible crime to deserve this.
>
> Pt: I want to have this for my children and me. [*Wipes tears.*]
>
> Th: So this system has been so hard on you. As soon as anything good could happen, you get this self-attack and expectation of negativity and then hate yourself. Like it's a crime to feel good. [*Recap: linking positive self-regard to self-torture.*]
>
> Pt: That's right.

Retreat from Positive Self-Regard

Pressing this woman to take in a positive self-regard mobilized complex feelings and a brief moment of positive feeling pushing back the self-punitive dictator. Is this acceptable? Is she allowed to feel good about herself? A minute later the backlash comes in the form of projection.

> Pt: I'm so self-conscious. I keep thinking my boyfriend must hate me.
>
> Th: Does that happen here, too, now? What thoughts pop into your mind here with me? [*Exploration of projection in the transference.*]

Pt: That you must hate me, too. [*Instant projection.*]

Th: What did you think I thought? [*Exploration of projection.*]

Pt: Thoughts that you think I'm stupid.

Th: What feelings stirred up with me [before she projected]?

Pt: I just got anxious [*Stares, slows down.*]

Feelings, Projection, Cognitive-Perceptual Disruption

Here we see a rapid wave of cognitive-perceptual disruption when I pressed on what feelings she had creating her projection. She flipped from instant projection to cognitive-perceptual disruption when I focused on her internal feelings. In essence, the focus on the projection blocked her from using projection and caused complex feelings to manifest as cognitive-perceptual disruption.

Th: Can you tell me what happened in your body? [*Recap to reduce anxiety and to self-reflect.*]

Pt: My heart is beating fast and my head got a bit cloudy. [*Cognitive-perceptual disruption.*]

Th: Okay, all this happened as I asked about the feelings here with me. First the focus was on the positive feeling you felt, and as soon as we did that, the idea came that I had a negative view of you. This thought stirred up some feelings that very quickly circled back into high anxiety. [*Global recap.*]

Pt: Yes, that's right. [*Slightly lower anxiety, tendency to hyperventilate.*]

Th: Did you get a look at the feelings before you got anxious and had this negative response toward yourself and fear of my reactions? [*Bracing: feelings to anxiety.*] What do you feel with me before you got anxious in your body? [*Pressure to identify feelings.*]

Objectives

Here I'm recapping, intellectualizing, and pressing in various areas. I keep moving and focusing on the rotating front. These actions are not aimed for breakthrough to the unconscious but rather to bring rise in complex transference feelings and to better understand her system with her. This process builds her ability to self-reflect and tolerate anxiety.

Pt: It was almost resentful. [*Declaration of negative feeling.*]

Th: Did you notice that in your body beforehand? [*Bracing.*]

Pt: Only a second, then the thing went all back on me. [*Improved self-observation of self-attack.*]

Th: Okay, there were some feelings with me: the positive and frustration, but this turned into thoughts I'd have a negative at you. This caused more resentment and that went back in on you. That's exactly the process. It's very fast. [*Recap: instant projection and self-attack.*]

Pt: Yes, exactly. It's like I felt bad about the resentment. [*Mild irritation, but listening and very engaged.*]

Th: Yes. It's like you had to get beat up for what you did to me. [*Recap: guilt and self-punishment.*]

Guilt: Psychic Glue

Here I'm pressing on the single emotion that integrates all the complex feelings and zeroes in on the causes of much of her psychopathology: guilt. If she can recognize and hold guilt consciously, her anxiety tolerance will increase, her need to suffer will reduce, and empathy for herself will increase. Even cognitive awareness of the guilt can be beneficial.

Th: What do you feel like you did to me? [*Pressure to hold all these things together and identify guilt.*]

Pt: Nothing. [*Smiles slightly.*] I know it doesn't make logical sense.

Th: Okay, it's like you did something to me and this caused a self-attack and the idea that I would also be mad at you. Then the whole circle went around again. [*Recap: guilt and projection.*]

Pt: Exactly.

Th: Then that drove up the anxiety, which can cloud up your thoughts or make your body react. [*Recap: guilt and anxiety.*]

Pt: Exactly.

Th: But when you feel positive for a second, your mind and body relax—but then that sets off this whole cycle. [*Recap: attachment drives feelings, anxiety, and projection.*]

Pt: Yes.

Th: Positive feeling pulls up some negative feelings and that makes guilt about the resentment. But the guilt and self-hating go into ideas that I'd be mad at you somehow. That immediately goes to more anger, which makes more guilt. So then the mixed feelings stir up guilt, as if you hurt me somehow? [*Recap: complex feeling-guilt-projection.*]

Pt: Yes.

Th: It's so fast, like one frame of a film: super fast going from one to the next.

Pt: That's right.

Th: So how would you feel if you had really been angry with me and put me down? [*Pressure to feel guilt.*]

Pt: Horrible. [*Cognitive awareness of guilt.*]

Th: So that's painful for you to think of putting someone down. [*Underscoring guilt.*]

Pt: Yes, anyone else but me. [*Looks sad.*]

Th: So guilt comes for having done nothing to me, but it's like you did. Then you go punishing yourself and putting yourself down and expecting others to do that, too. Then you have more anger at them, then more guilt, then more anger at yourself. [*Recap: instant projection and self-attack.*]

Pt: Exactly. It's a circle. [*Appears somewhat foggy headed and slows in the middle of this recap.*]

Th: Can you tell me about another time this type of thing happened?

Summary

This vignette is a typical piece of early work with severely fragile patients emphasizing complex feelings, guilt, anxiety, projection, splitting, and self-attack. This work builds capacity to self-reflect, isolate affect, and tolerate mixed feelings with me. It increases psychic integration and reduces splitting. It also opens the door to express and feel any emotions that rise in the treatment process.

First Experiences of Unconscious Anxiety

When primitive defenses diminish, unconscious anxiety will manifest for the first time, usually as cognitive-perceptual disruption. Restructuring the projective defenses helps patients to better contain themselves. Relationships start to improve as, for the first time, the patient begins to use his anxiety to self-regulate instead of projecting on others. For example, the patient will drift and fall asleep with rise in unconscious feelings instead of harming himself or others in response to projections. Confused about this new phenomenon, some patients will go to a doctor or neurologist; doctors may start new medications because of misunderstanding the meaning of this therapeutic development to a more integrated, anxious state.

DEACTIVATE SELF-ESCALATING PROJECTIVE PROCESSES: GUILT

Severely fragile patients can have cycles of projection and secondary emotional response to projection that in turn mobilize emotions that are projected. For example, if the patient perceives a hostile threat, she may respond with rage. Due to guilt about this rage, she will project that others will punish her. In response to the punishment she feels more rage and guilt that in turn cause more projection of punishment. (See fig. 17.2.) This cycle can lead to an acutely paranoid state or regressive behavior. The solution is to help the patient see that she has guilt about rage: pressure to feel guilt is a powerful, integrating, and empowering technique that de-escalates this process.

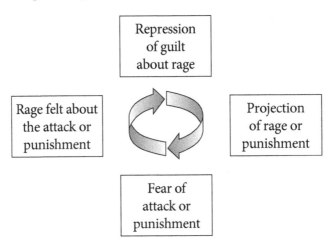

Figure 17.2 Cycles of guilt and projection

INTERRUPTION OF SELF-ESCALATION: VIGNETTE 1

The patient is a young man with a history of paranoid personality disorder with fragile character structure. He had a past episode of anger and guilt with a former boss that converted into auditory hallucinations telling him to hang himself. He was noted for becoming agitated and fighting what he projected. He would go to the coffee shop and begin to yell at people he perceived to be hostile. He would self-escalate into a paranoid state of hostility, isolation, and fear. This was then followed by depressive states with suicidal ideation. This process is common in patients with severe fragile character structure and in some patients with psychotic disorders. By session thirteen, this patient had improved awareness of his psychic processes and was having some bodily anxiety.

Focus on Specific Incident

With focused pressure, the patient was able to have a low-level experience of the somatic pathway of violent rage with an urge to punch his boss.

Th: How do you feel after you punched him down? [*Pressure toward guilt.*]

Pt: I'm thinking he deserved it for what he did.

Th: But how do you feel about you hurting him? [*Pressure toward guilt.*]

Pt: I don't care. You know, sometimes I think it would be better if I were a violent person. [*Still in projection the boss had harmed him.*]

Th: But how do you feel to hurt this man? [*Pressure toward guilt.*]

The Meaning of No Signals

This absence of signals means you need to examine where the dynamic forces are going. (See chapter 7.) In patients with severe fragility the lack of signals usually means they are using projection. No signals means worry and search!

Pt: Now when we are talking, I start to see the camera and . . . you have all these tapes about me beating people. [*Instant projection of guilt.*]

Th: What are your thoughts?

Pt: I keep thinking that someday these are going to be in court. That's not helping me, is it?

Th: Now why did that just come to your mind?

Pt: When I see a camera, I think about court and the recording being used against me.

Th: What you're telling me is your concern is someone is going to say you are guilty.

Pt: Yes. Yes.

Th: But whose idea is that? That's your idea. Your idea is you are guilty of damage. But you haven't done any damage.

Pt: Something may happen.

Th: But this came to your mind right now when we were talking about this rage. So I wonder where the guilt went?

Pt: [*Nods repeatedly in agreement.*]

Th: I wonder how you would really feel if this man is bleeding on the floor here and your knuckles had done it. How do you feel? This is another human.

Pt: I would feel anxious. [*A move away from projection to ambivalence about his action.*]

Th: Uh-huh.

Pt: I'd probably vomit. [*A move to smooth muscle anxiety away from projection.*]

Th: Uh-huh.

Pt: I'd feel a bit relieved to do it. [*Positive part of feeling the impulse.*]

Th: I understand [the positive aspect], but how else do you feel when you see his eyes and bleeding and your knuckles did it? [*Pressure to experience guilt.*]

Pt: [*Draws a large sigh, moving to striated muscle anxiety: projection is overcome!*] In today's world, that's not acceptable. [*Some guilt.*]

Th: So in one second you have both feelings: to hurt him and guilt about wanting to hurt him, as if you did it. [*Recap.*]

Pt: Yeah.

Th: What would you do with him if you did that?

Pt: I'd help him up. I don't hate him really.

Th: You see, the feelings are both there. Two feelings at the same time.

Pt: Uh-huh.

In this vignette he had a small experience of the complex feelings. This experience is adequate to link phenomena from the past to the present and to build greater anxiety tolerance. At the next session this patient reported a marked reduction in his anxiety symptoms, and he arrived with striated muscle anxiety.

INTERRUPTION OF SELF-ESCALATION: VIGNETTE 2

This young woman with borderline personality disorder had alternating self-harm, aggressive actions to others due to projection and depressive features. By session twelve she had improvement in capacity to self-reflect and she brought feelings about being wronged by her brother, who was the family "golden boy." He is split part number one.

>　*Pt:* I was thinking this week of going away to see him and get back the things he took from me in the past. I was thinking I want to go up there and kick the shit out of him. [*No signals of anxiety.*]

>　*Th:* To go see him, and how would that go in your mind?

>　*Pt:* I'd go up there and bring the police. [*Split part number two.*] That way he couldn't stop me from getting back my things.

>　*Th:* And then what happens?

>　*Pt:* Then he tries to fight back but I kick and punch him and he goes down the stairs. [*Smiles.*]

>　*Th:* Unconscious? Or how badly injured?

>　*Pt:* Unconscious and bleeding from his head.

Cognitive Process

Because we had spent previous sessions together working on a cognitive framework to examine situations, this lack of signals was not worrisome for me since the patient was attempting to intellectualize and isolate affect; she was defining the characters (split parts) for us to piece together.

>　*Th:* Then what happens?

>　*Pt:* Then I call my mother to come up, and I tell her to clean up the damn mess. [*Another split part: her mother.*]

>　*Th:* What happens when she arrives and sees your brother bleeding there?

>　*Pt:* She yells at me, but I kick her hard right in the chest.

>　*Th:* Then what?

>　*Pt:* She's on the floor holding herself, scared of me.

What to Do Next

Up to this point this woman has described three people who reflect split parts of herself (neglecting mother who should be punished,
ideal brother who should be arrested, police who should punish others) that she interacts with. Her actions tend to create these projected
attributes. Now that she has mentally done violence, I move to help her
see that she is missing aspects both of herself and others in this split-up
picture.

> *Th:* What do you do then with your brother there with a damaged
> head?
>
> *Pt:* I just want him to stay down [so she doesn't have to hit him more].
> [*Looks at the floor where he is lying.*]
>
> *Th:* How is that to see his eyes, your brother's eyes, after you do this to
> him? [*Pressure to recall the longing for attachment with the brother.*]
>
> *Pt:* I'm getting a headache right now.

Projective Identification and Symptom Formation

This is the process of sympathetic reaction called *projective identification and symptom formation* (Davanloo 2005). The guilt about the
rage takes the form of the identical symptoms the victim would have.
Here she develops a headache after damaging the brother's head. She
cannot yet consciously understand what is happening.

> *Th:* What about your mother? What happens when she is kicked in
> the chest and terrified? Does she have another . . .
>
> *Pt:* Yeah, maybe she would have another heart attack.
>
> *Th:* How is that when she has another heart attack after you beat her?
>
> *Pt:* I'm getting chest pain . . . on my left side. [*Slows down and looks to
> where her mother is on the floor.*]

Press for Guilt to Counter This Projective Process

Focusing on positive feeling for the mother will bring more structural integration that may eventually enable the patient to feel guilt
about the rage. Now I focus on the positive feelings for the mother,
pressing an integration of positive feelings and rage about the mother's
neglect.

> *Th:* How bad would you feel to do this to them? [*Pressure toward guilt.*]

Pt: I don't feel bad. They deserved it.

Th: How do you feel to see your mother's eyes with a heart attack and damaged brother? [*Pressure toward guilt.*]

Pt: I don't see that.

Th: What do you think is happening when you talk about this? What are we missing?

Pt: What do you mean? [*Sounds irritated; rise in complex feelings with me.*]

Th: Well, maybe part of you didn't want to do harm to them. [*Pressure toward guilt.*]

Pt: Well, I'm a logical person, so I prefer logic to violence. But when people are illogical then I have no choice.

Th: That's right? You prefer logic. So how bad is it for you to do harm to your mother and brother?

Pt: [*Sighs: move to striated muscle anxiety.*] I wouldn't want to.

Structural Change

Dramatic structural change is taking place by pressing for the patient to be *whole*: to realize she wants *love* and is so upset by the *interrupted attachments* of the past. She hasn't had the bond she needs to pull all this together and heal. We must help her see all of her self, including the buried drives for affection, pain, rage, and grief. Focusing on *guilt about rage* is a potent way to achieve this.

Th: We see this has been a very painful issue in your life: being second to your brother and always feeling like an outcast. You have always wanted to be loved and have been hurt so badly. [*Feeling of grief for her.*]

Pt: Yes. I remember just now a time I stabbed him in the face with a pencil when I was about nine. How terrible that would have been if it hurt him badly.

She experienced complex feelings on a primarily cognitive level; however, this is adequate to bring further psychic integration and gains in anxiety tolerance. The following session this woman arrived with positive feelings and striated muscle anxiety. This session was a turning point, a first small breakthrough to the unconscious enabling more anxiety tolerance.

Summary: Guilt and Healing

These key change sessions underscore the power of psychic integration and the nature of structural change in unconscious anxiety when love can be consciously experienced with rage. Helping the patient experience guilt about rage is a very potent approach to counter projection and self-escalation processes in fragile patients and select psychotic patients. Each time this process has been worked through, I've found it to have positive effects on patients' emotional capacities.

RESULTS OF PHASE 2 WORK: MORE INTEGRATION

During phase 2 we create integrated patients with unconscious anxiety and some growing capacity to self-reflect and isolate affect. They will structurally be akin to moderately fragile patients. Some patients will experience smooth muscle unconscious anxiety while on the way to higher anxiety tolerance. When the anxiety is in the smooth muscle, the cognitive-perceptual field is clear and projection has ceased, so this is a mark of clinical improvement. This advance should not result in the prescription of medication for somatic symptoms. (See fig. 17.3.) Instead, this development directs the therapist to use graded work to build anxiety tolerance.

Preparatory work done to this point provides a foundation, an internal structure, for the patient. It helps to develop capacity to be anxious and begin to tolerate this anxiety. This work helps the patient to begin to develop a more mature defensive system.

Now unconscious signaling will tell the therapist how to travel the road toward the unconscious. This road is without the major structural damage that previously prevented such a journey.

PHASES 3–5 WITH SEVERE FRAGILE CHARACTER STRUCTURE

All this preparatory work leads to the phase of *repeated unlocking* of the unconscious with dominance of the unconscious therapeutic alliance over the resistance. These unlocked feelings and impulses become increasingly intense and come from earlier and earlier stages of life. Early unlockings look similar to those in chapter 16. Later breakthroughs are more akin to those shown in chapter 15 with repeated high-level breakthroughs of intense rage for several minutes followed by distinct waves of intense, physically painful guilt. Primitive murderous rage precedes primitive torturous murderous rage and guilt. The unconscious therapeutic alliance operates at a high level producing images of the primitive unconscious, which enables passages of guilt. The unconscious therapeutic alliance also brings vivid memories of positive moments that in turn bring grief about thwarted attachment efforts and losses.

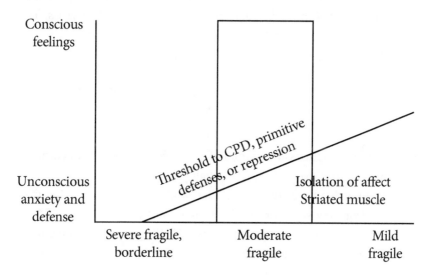

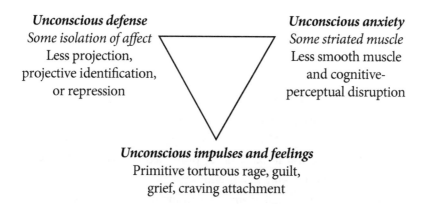

Figure 17.3 Early changes in severe fragile character structure

The phase of *working through* has a major emphasis on grief and pain of the losses associated with the attachment trauma. Love and understanding of the parents emerges. This understanding of self and others comes with increasing compassion for self. A process of de-shaming takes place where the patient can see that he had been projecting self-hatred to create a frightening world and to self-harm and deprive himself of love. Grief and guilt about self-harm is experienced as well as grief about delayed social development and lost years. This working through translates into greater physical self-care, occupational improvements, and new healthy relationships.

Vignette: Working Through in Patient with Severe Fragile Character Structure

This patient had paranoid personality disorder with past psychotic states. This vignette is after a total of nearly one hundred unlockings of the unconscious over one and one-half years.

Pt: One thing I've noticed in the last while is the guilt is coming apart from my sense of self. It's to the point that I ask myself "why would I punish myself that much?" The guilt has nothing to do with any bad behavior I've done either. It's been fused into my identity. It's all guilt based. Any guilt from anywhere, I would take in. Even if I did something to benefit me, it caused guilt. It was completely false and based on no reality.

Th: We saw that the love, rage, and guilt had been fused into a ball.

Pt: That's right.

Th: And what we've been doing is defusing these so the feelings can be felt.

Pt: That's exactly right; it's been separating these out.

Th: We saw this guilt can be projected out.

Pt: Or worse, I could become the scapegoat and take in everyone else's guilt. But now, I can see other people's roles and question them before taking in any guilt.

Th: It's been a tight ball of emotions from the very early phase of your life.

Pt: And the ball of feelings was so tight, I was just in it. I couldn't see it because it was all me. That ball of fused feelings has come apart now. I can see it. That [fusion] had a huge negative impact on my

life. With all that guilt in there, I couldn't be in the present moment; I was always guarded, not trusting, and anxious. I couldn't
make a move forward with any smoothness or fluidity.

Later in the session he described his positive feelings with his
parents.

Pt: I feel love toward my parents these days, too.

Th: You understand them now.

Pt: It's independent of understanding them; it's just a feeling of love
that cuts through everything else. [*Emergence of grief.*]

Th: That's very painful.

The session continues after three minutes of uninhibited grief and
wailing by the patient.

Pt: Love doesn't have sharpness to it; it's just an open feeling. That
love wasn't there at all when I was a child.

Th: It seems to have been buried with all the fused feelings. Love is
attached to this pain and also the rage and guilt. The love is at the
very center of you.

The patient experiences the hard passage of grief and wails for two
minutes.

The phase of *termination* is prolonged with severely fragile patients. The treatment is typically long-term, so the therapy bond is significant and a great loss to the patient. This loss brings any unresolved
grief and losses to the surface. The prospect of termination of a successful partnership mobilizes remaining repressed guilt-laden rage as
well so this is used therapeutically throughout treatment. Although
short treatment courses of even twenty sessions can yield lasting benefits, the entire treatment course tends to be two to three years. Thus,
it is no longer a "short-term" therapy model (usually meaning forty or
fewer sessions), rather a compressed psychoanalytic treatment format.

Vignette: Termination

The patient is a fifty-year-old woman. She had depression, severe
anxiety, and chronic mistrust of men after enduring abuse by men since
childhood. This excerpt is from a termination phase treatment session
after two years of weekly therapy. Through the treatment course she
had formed a very successful business relationship with a man and

had an entirely changed view of men in general. She reported a dream that summarized our treatment process and its upcoming termination.

> Pt: Last night I had a dream. I was in my car, buried in mud up to the roof. Then I saw you up on a big staircase, on a pedestal. The next thing I knew you were in my car driving it and the car was moving! I was so appreciative. The road was bumpy at first. Then I was driving the car and you were in the passenger seat and the road was better. Then you were in the backseat and there was another man in my car in the front seat with me. At the end, I dropped you off and said goodbye. I was so, so sad. [*Weeps with grief.*]

CONCLUSION

Hence, the ISTDP metapsychology and spectrum of techniques provide us with a framework to understand, integrate, and build capacity with patients with multiple thresholds toward a healthier and more resilient self. It is an approach that can be adapted to fit individuals with all levels of fragility within an integrated interpersonal, cognitive, and psychodynamic framework.

Patients with severe fragility require psychic integration, bracing, and graded work to build capacities to bear their intense underlying feelings. As primitive defenses are overcome these patients experience anxiety for the first time. All pathologic defenses must be replaced by positive self-regard, self-reflection, and isolation of affect that in turn produce striated muscle anxiety. The emotions are intense and the defenses are primitive; therefore, advanced skills and various supports are required to begin to use ISTDP with this patient group.

Empirical Basis of Short-Term Psychodynamic Psychotherapy and Intensive Short-Term Dynamic Psychotherapy

This appendix reviews the evidence base for short-term psychodynamic psychotherapy (STPP) and intensive short-term dynamic psychotherapy (ISTDP). This growing body of research contributes to the evidence that psychodynamic psychotherapy (Shedler 2010) and psychotherapy overall (American Psychological Association 2013) are efficacious treatments.

PROCESS STUDIES

Davanloo developed ISTDP based on a detailed study of a large case series. He used video-recording of the treatment processes as a research aid. Through this study he developed his metapsychology of the unconscious and his technique to work with the unconscious (Davanloo 1995b, 2001, 2005). He extended the research to include highly resistant, fragile, and somatizing patients in the 1970s to 1990s.

Since this groundbreaking research, approximately fifteen process studies have validated various aspects of ISTDP metapsychology (Abbass, Town, and Driessen 2013; Town, Abbass, and Bernier 2013; Abbass and Town 2013). These studies provide diverse evidence to support ISTDP therapist activity and treatment foci. These studies examined the concept of spectra of patients (Abbass 2002a; Abbass, Sheldon, et al. 2008; Johansson, Town, and Abbass 2014); the central role of "unlocking the unconscious" (Town, Abbass, and Bernier 2013;

Johansson, Town and Abbass 2014); the nature, function, and effects of the trial therapy (Abbass, Joffres, and Ogrodniczuk 2008, 2009); and the role of defense work and response to specific interventions (Abbass, Town, and Driessen 2013).

CASE SERIES OUTCOME RESEARCH

Case series outcome research has been carried out on several patient populations.

Mixed Patient Samples

Davanloo (1980, 2005) described that 83 percent of his initial case series of 172 patients had what he referred to as total resolution of symptom and character problems. Since then, numerous case series of diverse populations have revealed the breadth of applicability of the approach. I published data showing 86 percent of a series of 342 patients referred to a psychiatric outpatient practice were candidates for a trial therapy. I reported on 166 patients who were treated, and 80.6 percent derived and maintained gains in passive follow-up (Abbass 2002a). A subgroup of 89 of these patients were studied in depth and exhibited normalization of symptoms as well as three times the cost offset in one year of follow-up (Abbass 2002b). The largest-ever study of ISTDP was reported on 500 patients showing large, significant symptom and interpersonal gains (Johansson, Town, and Abbass 2014). This study found greater outcomes with major unlocking.

Treatment Resistant Samples

ISTDP is emerging as a first-line choice for treatment-resistant samples. I published a pilot study of ten patients with treatment-resistant depression (Abbass 2006) showing large and sustained effects. Hajkowski and Buller (2012) found ISTDP to yield good effects in a mixed group of treatment-resistant outpatients. ISTDP provided in residential programs has demonstrated great effects in complex and treatment-resistant samples in the Netherlands (Cornelissen and Verhuel 2002) and Norway (Solbakken and Abbass 2014).

Somatic Symptom Disorders

Case series have validated ISTDP as an effective treatment for a broad range of somatic disorders including medically unexplained symptoms (Abbass, Campbell, et al. 2009), headache (Abbass, Lovas, and Purdy 2008), and movement disorders (Hinson et al. 2006).

Anxiety Disorders

A case series has shown ISTDP to be effective with anxiety disorders and to result in changes on markers of character structure using the SWAP-200 method (Rocco et al. 2014).

New Indications

I reported on the effects of modified ISTDP in bipolar disorder (Abbass 2002c) and in a case of schizophrenia with OCD (Abbass, 2001). Nowoweiski, Arthey, and Bosanac (2011) reported the effects of ISTDP in eating disorders. ISTDP was found to be effective and cost-effective in treating psychiatric inpatients with depression, anxiety, and psychotic disorders: the need for electroconvulsive therapy reduced after ISTDP began to be used in one of the wards (Abbass, Town, and Bernier 2013). (See Abbass, Town, and Driessen 2012 for further details.)

RANDOMIZED CONTROLLED TRIALS

Over one hundred randomized controlled trials using short-term psychodynamic psychotherapy methods have been published. Currently nine randomized trials using Davanloo's intensive short-term dynamic psychotherapy have been published with more in progress.

Personality Disorders

Winston et al. (1994) published a randomized trial of the early version of Davanloo's method showing that it was more effective than a waitlist control for patients with personality disorders. Hellerstein et al. (1998) also compared Davanloo's early method to supportive dynamic therapy for patients with personality disorders and found the treatments to be equally effective. We (Abbass, Sheldon, et al. 2008) completed a randomized controlled trial of ISTDP for patients with personality disorders and found marked effects on employment, symptom reduction, interpersonal ratings, and overall costs compared to a minimal contact control. Gains were maintained in a two-year follow-up.

Somatic Symptom Disorders

Baldoni, Baldaro, and Trombini (1995) found STPP to be superior to usual medical treatment for pelvic pain and urethral syndrome. Gains were maintained in a four-year follow-up.

Panic

Wiborg and Dahl (1996) showed that STPP, including some of Davanloo's techniques, brought superior and persistent benefits compared to medication treatment alone for patients with panic disorder.

Immune Effects

Ghorbani et al. (2000) studied a small series of patients compared to a control group and found that ISTDP brought about an increase in T4 immune cell counts in normal samples.

Depression

Ajilchi et al. (2013) found ISTDP to outperform a waitlist control for major depression in a randomized controlled trial.

Depressed and Traumatized Adolescents

Trowell et al. (2002, 2007) reported successful application of modified STPP/ISTDP for adolescents with major depression and trauma in two randomized controlled trials.

META-ANALYSES

Many meta-analyses of STPP and ISTDP have now been published.

Short-Term Psychodynamic Psychotherapy

Meta-analyses show STPP to be effective with persistent effects for patients with mixed disorders (Abbass, Kisely et al. 2014), depression (Abbass and Driessen 2010; Driessen et al. 2010), personality disorders (Town, Abbass, and Hardy 2011), depression with personality disorders (Abbass, Town, and Driessen 2011), and somatic disorders (Abbass, Kisely, and Kroenke 2009). In addition, a meta-analysis of STPP for children and adolescents showed large gains that increase in follow-up (Abbass, Rabung, et al. 2013). STPP is as effective as other bona fide treatments, such as cognitive behavioral therapy, in these reviews and is superior to controls.

Intensive Short-Term Dynamic Psychotherapy

We have published a meta-analysis of all ISTDP studies (Abbass, Town, and Driessen 2012). The treatment effects were large and persisted in long-term follow-up. ISTDP outperformed controls. Subanalyses suggested that the newer version of ISTDP (Davanloo 2000) outperformed the earlier version of Davanloo's method, and broader patient samples were studied. In a second meta-analysis, Town and Driessen (2013) found moderate to large effects in patients with somatic symptom disorders and large effects in patients with personality disorders.

Comparisons between Models

In a subanalysis from the Cochrane review of STPP for common mental disorders, studies citing Davanloo or Malan had the greatest treatment effects, accounting for most of the benefits for the overall set of studies (Abbass, Kisely, et al. 2014). Current ISTDP (Davanloo 2000), as used in the most recent randomized controlled trials of the method for personality disorders (Abbass, Sheldon, et al. 2008), appears to have the broadest inclusion criteria of the STPP methods; it may also be more efficient and effective than other STPP methods (Winston et al. 1994; Hellerstein et al. 1998). This finding of superior treatment effects may be due to therapist effects because all therapists in our study had extensive training; amounts of therapist experience do relate to treatment outcomes in some studies of this method (Abbass, Kisely, et al. 2013; Johansson, Town, and Abbass 2014).

COST EFFECTIVENESS

Emotional factors stemming from attachment trauma and childhood adversity cost societies a fortune (Felitti et al. 1998). ISTDP reduces emotional and physical symptoms while saving money and resources. Several studies have shown ISTDP to be cost-effective, more than offsetting treatment costs overall through decreased medical service use, hospital use, medication, and disability costs. Most cost-effectiveness studies to date were recently reviewed (Abbass and Katzman 2013). Another recent study has shown the treatment to reduce costs related to electroconvulsive therapy (Abbass, Town, and Bernier 2013). Another reported greater cost reduction with major unlocking of the unconscious (Town, Abbass, and Bernier 2013). Finally, a study of 890 patients who were provided ISTDP showed an over $12,600-per-patient reduction in hospital and doctor costs after three years of follow-up; this reduction equaled over seventeen times the treatment cost (Abbass, Kisely, et al., forthcoming).

A growing body of evidence indicates that short-term psychodynamic psychotherapy can be broadly applied, efficient, and effective. ISTDP is one of the best studied and most broadly applicable of all the STPP methods with evidence to support its theoretical basis, efficacy, effectiveness, and cost-effectiveness.

Recommended Reading

Abbass, Allan. 2004. "Idealization and Devaluation as Barriers to Psychotherapy Learning." *Ad Hoc Bulletin of Short-Term Dynamic Psychotherapy—Practice and Theory* 8 (3): 46–55.

Abbass, Allan, and D'Arcy Bechard. 2007. "Bringing Character Changes with Davanloo's Intensive Short-Term Dynamic Psychotherapy." *Ad Hoc Bulletin of Short-Term Dynamic Psychotherapy* 11 (2): 26–40.

Abbass, Allan, and Jeffrey Katzman. 2013. "The Cost Effectiveness of Intensive Short-Term Dynamic Psychotherapy." *Psychiatric Annals* 43 (11): 496–501.

Abbass, Allan, David Lovas, and Allan Purdy. 2008. "Direct Diagnosis and Management of Emotional Factors in Chronic Headache Patients." *Cephalalgia* 28 (12): 1305–1314.

Abbass, Allan, Joel Town, and Ellen Driessen. 2012. "Intensive Short-Term Dynamic Psychotherapy: A Systematic Review and Meta-analysis of Outcome Research." *Harvard Review of Psychiatry* 20 (2): 97–108.

Davanloo Habib. 1990. *Unlocking the Unconscious: Selected Papers of Habib Davanloo, MD.* New York: Wiley.

———. 1995a. "Intensive Short-Term Dynamic Psychotherapy: Spectrum of Psychoneurotic Disorders." *International Journal of Short-Term Psychotherapy* 10 (3): 121–155.

———. 1999a. "Intensive Short-Term Dynamic Psychotherapy— Central Dynamic Sequence: Phase of Pressure." *International Journal of Intensive Short-Term Dynamic Psychotherapy* 13:211–236.

———. 1999b. "Intensive Short-Term Dynamic Psychotherapy— Central Dynamic Sequence: Head-On Collision with Resistance." *International Journal of Intensive Short-Term Dynamic Psychotherapy* 13:263–282.

————. 1999c. "Intensive Short-Term Dynamic Psychotherapy—Central Dynamic Sequence: Phase of Challenge." *International Journal of Intensive Short-Term Dynamic Psychotherapy* 13:237–262.

————. 2000. *Intensive Short-Term Dynamic Psychotherapy: Selected Papers of Habib Davanloo.* Chichester; New York: Wiley.

————. 2001. "Intensive Short-Term Dynamic Psychotherapy: Extended Major Direct Access to the Unconscious." *European Psychotherapy* 2 (1): 25–70.

————. 2005. "Intensive Short-Term Dynamic Psychotherapy." In *Kaplan & Sadock's Comprehensive Textbook of Psychiatry*, edited by B. J. Sadock and V. A. Sadock, 2628–2652. Philadelphia: Lippincott Williams & Wilkins.

Frederickson, Jon. 2013. *Co-Creating Change: Effective Dynamic Therapy Techniques.* Kansas City, MO: Seven Leaves.

Bibliography

Abbass, Allan. 2001. "Modified Intensive Short-Term Dynamic Psychotherapy of a Patient with OCD and Schizophrenia." *Quaderni di Psichiatria Pratica* December: 143–146.

———. 2002a. "Office Based Research in Intensive Short-Term Dynamic Psychotherapy (ISTDP): Data from the First 6 Years of Practice." *Ad Hoc Bulletin of Short-Term Dynamic Psychotherapy—Practice and Theory* 6 (2): 5–14.

———. 2002b. "Intensive Short-Term Dynamic Psychotherapy in a Private Psychiatric Office: Clinical and Cost Effectiveness." *American Journal of Psychotherapy* 56 (2): 225–232.

———. 2002c. "Modified Short-Term Dynamic Psychotherapy in Patients with Bipolar Disorder: Preliminary Report of a Case Series." *Canadian Child Psychiatry Review* 11 (1): 19–22.

———. 2004. "Idealization and Devaluation as Barriers to Psychotherapy Learning." *Ad Hoc Bulletin of Short-Term Dynamic Psychotherapy—Practice and Theory* 8 (3): 46–55.

———. 2005. "Somatization: Diagnosing It Sooner through Emotion-Focused Interviewing." *Journal of Family Practice* 54 (3): 231.

———. 2006. "Intensive Short-Term Dynamic Psychotherapy of Treatment-Resistant Depression: A Pilot Study." *Depression and Anxiety* 23 (7): 449–452. doi: 10.1002/da.20203.

———. 2012. "Proceedings of the 9th Halifax Immersion in Intensive Short-Term Dynamic Psychotherapy." Halifax, NS, Canada, 2010.

Abbass, Allan, Stephen Arthey, and Dion Nowoweiski. 2013. "Intensive Short Term Dynamic Psychotherapy for Severe Behaviour Disorders: A Focus on Eating Disorders." *Ad Hoc Bulletin of Short-Term Dynamic Psychotherapy—Practice and Theory* 17 (1): 5–22.

Abbass, Allan, and D'Arcy Bechard. 2007. "Bringing Character Changes with Davanloo's Intensive Short-Term Dynamic

Psychotherapy." *Ad Hoc Bulletin of Short-Term Dynamic Psychotherapy* 11 (2): 26–40.

Abbass, Allan, Samuel Campbell, Kirk Magee, and Robert Tarzwell. 2009. "Intensive Short-Term Dynamic Psychotherapy to Reduce Rates of Emergency Department Return Visits for Patients with Medically Unexplained Symptoms: Preliminary Evidence from a Pre-Post Intervention Study." *Canadian Journal of Emergency Medicine* 11 (6): 529–534.

Abbass, Allan, and Ellen Driessen. 2010. "The Efficacy of Short-Term Psychodynamic Psychotherapy for Depression: A Summary of Recent Findings." *Acta Psychiatrica Scandinavica* 121 (5): 398; author reply 398–399.

Abbass, Allan, Michel Joffres, and John Ogrodniczuk. 2008. "A Naturalistic Study of Intensive Short-Term Dynamic Psychotherapy Trial Therapy." *Brief Treatment and Crisis Intervention* 8 (2): 164–170.

———. 2009. "Intensive Short-Term Dynamic Psychotherapy Trial Therapy: Qualitative Description and Comparison to Standard Intake Assessments." *Ad Hoc Bulletin of Short-Term Dynamic Psychotherapy—Practice and Theory* 13(1): 6–14.

Abbass, Allan, and Jeffrey Katzman. 2013. "The Cost Effectiveness of Intensive Short-Term Dynamic Psychotherapy." *Psychiatric Annals* 43 (11): 496–501.

Abbass, Allan, Steve Kisely, and Kurt Kroenke. 2009. "Short-Term Psychodynamic Psychotherapy for Somatic Disorders: A Systematic Review and Meta-analysis." *Psychotherapy and Psychosomatics* 78:265–274.

Abbass, Allan, Steve Kisely, Daniel Rasic, and Jeffrey Katzman. 2013. "Residency Training in Intensive Short-Term Dynamic Psychotherapy: Methods and Cost-Effectiveness." *Psychiatric Annals* 43:508–512. doi: 10.3928/00485713-20131105-07.

Abbass, Allan, Steve Kisely, Daniel Rasic, Joel Town, and Robert Johansson. "Long-Term Healthcare Cost Reduction with Intensive Short-Term Dynamic Psychotherapy in a Tertiary Psychiatric Service." *Journal of Psychiatric Research* (forthcoming).

Abbass, Allan, Steve Kisely, Joel Town, Falk Leichsenring, Ellen Driessen, Saskia De Maat, Andrew Gerber, Jack Dekker, Sven

Rabung, Svitlana Rusalovska, and Elizabeth Crowe. 2014. "Short-Term Psychodynamic Psychotherapies for Common Mental Disorders." *Cochrane Database of Systematic Reviews* 7:CD004687. doi: 10.1002/14651858.CD004687.pub4.

Abbass, Allan, David Lovas, and Allan Purdy. 2008. "Direct Diagnosis and Management of Emotional Factors in Chronic Headache Patients." *Cephalalgia* 28 (12): 1305–1314.

Abbass, Allan, Sarah Nowoweiski, Denise Bernier, Robert Tarzwell, and Manfred Beutel. 2014. "Review of Psychodynamic Psychotherapy Neuroimaging Studies." *Psychotherapy and Psychosomatics* 83 (3): 142–147. doi: 10.1159/000358841.

Abbass, Allan, Sven Rabung, Falk Leichsenring, Johanne Refseth, and Nick Midgley. 2013. "Psychodynamic Psychotherapy for Children and Adolescents: A Meta-analysis of Short-Term Psychodynamic Models." *Journal of the American Academy of Child and Adolescent Psychiatry* 52 (8): 863–875. doi: 10.1016/j.jaac.2013.05.014.

Abbass, Allan, A. Terry Sheldon, John Gyra, and Allen Kalpin. 2008. "Intensive Short-Term Dynamic Psychotherapy for DSM-IV Personality Disorders: A Randomized Controlled Trial." *Journal of Nervous and Mental Disease* 196 (3): 211–216. doi: 10.1097/NMD.0b013e3181662ff0.

Abbass, Allan, and Joel Town. 2013. "Key Clinical Processes in Intensive Short-Term Dynamic Psychotherapy." *Psychotherapy* 50 (3): 433–437. doi: 10.1037/a0032166.

Abbass, Allan, Joel Town, and Denise Bernier. 2013. "Intensive Short-Term Dynamic Psychotherapy Associated with Decreases in Electroconvulsive Therapy on Adult Acute Care Inpatient Ward." *Psychotherapy and Psychosomatics* 82 (6): 406–407. doi: 10.1159/000350576.

Abbass, Allan, Joel Town, and Ellen Driessen. 2011. "The Efficacy of Short-Term Psychodynamic Psychotherapy for Depressive Disorders with Co-Morbid Personality Disorder." *Psychiatry* 74 (1): 58–71.

———. 2012. "Intensive Short-Term Dynamic Psychotherapy: A Systematic Review and Meta-analysis of Outcome Research." *Harvard Review of Psychiatry* 20 (2): 97–108.

———. 2013. "Intensive Short-Term Dynamic Psychotherapy: A Review of the Treatment Method and Empirical Basis." *Research in Psychotherapy: Psychopathology, Process and Outcome* 16 (1): 6–15.

Ajilchi, Bita, Hasan Ahadi, Vahid Najati, and Ali Delavar. 2013. "The Effectiveness of Intensive Short-Term Dynamic Psychotherapy in Decrease of Depression Level." *European Journal of Experimental Biology* 3 (2): 342–346.

American Psychological Association. 2013. Recognition of Psychotherapy Effectiveness. *Psychotherapy* 50 (1): 102–109.

Baldoni, Franco, Bruno Baldaro, and Giancarlo Trombini. 1995. "Psychotherapeutic Perspectives in Urethral Syndrome." *Stress Medicine* 11:79–84.

Cornelissen, Kees, and Roel Verhuel. 2002. "Treatment Outcome of Residential Treatment with ISTDP." *Ad Hoc Bulletin of Short-Term Dynamic Psychotherapy—Practice and Theory* 6 (2): 14–23.

Davanloo, Habib. 1980. *Short-Term Dynamic Psychotherapy*. New York: Jason Aronson.

———. 1987a. "Unconscious Therapeutic Alliance." In *Frontiers of Dynamic Psychotherapy*, edited by P. Buirski, 64–88. New York: Mazel & Brunner.

———. 1987b. "Clinical Manifestations of Superego Pathology." *International Journal of Short-Term Psychotherapy* 2 (4): 225–254.

———. 1988. "Clinical Manifestations of Superego Pathology. Part II: The Resistance of the Superego and the Liberation of the Paralyzed Ego." *International Journal of Short-Term Psychotherapy* 3 (1): 1–24.

———. 1990. *Unlocking the Unconscious: Selected Papers of Habib Davanloo, MD*. New York: Wiley.

———. 1995a. "Intensive Short-Term Dynamic Psychotherapy: Spectrum of Psychoneurotic Disorders." *International Journal of Short-Term Psychotherapy* 10 (3): 121–155.

———. 1995b. "The Technique of Unlocking the Unconscious in Patients Suffering from Functional Disorders. Part 1. Restructuring Ego's Defenses." In *Unlocking the Unconscious: Selected Papers of Habib Davanloo, MD*, edited by H. Davanloo, 283–306. New York: Wiley.

———. 1995c. "The Technique of Unlocking the Unconscious in Patients Suffering from Functional Disorders. Part 2. Direct View of the Dynamic Unconscious." In *Unlocking the Unconscious: Selected Papers of Habib Davanloo, MD*, edited by H. Davanloo. New York: Wiley.

———. 1995d. "Intensive Short-Term Dynamic Psychotherapy: Technique of Partial and Major Unlocking of the Unconscious with a Highly Resistant Patient: Part I—Partial Unlocking of the Unconscious." *International Journal of Short-Term Psychotherapy* 10 (3): 157–181.

———. 1996a. "Management of Tactical Defenses in Intensive Short-Term Dynamic Psychotherapy: Part I—Overview, Tactical Defenses of Cover Words and Indirect Speech." *International Journal of Short-Term Psychotherapy* 11 (3): 129–152.

———. 1996b. "Management of Tactical Defenses in Intensive Short-Term Dynamic Psychotherapy: Part II—Spectrum of Tactical Defenses." *International Journal of Short-Term Psychotherapy* 11 (3): 153–199.

———. 1999a. "Intensive Short-Term Dynamic Psychotherapy— Central Dynamic Sequence: Phase of Pressure." *International Journal of Intensive Short-Term Dynamic Psychotherapy* 13:211–236.

———. 1999b. "Intensive Short-Term Dynamic Psychotherapy— Central Dynamic Sequence: Head-On Collision with Resistance." *International Journal of Intensive Short-Term Dynamic Psychotherapy* 13:263–282.

———. 1999c. "Intensive Short-Term Dynamic Psychotherapy— Central Dynamic Sequence: Phase of Challenge." *International Journal of Intensive Short-Term Dynamic Psychotherapy* 13:237–262.

———. 2000. *Intensive Short-Term Dynamic Psychotherapy: Selected Papers of Habib Davanloo*. Chichester; New York: Wiley.

———. 2001. "Intensive Short-Term Dynamic Psychotherapy: Extended Major Direct Access to the Unconscious." *European Psychotherapy* 2 (1): 25–70.

———.2005. "Intensive Short-Term Dynamic Psychotherapy." In *Kaplan & Sadock's Comprehensive Textbook of Psychiatry*, edited by B. J. Sadock and V. A. Sadock, 2628–2652. Philadelphia: Lippincott Williams & Wilkins.

Driessen, Ellen, Pim Cuijpers, Saskia de Maat, Allan Abbass, Frans de Jonge, and Jack Dekker. 2010. "The Efficacy of Short-Term Psychodynamic Psychotherapy for Depression: A Meta-analysis." *Clinical Psychology Review* 30 (1): 25–36.

Felitti, Vincent, Robert Anda, Dale Nordenberg, David Williamson, Alison Spitz, Valeria Edwards, Mary Koss, and James Marks. 1998. "Relationship of Childhood Abuse and Household Dysfunction to Many of the Leading Causes of Death in Adults. The Adverse Childhood Experiences (ACE) Study." *American Journal of Preventive Medicine* 14 (4): 245–258.

Frederickson, Jon. 2013. *Co-Creating Change: Effective Dynamic Therapy Techniques.* Kansas City, MO: Seven Leaves.

Ghorbani, Nima, P. Dadsetan, J. Ejei, and H. Motiyan. 2000. "The Consequences of Overcoming Resistance and Emotional Disclosure on Lymphocyte T-helper and T-suppressor and Psychological Pathology." *Journal of Psychology* (3): 368–389.

Hajkowski, Susan, Stephen Buller. 2012. *Implementing Short-Term Psychodynamic Psychotherapy in a Tier 4 Pathfinder Service: Interim Report.* England: Derbyshire Healthcare NHS Foundation Trust.

Hellerstein, David, Richard Rosenthal, Henry Pinsker, Lisa Wallner Samstag, J. Chris Muran, and Arnold Winston. 1998. "A Randomized Prospective Study Comparing Supportive and Dynamic Therapies—Outcome and Alliance." *Journal of Psychotherapy Practice and Research* 7:261–271.

Hinson, Vanessa, Steven Weinstein, Bryan Bernard, Sue Leurgans, and Christopher Goetz. 2006. "Single-Blind Clinical Trial of Psychotherapy for Treatment of Psychogenic Movement Disorders." *Parkinsonism and Related Disorders* 12 (3): 177–180. doi: 10.1016/j.parkreldis.2005.10.006.

Johansson, Robert, Joel Town, and Allan Abbass. 2014. "Davanloo's Intensive Short-Term Dynamic Psychotherapy in a Tertiary Psychotherapy Service: Overall Effectiveness and Association between Unlocking the Unconscious and Outcome." *PeerJ* 2:e548. doi: 10.7717/peerj.548.

Kernberg, Otto F. 1976. 1965. "The Concept of Countertransference." *Journal of the American Psychoanalytic Association* 13:38–56.

———. 1976. "Technical Considerations in the Treatment of Borderline Personality Organization." *Journal of the American Psychoanalytic Association* 24 (4): 795–829.

Malan, David H. 1979. *Individual Psychotherapy and the Science of Psychodynamics*. London; Boston: Butterworths.

Nowoweiski, Dion, Stephen Arthey, and Peter Bosanac. 2011. "Evaluation of an Australian Day Treatment Program for Eating Disorders." *Behaviour Change* 28 (4): 206–220. doi: 10.1375/bech.28.4.206.

Rocco Diego, Allan Abbass, Vito Agrosì, Francesca Bergomi, Luce Maria Busetto, Silvia Marin, Giovanna Pezzetta, Luca Rossi, Lorenzo Zuccotti and Diego Zanelli. 2014. "The Efficacy of Intensive Short Term Dynamic Psychotherapy for Anxiety Disorders When Provided by Psychologists in Training." *Ad Hoc Bulletin of Short-Term Dynamic Psychotherapy—Practice and Theory* 18 (1): 5–15.

Shedler, Jonathan. 2010. "The Efficacy of Psychodynamic Psychotherapy." *American Psychologist* February-March: 98–109.

Solbakken, Ole Andre, and Allan Abbass. 2014. "Implementation of an Intensive Short-Term Dynamic Treatment Program for Patients with Treatment-Resistant Disorders in Residential Care." *BMC Psychiatry* 14:12. doi: 10.1186/1471-244X-14-12.

Town, Joel, Allan Abbass, and Denise Bernier. 2013. "Effectiveness and Cost-Effectiveness of Davanloo's Intensive Short-Term Dynamic Psychotherapy: Does Unlocking the Unconscious Make a Difference?" *American Journal of Psychotherapy* 67 (1): 89–108.

Town, Joel M., Allan Abbass, and Gillian Hardy. 2011. "Short-Term Psychodynamic Psychotherapy for Personality Disorders: A Critical Review of Randomized Controlled Trials." *Journal of Personality Disorders* 25 (6): 723–740.

Town, Joel, Marc Diener, Allan Abbass, Falk Leichsenring, Ellen Driessen, and Sven Rabung. 2012. "A Meta-Analysis of Psychodynamic Psychotherapy Outcomes: Evaluating the Effects of Research-Specific Procedures." *Psychotherapy* 49 (3): 276–290. doi: 10.1037/a0029564.

Town, Joel, and Ellen Driessen. 2013. "Emerging Evidence for Intensive Short-Term Dynamic Psychotherapy with Personality Disorders and Somatic Disorders." *Psychiatric Annals* 43 (11): 503–511. doi: 10.3928/00485713-20131105-05.

Trowell, Judith, Ilan Joffe, Jesse Campbell, Carmen Clemente, Fredrik Almqvist, Mika Soininen, Ulla Koskenranta-Aalto, Sheila Weintraub, Gerasimos Kolaitis, Vlassis Tomaras, Dimitris Anastasopoulos, Kate Grayson, Jacqueline Barnes, and John Tsiantis. 2007. "Childhood Depression: A Place for Psychotherapy. An Outcome Study Comparing Individual Psychodynamic Psychotherapy and Family Therapy." *European Child and Adolescent Psychiatry* 16 (3): 157–67. doi: 10.1007/s00787-006-0584-x.

Trowell, Judith, I. Kolvin, T. Weeramanthri, H. Sadowski, M. Berelowitz, D. Glaser, and I. Leitch. 2002. "Psychotherapy for Sexually Abused Girls: Psychopathological Outcome Findings and Patterns of Change." *British Journal of Psychiatry* 180:234–247.

Whittemore, Joan W. 1996. "Paving the Royal Road: An Overview of Conceptual and Technical Features in the Graded Format of Davanloo's Intensive Short-Term Dynamic Psychotherapy." *International Journal of Short-Term Psychotherapy* 11 (1): 21–39.

Wiborg, Ida, and Alv Dahl. 1996. "Does Brief Dynamic Psychotherapy Reduce the Relapse Rate of Panic Disorder?" *Archives of General Psychiatry* 53 (8): 689–694.

Winston, Arnold, Michael Laikin, Jerome Pollack, Lisa Samstag, Leigh McCullough, and J. Chris Muran. 1994. "Short-Term Psychotherapy of Personality Disorders." *American Journal of Psychiatry* 151 (2): 190–194.

Index

About the Author

Allan Abbass, MD, is a psychiatrist, teacher, and researcher. He is a professor of psychiatry and psychology and the founding director of the Centre for Emotions and Health at Dalhousie University in Halifax, Canada.

After completing medical school at Dalhousie University, Allan started his career as a family physician and emergency physician but soon became frustrated with the limits of traditional medicine. He observed that a large percentage of his patients experienced physical and mental symptoms that medications failed to address. So he decided to add a year of family medicine residency at McGill University to study a form of short-term psychotherapy.

Soon he was immersed in Dr. Habib Davanloo's training and research program, where he discovered what these symptomatic patients were actually looking for: an emotional corrective experience with a caring professional. With his first two patient contacts he had no doubt about the power of the human relationship to help heal old attachment trauma.

This experience had a dramatic effect on Allan, who decided to complete a psychiatry residency at the University of Toronto to teach and research in psychotherapy. From there he went to the University of British Columbia, where he established a university-based training program in ISTDP and led a provincial tertiary program for people with severe personality disorders.

In 1998 he returned home to Dalhousie University—first as director of psychotherapy and then director of education for the university's department of psychiatry. In his first seven years there, he won departmental, regional, and national awards for excellence in education. In 2013 he was awarded the Douglas Utting Prize for his contributions in the area of major depression. His innovative program to diagnose and treat emotional contributors to medically unexplained symptoms in the emergency department won a quality award and a national designation as a "Canadian Leading Practice." Similar programs have followed in other Canadian and international jurisdictions.

Since 2000 he has been consulted widely by governments, universities, and health agencies on the cost-effectiveness and applicability of short-term psychotherapy. He has provided over 250 invited presentations around the world as well as ongoing video-recording-based training to professionals in several countries. In addition, he has been awarded seventeen research grants and has over 150 publications.

He has been a consultant to the American Psychological Association on the Unified Psychotherapy Project and to the American Psychoanalytic Association, where he serves on the Scientific Committee. He was a board member of the International Experiential Dynamic Therapy Association. He has been an editorial board member for the American Psychological Association journal *Psychotherapy*. He is a visiting faculty member at institutions in the United States, England, and Italy.

An avid basketball fan and former player, Allan uses an approach that incorporates the notions of collaborative teamwork: practicing a lot, helping others perform their best, and teaching complex concepts in the simplest ways possible.

Please visit www.istdp.ca for further information about Allan, articles, and training opportunities. You can follow him on Twitter (twitter.com/ISTDP), Facebook (facebook.com/allan.abbass.7), LinkedIn, or ResearchGate.